WHERE TO
SELL IT!

WHERE TO SELL IT!

How to Find the Best Buyers
of Antiques, Collectibles, and Other
Undiscovered Treasures

Tony Hyman

Nationally known authority
on buying and selling
collectibles by mail

A PERIGEE BOOK

A Perigee Book
Published by The Berkley Publishing Group
200 Madison Avenue
New York, NY 10016

Library of Congress Cataloging-in-Publication Data

Hyman, Tony.
    Where to sell it!: how to find the best buyers of antiques, collectibles, and other undiscovered treasures / Tony Hyman.
        p.   cm.
    Rev. and updated ed. of: Dr. Tony Hyman's I'll buy that.
    Includes index.
    ISBN 0-399-51817-7
        1. Collectors and collecting—United States— Directories. 2. Antique dealers—United States—Directories. 3. Selling—Antiques—United States—Directories. 4. Selling— Collectibles—United States—Directories.
    I. Hyman, Tony, Dr. Tony Hyman's I'll buy that. II. Title.
AM303.H948   1993   93-9432 CIP
381'.45'0002973—dc20

Cover design by Jack Ribik
Cover: All collectibles courtesy of Hake's Americana & Collectibles
Interior design by Steve Gussman

The Putnam Berkley World Wide Web site address is
http://www.berkley.com

Printed in the United States of America
    10

ABOUT THIS BOOK

Where To Sell It! is designed to do three things:

✓ Help you identify objects around your home and work that are sought by collectors...literally millions of items you might own and not realize had value

✓ Help you find buyers for this amazing array of items from ancient coins to Melmac© dishes: 2,400 categories

✓ Help you get fair prices for what you sell by suggesting folks who will either buy your item or help you sell it to someone else

It's also designed to help 1,000 buyers actively looking to expand collections or inventory. *Where To Sell It!* puts the two of you together.

Where To Sell It! is the 6th in a series of similar guidebooks originally created to help the 93% of America who do not care about antiques and collectibles, but probably own something a collector would like and be willing to buy.

Everyday items that can be worth $250 or more include: model kits, fishing tackle, perfume bottles, G.I. Joe© dolls, electric trains, lunch boxes, fountain pens, mystery books, cookie jars, pocket knives, Levis© jackets, and countless others. Even file drawers full of old catalogs and business correspondence is useful to someone.

Finding buyers of some items can be difficult. Van Gogh paintings may be setting record prices, but competition for photographs of 19th Century funerals isn't exactly fierce. There is only one good buyer of cigar boxes in the country, and buyers of cap guns, corkscrews, and PEZ© dispensers were equally hard to find before this valuable series of guidebooks became available.

How the series began

I've been collecting, buying and selling for 40+ years while carrying on a professional career in media that has allowed me to travel in every state and Canadian province. My family has had the opportunity to live in nine states and more than 30 big cities, small towns, and rural hamlets.

While living in the Northeast, it was possible, by spending a lot of time driving to weekend flea markets, to visit 10,000 antique and collectibles dealers each year. As I shopped, I met fascinating people, authorities on obscure collecting topics, who were passionate about their hobbies. I enjoyed meeting folks whose approach to collecting was much like my own, and who, like me, enjoyed sharing information about what they collected.

Every time I met one of these serious but friendly folks, their name went into my "little black phone book." Over the years, while hunting for cigar boxes (my specialty), I'd run across things these other collectors wanted. I'd usually find them at bargain prices, which enabled me to make a profit while helping other people.

One snowbound New York evening, my wife was teasing me for the ease with which I bought a $50 sewing machine from an antique dealer, placed one phone call, sold it for $350 and made me and the buyer both very happy.

"Anyone could do the same thing if they knew who to call," I replied, and the idea for these guidebooks was born.

Where To Sell It! is an expanded version of my personal address book. The first edition proved that average folks who had never before bought and sold by mail could easily make money even if they didn't know what they had or what it was worth. Readers discovered, as I had, that asking collectors to make offers resulted in handsome profits, sometimes more than 100 times more money than expected.

It's now twelve years later, and the *Where To Sell It!* books have made millions of dollars for folks just like you by providing step-by-step instructions on how to turn your undiscovered treasures into cash.

What is Included

There are three parts to this book, designed to help you identify collectibles, find a buyer, and get a fair price.

The **index** lists 2,400 categories of things you can sell. The **body** of the book gives you names, addresses, and phone numbers of 1,000 top buyers in the U.S. and Canada who want those things. The **introduction** teaches you exactly what to say and what to do If you would like to sell your item at fair prices quickly and easily.

This all-new 1993-94 edition includes special features added to make it easy to use:

✓ Redesigned introduction, easier to understand and and follow, so you can make each contact a good one.

✓ Buyers are grouped with buyers of similar items, in ways logical to antiquers, and easy to follow for amateurs.

✓ Each major grouping opens with hints to help you sell, and additional advice can be found in boxes placed throughout the text.

✓ Items you can sell are printed in boldface type and other boldface type points out important other categories of items sought by collectors.

✓ For quick reference, section headings at the top of each page identify the type of buyers you'll find there.

✓ New compact format easier to carry in car and purse.

A closing note to readers

Congratulations on buying the buyers' guide experts themselves use. I hope you'll enjoy meeting and working with people you meet through *Where To Sell It!*

I'm sure you like dealing with people who are honest, helpful, and know what they're talking about. Me too. That's why I've done business with some of these folks for 20 years. The buyers in *Where To Sell It!* have made a lot of money for me. They have made a lot of money for readers. I can only hope your dealings with them will prove to be as pleasant and as profitable.

If you discover a listee has moved or died, please tell me. In general, collectors are more stable than average, but we live in a very mobile society, changes do occur, and busy folks sometimes forget to notify us. When you tell me about any changes, if you include a long self-addressed stamped envelope, I'll send you a free update sheet listing all changes reported by other readers since the last printing. This offer is good as long as this edition is in print.

If you know other buyers you think should be included, please don't be shy. I'm always glad to meet more folk who are expert in their fields, honest in their dealings and fair in their pricing.

If you'd like to tell me about your experiences selling to these folks by mail, drop me a line. I don't have time to answer personally, but I listen well, and I'll take what you say into consideration when doing radio, TV and future editions of *Where To Sell It!*

Good luck!

Tony Hyman
Box 3028
Shell Beach, CA 93448

WHERE TO SELL IT!

TABLE OF CONTENTS

TABLE OF CONTENTS

TABLE OF CONTENTS

TABLE OF CONTENTS

HOW TO USE THIS BOOK

Identifying what has value

If you want a quick overview of items you may own that are sought by collectors, take a few minutes to skim the entire index starting on page 451. Circle the index entry when you see something you own listed among the 2,400 categories it is possible to convert to cash. When you have finished reading the index, turn to the pages you have circled.

Each page in *Where To Sell It!* contains one or more entries for buyers. Each entry begins with bold type telling you the main category of things that person wants to buy. Read the entire entry because it often contains specific info about other things the person wants, how to describe what you have, what the buyer pays, what reference books are available, and what the buyer does not want. The more entries you read, the more likely you are to learn about things you own, but did not know had collector value.

Entries are grouped so that buyers with similar wants are on the same or nearby pages. By reading nearby entries, you may find three or four people who might be interested in things you have, as well as learn about yet more things that you can sell.

If you use the index to look up a specific item, you can increase your chances of making money by looking under several categories. For example, an art glass cigar box with a label depicting nude women playing poker in a railroad car would be desirable to buyers of art glass, cigar boxes, labels, advertising, nudes, card playing, gambling and railroads. A buyer may be found by looking under any of those categories. Circle possibilities as you go.

When reading entries, you will often see the words ephemera (ef-fem'-er-a) and memorabilia. **Ephemera** means things that are short lived, created to be thrown away, such as catalogs, theater tickets and programs. **Memorabilia** refers to items a bit more substantial, things designed to be saved, or to be used over time. For you, the differences are not important. The words are often used among collectors almost interchangeably.

Finding a Buyer

Once you've identified an item to sell, you need to find a buyer. You started the process of finding a buyer when you began reading the entries suggested in the index. Each entry describes, in varying amounts of detail, what that buyer wants.

Buyers listed in *Where To Sell It!* are private collectors, universities, museums, auctioneers, and specialty dealers. They have been selected for their experience, knowledge, scholarship, willingness to give information to amateur sellers, and commitment to pay fair prices. No one paid a fee to be included in this book.

Before you contact buyers, read their entries carefully. If an entry reads "No tribbles," you will not be able to sell your tribble to that buyer. Don't waste your time asking. If an entry reads "Tribbles considered," it means that tribbles are not a specialty, but if your tribble is particularly scarce and in fine condition, the buyer may make an offer.

If you believe you own something a buyer might want, it is easy to ask him or her by mail or by telephone. Each entry in *Where To Sell It!* gives you the buyer's name and address and, in many cases, their phone and fax number. Although you are dealing with experts, you'll find these buyers to be "just plain folks," friendly, and easy to talk to.

The buyers in *Where To Sell It!* are rooting for you. They want you to succeed. They want you to have something rare. They actually want to pay you. "I hate telling people I don't want what they have," said one buyer. "I'd much rather say, 'Thanks. I'm glad you sold it to me and here's a good sized check!'"

The majority of buyers prefer you to state clearly in your first letter what you have and its condition. They want you to set a price or to request an offer. Buyers want sellers, not pen pals.

There are a few exceptions, however. "I'm a lonely old retiree," admits one expert, "and I love getting and answering mail." A handful of others agree, and one Iowa buyer actually married a Pennsylvania reader who phoned him with an item for sale.

Most buyers provide their phone number. Phone calls are fast, easy, and let you get the most information to the buyer with the least effort. When you sell anything likely to be worth $50 or more, make the first contact by phone.

An important reason for using the telephone is to give the buyer an opportunity to ask questions, so have your item at hand, if possible, and be prepared to discuss details, including size, color, maker, distinguishing characteristics, and damage. An expert can often determine what you have based on a few simple questions.

A few buyers indicate specific hours during which they'd like you to call. Respect their wishes and you'll get off to a good start. If no hours are suggested, call during normal business hours for the time zone in which they live. If you don't reach them, try between 7 and 8 p.m. their time. Folks in California hate 6 a.m. calls from eager Easterners, just as Easterners don't appreciate 2 a.m. calls from Western night owls.

If leaving a message on an answering machine, be brief and specific about what you have. When you leave your name, it is helpful if you spell it. If you leave your number, make certain you say it slowly so it can be understood and written down when your message is played back.

If a buyer decides over the phone that your item is not of interest, don't waste time arguing. Ask if the buyer can recommend another collector or dealer who might be interested. If your item is in good condition, but potential buyers say your item is of no collector interest, you can safely sell it at a yard sale or donate it to a charity.

A few buyers now provide 800 numbers so you can call them for free. These 800 numbers are expensive to maintain, and you should not use them for idle chit-chat or to obtain free appraisals. They are business lines to make your selling easier. Respect them, do your business, and hang up.

Never call collect unless the buyer has given you specific permission to do so. Only a handful, like fishing tackle expert Rick Edmison, will accept collect calls.

Whether you write or phone, you must be prepared to describe what you have. A thorough description includes:

✓ What you have, as best as you know;

✓ What material(s) it is made from;

✓ Colors of the item. If the item is painted, estimate what percentage of original paint remains;

✓ All words and numbers embossed, incised, painted, or otherwise printed on your item. If the item has an ID plate (like most machines) give all information on the plate;

✓ Size of non-standard items, or items that come in more than one size. Measurements are important in many categories and should be accurate to the quarter inch;

✓ Condition, noting dents, scratches, tears, writing, fading, soil, stains, and everything else that was not there when the item was originally manufactured.

WHERE TO SELL IT!

Some buyers want additional, very specific, information. You will find this indicated in the "Tips on Selling" at the front of each section, or in that buyer's listing. See the Table of Contents to find various "Tips" pages.

Many buyers ask for a photograph or a photocopy.

Photographs are taken with a camera. The best photos are close-ups taken with a 35mm camera. If you do not have one, perhaps a friend who does can take pictures for you. Polaroid© and snapshot cameras frequently do not provide enough detail to be useful to a potential buyer. This is usually the fault of the person taking the picture. If you use one of these cameras you will get better results if you use a tripod, or rest your camera on a flat surface so the picture comes out sharp. Photos are particularly important when selling toy vehicles, banks, and other items where the percentage of paint remaining plays an important role in determining value.

Photocopies are made with a Xerox© type machine. I recommend you make a photocopy of what you have to sell whenever you can because it is the cheapest and easiest method of describing most items. Objects such as knives, small dolls, badges, medals, pipes, even pistols, will usually photocopy well enough for a buyer to know what you have. Copies are especially useful for describing china patterns. Copiers are found in businesses, banks and libraries, and cost from 4¢ to 25¢. Color copies are available at some copy centers, but for most items you'd like to sell are an unnecessary expense.

In addition to the above, always mention any historical connection, authentication, "family legends" or other oral history associated with the item. Don't forget your name, address, and telephone number, along with a photograph or photocopy if possible. Include a Self-Addressed Stamped

WHERE TO SELL IT!

Envelope if you want a reply. It's easier on everyone if you tell a prospective buyer not to bother answering if your item isn't marketable.

Self-Addressed Stamped Envelope (SASE)

When you write someone asking for information or an offer, include a long business size #10 envelope, address it to yourself, and put a stamp in the corner. This is a Self-Addressed Stamped Envelope (SASE). Use a long envelope because many buyers will send you pages of information which won't fit into smaller envelopes. If you do not include an SASE, you are telling buyers not to bother answering your letter if they are not interested in what you have to sell. "If my help isn't worth an envelope and stamp to the seller," said one expert, "it's not worth my time and money either."

A few buyers (of watches, tin cans, jewelry, among other things) will request you to ship your item before they send final payment or make a firm offer. There is nothing unusual about this, and it can often result in your receiving more money for your item. As one experienced appraiser said, "we always assume the worst, until we see exactly how good an item actually is."

Most buyers prefer you not bother them unless your item is for sale. If you contact them frivolously, they'll quit making offers and helping others. One musical instrument buyer explained, "We're a small company. We don't have time to spend with people who are not really selling."

Many readers would like an estimate of their item's value so they can decide whether to sell. As one reader put it, "I'd take a million dollars for anything I own, but would I take $50 when I'd like $250?" That's a question only you can answer. You need to give thought to your expectations before you begin trying to sell.

WHERE TO SELL IT!

CONDITION, CONDITION, CONDITION

It is vital that you examine and accurately describe the condition of your item. Some collectibles lose 40-50% of their value with their first scratch or dent. Stains, tears, wear, fading, foxing, thin spots, fraying, nicks, water stains, handwriting, and brittleness all affect value.

Low or medium quality items in only fair condition almost never have buyers at any price. Neither dealers nor collectors want to tie up cash in poor goods. Chips and cracks in most china and glass make values drop to almost nothing. Postcards, comic books, and sheet music are among those paper collectibles which become nearly valueless if not in excellent condition.

On the other hand, some less-than-perfect paper will sell. "Rock and roll concert posters and handbills tucked in the drawers of aging hippies are rare enough to be a cash windfall in any condition," says one expert.

Mechanical items will sell with parts and pieces missing. Jukeboxes, slot machines, radios, and the like can all be restored, although buyers warn you should never attempt restoration of anything you want to sell.

Whatever condition your item is in, if you fail to describe its condition accurately, the buyer will return it, costing you and the buyer money and wasted effort.

Amateur sellers are notorious for overestimating the quality of condition. As a result, many dealers and collectors will ask to see the item before they make a final offer. This is particularly true of buyers of paper goods like postcards, trade cards, match covers, sheet music, and stamps. Paper dealers want to see what you have, because very small variations in condition mean substantial difference in price. For example, paper money worth $50 in very fine condition might be worth only $5 in circulated condition. Postcards with creases, or match covers with their strikers removed, are worth little or nothing.

A few buyers will give free appraisals, whether your item is for sale or not, if you give a good enough description. A few others will charge a fee to estimate the value of some thing that is not for sale. It is not fair to pretend your item is for sale so you can get a free appraisal to learn how much to charge a friend or relative.

Make clear what you want when you contact someone listed in *Where To Sell It!* Appraisals done for insurance or other legal purposes require the appraiser to have the item physically in hand to make the appraisal, so you will need to ship your item for close inspection. When someone in *Where To Sell It!* normally charges for an appraisal, that is noted in his or her entry. A fair price for an informal appraisal for a simple item is $10 to $20. You'll usually pay a higher fee for formal written appraisals on collections or obscure and unusual items.

Getting a fair price

For most people, setting the price is the most difficult part of selling. Selling the *Where To Sell It!* way offers you an alternative to the hassle and guesswork of pricing.

Antiques, collectibles, and other items you sell are second-hand goods. They have no set value. Something is worth what the buyer and seller agree it is worth. Value is determined when someone hands you money and you hand them your item. Most people want to make certain that the amount of money they are handed is fair.

Amateur sellers don't know what's fair. If it's any comfort to you, I don't know what is a fair price for everything either, and neither do most antique dealers and flea marketers. A collector or dealer may (or may not) know a whole lot about a little bit, but there is no one who can keep up with the value of the hundreds of millions of items made in the last 150 years.

You can't rely on price guides to tell you what is fair. Values expressed in price guides are rarely the amount you will pocket when you sell that item. They are only estimates, often poor estimates, of what an item may actually sell for.

There are, however, a few informative price guides, some of the best of which were written by people listed in *Where To Sell It!* You can look up the values of your stamps and coins relatively easily because collectors everywhere use the same readily available price guides. Standard guides exist for phonograph records, comic books, Disney items, political buttons, Pez© dispensers, and a few other items as well, but books in many other hobbies have very limited distribution. Many fields have no good reference books, making research difficult.

How do you set a price if there are no price guides, or you weren't able to find your thing listed in guides that were available?

Forty years' experience has taught me the best way to get a fair price is to ask people who specialize in whatever I want to sell to set the price. I make the most money by trusting an expert to make a fair offer. The process is usually simple, quick, and the most profitable.

It's popular these days to be cynical about honesty and to assume everyone is crooked. Fortunately, that's simply not the case. The world is full of honest, knowledgeable, helpful people, many of whom you will meet in the pages of *Where To Sell It!* If you deal with good people, you don't need to know an item's value to get a fair price. You don't even need to know what your item is. The Midwestern lady who got $10,000 for her Japanese sword had no idea what she owned, nor did the Los Angeles widow who got $55,000 for Indian medals she had looked at only once in 30 years. An Ohio teen was stunned when my arrowhead expert paid $10,000 for points he found in the dump.

Fabulous finds like these happen more often than you think, and each was possible only because the seller turned to an expert for advice on pricing. Not everything you own is worth a fortune, however. When you offer something for sale, you must be prepared to discover your items are not worth as much as you hoped. If you fail to find a buyer immediately, don't give up. Last month, a reader wrote, "I made several contacts without making a sale, and got a little discouraged but then I hit the jackpot! I'm a single parent and earning a second income helps tremendously!"

When you offer an item for sale, any potential buyer will evaluate your item in terms of scarcity, desirability and condition. Dealing with an expert specialty buyer makes it more likely you will get an accurate assessment of what you have and a reasonable estimate of fair market value. Accuracy is important when a wrong appraisal can cost you hundreds, or even tens of thousands, of dollars.

The concept of "fair market value" is a hazy one. Every time something sells, it's value could be more, less, or the same as the day before. In the world of second hand goods, selling is always a bit of an adventure, with the possibility of differences of opinion.

Almost all the buyers in *Where To Sell It!* will make offers for desirable items you own. Buyers who do not make offers are usually people who feel they have been treated dishonestly by amateur sellers. They believe amateurs "fish for free information, don't really want to sell, or have outrageous expectations about the value of their objects."

When a buyer makes you an offer, weigh not only the amount of money you will get against how much you enjoy owning the object, but consider the satisfaction of helping a collector or researcher and the new home your cherished item will have. More often than not, I accept the offer, sell, and move on.

HOW MUCH DO PEOPLE PAY?

The typical collectible changes hands five to seven times as it moves up the ladder from the original owner to the final collector. Each person who handles it raises the price. If the final collector pays 100% of value, what do others pay?

Homeowners give things to charity, where alert shoppers and pickers snap up "the good stuff" within hours. Selling at yard sales may bring as much as 25% on children's clothes, but few other items fare as well. Homeowners selling items worth $3,000 to $250,000 at yard sales usually get from 1¢ to 6¢ for every $20 of value.

Pickers who buy from yard sales and local auctions generally pay from 1/2% to 20% of dollar value, often much less. Picking can be very profitable thanks to the many mistakes by homeowners, thrift stores, auctions, flea market dealers, and rummage sales.

Flea market dealers generally pay in the same range as pickers, from 1/2% to 20% as their knowledge and markets are limited. Flea markets are often great places to buy, but almost never good places to sell.

Mall dealers are frequently pickers, usually part-timers, and increasingly tend to specialize in a few types of goods, such as Western, books, ladies' things, etc. Profits are low, so the prices they pay must be low too. They do best when they pay under 5% and can seldom pay you more than 30%.

Shop owners come in all sizes, shapes, specialties and skill levels, so generalizations are difficult. From a business standpoint, the general or semi-specialist shop must try to pay from 5% to 30% to survive, with higher prices going only for good quality, fast moving goods. Shop owners make frequent mistakes, because their experience is usually limited to a few fields. When they buy outside their specialty, you may be lucky to get 1% for a rare item.

HOW MUCH DO PEOPLE PAY? (con't)

Auction houses exist at all levels of skill and clientele. The price you get will depend upon the quality of your item, its history, what is being auctioned with it, when the auction is held, where the auction is held, and, most important of all, who will be attracted to bid in the auction. Most sales at auctions are to **dealers**, who will double or triple the auction price when they sell to their customers. Prices range from as low as 1%, to a typical 15% to 60%. Top flight goods under perfect conditions in important auctions will sell for 50% to 100% of value, or more. Deduct the auction house share, typically 15% to 25% of the bid. Big mistakes in evaluation by auctioneers are more common than they would like you to know. A number of auction houses have recently succumbed to criminal charges, legal troubles, or financial woes, so investigating any auctioneer before turning over your goods makes sense.

Specialty dealers usually pay from 30% to 75% of an item's probable retail value. How much they pay depends on how much money the dealer has, how anxious he/she is to add your item to inventory, and how quickly your item is likely to resell. The more expensive the item, the higher percentage of retail you can expect to get.

Collectors tend to pay 50% to 100% of retail value. They, too, pay a higher percentage for expensive items. One collector explained: "If I'm offered a common item, worth only $5, I'll rarely pay more than a dollar or two, if I buy it at all. When someone offers me something rare, I'm willing to pay full value or even more because I'd rather overpay to make certain I get it. When I examine the item, if I find that it's better than either I or the seller thought, I'm glad to send another check."

The above are generalizations only, and not intended to describe any particular dealer, company, or individual.

Shipping what you sell

If you have accepted a buyer's offer, or the buyer has requested you to send the item for inspection, you will need to ship your item. Shipping is easier than you think. In the case of large items like furniture and juke boxes, the buyer will probably arrange to have all shipping done for you.

When packing smaller items you sell, always use sturdy boxes. You can buy boxes at most post offices, stationery stores, and packing companies, but heavy duty boxes can often be obtained free from book stores. Don't ship anything, even shoes, in shoe boxes.

When you sell many items, you may need additional packing supplies. You can order boxes, tape, styrofoam, and bubble wrap from stores which sell these items to the commercial market. Depending upon the size of your town's Yellow Pages, you'll find them listed under "Packing Supplies," "Paper," or "Boxes and Cartons." If it's hard for you to get around, you can order these supplies with a credit card and they will be delivered to you.

If you are shipping an item that is breakable, double boxing is the preferred method. Pack your item carefully in the smallest box that leave an inch or two of protection around your item. Write the name and address of the recipient on that box, then pack it inside a larger box, with two or three inches of padding. When you are packing breakables, never let two items touch. Wrap each item separately in styrofoam sheeting, bubble bags, or clean paper. Don't leave lids on cookie jars, sugar bowls, and the like. They are likely to chip if you do.

Never pack your item in direct contact with newsprint. Newsprint smears, and can damage clothing and ruin porous china like Wedgwood. Wrap breakables in tissue, paper towel or plain unprinted paper, then use newspaper to fill the carton.

Flat items should be shipped between two sheets of cardboard approximately one inch bigger on all sides than what you're sending. Put the grain of the two pieces of cardboard at right angles. Your package will be less likely to bend.

Ship by First Class Mail or by private carrier. Do not use parcel post. The difference in price between parcel post and first class is so small, the few pennies you save aren't worth the time delay and increased risk. If your package weighs under two pounds, you can ship anywhere in the U.S. for only $2.90.

When an item is worth more than $300, I ship it by Registered Mail, because packages receive special security handling in transit. Registered Mail can also be insured up to $25,000 and must be signed for by the addressee. All this for one $5 to $10 fee. Anything you sell that cannot be replaced should be sent Registered Mail.

There are a few special rules for Registered Mail, so check with your Post Office before you wrap. The most important differences are that you must use a clean box with no signs of damage or printed advertising. The address and return address must be written directly on the box, not on an applied paper label. Each seam of the box (where it was assembled) must be covered with brown paper tape. No plastic tape is allowed.

Always insure what you mail. Insurance up to $500 on a first class package costs about $5. Insurance on Registered Mail costs much less, because of the strict security under which Registered Mail is handled.

Questions people ask

The information in my buyer directories has become so valuable I've been invited to appear on 1,100 radio and TV shows, dubbed "America's most popular talk show guest" in *Talker* magazine, and host the nationally syndicated "Trash into Cash" radio show. I spend hundreds of hours each year on air answering people's questions about the disposing of their antiques and collectibles. Some years I receive 1,300 letters a week. It seems everyone wants to make money with their junk. It also seems people everywhere share many of the same questions and concerns.

1 "Why no pictures and prices in this book?"

In the last 200 years more than a billion different items have been manufactured. A book which pictures them all would be taller than the World Trade Center, an obvious impossibility, especially since no photos are available of 2/3 of the items which exist. For me to include a few hundred pictures in this book would help no one, yet make it more expensive to bring you this valuable reference book.

Pictures are essential only in price guides used by "do-it-yourself" evaluators curious about the "worth" of their item. *Where To Sell It!* believes you get accurate prices from expert buyers, not books. *Where To Sell It!* explains how and to whom to sell those items pictured in other books. It's your introduction to the people who write price guides.

You may find it interesting to note that not one of the seven most valuable things known to have been sold by my readers and listeners was pictured or listed in a price guide, yet they got as much as $200,000 for what they had. Photos seldom exist of the most valuable items.

2 "Why not sell to a local dealer?"

It may be in your best interest to sell some things to a local dealer, but only after you have made certain you don't have an item wanted by one of the specialty dealers and collectors dealers. The chart on page xxiii should explain why.

The problem with selling to anyone other than an expert is that the buyer may not know exactly what your item is. One dealer in a thousand might recognize the rarest stone spear point, but fewer yet would pay you the $10,000 you'd get by dealing with someone who knows and appreciates Indian stone. Dealing with an expert in Indian stone will require a phone call, a letter, and perhaps a photocopy or photo. The entire transaction may take less than an hour. Selling your spear point to the antique dealer around the corner will take about the same amount of time, but the difference in price could be substantial.

A Long Island antique dealer priced a $66,000 dish at $2, a Southern antique dealer sold his $22,000 Stickley table for $440, a Western NY antique dealer sold his $43,000 cast iron bank for $125. Every antique shop has one or more good things priced at less than 10% of value because the dealer doesn't know what an expert will pay for it. No one can know everything. You and I make mistakes, too. We all make fewer mistakes, however, when we do business, any business, with people who know what they're doing.

3 "Will I get cheated?"

What is to keep a buyer from cheating you and telling you your $5,000 watch is worth $5? Honesty, for one thing. Reputation for another. The world of collectibles is a small one. Word gets around fast, and dishonest buyers seldom stay in business long. "Why would I risk a reputation it took me thirty years to build, just to cheat some old lady out of

$500? It doesn't make sense," explains one veteran pro.

Some people feel a conflict of interest exists when the same person evaluates and sets the price. To some extent, that may be. But when you deal with people who have reputations for knowledge and integrity, you're likely to be many dollars ahead of selling at a yard sale, flea market, or local auction.

Dishonesty, misunderstandings, and disagreements are all possibilities in any human activity, but I've known some of these people personally for 20 years. I've been featuring buyers in books, newspapers, radio and television for a dozen years. Hundreds of thousands of transactions have taken place between readers and these buyers. I've received less than a dozen letters of complaint, all minor.

4 "Why not sell at a yard sale?"

Great idea, as long as you sell things appropriate to a yard sale: children's clothing, modern kitchen items, and newer household do-dads. If your item is fifteen or more years old, be cautious about selling it at a yard sale.

Some items should never be offered at yard sales unless you are certain of their worth. These include: Disney toys, electric guitars, briar pipes, advertising, wrist watches, hardback books from before 1950 with dust jackets, fishing tackle, fountain pens, perfume bottles, balloon tire boys' bi-cycles, plastic radios, tin cans, carnival glass, baseball cards, Indian artifacts, pocket knives, dolls, art prints signed in pencil, and just about anything related to TV or movies.

The problem with selling at a yard sale is that you must set the price, and most people are not qualified to do that. A Hollywood homeowner asked $15 for a perfume bottle at his yard sale. The woman who bought the $15 bottle drove two blocks to a gas station where she phoned my expert in perfume bottles. He asked her for an offer on the $15 bottle. "Would you take $4,000?" came the reply. In a few minutes, one seller got $15 for the bottle and another got $4,000. Which seller are you? *Where To Sell It!* gives you the power to be the person who profits most.

5 "Why didn't I get an answer to my inquiry?"

If you offer something rare for sale, you'll get an answer from any collector.

If you don't get a response to your inquiry from one of the people in *Where To Sell It!*, it may mean that your item was not collectible, or you didn't include a self-addressed stamped envelope, or the buyer hasn't had time to respond. Perhaps you wrote the wrong person, or offered something the buyer specifically said was not wanted. It's also possible that your letter got lost in the mail or that the buyer is out of town or sick. Remember, you're writing to real people. Like you, they have families, work long hours, and sometimes travel. You may not have gotten an answer because the person to whom you wrote has moved and mail was forwarded slowly, or not at all.

6 "Can I make money as a picker?"

Many readers discover they enjoy making money the *Where To Sell It!* way. So they begin adding income by reselling things they buy from yard sales and flea markets run by people who have not read *Where To Sell It!* If you would like to become a successful part time seller of collectibles with a minimum of effort, *Where To Sell It!* is the single most important book you can own. It tells you exactly where to go to obtain expert guidance and to sell your finds promptly and profitably. An Oregon reader who says, "I pick up a thousand dollars a month to help out Social Security" is not alone. Other people in their 70's claim anyone willing to work seriously at yard sale shopping can make money.

7 "Can I sell to Canadians?"

Yes. Canadians are good buyers, but request payment with a check in U.S. funds drawn on a U.S. bank. Canadian collectors frequently maintain accounts for this purpose.   If you receive a Canadian bank check, it can cost you up to $15 in charges to cash at your bank. If drawn in Canadian money, you will also lose on the exchange rate. Canadian Postal Money Orders in U.S. funds are an excellent method of payment as they are inexpensive and can be cashed at full value by any U.S. post office. Reminder: a one ounce first class letter to Canada is 40¢.

8 "Is Dr. Hyman available for consultation?"

Yes, Tony Hyman occasionally helps disburse important collections. You can get also get Dr. Tony Hyman in your own home on tape. Send long SASE for a catalog to: TH Tape, Box 3028, Pismo Beach, CA 93448.

9 "If I wait, won't prices go up more?"

Maybe. Maybe not. Many items sell for less today than they did a few years ago. Just as the value of gold or the stock market goes up and down constantly, so does the value of antiques and collectibles. A few years ago, a rare Edgar Alan Poe 1827 paperback was found in a pile of equipment catalogs for $15, and resold for $198,000. When that some book resold at auction in 1992, its price had plunged to under $150,000.

Items sold during 1987-89 when things soared upward in an inflationary spiral, are now often selling at half to three-quarters of those figures, and in a few hobbies only the very best items are selling at all. It's true that over the long haul, prices tend to rise. But they often rise far less than the benefits you gain by converting those items to cash now.

10 "Why not give it away?"

No matter where you live, there are local churches and organizations looking for good usable second hand goods to either use or resell in thrift shops or at fund-raising rummage sales. Public libraries everywhere hold book sales, and can use donations of books of all sorts.

The Disabled American Veterans are one of many groups looking for cars in good condition for use or resale. When you are purchasing a new car, consider donating your present vehicle instead of trading it in. With tax breaks, you may be dollars ahead.

When we make donations, we give things away without strings. Recipients want the freedom to dispose of your gifts as they see fit. Get a signed, dated, and itemized receipt in the event the donation proves to be tax deductible. If substantial sums of money or valuable items are involved, it is a good idea to talk with your attorney or tax advisor.

Obsolete corporate inventory, services, or other assets can be donated to EAL, a non-profit group who barters your donations with colleges in exchange for tuition scholarships for disadvantaged youth. Donations can range from hard goods such as paint, paper products, office furniture, computers, and lab equipment to such intangibles as catering, conference centers, hotel rooms, transportation, and the like. EAL is a 501(c)(3) tax-exempt organization. For information: Peter Roskam or Eric Anderson, P.O. Box 3021 Glen Ellyn, IL 60138 (708) 690-0010   Fax: (708) 690-0565.

Each reader must decide for himself or herself whether to sell or give away an item to anyone listed in this book. Neither I nor the publisher can guarantee the results of any transaction. We can only provide the most accurate information available on potential buyers, and share with you the sources I use when I wish to sell.

Furniture, rugs and lamps

Yes, you can sell big heavy things like furniture, lamps and rugs by telephone or through the mail.

If you own "furniture store" bedroom or dining room suites from the 1920-1960 era, unless they were originally expensive designer pieces, they probably have little if any collector value. The best way for you to sell these is through classified ads in your local newspaper. Older furniture should be checked by an expert, as should all items of designer furniture no matter how new. Chairs and tables from the 1940's and 50's can be worth in excess of $2,000 if they were created by the right designers. Many classic designs have been reproduced or copied. As a result, some pieces must be seen in person to determine their value.

Many leaded lamps have also been reproduced. These reproductions sell new for around $250 and are worth only $20 to $100 in local markets. If you have original leaded or painted lamps from before 1930, however, the value can run into the multiple thousands of dollars, so don't be hesitant to ask an expert for assistance.

Damaged rugs seldom have buyers, but broken lamps and lamp parts before 1930 almost always can be worth some cash to you. After saying that about damaged rugs, I must report that a small scrap of a 15th century rug just sold in excess of $10,000. Contrary to popular belief the finest Oriental rugs are not thickly piled carpets, but are in fact rather thin (it's the way they are preferred in the Middle East) so don't be fooled into thinking your carpet has no value just because the threads aren't long and lush. Every very large or very old rug must be checked out by an expert. All you need to avoid expensive mistakes is a good photo and *Where To Sell It!*

Because furniture, lamps, and rugs have the potential to be worth hundreds, even thousands or tens of thousands, of dollars, the fuss of taking a photograph is justified and almost always required by buyers. If possible, your photos should be 35mm slides or prints. If you don't own a 35mm camera, ask a friend to take the photos for you, but don't go to the expense of hiring a professional photographer as that cost is seldom justified. You should send buyers close-ups of details, such as inlay and drawer pulls on furniture, patterns, edging and Arabic signatures on rugs, and the colors of shades and configuration of the base of lamps.

If sending a photo is not possible, you may wish to telephone the buyer and discuss your item. Be prepared to answer specific questions about colors, dimensions, type of wood, labels, etc.

Make certain when selling large or heavy items that you and the buyer agree who has responsibility for packing and shipping. This cost is normally born by the buyer.

Large furniture pieces can often be handled by moving companies or other truckers and freight haulers. As a rule, you should request the buyer to have large items picked up as part of the sale. This is particularly important if you are elderly, have difficulty getting around, find it hard to use a telephone, or if you live outside a big city.

In many American towns and cities there are "packing stores" which can ship almost any small or medium sized item, such as lamps and accessories. Most packer/shippers will pick up items for a small fee if you are not too far away from their place of business. Look under "Packaging Service" in the local Yellow Pages.

FURNITURE

★ **Entire estates including furniture and accessories from the American colonial period,** art, or important collections of toys, dolls, guns, decoys, miniature lamps, art glass, advertising, or other specialties. Your estate or collection must have a value in excess of $50,000 to be handled by this important firm. No interest in minor collectibles, limited edition plates, or common items.
>   James D. Julia Auctioneers
>   PO Box 80
>   Fairfield, ME 04937
>   (207) 453-7904   Fax: (207) 453-2502

★ **Heavily carved or decorated American furniture made between 1820-80** including fancy Empire, Gothic revival, American Renaissance, rococo, etc., especially furniture made by *Belter, Roux,* or *Meeks.* Also **gas chandeliers and *Argand Astral* lamps.** This prestigious dealer does not make offers so research is in order since many of these pieces can be very valuable. Send her a photo of the furniture plus a copy of every label or maker's mark you can find. She will help an amateur seller if you're really *selling* and not fishing for free appraisals.
>   Joan Bogart
>   PO Box 265
>   Rockville Centre, NY 11571
>   (516) 764 0529

★ **Furniture and accessories from the Arts & Crafts or "Mission" period.** Buys oak furniture, light fixtures, and metalwork by *L. & J.G. Stickley, Gustav Stickley, Roycroft, Limberts, Lifetime, Charles Stickley, Rohlfs, Stickley Brothers,* and *Dirk Van Erp,* especially unusual pieces, custom made pieces, and items inlaid with silver, pewter or copper. Also textiles, various publications, and catalogs from these firms. "If you have any doubts, please call. I will be glad to help."
>   Robert Berman, Le Poulaille
>   441 South Jackson Street
>   Media, PA 19063
>   (215) 566-1516

★ *Roycroft* **furniture and accessories including lamps,** waste baskets, clocks, frames, art, pottery, china, glassware, and all books and paper ephemera associated with the *Roycroft* company or its founder, Elbert Hubbard. When you write, make certain to state honestly whether the item is for sale or whether you are seeking identification and appraisal. Please give the source of the item for sale and include any stories or history you know about the piece(s).
>   Tom Knopke, House of Roycroft
>   1430 East Brookdale Place
>   Fullerton, CA 92631
>   (714) 526-1749

★ **Adirondack and other rustic furniture.** "I'll buy rustic furniture made of roots, twigs, antlers, diamond willow, or birch bark, and hickory furniture from the *Old Hickory Company*. Dealers must price their goods but I will help amateur sellers set a price, as long as their letter includes a photo and a complete description, including all damage."

    Barry Friedman
    22725 Garzota Drive
    Valencia, CA 91355
       (805) 296-2318

★ **Twig furniture.** "I'm interested in any type of rustic or Adirondack furniture. This includes pieces by *Old Hickory* and *Twig Furniture*. The wilder the style, the more I will want it. As always the better the condition, the more I will pay. If you have any doubts, call."

    Robert Berman, Le Poulaille
    441 South Jackson Street
    Media, PA 19063
       (215) 566-1516

★ **Wicker furniture and luggage.** "I'll consider any good condition old wicker, but am most interested in Bar Harbor Victorian characterized by curled arms and an open weave that you can see through. Pieces can be in any color, but natural is usually best. **Wicker luggage** can have either leather or brass trim, but should be in fine condition, inside and out, suitable for resale. Give the dimensions, status and color of the lining, condition of the wicker, hardware, and the leather trim."

    Joan Brady
    834 Central Ave.
    Pawtucket, RI 02861
       (401) 725-5753

★ **Designer furniture from the 1940's and 50's** by Herman Miller, Knoll, Eames, Nelson, Gilbert Rohde, Frank Lloyd Wright, Heywood Wakefield, Noguchi, Thonet, and other national and international designers. Most pieces are signed on the bottom. Primarily interested in bent plywood chairs, tables, couches, desks, and dressers as well as chrome furniture by Frank Lloyd Wright.

    Frank Novak
    7386 Beverly Blvd.
    Los Angeles, CA 90036
       (213) 683-1963   Fax: (213) 683-1312

★ **Folding chairs.** Interested in everything dealing with folding chairs, including photographs of chairs in use in lodges, churches, picnics or other events. Send a photo or photocopy of offered chairs, catalogs or photographs. Especially wants chairs with advertising on the back.

    Richard Bueschel
    414 North Prospect Manor Ave.
    Mt. Prospect, IL 60056

RUGS

★ **High quality rugs and tapestries.** Oriental, Chinese, European, American Indian, and large hooked rugs are all of interest if of sufficient quality and condition. Interested in Art Deco, art nouveau, and arts and crafts rugs and textiles as well. Worldwide interest in fine tapestries, textiles, embroideries, and weavings as well as paisley and Kashmir shawls. A good clear color photograph is important. Make certain to mention wear or stains. Appraisals and offers are made *only* after actually seeing your rug. Gallery open by appointment only.
    Renate Halpern Galleries
    325 East 79th Street
    New York, NY 10021
        (212) 988-9316

★ **Oriental rugs.** Claims "highest prices paid" for Oriental rugs of all types: antique, used, or just old.
    David Tiftickjian, Jr.
    260 Delaware Ave.
    Buffalo, NY 14202
        (716) 852-0556

★ **Rugs with advertising logos, cartoons or images** such as Buster Brown, *Coca-Cola,* etc.
    Charles Martignette
    PO Box 293
    Hallandale, FL 33009
        (305) 454-3474

★ **Greenfell hooked mats/rugs.** "I'll buy any tightly hooked textile, mat, or rug labeled GREENFELL LABRADOR INDUSTRIES as long as it is in excellent condition. These always depict Northern scenes like polar bears, igloos, Eskimos, etc. Please send dimensions and a photo with your first letter. Dealers are expected to price their goods, but amateurs may request an offer."
    Barry Friedman
    22725 Garzota Drive
    Valencia, CA 91355
        (805) 296-2318

LAMPS

★ **Lamps and lamp parts of all types from all periods.** Buys a wide range of wall, floor, and table lamps from the Betty lamps of the 1700's right through to the 1950's. Will buy kerosene, whale oil, electric, *Aladdin*, organ, marriage, student, desk, and other lamps. Also interested in *Tiffany* and other high quality leaded and painted lamps. This major Western dealer can be very helpful to amateurs with just about any type of lamp to sell. **Especially wants *Aladdin* lamps and parts** including galleries, chimney cleaners, bug screens, flame spreaders, wick cleaners, wick raisers, finials, and anything else made by *Aladdin*. Also buys parts from other lamp makers. If you have lamps or parts for sale, please note whether they are brass or nickel plated and give all numbers and wording. A photo is very helpful if asking for an offer.

    Richard Melcher
    1206 Okanogan Street
    Wenatchee, WA 98807
    (509) 662-0386

★ **Lamps and light fixtures from the early 1800's to the early 1940's** are wanted by this veteran lighting restoration dealer. He buys old iron, brass, or tin electric or gas fixtures, wall sconces, chandeliers, colored glass shades from fixtures, and damaged fixtures suitable for scavenging parts. He will buy inside or **outside lighting fixtures**, (including street lights) and has particular interest in those from commercial buildings as well as homes. He notes that large fixtures can be disassembled and shipped at his expense. Note all cracks or chips in glass. He is not interested in reproduction shades or in any fluorescent fixtures. He is, however, strongly interested in **catalogs from manufacturers** or retailers which depict large numbers of lighting fixtures from before 1920.

    Robert Daly, Historic Lighting Restoration Sales & Service
    10341 Jewell Lake Court
    Fenton, MI 48430
    (313) 629-4934

★ **Reverse painted, leaded glass, or art glass lamps** including table lamps, boudoir lamps, and floor lamps. "I am interested in buying shades, bases or parts for lamps of these types. I have a special interest in *Moe-Bridges*, *Classique Studios*, or *Phoenix Light Co*. I am also interested in buying catalogs from lamp and lighting fixture manufacturers (not retailers) before 1935." Does not want oil lamps, hurricane lamps, Gone With the Wind lamps, etc. No lamps after 1920's. Give all names and numbers found anywhere on the lamp or shade, and all dimensions. He prefers you to set your own price, but will make offers.

    Merlin Merline
    PO Box 16265
    Milwaukee, WI 53216
    (414) 871-6261

★ *Tiffany* **and other high quality glass lamps.** "I believe we are the only auction firm in North America that conducts specialty auctions for rare lamps only." Collections, large or small, of *Tiffany, Handel, Jefferson, Pairpoint,* and other quality lamps, lamp bases, and lamp shades from both **large and small oil and electric lamps** will be considered by this record setting auctioneer. Photos are a must. Telephone if you have a large group of lamps to sell.

>James D. Julia Auctioneers
>PO Box 80
>Fairfield, ME 04937
>(207) 453-7904 Fax: (207) 453-2502

★ **Lamps and light fixtures** in fine or restorable condition are sought by this restoration house.

>Helene Hilton, Bright Idea Home Lighting Center
>8563 Oswego Road, Route 57
>Baldwinsville, NY 13027

★ **Small bedroom lamps made of art glass.**

>Madeleine France
>PO Box 15555
>Plantation, FL 33316

★ *Tiffany* **lamps, chandeliers, and other high quality glass lighting fixtures.** Please include photos and your phone number.

>Carl Heck
>PO Box 8416
>Aspen, CO 81612
>(303) 925-8011

Lamp collectors want to know if your lamp is original and complete, and if there is anything wrong with it.

You should mention if it shows any signs of repair or of being a marriage of parts from different lamps. Describe the quality of the finish on the base and whether the glass shows any cracks or chips.

A signature on the base or shade usually makes a lamp worth more. Look carefully, as signatures can be very hard to locate on some valuable lamps.

★ *Tiffany* **lamps and grapevine picture frames.** Lamps bring from $2,500 up. Frames are worth from $300 to $1,500 depending upon their size and condition. Dawson requests a complete description of condition and return privileges if judged not to be as described. He prefers you to set the price, but will help amateur sellers if their item is for sale.

> T. O. Dawson
> 2110 Noel Drive
> Champaign, IL 61821
> (217) 352-7373 eves

★ **Lamps and light fixtures from the "Mission" or Arts & Crafts period.** Anything signed by *L. & J.G. Stickley, Gustav Stickley, Roycroft, Limberts, Lifetime, Charles Stickley, Rohlfs, Stickley Brothers,* and *Dirk Van Erp*, especially unusual pieces, custom made pieces, and items inlaid with silver pewter or copper. Also catalogs from these firms. "If you have any doubts, please call. I will be glad to help."

> Robert Berman, Le Poulaille
> 441 South Jackson Street
> Media, PA 19063
> (215) 566-1516

★ *Emeralite* **and** *Bellova* **lamps,** 1909 to 1940's, wall, desk, table, and floor models, either green-shaded, acid etched or reverse painted models. These are found with brass or with other metal bases. Prefers signed pieces. Unsigned pieces must be heavily decorated to be of interest. A photo "is essential."

> Bruce Bleier
> 73 Riverdale Road
> Valley Stream, NY 11581
> (516) 791-4353

★ **Revolving radio and TV lamps** from the 1930's, 40's, and 50's that are driven by the heat of the light bulb. These were made by *Econolite Corp, Scene In Action,* and *Rev-O-Lite* among others. "I will pay $350 for the scene in a fish bowl, and other substantial amounts for mermaids, motorcycles, snow skiers, sailing ships, water skiers, Santa Claus, and many others. Please call if you have one for sale."

> Bill and Linda Montgomery
> PO Box 68572
> Portland, OR 97268
> (503) 652-2992

★ **Lamp shades of cloth or beaded silk** from 1890 to 1930's that are in near perfect condition. He'd like you to send a photo, the dimensions, and your asking price.

> Charles Martignette
> PO Box 293
> Hallandale, FL 33009
> (305) 454-3474

Pottery and glass

Pottery, porcelain, china, bisque, parian, and stoneware are names often misunderstood by most amateur sellers. Fortunately, to sell the *Where To Sell It!* way, you don't need to know much more than the basics.

Essentially, all these products are "earthenware" made from one form or another of clay. The different names signify the quality and colors of the raw materials and the processes under which they are fired and decorated. Earthenware takes many forms, such as dinner dishes, vases, flower pots, bottles, sculpture, decorative objects, figurines, crocks, tiles, as well as commercial products such as insulators.

Artists and manufacturers worldwide, large and small, have worked in clay for centuries. Their surviving work ranges in value, from a few pennies to tens of thousands of dollars. Collectors frequently treasure items once thought ordinary, so take caution when disposing of pottery items of all types, as those that are valuable are not always easy for the untrained eye to detect.

The output of a few dozen 20th century factories such as *Cowan, Fulper,* and *Weller* have become popular, while the work of other makers is often ignored by collectors. Some "companies" were one-person operations, like that of the eccentric George Ohr, "The Mad Potter of Biloxi." His strange unusually shaped and glazed pottery tends to start at $300 and escalate rapidly. Blue decorated stoneware crocks, with less imaginative shapes, but with interesting folk art decorations start at that same price level and can climb to even higher values.

When attempting to determine the monetary worth of your bowl or figure, remember that the quality of the clay and the delicacy of the painting do not guarantee collector acceptability and high prices. Popularity and scarcity do.

Similar conditions prevail in the world of buying, selling, and collecting glass. The work of some companies and periods is hotly sought after, while other, often older and rarer types of glass go relatively ignored.

Glass, like clay, is manufactured into many forms and colors, some worth hundreds of thousands of dollars, others worth only recycling! Advice in selling glass is essential since it is difficult for the amateur to tell the good from the bad, the common from that worth $100 or more.

Because color has so much to do with value of both glass and earthenware, a photo is almost essential to sell anything other than a stock item from a well-known factory. An otherwise identical piece of glass or pottery can be worth fifty times as much in one color as in another. If you can't send a photo, "at the very least," advises Majolica buyer Denise Sater, "accurately describe the color, give the dimensions, patterns, and marks, along with a statement of condition."

Whether purchasing earthenware or glass, buyers seldom want chipped, stained, or damaged items, although a few very large and/or rare "bruised" pieces may find a market. Bruised pieces always sell for a great deal less than perfect ones, however.

Pottery and glass can be shipped safely. Make certain you get specific instructions from the buyer on how he or she wants the newly purchased item packed. Follow the simple steps for double-boxing explained in the Introduction to *Where To Sell It!* and you'll usually be safe.

POTTERY (earthenware)

★ **American art pottery of all types.** "I'll buy pottery from *Fulper, Paul Revere, Rookwood, Grueby, Dedham, TECO, Tiffany, Clewell, Marblehead, Saturday Evening Girls, Newcomb College, George Ohr, Van Briggle, Cowan, Grand Feu, Losanti, New Orleans Art Pottery, Robineau,* and other quality American art pottery. I'll also buy good **quality European pottery** such as *Martin Bros, Moorcroft,* and others." Especially likes large and unusual pieces, and has been known to consider damaged pieces if they are important. "If you have any doubts, phone me and I will be glad to be of assistance."
    Robert Berman, Le Poulaille
    441 South Jackson Street
    Media, PA 19063
    (215) 566-1516

★ *Van Briggle* **and other American art pottery.** A variety of fine pottery will be considered, including *Rookwood* that is artist signed, *North Dakota School of Mines* pottery "with good color contrast," *Hylong, Newcombe,* decorated *Marblehead,* and the like. But his primary interest is in pre-1913 *Van Briggle* pottery, the man who created it, and the company that produced it. Wants company records and catalogs, as well as paintings and pots signed by Van Briggle. Will even accept damaged pre-1913 pieces "if priced accordingly." Is not interested in undated *Van Briggle* or in *ND School of Mines* that is plain. Describe the size, shape, colors, glaze quality, bottom markings, and condition. Scott is a former president of the American Art Pottery Association and author of *The Collector's Guide to Van Briggle,* available from him for $35 and a *Van Briggle Price Guide* for $6.50. He does appraisals for a fee, and expects you to price your own goods.
    Scott Nelson
    PO Box 6081
    Santa Fe, NM 87502
    (505) 986-1176

★ *Stangl* **pottery.** "We especially want *Stangl* toby mugs with ashtray hats, *Stangl* birds and animals, flower pots, and flower ashtrays. We want "rainbow ware," and drippy blue, green, orange, and yellow artware. Also the following dinnerware patterns: Fruit, Fruit and Flowers, Country Gardens, Country Life, Blueberry, Garden Flower, Thistle, Town and Country, Chicory, Yellow and Blue Tulip, Wild Rose, and all Christmas patterns. We don't want brown stains, chips, or cracks, but minor flaws are acceptable."
    Bob and Nancy Perzel, Popkorn Antiques
    PO Box 1057
    Flemington, NJ 08822
    (908) 782-9631

★ **Weller, TECO and other American art pottery.** *"TECO* pottery is my favorite. I'll buy geometric and organic vases with square or built in handles. Sculptural leaves and plant forms, usually in matte finish with green tones, but also brown, yellows, grays, etc. This is often highlighted in a black/gray gunmetal color. I am also a strong buyer of *Weller* vases with raised figures, lizards, snakes, nudes, etc. *Weller* also comes in strong geometrics. Colors are rose, pink, blue, gray, yellow, brown and matte green, often mixed, often veined with gun-metal. Normally signed. I buy a great deal of *Weller*, including many of their other lines." He also buys a wide range of other art pottery including *Grueby, Saturday Evening Girls, Newcomb College, University of North Dakota, Jervis, American Art Clay, Fulper, George Ohr, Arequipa, California Faience, Chelsea Keramic, Clewell, Clifton* (large vases only), and many more. Strongly suggests you take a picture since the form and color of pottery determines value. When you send your photo, write down carefully all the marks you find on the bottom of your pottery.

Gary Struncius
PO Box 1374
Lakewood, NJ 08701
(800) 272-2529

★ **Ceramic flower frogs and candelabra** depicting ladies dancing or posing in the Art Deco style. "I'm especially interested in those made by the Ohio pottery company called *Cowan*, but will buy European makers as well." He especially seeks *Cowan* frogs number 708, 717, 803, 804, 805, 812, and 853 as well as the figural dancing candelabra #752. These can bring from $150 to $600, depending on the figure, colors, and condition, so are definitely worth your time. To sell your frog, note all the markings you can find.

William Sommer
9 West 10th Street
New York, NY 10011
(212) 260-0999

★ **Weller flower frogs.** "I buy *Weller* flower frogs. How do you tell a *Weller* frog? Pottery flower frogs with bees, butterflies, frogs, fish, women, lily pads, etc. sitting on top a base are probably *Weller* if they are colored with greens, beiges, white, and muted orange. Those are basic *Weller* colors."

Susan Cox
800 Murray Drive
El Cajon, CA 92020
(619) 447-0800 days

★ **Stoneware crocks and jugs with blue decorations.** Especially likes pottery with clear incised markings from NY, NJ, OH, PA, and New England. "I'll pay top dollar for unusual forms decorated with people, animals, ships, trees, houses, strong blue florals, etc. Dated pieces are particularly desirable. I pay from $100 to as much as $10,000 for the right items." He emphasizes that he is interested only in stoneware that is blue decorated, not brown or white. Also buys inkwells, flasks, and unusual small items made of blue decorated stoneware. Needs to know the size of the piece in quarts or gallons if marked, in inches if not. Take a photo or make a good sketch of the decoration because the more unusual the decoration, the more he pays. Mention the darkness of the blue. He will help amateur sellers determine what they have.

    Richard Hume
    1300 Northstream Parkway
    Point Pleasant, NJ 08742
       (908) 899-8707 eves

★ **Spongeware, stoneware, and redware pottery and crockery.** Note all markings on the sides and bottoms, please, if you'd like this important dealer to evaluate what you have. These are often incised with the name of the maker or user, and their city and town, as well as the size of the container. Minor damage and cracks are acceptable in very rare pieces, but you must note all damage, no matter how small. The decoration is the key to value, so photos are essential.

    Louis Picek, Main Street Antiques and Art
    PO Box 340
    West Branch, IA 52358

★ **Stoneware pottery.** "I'll buy pre-1900 stoneware pottery crocks, jugs, pitchers, flasks, churns, and bottles with cobalt blue decoration, especially those depicting birds, animals, people, flowers, buildings, flags, or dates. I also buy pottery marked ROBINSON CLAY PRODUCTS, OLD SLEEPY EYE, or with elongated (stretched out) numbers on the bottom. I do not buy *Red Wing* pottery." Please send a photo, dimensions, and list of any defects. Dealers are expected to price their goods, but he will help amateur sellers. "Nobody answers faster."

    Barry Friedman
    22725 Garzota Drive
    Valencia, CA 91355
       (805) 296-2318

★ **Redware plates, bowls, and other pieces.** When describing, mention all marks on the bottom and take a photo or make a sketch of the pattern, indicating what part of the pattern is yellow or green. Make certain you note if there are any cracks or chips.

    Richard Hume
    1300 Northstream Parkway
    Point Pleasant, NJ 08742
       (908) 899-8707 eves

★ **Pottery made in Georgia, Alabama and the Carolinas.** Wants utilitarian items made 1870 to 1930, such as bowls, face jugs, churns, etc.
Allen Woodall
PO Box 1646
Columbus, GA 31994

★ **Pottery by the Buffalo Pottery Company.** Also wants catalogs and other Buffalo Pottery Company ephemera.
Thomas Knopke
1430 East Brookdale Place
Fullerton, CA 92631
(714) 526-1749

★ **Buffalo Pottery.** "I'll buy almost any marked piece."
Seymour Altman
8970 Main Street
Clarence, NY 14031
(716) 634-4488

MAJOLICA

★ **Italian pottery (Majolica)** of all types, such as flower pots, vases, dinnerware, bottles, lamps, tiles, dishes, figurines, pockets, etc. "The pieces are all hand-painted in bright colors, often on a white background. There are hundreds of types of decoration: fruit, flowers, people, mythical and religious themes, architecture, etc, but always in bright reds, blues, yellows, greens, and rose (usually all of the above!). Many are reproductions of pieces created during the Renaissance, others are more modern and look like souvenirs. I am interested in all types if they are marked MADE IN ITALY on the bottom. Sometimes the markings also identify the region where they were made, such as GUBBIO, DERUTA, ASSISI, etc." A photo is "very helpful," but at the very least, give the dimensions, patterns, colors, and marks, along with a statement of condition. The price you'd like is "helpful" but not required.
Denise Sater
PO Box 591
Maytown, PA 17550
(717) 426-2957

★ **Majolica pottery.** Interested in all 19th century Majolica pieces from any country. Claims to pay top dollar for this brightly colored pottery. Asks you to send a photo.
Rick Kranz
702 West Olive
Stillwater, MN 55082
(612) 430-3016

GLASS

★ **Antique and 20th century art glass.** This well known auctioneer conducts cataloged auctions of art glass, so can handle collections and fine individual pieces of *Daum Nancy, Steuben, Galle, Tiffany* and other art glass, as well as collections and fine pieces of *Wedgwood* and other fine porcelain.

> James D. Julia Auctioneers
> PO Box 80
> Fairfield, ME 04937
> (207) 453-7904   Fax: (207) 453-2502

★ **Antique Bohemian glass goblets, beakers,** and other types of drinking vessels. "I'll buy colored or clear glass with wheel engraved landscape scenes, portraits, animals, spa scenes, religious themes, etc. In addition to wheel engraved items, I'm seeking pieces decorated with transparent or opaque enamels, overlays, gilt work, cutting, paintings, etc. Cameos are particularly desirable." Not interested in any other glass. He notes, "There are many, many reproductions of this glass. It takes a trained eye to tell the difference." Common, and not desirable, pieces include deer and castle, deer and pine trees, and bird and castle. Later pieces are simple and the engraving lacks detail in the animals. You must send a close-up photo of this potentially valuable glass and note every chip, flake, or crack. Dealers are expected to price their goods, but he will make offers to amateur sellers. You must include an SASE if you wish your photos back.

> Tom Bradshaw
> 325 Carol Drive
> Ventura, CA 93003

★ **Antique glass paperweights,** 1845-1900. "I will buy fine French (*Baccarat, Clichy, St. Louis*), American (*New England Glass Company, Sandwich*), English, and Bohemian paperweights. I am looking for millefiori, flowers, sulfides, fruit and animals." Among the most valuable are large 19th century French paperweights by *Pantin* which contain a lizard on rocky ground with flowers and plants around it. These can be worth as much as $50,000 but have been widely copied and the copies are worth as little as $50. It takes an expert to tell the difference. Other paperweights have also been copied, often including fake dates and wear. "I don't want china paperweights, Italian copies, plain glass, weights with photos, mottoes, or advertising, and no weights with air bubbles as part of the design." A close up color photo of your weight is important and should be accompanied by a good description. "I don't mind surface wear and nicks, but cracks in the glass are not acceptable." Include an SASE if you want photos returned. "I will make offers to amateur sellers, but dealers are expected to price their goods."

> Tom Bradshaw
> 325 Carol Drive
> Ventura, CA 93003

★ **Antique glass paperweights,** 1845-1900. "I will buy fine French (*Pantin, Baccarat, Clichy, St. Louis*), American (*Boston Glass Co., Sandwich Glass Co., New England Glass Co., Gillinoer, Mt. Washington*), English (*Bacchus, Whitefriars*), Russian and Bohemian paperweights. I am especially looking for *Pantin* paperweights from the late 1870's for which I will pay from $2,000 to $35,000. I also seek early *Clichy* bouquet on a moss background which can be worth as much as $40,000. I don't want paperweights with blobs of colored glass or with large bubbles in the design." A close up color photo of your weight is important and should be accompanied by a good description, including the diameter. This well known author and collector does not send out a wants list because, he explains, "I will purchase all top quality weights."
Paul Dunlop, The Dunlop Collection
PO Box 82370
Phoenix, AZ 85071
(800) 227-1996

★ **Antique glass items** including paperweights, art glass, glass pens, canes, and whimsies. Looks for the old and rare. Make certain to note all damage, no matter how small.
Stanley Block
PO Box 51
Trumbull, CT 06611
(203) 261-3223

When looking for something to sell, do not overlook the colored glass dinnerware of 1910-1940, commonly called "Depression glass," as a few pieces are surprisingly valuable. Covered butter dishes, for example, usually bring you $100 - $400 each. Candy dishes and water pitchers also bring better than average prices. Expert advice is essential, because pieces that have little value in one color or pattern can be worth $100 in another.

Be careful attempting to set a price on carnival glass, which ranges from $10 to $10,000. Work with the buyer when it comes to pricing, as rarities are very hard for anyone but an expert to recognize. A North Carolina woman sold a carnival glass plate for $1. The picker who bought it, resold it by telephone for $10,000 to one of the buyers listed in this book. That same buyer paid $10,000 for a pitcher I discovered during a radio talk show.

★ **Many kinds of glassware and china** are sought by one of the country's larger auction firms specializing in post-Victorian glass. He buys outright or accepts on consignment for auction:

  Carnival glass especially pitcher sets, tumblers, whimsies, opalescent pieces, and common items in rare patterns and colors. He encourages you to contact him with one item or a giant collection since there are many valuable pieces that only an expert will recognize;

  Victorian pattern glass;

  Cameo glass vases, plates, urns, and other glass items made by the *Phoenix Glass Co.*;

  RS Prussia china with scenes, portraits, or pearlized florals;

  Noritake **china** with geometric designs;

  Nippon china humidors and large high relief "blown out" vases depicting birds, animals, or figures;

  Mandarin red glassware by *Fenton Glass Company.*

Include your phone number if the piece is for sale. Tom has a reputation for being slow to respond, but helpful with amateur sellers. Phone him midweek if you think you have something good.

  Tom Burns, Burns Auction Service
  109 East Steuben Street
  Bath, NY 14810
    (607) 776-7942

★ **Carnival glass** is wanted "in any amount and any color." Prefers you to price, but may help amateurs "who are actually selling, not fishing for a price."

  Dick Hatscher
  142 Walnut Hill Road
  Bethel, CT 06801
    (203) 743-1468 eves

★ **Carnival glass.** "I'll buy one piece or a collection, in any colors." Prefers you to set the price.

  W. J. Warren
  38 Mosher Drive
  Tonawanda, NY 14150
    (716) 692-2886

★ **Depression glass** in various makers, colors, and patterns.

  Nadine Pankow
  207 South Oakwood
  Willow Springs, IL 60480
    (312) 839-5231

★ *Fostoria* **glass and memorabilia** are wanted by the founder of the *Fostoria* Glass Society in Southern California. "I'll buy dealer signs, dealer catalogs from before 1940, postcards, displays, trade cards, calendars, magazine ads (1924 to 1931 only), and any other *Fostoria* Glass Company memorabilia that's in mint condition." His glass wants are more restricted as he only buys frosted or clear **Victoria** (pattern #183) and rare pieces of pattern #2412 called **Colony**. He is not interested in common Colony glassware or other *Fostoria* patterns, but finding a Victoria oil lamp is high on his list. "All items must be in mint condition or don't bother."

    Gary Schneider
    7301 Topanga Canyon Blvd. #202
    Canoga Park, CA 91303
       (818) 998-4588 or (818) 702-9967

★ **Glass toothpick holders** in mint condition. There are numerous patterns she is still seeking. Make a photocopy or photo of your holder if you don't know the name of its pattern, and describe the color as best you can. There are many reproduction holders, so she'll have to examine yours before making a final offer. Judy is founder of the Toothpick Holder Collectors Society and published their newsletter for 20 years.

    Judy Knauer
    1224 Spring Valley Lane
    West Chester, PA 19380
       (215) 431-3477

★ **Early American glass in** *Willow Oak* **pattern** in amber, blue, or Vaseline colors.

    Audrey Buffington
    2 Old Farm Road
    Wayland, MA 01778
       (508) 358-2644

★ **Fine crystal.** David runs a restoration service which repairs glass, crystal, porcelain, bisque, and figurines. He also buys damaged and undamaged figurines, *Hummels*, china and crystal for resale.

    David Jasper
    Rural Route 3 Box 330
    Sioux Falls, SD 57106
       (605) 361-7524

China and tableware

The first step in selling china and tableware is to ask yourself, "Would I want to buy this and use it?" No one wants chipped, stained, or damaged items. Unless your china dates before the Civil War (1860 or before), pieces must be in perfect condition to find a buyer.

China and crystal glassware is often purchased for resale by pattern matching services. From their point of view, the best china is unchipped service for 12 in a classic pattern by an important maker bought by your great grandmother in England or France and has since sat packed and unused.

On the other hand, if you raise a family, service for 12 becomes service for 7 in a surprisingly short time. But never fear, as one of the advantages of selling to matching services is that sets in a popular pattern do not have to be complete to have some value.

Don't expect to be paid a fortune for old china just because it's pretty or it belonged to great granny. China patterns and companies fall in and out of favor. One decade, plain patterns are in, the next decade may prefer elegant or flowery or formal. Because of recent social trends toward informality, you can't assume hordes of people are waiting to purchase your old china, silver, or glassware, no matter how lovely.

I don't mean to discourage you. Fine china, like fine anything, always has value. Serving pieces, especially large pieces and those with lids (like soup tureens) are harder to find and as a result worth more than ordinary table settings. The more unusual the piece, the more likely it is to have a market.

To sell china, begin by listing the pieces, and how many of each you have. Do not list pieces with cracks or chips. You should note all crazing, knife scratches and pattern wear on the pieces you choose to list.

If you don't know the pattern name, send a photocopy of the front and back of a small plate. Indicate the colors in your pattern and the color of the maker's mark on the back (as some companies use color codes). Photocopies usually give much more detail, hence give an expert an accurate look at what you have. If you are able to take sharp, close-up 35mm photographs, include a photo which shows the shape of a cup handle. If you can't take photos, a sketch which shows the shape of the handle and base of the cup compared to the bowl is sometimes very useful.

If you sell your china, the buyer will usually provide detailed packing instructions. If packed properly, china can be shipped around the world safely. In addition to the buyer's instructions, always remember one important rule: never let two pieces of china touch while packed. Padding such as bubble pack, styrofoam sheets, or similar material must separate every packed piece. Lids are almost certain to chip or break if they are left on sugar bowls and other covered dishes while they are being shipped.

CHINA

★ **Obsolete sets and pieces of fine English dinner china** including *Aynsley, Coalport, Lenox, Minton, Oxford, Paragon, Rosenthal, Spode, Royal Albert, Royal Crown Derby, Royal Doulton, Royal Worcester, Shelley, Wedgwood*, and some patterns in *Elite* and *Haviland*. Also buys and sells **popular patterns by American, French and German makers.** Margaret does business worldwide and will make offers for items she can use. Items *must* be in excellent condition. If you wish things appraised, there is a fee, which is refundable if and when they buy your dishes.

    Margaret Roe, Old China Patterns Unlimited
    1560 Brimley Road
    Scarborough, Ontario
    M1P 3G9, CANADA
    (416) 299-8880

★ *Wedgwood, Royal Doulton* and *Lenox* **china**. Also wants *Spode, Castleton, Coalport, Franciscan, Gorham, Pickard, Royal Worcester, Minton*, and *Flintridge* china. No giftware. Ives offers a free pamphlet *On Caring for your China* if you send her a business size SASE.

    Jacquelynn Ives, China Match
    219 North Milwaukee Street
    Milwaukee, WI 53202
    (414) 272-8880

★ **Discontinued English and American china patterns** in perfect condition, produced by *Castleton, Franciscan, French Haviland, Lenox, Spode, Minton, Pickard, Royal Doulton, Royal Worcester, Syracuse, Wedgwood*, etc. "We buy sets or incomplete sets consisting of ten pieces or more. For patterns in demand we buy outright; others are listed in our computer system and customers notified as to availability and prices. They do not want to buy Japanese china or *anything* that is imperfect. Roundhill personally collects 100+ year old museum quality *Worcester* products. He prefers you to set the selling price, but will make offers.

    J. Warren Roundhill, Patterns Unlimited WTS
    PO Box 15238
    Seattle, WA 98115

★ *Wedgwood, Adams, Coalport* and *Midwinter* **china in discontinued patterns** in mint condition. Especially likes to find Patrician, Wellesley, and quince patterns. Please state how many of each type piece you have, the manufacturer, and the name of the pattern. If you don't know the pattern, photocopy both sides of a small plate. This *Wedgwood* expert does not buy china by Johnson Brothers, Franciscan, Enoch Wedgwood or Wedgwood, Ltd., and is not interested in glassware.

    Gloria Voss Beyer, A Wedgwood China Cupboard
    740 Honey Creek Parkway
    Milwaukee, WI 53213
    (404) 259-1025

★ *Wedgwood* **commemorative ware transfer print china.** Earthenware or bone china plates, trivets, tiles, etc., that contain American scenes, calendars, views of historic places, children's topics, or scenes from literature. "We mainly want items of American interest, but will also buy some Canadian and Australian scenes." These pieces almost always bear backstamps marked JOSIAH WEDGWOOD & SONS, WEDGWOOD, ETRURIA or ETRURIA & BARLASTON. Calendar tiles from the 1870's and 80's are worth up to $200, and tiles honoring the Washington Light Infantry and President Garfield are worth in excess of $400 each. "It's hard to give advice as to what we don't want. People are better off to inquire by giving a good description, photo, description of the back markings and sending a photocopy of their tile. Some items will have to be seen before we can make an offer."

> Benton & Beverly Rosen, Mansion House
> 9 Kenilworth Way
> Pawtucket, RI 02860
> (401) 722-2927 or (508) 759-4303

★ **Sets or pieces of German, Bavarian, Czechoslovakian, and Austrian china** in fine condition. Companies stocked include *Johann Haviland, Bavarian, Heinrich, Fronconia, Meissen, Rosenthal Thomas, Royal Heidelberg, Krautheim,* and many more. China need not be old, just discontinued. They also purchase **some French patterns**, but want no French *Haviland*, Japanese china, or English china. "We buy no china with cracks, crazing, or chips, or china with the color in a pattern worn off, although we will accept pieces with a slight amount of gold wear. We ask that anyone wishing to sell would send us a colored photocopy of a six inch or eight inch plate. Copy the front for the design and the back so we can see the hallmark. We also need a good color photo of a plate and a cup. The cup should be photographed in silhouette so we can see the shape of the handle and if the cup is footed or flat. We will quote a fair purchase price for any items we can use. If we cannot use what you have, we will try to tell you how you can sell it in your locality."

> Joan Nackman
> 56 Meadowbrook
> Ballwin, MO 63011
> (314) 227-3444

★ **Sets or pieces of French, American, or English china and stemware** especially pieces by *Haviland, Castleton, Franciscan, Oxford, Royal Doulton, Lenox, Spode, Syracuse,* and *Wedgwood*. Wants **stemware** by *Cambridge, Duncan, Fostoria, Heisey, Imperial, Lenox, Rock Sharp,* and *Tiffin*. List only the perfect pieces, and give the measurements of all serving pieces. She does not buy German or Japanese china. Medley has been a dealer for 20 years.

> Laura Medley, Laura's China & Crystal
> 2625 West Britton Road
> Oklahoma City, OK 73120
> (405) 755-0582

★ *Haviland* **china for resale.** Buys sets or single unusual pieces. Especially wants jardiniers, claret jugs, unusual tea or toast sets, free form salads, syrup jugs, spoon trays, tea caddies, lemonade sets, and other unusual pieces. No individual saucers. If your Limoge china isn't marked *Haviland*, she doesn't want it. Pieces must be in mint condition with no wear or scratches. To sell your dishes, give the pattern name on the backstamp, a photocopy of the pattern, and note the colors. Eleanor has 22,000 pieces in stock and has a computerized search service to help customers find other dishes.
> Eleanor Thomas, Auld Lang Syne
> 7600 Highway 120
> Jamestown, CA 95327
> (209) 984-DISH

★ *Royal Doulton, Royal Worcester, Minton* **and other fine china and stoneware.** This 12 year veteran matching service also buys **most fine crystal** in popular patterns.
> Freda Bell's China Match
> 9 Elmford Road
> Rochester, NY 14606
> (716) 426-2783

★ **Nippon and** *Noritake* **china.** "We're seeking large vases, urns, portrait pieces, dolls, chocolate and tea sets, jugs, wall plaques, smoke sets, humidors, and anything else that's quality and perfect. We'll buy *Coralene, Moriage*, blown-outs, rectangulars, pieces with silver overlay, you name it! We're also in the market for *Noritake* with Art Deco decorations of men and women. Call or write if you have any."
> Mark Griffin and Earl Smith
> 1768 Maple Avenue
> Fort Myers, FL 33901
> (813) 334-0083

★ *Royal Doulton* **"logo china"** from hotels, restaurants, ships, railroads, airlines, and private companies of all types.
> Diane Alexander
> 20834 San Simeon Way #70-C
> North Miami Beach, FL 33179
> (305) 770-4422

★ *Buffalo Pottery* **or** *Buffalo* **china.** "I'll buy almost any marked piece made in that factory," he says.
> Seymour Altman
> 8970 Main Street
> Clarence, NY 14031
> (716) 634-4488

★ *Deldare Ware* made by the *Buffalo Pottery Company.* No damaged pieces, please.
>   Jerome Puma
>   78 Brinton Street
>   Buffalo, NY 14214
>   (716) 838-5674

★ *Warwick* **china, especially portrait items.** Include a photo with your complete description, and he'll return it. Promises to answer every letter regarding the work of this fine American china maker. Prefers you to set the price wanted, but "amateurs should still write."
>   Jeff Mauck
>   142 North 19th Street
>   Wheeling WV 26003
>   (304) 277-2356

★ **Cowboy theme dinnerware.** Sets or single pieces of pictorial china or pottery dinnerware which features cowboys or brand marks. Makers include *Wallace, Red Wing,* and *Tepco.*
>   Frank Novak
>   7386 Beverly Blvd.
>   Los Angeles, CA 90036
>   (213) 933-0383   Fax: (213) 683-1312

★ *Goss* **china** especially pictorials, cottages, busts, animals, military commemoratives and foreign crests.
>   Jeanne Goss Spaulding
>   1325 West Ave.
>   Hilton, NY 14468

★ **Pictorial souvenir china** with views of towns, streets, and places of interest. Especially interested in pictorial china with New England views, but all are considered. Indicate what the scene is, where the item was made, and whether there are any cracks or chips. Gary publishes *Antique Souvenir Collectors News,* the marketplace for antique souvenirs.
>   Gary Leveille
>   PO Box 562
>   Great Barrington, MA 01230
>   (413) 528-5490

★ *Wheelock* **souvenir china.** Bill buys this German made blue and green scenic souvenir china.
>   Bill Copeland
>   2 Clifton Park Court
>   Melrose, MA 02176

★ *Clarus Ware* **plates, bowls, vases and other china.** "We also buy old pieces of *Pope Gosser China Ware* and want any vase, bowl, plate, or other china signed AST VAN HISE."
C.W. and Hilda Roderick
27858 TR 31
Warsaw, OH 43844

★ **Series Ware by** *Royal Doulton* includes hundreds of shapes and patterns of pitchers, mugs, plates, and other useful, but highly decorated items. This popular transfer ware with a hand-painted look includes a wide variety of themes such as motoring, golfing, fishing, and coaching. Value is dependent on the rarity and desirability of the form and the image. There have been four books written on *Doulton* Series Ware, so you can get information at your local public library. If your item is for sale, call Ed, who lectures frequently in the U.S. and England, and has edited price guides to *Royal Doulton*. Also buys *Royal Doulton* **figurines, figural bottles and red animals** (see his listings in this book under Animals, Whiskey, and Figurines for more information). He is not interested in buying dinnerware, and does not do pattern matching.
Ed Pascoe, Pascoe & Co.
545 Michigan Ave.
Miami Beach, FL 33139
    (800) 872-0195   Fax: (305) 532-8543

★ *Clarice Cliff Bizarre Ware.* This English hand painted pottery is decorated with fanciful, geometric, and floral themes. Most pieces are marked, often with the name of the artist, but usually CLARICE CLIFF or BIZARE. Does not want transfer patterns, only painted ones such as Crocus, Fantasque, Delecia, Caprice, Ravel, and many others. A photo or photocopy is very important as the company made so many patterns, they're almost impossible to know which you have without seeing it.
Darryl Rehr
2591 Military Ave.
Los Angeles, CA 90064
    (310) 477-5229

WHEN OFFERING CHINA FOR SALE, ALWAYS:

(1) List how many of each type item (plates, saucers, cups, etc.) you have;

(2) Include a color photograph or a b/w photocopy which indicates the colors and patterns;

(3) Include a drawing or photocopy of what all mark(s) on the bottom of the china look like, and the color of those marks.

★ *Coors* **pottery and porcelain.** "I'll buy any dinnerware made by the Coors Company of Golden, CO. Decalware made in the *Thermo Porcelain* line is of particular interest, as are malted milk jars, **figurines,** art pottery, and advertising items *Coors* made for other companies. Among desirable figures are monks, turkeys, buffaloes, clown banks, and vases especially those more than 10" tall. *Coors* items made for the 1939 Colorado State Fair are among my favorite finds as well. I do not buy pharmaceutical or industrial items, common ashtrays, *Coorsite*, or things made by HF Coors. If you want to sell, I'll need to know what you have, its size, color, markings, and condition. It's helpful if you price, but not essential."

    Jo Ellen Winther
    8449 West 75th Way
    Arvada, CO 80005
        (800) 872-2345 days   (303) 421-2371 eves

★ **Oyster plates.** Nothing damaged, please.

    Sheldon Katz
    211 Roanoke Ave.
    Riverhead, NY 11901
        (516) 369-1100

★ **Eggcups.** If you have a fine eggcup to sell, the *Eggcup Collectors Corner* may be your best source of information. Sample copies of this club newsletter cost only $5 and will give you insights into cups and their prices, plus a bibliography. When you order your sample, tell Joan why you want one and she'll pick an appropriate issue. Members of the Eggcup Collector's Club share information about buying and selling.

    Joan George, editor, *Eggcup Collectors Corner*
    67 Stevens Ave.
    Old Bridge, NJ 08857

★ **Presidential and patriotic English urns, vases and mugs** with American historical motifs, pictures of political figures, battles, or famous events. May be any type of china by any maker. A delft teapot advocating NO STAMP ACT would bring around $6,000.

    Rex Stark
    49 Wethersfield Road
    Bellingham, MA 02019
        (508) 966-0994

    Packing china for shipment is not as hard as you might think, but does require proper care. Never allow two pieces to touch. Ask your buyer for specific packing instructions and read the section on "packing" in the front of *Where To Sell It!*

Household items

From flashlights to perfume bottles, this amazing array of items has three things in common. For the most part they are small, found around the home, and owned by people with little idea of their value.

These items litter the lawns of America each weekend, selling for a penny on the dollar. These are the fodder for legions of yard sale shoppers seriously stalking bargains.

In previous chapters, you discovered furniture and lamps worth in excess of $10,000, then learned that some pottery is also worth that much or more and that glass paperweights can be worth a quarter of a million dollars!

In this lengthy section of *Where To Sell It!* you will read about many hundreds of less expensive items worth $50 to $300, and a handful worth $1,000 or more. The odds are good that you already own one or more of these items, and that a relatively little amount of effort might put hundreds of dollars in your pocket.

If you are considering selling or giving away any of the items listed in the Household items section, you should exercise caution. An excellent way to exercise that caution is to deal with experts who can help you identify what's good and what's not.

Be especially careful when disposing of perfume bottles, clocks, quilts, samplers, and jewelry, as mistakes can be easily made and be very costly. In those few cases when you are dealing with buyers who will not make offers, it is essential you research what you plan to sell.

There is no special knack to selling small household items found in this section of the book. When offering any of these items to a *Where To Sell It!* buyer, follow the basic steps.

(1) Describe your item, noting colors, dimensions, and the materials from which it is made;

(2) Include a photograph or a photocopy. These items often photocopy easily because of their size.

(3) Be honest in your description of what's wrong with your item. Note all flaws.

(4) Be realistic in your expectations.

Many of the collecting hobbies represented in this chapter have only a handful of devotees. Some of these hobbies are only a few years old, and their ultimate fate, and the ultimate value of the items, will remain unresolved for years to come. Because some of these hobbies are so new, many items remain uncataloged and unknown. Other people find these items all the time. Why not you?

SPECIAL INCOME OPPORTUNITY TIP

I didn't write this book to encourage readers to purchase collectibles for speculation. It has become, however, the basic guide for pickers, people who make a living (or second income) out of shopping at yard sales and second hand stores. Since picking can be done by people of any age, it has become a popular way to supplement Social Security. If you'd like to make money by shopping and yard sales, flea markets, and second hand stores then reselling what you find to specialty buyers in *Where To Sell It!*, read every entry in this section on Household items. These items are frequently found priced well below value, even in antique shops. Other types of collectibles worth particular attention are found in Pottery, Pop Culture, Sports, Transportation, and Advertising. In each of those categories, you will occasionally find things you can resell to a *Where To Sell It!* buyer for fifty times what you paid. With a bit of work and study, it is possible for you to supplement your income significantly.

ACCESSORIES

★ **Accessories and personal items made of early thermoplastic,** often mistakenly called "gutta percha." "I'll buy any small thermoplastic items made between 1850 and 1900, including photo cases, **picture frames** in shapes other than rectangular, **mirrors** with figural scenes or unusual geometric designs, vanity sets (other than those rimmed in metal), **desk sets, wall plaques, boxes** of all types, **clocks** with this early plastic as part of the decoration, **jewelry,** and other items, from religious objects to door knobs. Please send a photo or photocopy, along with a description of color, condition, and the price you'd like." Amateur sellers may request offers.
    Mike Semegran
    3711 West 230th Street #207
    Torrance, CA 90505
    (310) 373-0464

ACCESSORIES

Accessories are useful objects that are also decorative. Collectors seek high quality items in good condition from important makers. Damaged items are almost never of interest. Values can run into the hundreds of dollars, with a few lamps bringing more.

★ **Art Deco accessories.** "I'll buy Deco items that compliment my collection of radios." Ed is interested in a wide range of distinctive Deco items, so give him a try for items like clocks, **picture frames**, and **lamps**. If you are the original owner, he'd appreciate the item's history. He prefers you to set your price but will make offers if you are an amateur seller intending to sell.
    Ed Sage
    PO Box 1234
    Benicia, CA 94510
    (707) 746-5659

★ **Items made of banded agate.** Will purchase **pens, button hooks, snuff boxes**, and **small decorative items** made entirely or mostly of banded agate. If you want to sell, give dimensions and condition.
    Stanley Block
    PO Box 51
    Trumbull, CT 06611
    (203) 261-3223

★ **Gold bearing quartz items.** Masculine items made from or decorated with quartz containing gold flakes and nuggets are sought. Items include **matchsafes, cane handles, watch fobs, watches, desk sets, money clips**, etc. Sandra doesn't have much interest in jewelry, "unless it's exceptional." Sending a photocopy or photograph is the best way to sell.

> Sandra Whitson
> PO Box 272
> Lititz, PA 17543
> (717) 626-4978

★ **Indian motif sterling silver** items made for men by *Unger Bros.* Items she seeks include **desk sets, clothes brushes, matchsafes**, etc. Has only limited interest in women's items and jewelry by *Unger*, but will buy some items.

> Sandra Whitson
> PO Box 272
> Lititz, PA 17543
> (717) 626-4978

★ **Arts and crafts period lamps and accessories** made by *Van Erp, Roycroft, Limberts, Stickley,* and others. Lamps are often copper and colored glass, as are **cigarette boxes, bookends, ashtrays, humidors, desk sets**, and other items. Better pieces are often inlaid with silver. This active arts and crafts expert also buys **furniture** by these makers, whose work tends to be massive square oak furniture, often with dark finishes, visible pegs and hinges, and simple unornamented lines. Many people call it "mission oak." Send a photo or call if you think you have one of these pieces, as some can be quite valuable.

> David Rago
> PO Box 3592, Station E
> Trenton, NJ 08629
> (609) 585-2546

★ **Accessories from the Mission or Arts & Crafts period** including light fixtures and metalwork by *L. & J.G. Stickley, Gustav Stickley, Roycroft, Limberts, Lifetime, Charles Stickley, Rohlfs,* and *Dirk Van Erp,* especially unusual pieces, custom made pieces, and items inlaid with silver, pewter or copper. He is also interested in catalogs from these firms. "If you have any doubts about what you have, please call. I will be glad to help."

> Robert Berman
> Le Poulaille
> 441 South Jackson Street
> Media, PA 19063
> (215) 566-1516

KITCHEN CERAMICS & GLASS

★ **Figural cookie jars** are wanted by Chicago's only shop devoted exclusively to kitchen counter novelties. Wants figural ceramic jars and jar tops, but nothing cracked or repaired. Jars that aren't figural aren't of interest. She also buys **figural salt and pepper shakers.** She declares a photo to be essential, plus wants you to describe all markings on the bottoms of jars or salt sets. Make certain to mention every chip! Prefers you to price what you want to sell. She charges $10 per jar to make appraisals for insurance or estate purposes.
>Mercedes DiRenzo, Jazz'e Junque
>3831 North Lincoln Ave.
>Chicago, IL 60613
>   (312) 472-1500

★ **Figural cookie jars.** "I'll buy amusing, colorful jars in the shape of various people and animals, usually dating before 1950. Especially want those depicting fairy tales, nursery rhyme and cartoon characters such as Li'l Audrey or the Pearl China chef. I do not buy jars if they have any damage at all." This collector wants a photo or good description.
>Kier Linn
>2591 Military Ave.
>Los Angeles, CA 90064
>   (310) 477-5229

★ **Kitchenware by the *Shawnee Pottery Co.*** is wanted, but only their gold trimmed (with flower decals) cookie jars, creamers, pitchers, and teapots. Most pieces are marked SHAWNEE or MADE IN USA. This small popular company operated between 1937 and 1961.
>Van Stueart
>Route 3   Box 216
>Nashville, AR 71852
>   (501) 845-4864

★ **Teapots and pitchers from the Art Deco era.** "I'll buy solid color Deco era teapots and pitchers that exemplify the wonderful streamlined, geometric designs of the late Art Deco/moderne period." Makers to look for include *Hall, Fiesta, Riviera, Harlequin,* and others. Especially interested in *Hall* teapots. Not interested in items with gold trim or other decoration. No damaged items, no matter how small the damage. Please include a good description and sketch or photo.
>Kier Linn
>2591 Military Ave.
>Los Angeles, CA 90064
>   (310) 477-5229

★ **Unusual condiment sets.** Combination salt, pepper, and mustard sets are wanted if they are unusual and figural. Wants pieces without chips or repairs, but will consider slightly damaged goods if the piece is extremely unusual. Especially likes German sets, and those with designs related to water. A picture is important.

> Sylvia Tompkins
> 25-C Center Drive
> Lancaster, PA 17601
> (717) 569-9788

★ **Novelty figural salt and pepper shakers related to water.** She'll buy fish, frogs, ducks, penguins, seals, umbrellas, bridges, mermaids, sailors, firemen, fishermen, pirates, boats, lighthouses, shells, lobsters, crabs, alligators, seagulls, pelicans, dinosaurs, watermelons, sea serpents, and more! Generally doesn't want sets with chips or repairs, unless they are very rare. "Pictures are the only way to describe things. I have several thousand sets and it's impossible to know whether I have it without seeing a picture." (Photocopies would probably be fine). Likes you to set the price, but will make offers. Editor of the quarterly newsletter of the Novelty Salt & Pepper Shakers Club, she also issues catalogs of salt and peppers.

> Sylvia Tompkins
> 25-C Center Drive
> Lancaster, PA 17601
> (717) 569-9788

★ **Jadite green (a milky light green) or delphite blue (a similar blue) kitchen ware.** Wants bowls, reamers, canisters, salt and peppers and "anything else." A wide range of items, often in a variety of shapes, were made. Green pieces start at $4, with rare pieces reaching $100, whereas the blue is much more scarce with most pieces starting around $75. Tell what piece you have, its size, whether it is marked on the bottom (most weren't), and the condition, indicating any flakes or chips in the rim and base, and the condition of the painted decoration on canisters, salts, etc.

> Steve Kelley
> PO Box 695
> Desert Hot Springs, CA 92240
> (619) 329-3206

★ **Ceramic or chalk figural string holders,** in wall or counter style. Wants figures of fruits or people (full figure or face) including Indians, Chinamen, Black mammies, Black men, animals, cows, dogs, cats, or birds. Does not want apples, pears, Dutch girls, or chefs.

> Emma Kretchek
> 5726 Terrace Park Drive
> Dayton, OH 45429
> (513) 434-9126

★ **Older fruit (canning) jars with unusual closures or in unusual colors** other than aqua or clear. Colors wanted include amber, brown, deep green, and shades of cobalt blue. Is willing to pay up to $400 for a pint size jar embossed CADIZ JAR with a glass screw top. Also want pre-1960 **advertising**, promotional brochures, letterheads, signs and paperweights from jar and bottle manufacturers, including **wooden canning jar boxes** or box ends, which generally bring $10-30. Give the size, color, and report *exactly* what is embossed on the jar. Note all cracks, chips, dings, or unwashable stains.

> Tom and Deena Caniff
> 1223 Oak Grove Ave.
> Steubenville, OH 43952
> (614) 282-8918

★ **Glass knives** are wanted in any configuration or color, especially with original painted decoration in original box. Values run from $25 to $100 or more. Send a photocopy and describe color. She edits a quarterly newsletter about glass knives.

> Adrienne Escoe
> PO Box 342
> Los Alamitos, CA 90720

★ **Glass knives** are wanted, especially those colored amber, emerald green, opal, and cobalt blue, as well as those with ribbed handles or combinations of clear blades with colored handles. "I would really love to find a 6.5" *Westmoreland* with a certain type of thumb guard. I'd also love to find a 'glass pig,' the blob of glass with two of three knives attached, before they were broken off." Buys printed material, catalogs, photos, etc. on all aspects of 1920 to 1940's glass knives. Brands include *Kitchen Gadget Company, Kitchen Novelty Company, Buffalo Knife, ES Pease, John Didio*, and a number of others. Please describe the size, colors, pattern on the handle and the condition. You must price your knife.

> Michele Rosewitz
> PO Box 3843
> San Bernardino, CA 92413
> (714) 862-8534

CAST IRON COOKWARE

★ **Cast iron muffin pans,** gem pans, popover pans, and maple sugar molds in unusual patterns and shapes. Also interested in old catalogs, etc., which list multi-sectioned baking or muffin pans. Buys *any* cast iron item marked *Griswold*. Will pay $300+ for *Griswold* #13, 50, and 2800 pans. If you're a dealer, send for his wants list.

David "the Pan Man" Smith
PO Box B
Perrysburg, NY 14129
(716) 532-5154

★ **Early kitchen items made of cast iron** or of wood which has been folk carved or decorated are wanted by this important dealer.

Louis Picek
PO Box 340
West Branch, IA 52358
(319) 643-2065

★ **Iron pans and broilers in odd or decorative shapes,** including pans for muffins, popovers, rolls, and maple sugar molds. Roll pans shaped like hearts bring $100 and up, while those like fruits and vegetables are worth $150. Pans made by *GF Filley* start at $75. Cast iron broilers look like strange frying pans with grid work, slots, and holes. Not interested in reproductions (they have rough surface and grind marks) or in tin pans of any type. Trace your pans or photocopy.

David Smith
PO Box B
Perrysburg, NY 14129
(716) 532-5154

★ *Griswold* **cast iron pots and pans,** including skillets, lids, Dutch ovens, etc. Any items marked as being made by *Griswold* are likely to be of interest.

Alan Stone
PO Box 500
Honeoye, NY 14471
(716) 229-2700

KITCHEN TOOLS

★ **Russian samovars** from before 1930. Please send picture with descriptive information and a statement of condition. He needs to know the size, shape, type of metal, markings, condition, and whether there are any additional matching pieces. He prefers that you price what you have. Also interested in any written material on samovars, especially catalogs.

Jerome Marks
120 Corporate Woods, #260
Rochester, NY 14623
(716) 475-0220   Fax: (716) 475-0208

★ **Toasters.** "I'll buy old or unusual electric toasters in good, non-corroded condition, as long as there are no pieces missing. I am especially interested in very old or very unusual toasters, porcelain models and ones with toast racks. Prices vary greatly, according to rarity, but mint condition examples and ones with original boxes bring the best prices, but toasters do not have to work to be desirable. I am not interested in pop-up toasters unless they are very unusual. Please call or write if you have specific questions." Give the maker's name and model number. A sketch is helpful, but a photo is best. An accurate description of condition is essential. Toasters bring from $10 and up, with rare ones bringing you $100 or more.

Joe Lukach
7111 Deframe Court
Arvada, CO 80004
(303) 422-8970

★ **Hand can openers.**
Craig Dinner
PO Box 4399
Sunnyside, NY 11104
(718) 729-3850

★ **Tin can openers.** Will consider wall, counter, or hand operated kinds, but he wants old ones (1810-1940), not modern openers. There are more than 1,200 patents for can openers! Give all information that is stamped on the opener.

Joe Young
PO Box 587
Elgin, IL 60123
(708) 695-0108

★ **Fancy or unusual nutcrackers,** big or small, made of iron, brass, wood, or any other material. A sketch or photocopy is suggested. Include dimensions, colors, and all writing or marks.

C. J. Davis
East 4400 English Point Road
Hayden Lake, ID 83835

★ **Hand operated egg beaters, cream whips, and glass bottomed mixers** are wanted, if they are American made and before 1920. Buys either rotary or dasher (up and down) type, wall or table style. Cast iron beaters are particularly desirable, especially those with "Flat fold" beaters. There are a great many beaters he'll buy, and quite a few he won't. No beaters with plastic handles or stainless steel dashes. No *A&J* hand held rotary egg beaters, no *Ladd* hand beaters, no *Ekco* or *Maynard* brand beaters, nor butter churns (except *Dazey* models 10, 20, or 30). "No electric beaters," he says, but is willing to make exception for pre-1920 electric beaters in excellent condition. Nearly all had dates and maker's marks to help you describe them. A photo is requested, but "even a pencil sketch or outline will help." Include all dates and everything printed. Describe condition accurately, including the glass jar. "I pay a premium for original labels, containers or pamphlets accompanying desirable mixers. The more nearly perfect, the higher its value."

    Reid Cooper
    PO Box 900868
    San Diego, CA 92190
       (619) 286-1563 eves

★ **Tunbridge Ware** is attractive woodware with geometric or mosaic designs, or with embedded pictures created with cut woods of different colors. She buys boxes, candlestick holders, tea caddies, etc. made in Tunbridge. These pieces are rarely marked. If in doubt, send a good photo or a photocopy of the patterned portion of the item.

    Lucille Malitz, Lucid Antiques
    PO Box KH
    Scarsdale, NY 10583
       (914) 636-3367

★ **Twentieth century plastic items.** "Don't donate your old plastic dishes to a thrift shop, I'll buy them," says this veteran collector and one of the few people who care about *Bakelite* and other kitchen plastic.

    Dishes, singles or sets, especially serving pieces. Look for
       Branchell, Color-Flyte, Arrowhead, Russel Wright Ideal Ware, others;
    Salt & peppers, especially boxed figurals or geometrics;
    Character mugs of people or animals, especially *Dennis the Menace* by *F&F;*
    Soaky **Bubble Bath** and other figural bottles;
    Cookie jar figurals in plastic;
    Funny Face, Big Pitcher, Tony the Tiger and other characters.
Give the dimensions, colors, and maker (if you can), as well as a piece count and statement of condition.

    Mary Anne Enriquez
    716 West 17th Place Rear
    Chicago, IL 60616
       (312) 243-3425

★ *Melmac* is wanted, but generally only in sets. He's looking for "heavy colorful stuff" like *Arrowhead, Brook Park, Color-Flyte, Russel Wright*, and others. Wants to know the maker and condition of what you have, including whether or not you have the original box and paperwork. Dealers are to price their goods.

> "Melmac Mack"
> 443 West 21st Street
> New York, NY 10011

COOKBOOKS

★ **Cookbooks published as advertising** by various companies pre-1930, especially those from before 1900. Love to find pre-1920 JELL-O cookbooks. Also **fund raising cookbooks** from before 1940. Also buys pre-1920 grocer's catalogs, pre-1920 cooking magazines, reference books and bibliographies of cookbooks. **Unusual cookbooks** of any vintage including those assembled by movie stars, famous artists, etc., are also sought. Also wants **historical information concerning commercial food companies.**

> Roberta Deal
> PO Box 17
> Mecklenburg, NY 14863

★ **Hard and soft covered cookbooks,** especially soft cover advertising recipe books published by various food companies, such as JELL-O, *Rumford* baking powder, etc., especially fine condition ones from before 1900. Will pay $50 each for the 1930's JELL-O cookbooks based on the OZ books by Frank Baum. The founder of the Cook Book Collectors Club, and editor of its newsletter, does not want appliance company recipe books, diet books, or other modern health cookbooks such as heart and cholesterol related cookbooks. As with all books for sale, sellers should give complete bibliographic information. Sellers must price the books they offer.

> Col. Bob Allen, Cookbook Collectors Club of America
> PO Box 56
> St. James, MO 65559
>   (314) 265-8296 anytime

★ **Spiral bound church, community, or privately published cookbooks.** Will buy singles, collections, or multiple copies of the same title. Please indicate the sponsoring organization and the number of recipes. Mention the quantity you have, the original retail price, and the price you want for them all wholesale. Helen publishes cookbooks and a newsletter for recipe collectors.

> Helen Jump
> PO Box 171
> Zionsville, IN 46077

★ **Spiral bound church, community, charity, fund raiser, ethnic and other privately published cookbooks** with limited distribution.
Bob Roberts
PO Box 152
Guilderland, NY 12084

★ **Cookbooks and related pamphlets** from before 1950. State condition and price or just ship for immediate offer.
Alan Levine
PO Box 1577
Bloomfield, NJ 07003

★ **Cookbooks and commercial booklets in any language.** Especially wants early out-of-print items, including **hand written cookbooks**. Also wine, candy, chocolate, baking and specialty cooking books and booklets. Give standard bibliographic information on books. Condition is very important, and wants books to have tight bindings. Please don't ask for free appraisals unless you are actually selling your books.
Kay Caughren
284 Purdue Ave.
Kensington, CA 94708
   (415) 524-8859

SELLING COOKBOOKS

Selling cookbooks is no different from selling any other book. You must provide what the book world calls Standard Bibliographic Information:

  (1) Title as on the title page, not the spine;
  (2) Author;
  (3) Publisher and place of publication;
  (4) Date of copyright and of publication (list all);
  (5) Number of pages and illustrations;

Give the condition of the binding, spine, pages, and the dust jacket. Note bookplates, writing, and other damage to the book. A photocopy of the title page will save you lots of writing.

SILVERWARE

★ **Sterling flatware and serving pieces** are wanted by the nation's largest buyer and seller of second hand sterling tableware. "If a customer sends a SASE and the name of their pattern and its maker, we will send a written offer." If you do not know the name of the pattern, make a picture on a copy machine and list how many pieces you have. "Most sterling is standard, so if you know the name of the pattern, we know exactly what you have. As a result, we do not need to see what you have before buying. Please note, we do not make offers on non-standard items. We don't offer on coin silver, souvenir items, old unmarked tea sets, and the like, although we will consider them for purchase if you send a photograph or photocopy and set the price you want. We only make offers on standard items." If an item is damaged, worn, or monogrammed, be certain to note that fact. The company also repairs flatware, so if you have a favorite that needs fixing or restoration, they may be the folks who can do it.

> Thomas Ridley, Head Buyer, MidweSterling
> 4311 NE Vivion Road, Dept HY
> Kansas City, MO 64119
>   (816) 454 1990   Fax: (816) 454-1605

★ **Sterling and silver plated flatware,** especially made by *1847 Rogers, Community,* and *Holmes & Edwards.* Also all old grape patterns. Send the information on the back of your silver, and a photocopy if you don't know the name of the pattern. An SASE will get you a pattern guide. Particularly interested in more unusual pieces such as pie forks, punch ladles, ice tongs, sardine forks, etc. "We do not want monogrammed, damaged or worn silver except large serving pieces or very rare patterns." A 30 year veteran of buying through the mail.

> L.C. Fisher, Silver Exchange
> Route 8 Box 554 (Hwy 190 East)
> Huntsville, TX 77340
>   (409) 295-7661

★ **Sterling silver flatware, holloware, jewelry** and novelty items, such as goblets, mint julep cups, trays, etc., especially in old elaborate patterns. **Will also buy unusual pieces of old silver plate**, such as tea services, large trays, and elaborate epergnes (multi-branched center-pieces holding dishes, trays, or candles). You should take photos of larger pieces, and make photocopies of flatware. Everything must be in fine condition, cautions this 22 year veteran dealer. She is not interested in silver coins.

> Helen Cox, As You Like It Silver Shop
> 3025 Magazine Street
> New Orleans, LA 70117
>   (800) 828-2311   Fax: (504) 897-9310

★ **Victorian figural silverplate napkin rings.** Wants small figural napkin rings. Describe your rings to her well, including all markings, and "I'll probably know what you have."
> Sandra Whitson
> PO Box 272
> Lititz, PA 17543
> (717) 626-4978

★ **European sterling silver and silverplate** from companies like *Christophle, Buccellatti, Puiforcat*, etc. Buys and sells.
> Russ Burkett
> PO Box 4231
> Mission Viejo, CA 92690
> (714) 364-3844

★ **Gold or sterling silver open salt dishes,** American or European, in any size, with or without glass liners, as long as they are in fine condition. Describe well, and include your asking price if possible.
> Monica Murphy, Savannah's Antiques
> 1419 Fern
> New Orleans, LA 70118
> (504) 866-2221

★ **American and European open salt dishes in glass, sterling, or silver plate** if rare and unusual. No common or repro salts are wanted. Johnson is author of *5000 Open Salts*, available with a price guide from her for $52 postpaid.
> Patricia Johnson
> PO Box 1221
> Torrance, CA 90505
> (310) 373-5262

★ **Sterling spoons with "cute" Negro figures.** Will pay up to $150 for enameled spoons.
> Elijah Singley
> 2301 Noble Ave.
> Springfield, IL 62704
> (217) 546-5143 eves

★ **Silver spoons with advertising** on them. Either sterling or plate.
> W.T. Atkinson
> 1217 Bayside Circle West
> Wilmington, NC 28405

★ **Souvenir spoons** from before 1930, especially with hand engraving.
> T. K. Treadwell, Tower House Antiques
> 4201 Nagle Road
> Bryan, TX 77801
> (409) 846-0209

HOUSEHOLD MISCELLANY

★ **Vacuum cleaners** that are hand powered. "I pay well for information leading to the location of unusual and scarce items, and am prepared to travel anywhere. For the right items, I pay in cash immediately without fuss or bother. I am happy to buy single items or entire collections."
Peter Frei
PO Box 500
Brimfield, MA 01010
(800) 942-8968 or (413) 245-4660 in Massachusetts

★ **Flashlights.** Old flashlights, advertising, and catalogs are wanted, especially anything early marked *Eveready.*
Bill Utley
7616 Brookmill
Downey, CA 90241
(310) 861-6247

★ **Desk, ceiling, or pedestal fans** that are antique or unusual, especially mechanical fans not powered by electricity. Wants brands like *G.E., Westinghouse, Emerson, Peerless, Diehl* and others, but especially those made before 1920 or with unusual mechanisms. These early fans are usually cast iron and brass. Also wants literature, catalogs, ads and other information about fans and the companies that made them. He has no interest in steel fans made after 1940. If you want to sell your fan, include the brand, nameplate information, dimensions of the blades, number of blades, and what the various parts are made of, if you can. When describing condition, indicate whether your fan operates. Michael is the President of the American Fan Collectors Association and editor of its quarterly newsletter.
Michael Breedlove, Antique Fans of Indiana
15633 Cold Spring Court
Granger, IN 46530
(800) 858-3267

★ **Early and unusual floor and desk fans.** Buys electric fans from before 1915 (check your patent dates). Very interested in fans not propelled by electricity, such as wind-up, heat engine, water power, battery powered, etc. Some interest in ceiling fans, but does not want fans by *G.E.* or fans made in the 1920's or later.
Kevin Shail
30 Old Middle Road
Brookfield, CT 06804
(203) 775-7017

★ **Globes of the world.** Will buy unusual or oversized globes, black globes, and, especially, globes that are lit from the inside. "No ordinary globes, please." Send a photo, stamped self-addressed envelope, and your phone number. Prefers you to set price wanted, but will make offers to amateur sellers.

> Jay Novak
> 7386 Beverly Blvd.
> Los Angeles, CA 90036
> (213) 933-0383   Fax: (213) 683-1312

★ **Thermometers and thermostats,** pre-1940, especially ornate Victorian desk or mantle types. "I buy just about every *non advertising* one I can locate," but outdoor and decorative models are particularly prized, and can bring more than $100 each. "I have the largest antique thermometer collection in the world but am always looking for more." Thermometer ephemera and catalogs are sought. No commercial, industrial, clinical, advertising or "cutesy" thermometers are wanted. Give the maker, condition and whether it has mercury or red liquid in the bulb. "All the items bought are placed in the American Thermometer Museum in Sacramento."

> Warren Harris
> 6130 Rampart Drive
> Carmichael, CA 95608
> (916) 966-3490

★ **Decorative and figural light bulbs.** Wants all unusual light bulbs including neon bulbs (a metal image inside the bulb glows when lit), Christmas bulbs (figural or bubble type), unusually shaped bulbs, and those made of colored glass (not coated) that have a standard base. Also wants display devices for bulbs and **wired artificial Christmas trees**. Prices range from $10 to as much as $600 for a Statue of Liberty bulb. A boxed set of Disney's Snow White and the Seven Dwarfs bulbs will bring $600. Santa bulbs are worth from $15-$150. Does not want *Paramount* brand Disney character lights or old utility, auto, or industrial light bulbs. Photo or sketch required. "I will beat any legitimate offer if it's a bulb I want."

> Joseph Kimbell
> 708 Bay Street
> San Francisco, CA 94109
> (415) 346-8273

★ **Strap type watch fobs picturing machinery or advertising products.** No lodge, American Legion, or VFW, and similar fobs. He'd like you to tell him how much wear it shows and the name of the stamper, usually found at the bottom. No fakes or modern fobs.

> Albert Goetz
> 1763 Poplar Ave.
> South Milwaukee, WI 53172
> (414) 762-4111

WOODEN ITEMS

★ **Small hand painted American boxes.**
   Louis Picek
   Main Street Antiques
   PO Box 340,
   West Branch, IA 52358
       (319) 643-2065

★ **Wooden picture frames** that are early, unusual, and in perfect condition. A photograph is very helpful. Give a call if you're nearby.
   Craig Dinner
   PO Box 4399
   Sunnyside, NY 11104
       (718) 729-3850

STAMPED SELF-ADDRESSED ENVELOPE

If you want an answer when you write to a potential buyer, include a self-addressed stamped envelope.

GADGETS & POCKET PIECES

★ **Gadgets.** "I'll buy interesting old small mechanical devices such as:
  Pocket typewriters or sewing machines;
  Pocket size calculators;
  Miniature cameras;
  Optical devices;
  Personal check protectors;
  Combination pen-pencil-rulers;
  Adding machines.
"I'm interested in everything that whirs, buzzes, clanks, or just looks interesting." Darryl is particularly fond of typewriters and adders, paying $1,500 for important pocket typewriters. A photo is generally a good idea, and your description should include a detailed statement of condition. Will respond promptly to all offers.
  Darryl Rehr
  2591 Military Ave.
  Los Angeles, CA 90064
    (310) 477-5229

★ **Pocket items** designed to fit in the pocket and to be carried and used. Wants "mechanically interesting functional things" not just pretty things. "The items I like are usually made before 1930, so modern plastic stuff is of little interest." His wants include:
  Mini books (less than 4") on practical topics;
  Tool and gadget knives;
  Trick or special purpose knives;
  Folding cups, silverware, and tools;
  Vest pocket flashlights;
  Hand warmers;
  Lighters, compacts, and other pocket items that are
    combined with other tools;
  Pocket sewing machines;
  Optical devices, like sundials and instruments;
  Scientific devices;
  Things that look like pocket watches but aren't;
  Any device that says "pocket" on it.
Send a photocopy or photograph, a description of any damage or other problems, and a copy of any writing, embossing, or other markings found on the item.
  B.H. Axler
  PO Box 1288
  Ansonia Station, NY 10023

STANHOPE VIEWERS

★ **Stanhope viewers** are small objects with a peep hole and tiny pictures inside. They come in a wide variety of shapes and materials including alabaster urns, crucifixes, pens, and letter openers and Don will consider all types.
    Donald Gorlick
    PO Box 24541
    Seattle, WA 98124
    (206) 824-0508

★ **Unusual Stanhopes.** Stanhopes are objects with tiny holes which show a picture when you look inside. Wants rings, sewing items, figurals, pipes, and naughty ones. Does not want Stanhopes in pens, rosaries, or crucifixes, as those are the most common forms.
    Lucille Malitz
    Lucid Antiques
    PO Box KH
    Scarsdale, NY 10583
    (914) 636-3367

LITHOPANES

★ **Lithopanes** are figures and scenes viewed through transparent porcelain. Like Stanhopes, they are found in a wide variety of objects. Don wants them all *except* steins or cups, which are the most commonly found form.
    Donald Gorlick
    PO Box 24541
    Seattle, WA 98124
    (206) 824-0508

★ **Lithopanes (porcelain transparencies)** in any size or shape, colored or uncolored, used in a lamp, plaque, stein, cup, or other object. Describe the object and the picture, and give any letters or numbers appearing on either or both.
    Laurel Blair
    PO Box 4557
    Toledo, OH 43620
    (419) 243-4115

EYEGLASSES

★ **Eyeglasses, spectacles, and lorgnettes,** but only old, rare, and unusual. Not interested in any common eyeglasses or in buying them for their gold content. "I only want the exotic or pre-1850, with unusual lenses, frames, or history." A photocopy machine will make a good picture of most eyeglasses. Describe all writing on frames.

> W.H. Marshall
> 727 SW 27th Street
> Gainesville, FL 32607
> (904) 373-0556

★ **Antique eyeglasses and spectacles** are sought. Also would like to purchase early catalogs and trade cards featuring eyeglasses, unusual reading glasses, antique opthalmoscopes, and any material from the *McAllister Optical Co.* He has some interest in text books on ophthalmology from before 1890. Please describe the condition thoroughly.

> Charles Letocha
> 444 Rathton Road
> York, PA 17403
> (717) 846-0428

CANES

★ **Canes.** Especially likes dual purpose, container, weapon, gadget, and fancy carved canes made with ivory, gold, or silver. "Any cane or walking stick that does something, or has something enclosed or attached to the shaft for purposes other than support, is of interest, as are well executed hand-carved canes." Describe the tip of the cane and indicate whether it gives any evidence of having been shortened. Is there a hole in the shaft? What materials?

> Arnold Scher
> 1637 Market Street
> San Francisco, CA 94103
> (415) 863-4344

★ **Canes and walking sticks** made of either wood or ivory, but only those that have been carved into figures.

> Bruce Thalberg
> 23 Mountain View Drive
> Weston, CT 06883
> (203) 227-8175

PEST TRAPS

★ **Traps of all types and sizes from fly to grizzly bear.** Wants fine examples of fly, mouse, rat, mole, gopher, glass minnow traps, and spring operated fish traps. Will purchase anything unusual in any material including plastic, wood, wire, cast iron, glass, cardboard, and tin. Is especially fond of old and unusual mouse traps. He also buys patent models, books, catalogs, and advertising (pre-1940) related to traps. Does not want rusty or broken traps unless they are odd 19th century items. Send a picture or drawing, a good description, and an SASE and he promises to answer.
> Boyd Nedry
> 728 Buth Drive NE
> Comstock Park, MI 49321
>   (616) 784-1513

★ **Rare and unusual traps and trap guns.**
> Ron Willoughby
> 1072 Route 171
> Woodstock, CT 06281
>   (203) 974-1226

★ **Glass flytraps or flycatchers,** especially early or unusual ones. Will consider interesting traps in other materials. Also advertising and paper ephemera related to early flytraps.
> Maris Zuika
> PO Box 175
> Kalamazoo, MI 49004
>   (616) 344-7473

KEYS & LOCKS

★ **Keys and locks.** Don is author of the *Standard Guide to Key Collecting*, available for $21 from the author.
> Don Stewart
> PO Box 9397
> Phoenix, AZ 85068
>   (602) 493-8392

★ **Antique and unusual padlocks.** "We'll buy padlocks of all kinds and types, those that are odd shaped or made of cast iron, brass, figural, *Wells Fargo, Winchester*, railroad, miniature, and many others." If you want so sell your lock, a photocopy will help them know what you have. Indicate whether your lock has a key.
> Joe and Pam Tanner, Tanner Escapes
> PO Box 349
> Great Falls, MT 59403

KNIVES

★ **Pocket, hunting, and military knives.** Brands to look for include: *New York Knife, Canastota, Remington, Wabash, Winchester, Honk Falls, Napanoch, Henry Sears, Shapleigh, Union Cut, Keen Kutter, Bingham, American Knife, Bridge, Capitol, Case, Cattaraugus, Phoenix, James Price, Platts, Press Button, India Steel Works, Wallkill, Walden, Van Camp, Union Razon, Standard, Zenith, Northfield, Crandall,* and others. "This is only a small listing of the many good brands to be found. I love to find large bone-handled knives made in the U.S." **If your knife is one of the following brands, it is not of interest:** *Ambassador, Atco, Camco, Colonial, Executive, Frontier, Hit, Ideal, Klien, Richards, U.S.A., Pakistan,* and *Sabre.* Stapp is an advisor on knives for one of the popular price guides. For an evaluation of your knife and an offer, it is best to photocopy knives with the blade(s) open. Write down everything found on the blades and handles. Describe the handle material as best you can. Include a stamped self-addressed envelope.

> Charles Stapp
> 7037 Haynes Road
> Georgetown, In 47122
> (812) 923-3483

★ **Pocket knives** over 50 years old, especially those with multi-colored celluloid handles. Celluloid is a synthetic plastic with a variety of colors, usually looking swirly or in some type of pattern, and could resemble stone, wood, horn, pearl or marble, and may be opaque or translucent. To sell your knife, make a photocopy with the blade[s] open. If you don't, it is essential to give very accurate measurements of the knife open and closed. Provide all information stamped on the blades or handle. Include an SASE. If you have a price you'd like, tell him. If not, this 25 year veteran will make offers to amateur sellers. He is not interested in knives that are badly rusted or which have broken blades or handles. Never attempt to clean or sharpen an old rusted or broken knife, as you usually destroy all its possible value. "It's worth more when it looks worthless than when you make it worthless." Cleaning and restoration must be done by a knife expert.

> "Mr. T.C."
> PO Box 6694
> Woodland Hills, CA 91365

★ **Knives less than 1" long** are wanted, especially multi-bladed knives with mother-of-pearl, sterling, stag, or horn handles. To sell your knife, give as much information as possible, including number of blades, maker, condition, etc. Old knives only. No new items or reproductions. Says he also "buys and trades swords and razors."

> Jim Kegebein
> 6831 Colton Blvd.
> Oakland, CA 94611

★ **Unusually shaped figural pocket knives** shaped like objects such as dogs, cats, hats, baseball bats, ladies' legs, etc., from the 1800's or early 1900's. Value depends upon the shape, condition and maker. "Knives in unusual shapes made by *Remington, Winchester,* and *Case* may be worth several hundred dollars. I am also interested in any old advertising signs, pinback buttons, postcards, etc., related to the cutlery industry. Please phone or write." If you want to sell your knife, give the maker's name, shape, number of blades, and material from which the handle is made. John does not make offers, so you will have to set the price you want for your knife. Standard price guides may help you.

> John Baron
> 2928 Marshall Ave.
> Cincinnati, OH 45220
> (513) 751-6631

PENS & PENCILS

★ **Unusual quality fountain pens,** pre-1940, by makers such as *Eversharp, Waterman, Swan, Dunn, MacKinnon, Laughlin, Shaeffer, Chilton, Wahl, Moore, Camel* and many others. Some of these can be worth several hundred dollars. She also buys old **quill cutters, stylus pens,** and **glass pens. Advertising related to pens** is also wanted, including signs, trade catalogs, repair manuals, and spare parts. Also wants packaged powdered ink. To sell your pen, tell her the maker's name, model, color, and length of your pen. Describe the pen point and all decorations on the pen. Best to make a photocopy. Pens will have to be inspected before final price offered. No unbranded pens, *Wearever, Esterbrook,* ball point pens, or magazine ads. She will send a guide to help you describe pens.

> Mrs. Ky
> PO Box J
> Port Jefferson Station, NY 11776

★ **Fountain pens.** "I'm looking for quality old pens, not junk or common stuff," says this 22 year veteran.

> C. Ray Erler
> Box 140, Miles Run Road
> Spring Creek, PA 16436

★ **Fountain pens, mechanical pencils, and pen and pencil desk sets** are wanted by this aggressive collector. He will do appraisals for free if you mail your item(s) to him and include enough postage for him to return your item(s). He says he'll buy both vintage and modern pens and claims "nobody pays higher."

> Steven Alpert
> PO Box 6522
> Orange, CA 92613
> (714) 771-5500

★ **Inkwells,** either U.S. or foreign, figural or traveling, whether made of pottery, glass, or wood. Especially would like one made by *Tiffany*. He does not buy desk sets or fountain pens.

Eli Hecht
19 Evelyn Lane
Syosset, NY 11791

★ **Mechanical pencils with advertising on them** are wanted. Most advertising mechanical pencils are modestly priced 50¢ to $3, with some national ads worth $10, and a few as much as $20. Some non-advertising pencils are wanted including brands like *Parker, Conklin, Shaffer, Wahl, Eversharp, Swan* and others. Prices on these can range as high as $200 for rare, high quality pencils. He enjoys finding dual-purpose pencils, such as those combined with knives, magnifying glasses, etc. "I will consider **all items related to pencils, pre-1960,** such as catalogs, brochures, display cases, salesman's samples, sample cases, or signs that relate to mechanical pencils, but no magazine ads, please. I do not want new mechanical pencils or those with Bible verses. I am **not** interested in wood pencils, ink pens or fountain pens unless they are part of a set that includes a mechanical pencil. I will accept shipments up to 50 pencils for immediate response and payment. Please phone first if you have more than 50." He cautions "do not clean dirty or frozen pencils as you are more likely to destroy their value than to help it." He will make offers on collections of mechanical pencils, but only after inspecting them in person.

Tom Basore
715 West 20th Street
Hutchinson, KS 67502
    (316) 665-3613 eves

★ **Pencils with advertising.** Wants unusual and older unsharpened pencils. No pens. "They're not high value items, but at least they'll get into the hands of someone who will appreciate and take care of them."

Susan Cox
800 Murray Drive
El Cajon, CA 92020
    (619) 447-0800 days

★ **Pencil sharpeners.** Wants small hand-held figural pencil sharpeners made of metal, celluloid or *Bakelite*. She is only looking for those made in Germany or Japan during the 1930's and 40's. Don't offer her the small bronze colored sharpeners from Hong Kong made in the shape of various antiques. To sell your sharpener, give the shape, condition, country of origin, size, condition of the blade, and price.

Martha Crouse
4516 Brandon Lane
Beltsville, MD 20705

CAST IRON

★ **All useful items made from cast iron in the shape of figures.** "I'll buy **doorstops, bottle openers, lawn sprinklers, paperweights, pencil holders, match holders, string holders, windmill weights, horse weights, shooting gallery targets,** and **firemarks**. I have no interest in buying modern reproductions and castings." Include your phone number.
>   Craig Dinner
>   PO Box 4399
>   Sunnyside, NY 11104
>   (718) 729-3850

★ **Cast iron doorstops and windmill weights** are sought by this prominent dealer. No reproductions or modern pieces.
>   Louis Picek, Main Street Antiques
>   PO Box 340
>   West Branch, IA 52358
>   (319) 643-2065

★ **Cast iron lawn sprinklers, doorstops, windmill weights, shooting gallery targets** and other figural cast iron. Does not want reproductions, damaged and repaired items, or items with new paint. He is also not interested in "small shooting gallery targets such as ducks and birds." Please include color photo, phone number, and price range you'd like.
>   Richard Tucker, Argyle Antiques
>   PO Box 262
>   Argyle, TX 76226
>   (817) 464-3752

★ **Antique pressing irons of all kinds** including sad irons, polishing irons, hat irons, fluters, goffering irons, charcoal irons, alcohol irons, gasoline irons, boxed sets of irons, miniature and **toy irons,** and **all iron related items** such as postcards, trade cards, advertising giveaways by iron companies, and the like. Single items or entire collections wanted. Describe the condition. A photo is a good idea. Trace your iron and give the height. You tell her how much you want as she does not make offers.
>   Carol Walker, The Iron Lady
>   501 North 5th Street
>   Waelder, TX 78959
>   (512) 665-7166

★ **Miniature sad (flat) irons.** Wants irons smaller than 4 inches, but nothing bigger. No electric irons, please, no matter how early.
>   George Fougere
>   67 East Street
>   North Grafton, MA 01536
>   (508) 839-2701

CHRISTMAS DECORATIONS

★ **Christmas decorations** from before 1920, and related items like:
> **Figural ornaments**, made of paper, tinsel, pressed cardboard, cotton batting, glass or other material;
> **Board games** with lithographed boxes depicting Santa;
> **Santa toys** and **other ephemera:** anything based on St. Nick, including advertising, banners, greeting cards, paintings, die-cuts, chromoliths, and prints;
> **Die cut children's books** 1880-1900 about Santa;
> **Litho on tin candle holders** for Christmas trees;

He does not want anything made after 1920. There are many reproductions of Santa items, some of which are quite good and require an expert to authenticate. This 25 year veteran requests a photo or photocopy of what you'd like to sell.
> Dolph "Father Christmas" Gotelli
> PO Box 8009
> Sacramento, CA 95818
> (916) 456-9734

★ **German glass Christmas ornaments,** pre-1920, in the shape of animals, people, and cartoon characters. Also wants painted cotton ornaments, paper Dresdens, and old **candy containers** shaped like Santa. Also buys pre-1930 **postcards and photos of Christmas** events.
> Jim Bohenstengel
> PO Box 623
> Oak Park, IL 60303
> (312) 524-8870 or 386-5319

★ **Early handmade folk art Christmas decorations.**
> Louis Picek, Main Street Antiques
> PO Box 340
> West Branch, IA 52358

★ **Christmas tree ornaments.** Buys a variety of antique ornaments including *Kugel* ornaments; glass birds with spun glass wings, tails, or crests; Czech beaded ornaments with satin glass rings; birds perched in glass rings; unusual strings of glass beads; spun glass and paper decorations; chandelier or fantasy ornaments (where two or three small bells, pine cones, or other items hang from a larger ornament); and other delicate and unusual figural ornaments. Also buys catalogs and manufacturer's sales literature from manufacturers in any language.
> David Speck
> 35 Franklin Street
> Auburn, NY 13021
> (315) 252-8566 eves

★ *Matchless Wonder Stars* **Christmas lights.** "I'll buy all stars, working, dead, or broken. Boxed sets are particularly desirable, but even empty boxes have value, especially those with attractive decorations." This historian of the industry wants all factory wholesale literature and price sheets, as well as store display stands. He also buys other *Matchless* products plus lights by *Paramount, Sylvania, Alps, Royal, Peerless, Mazda, Majestic* and others. Especially interested in nice boxed light sets by *Propp* and *Clemco.* If you have any old light sets, especially those that twinkle, bubble, or whatever, drop him a line. He wants a good description and if you still have the box, the information on it. "I generally avoid plastic items, and Christmas lights later than the mid 1950's. I don't need any more common *NOMA* or *Royal* bubble lights." Although he buys dead bulbs (except *Sylvania* fluorescents), he requests return privilege if things aren't as described.

David Speck
35 Franklin Street
Auburn, NY 13021
(315) 253-8495 days

★ *Hallmark* **figural ornaments** from 1973-1986. Excellent condition only. In original box preferred. No ball ornaments.

Sharon Vohs-Mohammed
Box 14192
Tallahassee, FL 32317
(904) 385-3595

★ **Christmas reindeer.** "I buy hard or soft plastic Christmas reindeer from the 1960's and 70's, and pay $2 to $5 apiece for these dimestore animals which originally sold for less than a buck. They must be in good condition. I'm not interested in metal, glass, ceramic, or plaster deer."

Arnie Starkey, Starkey Art
11054 Otsego Street #5
North Hollywood, CA 91601

★ **Holiday decorations from Christmas, Easter, Halloween, or other holiday.** "I'll buy a wide range of fine condition attractive holiday decorations made between 1890 and 1930, for any season. Items such as **candy containers,** celluloid pieces, papier maché, cotton batting tree ornaments, Halloween pumpkins, centerpieces, displays, are all wanted." Of particular interest are **German china figurines of Santa** engaged in various activities, which she buys in excellent condition and full paint only, paying $40 to $100+ apiece. "I pay fair asking prices."

Linda Vines
PO Box 721
Upper Montclair, NJ 07043
(201) 746-5206

EASTER EGGS & DECORATIONS

★ **Russian Easter eggs** made of solid glass, silvered hollow glass, porcelain, and other materials. They are characterized by the letters "XB" which stands for XHRISTOS VOSKRECE (Christ is risen) in paint, enamel, or other material. Value depends upon rarity, authenticity and condition.
>David Speck
>35 Franklin Street
>Auburn, NY 13021
>>(315) 253-8495 days 252-8566 eves

★ **Papier maché or composition Easter rabbit candy containers** of rabbits wearing clothes.
>Dolph Gotelli
>PO Box 8009
>Sacramento, CA 95818
>>(916) 456-9734

★ **High quality Easter decorations** of all types in fine condition, but only dating from 1890 to 1930. Great old Easter Bunnies are especially sought. No modern items.
>Linda Vines
>PO Box 721
>Upper Montclair, NJ 07043
>>(201) 746-5206

VALENTINE'S DAY CARDS

★ **Fine Valentines,** including handmade valentines from before 1940, interesting mechanical valentines, and any unusual ones. Evalene likes lacy 8 x 10's and large fan shaped cards from the 1800's, particularly if they say A TOKEN OF LOVE. Pays $25-$50 for folding ships, planes, and better fans. She asks that you send a photocopy of what you wish to sell. She does not want children's penny valentines from any era. Evalene no longer has a shop, but runs an extensive mail auction of valentines. She is available for talks and displays of valentines.
>Evalene Pulati
>Valentine Collector's Association
>PO Box 1404
>Santa Ana, CA 92702
>>(714) 547-1355

★ **Valentines.** Wants early die-cut and elaborate valentines made before 1910, but buys others "if reasonable."
Madalaine Selfridge, Forgotten Magic
33710 Almond Street
Lake Elsinore, CA 92330
(909) 674-9221

★ **Valentines** dating from 1889 to about 1920, but only the three dimensional fold-out stand-up type.
James Conley
2405 Brentwood Road NW
Canton, OH 44708
(216) 477-7725

HALLOWEEN ITEMS

★ **Halloween.** "I'll buy older paper items, *Dennison Boogie Books*, Halloween pins, jewelry, decorations, etc, if before 1945. Nothing new."
Stuart Schneider
PO Box 64
Teaneck, NJ 07666

★ **Halloween.** "I'll buy a wide range of fine condition attractive decorations made between 1890 and 1940. Pumpkins, centerpieces, etc., are all wanted. I pay fair asking prices."
Linda Vines
PO Box 721
Upper Montclair, NJ 07043
(201) 746-5206

★ **Candy containers in glass or plastic** especially scarce glass items and early 1950's figural headed plastic *PEZ* dispensers. Pays to $300 for pumpkin headed witches, goblins, or a pop-eyed Jack-0-Lantern. No paper or tin items.
Ross Hartsough
98 Bryn Mawr Road
Winnipeg, MB R3T 3P5 CANADA

★ **Halloween candy containers** in glass, composition or papier maché.
Dolph Gotelli
PO Box 8009
Sacramento, CA 95818
(916) 456-9734

4TH OF JULY MEMORABILIA

★ **Anything with a fireworks company name** on it including:
Fireworks, rockets, and Roman candles;
Firecracker packs and **labels**;
Fireworks boxes that held salutes, torpedoes, sparklers, etc.;
Salesmen's display boards and samples;
Fireworks **catalogs** from before 1969 (often $100 up);
Paper ephemera: stock certificates, posters, banners, photos,
letters, billheads, magazine articles, and other paper about
American fireworks companies.
Would like to hear from former employees of U.S. fireworks companies.
Please include your phone number when you write.
Barry Zecker
PO Box 217
Martinsville, NJ 08836
(908) 253-3400 from 8 to 8

★ **Fireworks related items,** especially American and Chinese made.
"I'll buy boxes, labels, advertising, catalogs, salesman's samples, display
boards, company letters, patents, and posters." Colorful labels are worth
from $5-$50 each. Hal does **not** want those marked "DOT."
Hal Kantrud
Route 7
Jamestown, ND 58401
(701) 252-5639 eves

★ **Firecracker labels.** "I'll buy pre-1940 labels with aviation, space,
atom bomb, animals, and Americana themes." Also fireworks catalogs.
Send a photocopy of what you have. No modern labels.
Stuart Schneider
PO Box 64
Teaneck, NJ 07666
(201) 261-1983

★ **Fourth of July fireworks, firecrackers, and firecracker labels.**
Wants "anything prior to the early 1970's, especially packs of *Golliwog,
Picnic, Tank, Oh Boy, Typewriter, Evergreen, Lone Eagle, Spirit of 76,
Minute Man, Columbia, Crab, Blue Dragon, Golden Bear, Green Jade,
Santa Claus, Watermelon, Dwarf, China Clipper,* and many others." He
wants most of these badly enough to pay $50 or more per pack! NOTE:
if your package or label contains the letters "DOT" and/or "Contents do
not exceed 60 mg," he's probably not interested. He eagerly buys catalogs of fireworks too. Use photocopies whenever possible.
William Scales
130 Fordham Circle
Pueblo, CO 81005
(719) 561-0603

DOG RELATED ITEMS

★ **Dog figurines** in porcelain made by one of the following makers: *Boehm, Hutschenreuther, Mortens Studio, Royal Doulton, Nymphenburg,* or *Anri-Wood.* A few others will be considered. Will pay $175 for a *Boehm* cocker spaniel made from 1980 to 83. "I do not want Japanese porcelain animals, cloisonne made in China, or small metal dogs. Give the breed if you know it, the manufacturer's marks and numbers, the dimensions, and the condition. A photo is helpful."
> Jeffrey Jacobson
> 6424 Jefferson Ave.
> Hammond, IN 46324

★ **Great Dane items** including prints, lithographs, bronzes, calendars, magazine covers, and porcelains (especially *Boehm*). Pre-1940 only. Give the material, size, color, markings, condition and approximate age.
> Leon Reimert
> 9 Highland Drive
> Coatesville, PA 19320
> (215) 383-6969

★ **Greyhounds** and **whippets.** "I'm interested in paper, porcelain, pewter, wood, and ceramics. But not in recent pottery, reproductions, or damaged items. Give the marks on your item."
> June Mastrocola
> W137 N9332 Hwy 145
> Menomonee Falls, WI 53051
> (414) 251-8347

★ **Borzoi, Russian wolfhound**, and **greyhound collectibles.** Buys for resale some items from other purebreds ("no mutts"). Wants "everything from old postcards to bronzes but antique porcelain figurines are a favorite, as are all *Morten Studio* and *Erphila* dogs." Give her the breed, the dimensions, the material and list any damage. Photo or photocopy is helpful. She prefers you price what you have. SASE gets her catalog of items for sale in your favorite breed.
> Denise Hamilton
> 2835 Carson Drive
> Elmira, NY 14903
> (607) 562-8564

★ **Pekingese, Japanese spaniel**, and **pug dog collectibles** including Vienna bronze figures, doorstops, and books. Will also buy quality **paintings depicting small dogs**, and **dog show medals** with any breed of dog on them. Give condition and approximate age.
> Elenore Chaya
> 4003 South Indian River Drive
> Ft. Pierce, FL 34982
> (407) 465-1789

★ **Bull terrier dog material** including books, manuscripts, photos and relevant ephemera.
  Frank Klein, Bookseller
  521 West Exchange Street
  Akron, OH 44302
    (216) 762-3101

★ **Bull terriers** and **dog fighting.** Especially wants prints, paintings, and statuary. Books on dog fighting also wanted.
  Ron Lieberman
  RD #1   Box 42
  Glen Rock, PA 17327
    (717) 235-2134

★ **Labrador retriever books, art, figurines,** and **cigarette cards.** He is not interested in repros, fakes, reprints, or common items, nor is he interested in any other breed of dog. Please provide a detailed description of what you have.
  Bill Eberhardt
  682 Ranch Wood Trail
  Orange, CA 92669
    (714) 639-0882

PET LICENSES

★ **Pet license tags, rabies tags, and all other metal tags related to animals.** Especially interested in Illinois tags. Especially wants tags pre-1900 for which he pays $15 and up.
  Rich Hartzog
  PO Box 4143 BFT
  Rockford, IL 61110

★ **Dog license tags** including: (1) tags from any state if they are shaped like the date of issue; (2) tags from anywhere in the world pre-1910; (3) all NY tags issued before 1918; and (4) NY Conservation Dept. tags, 1917-35, which are worth from $10-$40. Dog tags from before the Civil War can bring up to $150, and pre-1900 tags start at $5.
  James Case
  Route 1   Box 68, Crane Road
  Lindley, NY 14858

★ **Dog and cat licenses,** especially colored ones or those cut into shapes. Will pay $8 each for all dog tags older than 1910 and will buy all cat tags in any quantity.
  George Chartrand
  PO Box 334
  Winnipeg, MB R3C 2H6, CANADA

ANIMAL COLLECTIBLES

★ *Royal Doulton* **flambe animal figurines.** Hundreds of different animals, both wild and domestic, are be found in these attractive red pottery figures which range from 2" to 14" in size. They are still made today, so it's the older figures that are most sought after and bring the best prices from this 20 year veteran collector. Have the figure(s) in front of you when you call, or send a good description.
Ed Pascoe
545 Michigan Ave.
Miami Beach, FL 33139
(800) 872-0195   Fax: (305) 532-8543

★ **Cat items of any sort** including porcelain, carvings, prints, Orientalia, needlework, pottery, jade, ivory, jewelry, cookie jars, calendars, Art Deco, advertising, steins, medals, doorstops, bronzes, crystal, postcards, playing cards, prints and fine art, etc. Buys some cartoon cats (**Felix the Cat**, Sylvester, Kliban cats) but does not want any Garfield figures or reproductions in any form.   Also she does not buy chalk figures, or anything broken or damaged.
Marilyn Dipboye
31311 Blair Drive
Warren, MI 48092
(313) 264-0285

★ **Horses.** Everything related to work or recreation horses including polo, horseback riding, carriage driving, sidesaddle, draft horses, **horseshoeing, veterinary**, etc. Wants posters, prints of riding and recognized horse breeds, books (1st editions in their original dust jacket only), magazines, stud books, and breed registers. "I don't buy common books still in print, book club editions, *Diseases of the Horse,* or books on horse betting. If you want to sell to me, everything you have must be in fine condition, as I buy for resale."
Barbara Cole, October Farm
Route 2, Box 183-C
Raleigh, NC 27610
(919) 772-0482

★ **Zebras in many different forms,** including porcelain, carvings, paintings, folk art, etc. To be of interest, an item must be of a zebra, not just zebra striped. Please, no hides or parts of dead zebras.
Dave Galt
302 West 78th Street
New York, NY 10024
(212) 769-2514

★ **Musk oxen figurines, prints, book plates, and other small ephemera,** 1750-1930. Especially wants postcards, cigarette silks, trading cards, pottery, stamps and other small paper items. Will pay up to $100 each for illustrations from *History of Quadrupeds* (1781) or *Arctic Zoology* (1784) both by Thomas Pennant.
> Ross Hartsough
> 98 Bryn Mawr Road
> Winnipeg, MB R3T 3P5, CANADA

★ **Pigeon related items** including books, magazines, postcards, and prints, dating from before 1960.
> Stan and Monty Luden
> 11908 Abingdon Street
> Norwalk, CA 90650
> (310) 863-0123

★ **Owls.** Donna buys owls, but only only a very select few: (1) owls made by American Indians, (2) owls on postcards, (3) *Sclarrafia* owls, (4) *Zsolnay* owls, (5) *Meissen* owls, or (6) owl decoys. She does not want anything current or produced for the mass market. You must include a detailed description of all damage, plus a photograph. "We will not respond to offers that do not indicate the price wanted." She publishes a bimonthly newsletter for owl collectors. Sample copy $3.
> Donna Howard
> PO Box 5491
> Fresno, CA 93755
> (209) 439-4845

★ **Wild boar ephemera.** "I'll buy paintings, bronzes, ceramics, advertising, anything featuring the wild European boar or its American counterparts, the peccary or javelina." Describe condition.
> Henry Winningham
> 3205 South Morgan Street
> Chicago, IL 60608

★ **Worms and caterpillars.** "Not real ones," she hastens to add, "but just about any figural in any material. I prefer small ones that can fit on a shelf, but I'll buy cookie jars, bookends, figurines, books, toys, dolls, novelties...any worm or caterpillar I don't have. I'm especially looking for a *Lowly Worm* in a car figure based on the *Lowly Worm* books." Give size, material, and general description.
> Nita Markham
> 529 Wave Street
> Monterey, CA 93940

★ **Oyster memorabilia.** Got anything related to oysters? Cans, figurines, what have you?
Sheldon Katz
211 Roanoke Ave.
Riverhead, NY 11901
(516) 369-1100

★ **Tropical fish tanks, equipment and ephemera.** Wants old books, magazines, catalogs directly related to tropical fish, as well as "pet shop" or turtle magazines and other paper relevant to the hobby. Photocopy what you have. Priced items preferred but will make offers.
Gary Bagnall
1615 East St. Gertrude
Santa Ana, CA 92705

★ **Snakes and other reptiles made of wrought iron.** Wants wrought iron snakes and other reptiles created by blacksmiths as whimsies or useful items (such as pot or watch holders, for example). Can depict one snake or several, or other reptiles such as alligators and turtles. **Other figural animal and human whimsies made of iron** are also sought, especially weird forms of dogs. Most of these iron figures are under 9" high. A photo or drawing and description are necessary. Please don't contact her unless your item is for sale.
Linda Campbell Franklin
2716 Northfield Road
Charlottesville, VA 22901

PET PUBLICATIONS

Canine Collector's Companion, a 20 page bimonthly is $20 a year from PO Box 2948, Portland, OR 97208.

Canine Collectibles, a quarterly newsletter for $28 from 736 N. Western Ave, #314, Lake Forest, IL 60045

Cat Talk, a 16 page bimonthly is $15 a year from 31311 Blair Drive, Warren, MI 48092.

The Owl's Nest, a 20 page bimonthly is $15 a year from PO Box 5491, Fresno, CA 93755

RAZORS & ACCESSORIES

★ **Straight razors with fancy handles** made of gold or sterling silver. Also razors with figural handles, multiple blades, fancy etching on the blade, or with fraternal emblems or advertising on the handle. Handles may be made of horn, mother-of-pearl, or multi-colored celluloid. Rare razors will be considered even if they are slightly damaged. Also **razor and cutlery advertising** and memorabilia, catalogs, trade cards, etc., including oversize displays.

> William Campesi
> PO Box 140
> Merrick, NY 11566
> (516) 546-9630

★ **Straight razors with handles of sterling, rough bone, mother-of-pearl, or aluminum.** Celluloid or pressed horn razors with several characters are also wanted. Good razors generally bring from $50-$75, with some higher, some less. Please provide all information found on the blade or handle. He does not want plain handled razors from Solingen, Germany. Make photocopies with the blade(s) open. Indicate the material from which the handle is made.

> Charles Stapp
> 7037 Haynes Road
> Georgetown, In 47122
> (812) 923-3483

★ **Safety razors and accessories.** This 20 year veteran collector wants to buy odd safety razors and advertising for razors including posters, magazine ads, and signs. He'd love to find oversize store display razors or oversize shaving mugs or brushes. Give all colors and metals and note "all writing on the items. A good clear photo is best," he says, but photocopies will suffice. Also buys **razor blades** and **blade sharpeners.** "I'll buy U.S. or foreign blades, in singles, packages, or on cards as well as interesting advertising signs, posters, and displays related to razor blades." Describe your sharpener carefully, pointing out all damage, and noting any words or numbers on it.

> Cary Basse
> 6927 Forbes Ave.
> Van Nuys, CA 91406
> (818) 781-4856

★ **Shaving related items** such as stropping machines, **packs of blades**, blade banks, and early or unique **safety razors**, "with highest prices paid for safety razors with unusual or oddly shaped blades."

> Phillip Krumholz
> PO Box 4050
> Bartonville, IL 61607

SEWING & TEXTILES

★ **Handmade lace** from 1500-1900. "Unless you are a lace scholar or have access to important reference books on lace, the best thing is to photocopy as much of the piece as possible. From a photocopy I can often tell whether a full appraisal is warranted or if it is a piece I might like to buy. Even small pieces are worth your attention." She does not want lace known to be machine made or ordinary crochet and tatting. She prefers sellers to set the price, but will assist genuine amateurs to identify what they have "if it's for sale." Produces an interesting newsletter for lace fanciers for $20 a year.

"A great deal of valuable lace is lost each year because people don't take time to inquire."

> Elizabeth Kurella
> Lace Merchant
> PO Box 222
> Plainwell, MI 49080
> (616) 685-9792

★ **Lace, linens, and stichery** including:
> **Table linens** especially with large napkins, lace, or handiwork;
> **Lace curtains, panels** and **hankies,** if fine quality;
> **Embroidered pictures** and **samplers;**
> **Lace collars** and **lace yardage** from before 1940;
> **Pillow cases** and **sheets** with hand stitchery or lace before 1925;
> **Embroideries** and **printed fabrics** of the Arts and Crafts period;
> **Unusual weaving, textiles and stitchery** from before 1930.

No hand towels, plain linen, Damask, damaged goods, or items made after 1960 are wanted. If Paul is interested in buying your items, he will request you ship on approval. Photographs or photocopies are useful.

> Paul Freeman
> PO Box 225 or 13 Circular Ave.
> Pittsfield, MA 01201

★ **Lace, trimmings, embroidery** and **stitchery.** Wants assortments of pre-1920 rosettes, fabric or ribbon trims for clothing or hats, tatted items that are more than 5" in size (including doilies), white on white stitchery, red stitchery on white, **beaded clothing and accessories,** and clothing (including pantaloons, skirts, and dresses) with decorative handiwork. Also buys quilt tops, crazy quilts, and other handmade cloth items. Send a good photograph or photocopy of what you wish to sell. "Items can be partially damaged if I use them to make other things. Please, no hankies or crochet items." Please include an SASE for response.

> Linda Gibbs, Heirloom Keepsakes
> 10380 Miranda
> Buena Park, CA 90620
> (714) 827-6488

★ **Quilting and patchwork patterns, books** and **tools** from before 1950. Also wants vintage fabric, cloth scraps, patterned flour and feed sacks, and other material useful for old style quilting.

> Judy Speezak
> Box 2528 Rockefeller Center Station
> New York, NY 10185

★ **Indian pattern blankets** made by *Beacon, Buell, Candelario, Capps, Esmond, Hamilton, Oregon City, Pendleton*, and *Racine (Badger State)*. "I'm writing a book on these blankets and am buying blankets, catalogs, and promotional advertising pieces, especially swatch books. I prefer all material to be priced, but will make offers to people who are not dealers. I answer calls and letters promptly." A photograph or photocopy is a must, and you are requested to list all flaws, holes, etc., in your first letter. Because blankets are often washed improperly, shrunk, and therefore undesirable, dimensions are a must.

> Barry Friedman
> 22725 Garzota Drive
> Valencia, CA 91355
> (805) 296-2318

★ **Fabrics from the 1940's and 1950's.** If you have at least three yards of any floral or tropical patterned fabric, and it's in perfect condition, you may well find a buyer in Leda.

> Leda Andrews
> 2110 Staples Ave.
> Key West, FL 33040

★ **American sewing machines from before 1875,** especially rare early treadle machines with low serial numbers for which he will pay from $1,000-$10,000. Small hand operated machines in the shape of animals are of particular interest. Also photographs of sewing machines in use before 1890. Tell him the maker and the serial number as well as the condition. If there is no name, send a photograph. Carter does not buy *Singer, White, Wheeler & Wilson, Willcox & Gibbs*, or other machines with brand names you recognize, nor does he buy treadle machines in oak cases, or any sewing machine with a chrome or nickel plated fly wheel. "High serial numbers on your machine mean it's a common one and of no collector interest."

> Carter Bays
> 143 Springlake Road
> Columbia, SC 29206
> (800) 332-2297

CLOTHING & ACCESSORIES

★ *Levis, Lee,* **and** *Wrangler* **jeans and jackets** for resale. "I'll buy all pre-1970 *Levi Strauss* jeans and jackets and some older *Wrangler* and *Lee* jeans and jackets. The *Levis* he wants all have a small red tag on the front pocket [jackets left, pants right] which spells out LEvis. That capitol "E" makes these called "Big E" jeans, and they are a hot fad item in some places today. Jackets from 1920-1949 bring $500 to $1,500; if heavily worn, still $100 to $300. Others jackets, with two front pockets, bring from $25 to $500. Does not want *Levis* with tags of any color other than red. Pants with waists larger than 34" are not of interest either. If you have a red Big E *Levis* tag in one of your front pockets, and want an immediate cash offer, describe condition carefully noting stains, holes, wear, the condition of the leather ID tag. The serial number on the back pocket leather ID tag would be helpful. Also buys advertising signs or figures from these same companies.

> David Bailey, Bailey's Antiques & Thrift
> 2580 La-i Road
> Honolulu, HI 96816
> (808) 734-7628

★ **Vintage Hawaiian shirts, 1930-1955.** The label, size, coloration, and pattern are important, as is the material, so include all that when you write. Shirts can be made of cotton, rayon, or silk. A silk shirt with a fish pattern (his personal favorite) could bring as high as $500. Most are considerably less, but well worth your time. "I'm willing to answer questions and provide information to people who are not sure if their shirts are old enough." A photograph or photocopy is helpful.

> Evan Olins, Flamingo's
> 75-5744 Alii Drive
> Kailau-Kona, HI 96740
> (808) 329-4122

★ **Hawaiian shirts made before 1960.**

> David Bailey
> 2580 La-i Road
> Honolulu, HI 96816
> (808) 734-7628

TIPS ON SELLING CLOTHING

Stained or torn clothing is not wanted. Always describe the style, color, material, size, and label. Clothes with designer labels are particularly desirable, but old *Levi's* may prove to be as valuable.

★ **Men's and women's clothing and accessories,** 1900-1940. Wants average sizes in good condition. Very interested in old warehouse stock and in rayon yardage.
> The Way We Wore
> 1094 Revere Ave #A-29
> San Francisco, CA 94124
> (415) 822-1800 10 a.m. to 5 p.m.

★ **Vintage clothes made before 1950** such as beaded sweaters and **beaded purses and bags,** evening gowns, prom dresses, men's tuxedos and hats, etc. Also buys **parasols** and **piano shawls.** No damaged or stained items as items are purchased for resale in her 2,000 sq.ft. shop. Price your goods when possible.
> Bird In the Cage
> 118 King Street
> Alexandria, VA 22314
> (703) 549-5114

★ **Alligator and crocodile handbags and luggage.** In addition to fancy leather bags, she wants designer luggage by *Hermes, Chanel,* and *Vuitton.* Everything must be in resale condition. Send measurements and sketch or photo. Describe condition inside and out including handles and hardware. Give the color of the bag and lining, and any special features. Also wants some **unusual vintage purses** suitable for resale.
> Joy Horvath
> 12 Belair Road
> Norwalk, CT 06850
> (203) 847-9035

★ **Women's spiked or high heeled shoes** in excellent condition from the 20's through the 60's. Please send photos, shoe size, and the height of the heels.
> Charles Martignette
> PO Box 293
> Hallandale, FL 33009
> (305) 454-3474

★ **Clothing worn by famous people,** such as U.S. Presidents, first ladies and well know entertainers.
> Paul Hartunian
> 127B East Bradford Ave.
> Cedar Grove, NJ 07009
> (201) 857-7275

★ **Hand painted ties** from the 1930's and 40's. These are easy to describe by making a photocopy.
> Barry Pener
> 9254 High Drive
> Leawood, KS 66206

★ **Hand painted neckties** from the 1930's and 40's. These are easy to describe by making a photocopy.
Barry Pener
9254 High Drive
Leawood, KS 66206

★ **Neckties by Dali.** "Will pay well. Please leave a message."
David Wilcox
Box 11203
Indianapolis, IN 46201
(317) 359-9342

★ **Ladies hand fans** from 1600 to 1900 are wanted in ivory, mother-of-pearl, tortoise shell, horn, or wooden sticks with painting or decor on silk, lace, paper, or chicken skin. All origins are sought: French, German, English, American, Chinese, Viennese, and Spanish, but only in good to mint condition. Send a photocopy.
Monica Murphy, Savannah's Antiques
1419 Fern
New Orleans, LA 70118
(504) 866-2221

★ **Antique fancy buttons.** Wants those with metal pictures, Oriental, pearl, *Bakelite*, etc. The way to tell whether she wants your buttons is to ask two questions before contacting her:
    (1) Does the button have holes through it? If yes, she is not
        interested in your button. If no, ask question #2.
    (2) Is it fancy or unusual? If yes, she wants it.
She does not want shirt buttons or ordinary plastic buttons with visible sewing holes. Almost all the buttons she buys are shank type. Please price your buttons for resale. Photocopies or approvals are suggested.
Barbara Bronzoulis, Barbara's Button Bracelets
1931 Laurel Hill
Kingwood, TX 77339
(713) 358-1518

★ **Buttons,** especially U.S. military, Confederate, military school, and uniform buttons with state seals. He also buys "high quality clothing buttons of porcelain, satsuma, or with pictures." He does not want WWI or WWII buttons or "simple clothing buttons made of plastic or bone." Please describe the design, and note anything stamped on the back. This director of the National Button Society prefers that you ship for inspection prior to final offer.
Warren Tice
PO Box 8491
Essex, VT 05451
(802) 878-3835 phone and fax

PERFUME

★ **Perfume bottles with glass stoppers.** Wants art glass bottles, large department store display bottles, and samples. Give the brand of perfume and photocopy the bottle. No *Avon* bottles are wanted.
Annette Chaussee
PO Box 22
Calhan, CO 80808

★ **Perfume bottles, decanters, and vases with silver overlay.** Describe all markings and give dimensions and colors.
Arnold Reamer, Timepiece Antiques
PO Box 26416
Baltimore, MD 21207
(410) 944-6414 or (410) 486-8412

★ **Perfume bottles made of blown or cut art glass**, singles or matching sets. Wants fine beautiful bottles including those with atomizers. Some important makers include *DeVilbiss, Daum Nancy, Galle, Baccarat, Webb, Moser, Czechoslovakian, Lalique*, and *Steuben*. Also English scents, bottles with sterling overlay, and figurals. Also **Sterling silver dresser sets, hair brushes, mirrors and other boudoir items**. The proprietor of this unusual shop for women does not make offers, nor does she buy *Avon* bottles.
Madeleine France
Past Pleasures for the 20th Century Woman
PO Box 15555
Plantation, FL 33316
(305) 584-0009

PERFUME BOTTLES

Collectors seek a great many perfume bottles from the 1920's, 30's, and 40's. Since these bottles were designed and made by top European art glass companies, they are frequently worth in excess of $100 and a few bring $1,000 or more. Look for pretty shapes, colored and clear glass, silver trim, atomizers, glass stoppers, and anything unusual, figural, or particularly decorative.

Avon perfume and toiletry bottles have little resale value.

★ *DeVilbis* **atomizers,** with or without original bulb, tube, and cord. Describe the size, colors, and condition. A detailed sketch or close up photo is essential. "If you have items to sell me, I prefer you to write rather than phone."

Bruce Bleier
73 Riverdale Road
Valley Stream, NY 11581
(516) 791-4353

★ *California Perfume Company* **(CPC) products made between 1886 and 1929,** especially *Natoma Rose* fragrances. He also wants CPC products marketed as *Goetting and Company, Savoi Et Cie, Gertrude Recordon, Marvel Electric Silver Cleaner,* and the *Easy Day Automatic Clothes Washer.* Dick does not want anything with *Avon* on the label, although he will answer specific questions about *Avon* if you include a Self-Addressed Stamped Envelope. Please give a complete description of the item you have for sale, including its condition and whether or not it has its original box. Is there a label and/or a neck band? Are there cracks or chips? Photocopy is helpful. Dick's collection is open to the public by advance appointment.

Dick Pardini
3107 North El Dorado Street
Stockton, CA 95204
(209) 466-5550 7am to 11pm

★ *Avon* **bottles** remain a popular collectible, but there are few people buying *Avons* through the mail, except very rare ones. If you want to learn about the world of *Avon* collecting, for $11 Western World Publishing offers six bimonthly issues of *Avon Collectors Marketplace,* each of which contains pages of WANTED and FOR SALE ads. Your subscription includes club membership and free classified advertising for a year. They also publish *Avon 8 Supplimnent #1,* available to owners of *Avon 8,* their illustrated popular price guide to *Avon* collectibles, for $9.

Western World Publishing
PO Box 23785-T
Pleasant Hill, CA 94523
(510) 825-1042

★ **Women's powder compacts,** from before 1950. All types of attractive compacts are wanted, as long as the condition is good and the compact complete. Unusual, Art Deco, and precious metals are preferred. Most others are less than five dollars.

Bird In the Cage
118 King Street
Alexandria, VA 22314
(703) 549-5114

TIPS ON SELLING

Jewelry

Diamonds are often mistaken for glass in old jewelry. So are emeralds, rubies, and many precious and semi-precious stones. 19th century gemstones were cut differently than is popular today. One reader showed me a two and a half carat diamond ring he bought at a yard sale for a quarter. I hope he wasn't shopping at your house!

Jewelry buyers want to know:

(1) The basic material from which your item is made, such as silver, gold, brass, plastic or a material you don't recognize.
(2) All names, numbers, and markings;
(3) Shape, color, and number of any stones.

The dimensions are helpful. Photocopying is a good way to describe pins, hatpins, brooches, and some bracelets.

Be prepared to ship your jewelry with a five day return privilege. Buyers usually want to inspect jewelry before they commit to buy. Many buyers are reluctant to pay before they see what you have. If they do pay first, you must be willing to give the money back if the buyer is not happy for any reason with what you send.

When mailing items worth more than $500, send them Registered Mail. It costs between $5-$10 to mail safely throughout the U.S. with insurance as high as $25,000. All recipients must sign for Registered Mail. Reread the Introduction for more information about Registered Mail.

JEWELRY

★ **Old and antique jewelry** especially
> **Karat gold pieces**, particularly signed pieces with art nouveau
> and Art Deco designs;
> **Sterling silver items** signed by *Unger Brothers* or *Kerr*, mostly
> art nouveau brooches featuring female faces;
> **Designer costume jewelry** signed by *Coro, Trifari, Mariam
> Haskell, Hattie Carnegie,* or *Eisenberg Original*
> *Georg Jensen* **jewelry**;
> **Silver puffed heart fancy charms**.

Describe your items completely, or make a photocopy. If you know the
item's ownership history, please give it. Note all markings.
> Arnold Reamer, Timepiece Antiques
> PO Box 26416
> Baltimore, MD 21207
> (410) 944-6414 or (410) 486-8412

★ **Antique jewelry** made of 8K to 22K gold with any type of stones,
made before 1900. Especially wants earrings, but also complete suites,
hair and mourning jewelry, cameos (shell or stone), seed pearls,
miniature ivory portraits, tiaras, tortoise shell jewelry, fine hair combs,
"anything worn from head to toe." She requests photo and/or description
with your asking price, and pledges "willing to pay for rarity."
> Monica Murphy, Savannah's Antiques
> 1419 Fern
> New Orleans, LA 70118
> (504) 866-2221

★ **Hatpins and hatpin holders** and related objects such as pincushion
dolls from before 1930. "Especially interested in plique-a-jour hatpins
for which I'll pay up to $350 or more if artist signed. I also like sterling
hatpins marked "C.H." and will pay $45-$110. Always interested in
vanity or figural hatpins such as compacts, pin-holders, perfume tops,
thimble with needle, etc., especially if art nouveau design atop 12" pin
stems. My special want is a hatpin hinged on the top ornament which
opens to reveal a teeny nude baby and I would pay up to $500 for a per-
fect one on a long pin. I also want to buy **figural hatpin holders** by
Royal Bayreuth, RS Prussia (red mark only), *Oriental, Schafer & Vater*
(S&V), others." Mrs. Baker has written books on jewelry and an encyclopedia of hatpins available from her for $79 postpaid. She founded the
International Club for Hatpin Collectors. Give the history of your hatpin,
and whether it has any flaws. Will make offers to amateurs only after inspection. An SASE brings information about the club and her books.
> Lillian Baker, The Hatpin Lady
> 15237 Chanera Ave.
> Gardena, CA 90249
> (310) 329-2619

★ **Tassie cameos** made of marble dust with gold colored paper wrapped around it. These are most often of mythological characters. Also want the molds in which the cameos were made. Very rare and hard to find, Tassie cameos are named after James Tassie of Scotland who, in the 1700's, invented glass cameo molds used by *Wedgwood* to make the decorations on their pottery. Tassie cameos are most often hung in picture frames. Pledges to pay premium prices for these rarities. Send a photo and/or description.

>Monica Murphy, Savannah's Antiques
>1419 Fern
>New Orleans, LA 70118
>   (504) 866-2221

★ **Old jewelry before 1930,** garnets, black jets, cameos, rings, **lockets, charms,** filigree beads, glass beads, and glass buttons. Craftsmanship and detail ("ornate and unusual") is more important than whether it's made of gold or not. **Lockets, hearts**, stars, flowers and other keepsake jewelry is wanted in gold or silver. "I look for all unusual items of clothing, jewelry, and accessories." Photocopy is suggested. Jewelry may be broken and need repair.

>Linda Gibbs
>10380 Miranda Ave.
>Buena Park, CA 90620
>   (714) 827-6488

★ **Plastic or metal** *Hummel* **jewelry** from 1940's in shapes similar to their figurines. She buys both painted and unpainted jewelry.

>Sharon Vohs-Mohammed
>PO Box 14192
>Tallahassee, FL 32317

★ **Woodburned glove and jewelry boxes** are purchased for resale, as are **jewelry boxes made of cast iron,** particularly those that are silk lined. Please give a thorough description.

>Linda Gibbs
>10380 Miranda Ave.
>Buena Park, CA 90620
>   (714) 827-6488

★ **Gold scrap.** "I buy all marked and unmarked gold and silver rings, wedding bands, and scrap," says this giant dealer in coins, medals, and tokens. Hartzog says you may ship whatever you have for his offer.

>Rich Hartzog, World Exonumia
>PO Box 4143 BFT
>Rockford, IL 61110
>   (815) 226-0771

Watches and clocks

Be cautious about selling watches locally. It is unlikely your local jeweler is expert in evaluating and pricing old watches, even though he sells new ones. There is a great deal of money at stake, and you may put five or ten times as much money in your pocket when you deal with watch buyers who keep up with the international watch market. One lucky reader bought a watch at a yard sale for $10 because he thought it was "curious looking." One of our buyers paid him $4,500 for that watch!

To describe a watch or clock, answer as many of the following as you can:

Is there anything unusual about its appearance?
What name is on the dial?
What name is on the movement (internal mechanism)?
Does it say how many jewels?
What is the size of the case?
What is the case made of?
Is the case decorated or engraved?
Is there a label inside the case?
Is there a serial number?
How is it wound or activated?
Do you have the key and weights?
Is it presently running?

In most cases, watch buyers will want to inspect your timepiece before making a final offer. Send watches via Registered US Mail, insured. This is a safe way to ship, and requires the recipient to sign for the package. Always discuss exact shipping procedures with the buyer.

WATCHES

★ **Vintage wristwatches and better antique pocket watches,** especially *Patek Philippe, Cartier, Rolex, Vacheron & Constantin, Audemars Piguet, E. Howard, Hamilton, Reed,* and *Illinois.* Also wants chronographs, watches that chime, enamels, phases of the moon, calendar watches, historical watches, gold cases, character watches, sports watches, oddly shaped watches, both U.S. and foreign. Exceptional prices paid for fine and rare vintage wristwatches and pocket watches, running or not. Call toll free if you have a watch to sell or know someone who does. "We pay a $ignificant finder$ fee for leads on large collections, estates, or accumulations." Not buying *Timex,* electronic, or inexpensive watches made after 1965. Describe your watch according to instructions on previous page. Ask for his wants list.

    Miles Sandler, Maundy International
    PO Box 13028 TH
    Overland Park, KS 66212
       (800) 235-2866

★ **High quality and collectible watches** by *Patek Phillipe, Rolex, Cartier, Tiffany, Audemars* and types of watches like chronographs, repeaters, alarm, doctor's watches, two time zone, and rectangular faces made between 1870 and 1960. **Also advertising items relating to watches.** Irv deals in watches from rare to common. Buys parts, cases, boxes, movements, dials, bands, from all *Rolex, Patek* or *Cartier* watches. If you are thinking of auction, Irv says, "We will buy any piece that interests us at 95% of anticipated net sellers hammer proceeds." Irv promises: "Fair prices, next day payment, postage refunded, and free appraisals," adding "I will come to you if what you have is very valuable or if you have many good pieces." Describe metal, shape, details, all names and numbers, as indicated on previous page. Irv offers a priced wants list.

    Irv Temes, American International Watch Exchange
    113 North Charles Street
    Baltimore, MD 21201
       (410) 882-0580

★ **Wrist and pocket watches,** both men's and women's, in gold, silver, or gold fill. Pocket watches may be in other metals if they date before 1940. Doesn't matter whether running or not. Describe all markings and give dimensions.

    Arnold Reamer, Timepiece Antiques
    PO Box 26416
    Baltimore, MD 21207
       (410) 944-6414 or (410) 486-8412

★ **Racing stopwatches, pocket watches, dashboard clocks, and schoolhouse clocks** with the name of a horse, horse race, carriage company, or automobile manufacturer on the face. Also sterling silver clock cases, with or without clocks. Also leather cases for car clocks that clip over the dashboard of a carriage. "When in doubt, please write and inquire, or send your watch on approval for an immediate response."

> Donald Sawyer
> 40 Bachelor Street
> West Newbury, MA 01985
> (508) 346-4724 days

★ **Watches and clocks with cartoon characters or product advertising on the face.** Any pre-1975 items that are mint in their original box are particularly desirable. "I'll pay $1,000 for a mint in the box 1934 *Ingersoll* Tom Mix pocket or wrist watch." Wants to know whether the face is round or rectangular, any wording on the face or back of the watch, defects (including scratches), the condition of the box (if any), and whether or not it is working. Don't overwind! Free appraisals available for amateur sellers.

> Maggie Kenyon
> Maggie's Place
> One Christopher Street #14G
> New York, NY 10013
> (212) 675-3213

★ *Hamilton* **"electric" wristwatches.** "I'm particularly interested in those with odd and asymmetrically shaped cases." An electric watch specialist and repairman, he also wants parts, movements, **advertising materials, catalogs**, and most anything else related to the *Hamilton Electric* watch, particularly dealer's stock, early prototypes, and calendar models. No *Hamilton Electronic* watches, or watches marked "Swiss." Only American made pre-1970 electric watches. Rene has produced a handsome and comprehensive book on *Hamilton* electric watches which you can obtain from him for $30 postpaid.

> Rene Rondeau
> 120 Harbor Drive
> Corte Madera, CA 94925

★ **Pocket watches,** better quality wristwatches, and clocks are wanted. Please give a thorough description.

> Robert Kolbe's Clock Repair
> 1301 South Duluth
> Sioux Falls, SD 57105
> (605) 332-9662

CLOCKS

★ **American wall and mantle clocks** from the 1700's through the Arts and Crafts movement of the early 20th century. "I'll buy, sell, or trade a wide range of clocks, but my specialties are weight driven calendar and regulator clocks that hang on a wall. I also buy interesting, unusual, and better grades of shelf (mantle) and other wall clocks of the 1800's. Especially like to find clocks with multiple dials or faces, in either plain or fancy cases." Some of the many names to look for include *Simon-Willard, E.N. Welch, Howard, Ithaca, Waterbury, Seth Thomas, New Haven*, and other early Connecticut makers. Bruce is well versed in clocks of all types so can be helpful to the amateur seller. "If I'm offered something I can't use, I try to refer folks to someone who might like to buy it. Early electric clocks don't interest me much, but I may be able to give readers some help in identifying or evaluating them." Provide a full description. Bruce says, "For my own collection, I like to find ones that are a little out of the ordinary." Some interest in **European clocks with porcelain dials, or with fine cases with gilt, inlay, or marble.**

> Bruce Austin
> RIT College of Liberal Arts
> Rochester, NY 14623
> (716) 223-0711 eves

★ **Grandfather clocks made in America.** "I want tall floor clocks made in the United States, especially in Pennsylvania. I generally don't buy them myself, but I screen clocks for one of the world's expert buyers of good clocks. If you have something good in the way of an old tall case clock, we will put you in touch with the buyer." European tall clocks are not wanted, no matter how pretty.

> Old Timers
> PO Box 392
> Camp Hill, PA 17001-0392
> (717) 761-1908

★ **Fine European clocks.** Buys high quality French, English and German wall, floor, and shelf clocks from 1600 to 1900, especially those with fancy inlay, gilded, bronze, porcelain, Meissen, and Sevres cases. Also wants musical clocks of any type, skeleton clocks with works that show; and many other unusual, highly decorated, or artistic types of clocks, dials, and/or cases. This company buys European, not American clocks of any kind! They want a clear photo and a description of the case, including dimensions, where and when you got it, and anything you know about repairs, internal or external. Mention names on the dial. Give your phone and best time to call. Does not return photos.

> Fraser Cameron, Ltd.
> PO Box 27162
> Minneapolis, MN 55427
> (612) 926-6609   Fax: (612) 949-1177

★ **Old wall and shelf clocks.** This respected Pennsylvania company buys a wide range of 18th and 19th century shelf and wall clocks, but are especially interested in the following:

Victorian shelf clocks. Wants ornate ones, with hanging tear drops, busts (such as Jenny Lind), cherubs or side mirrors;

Reverse painting on glass pillar and scroll clocks about 36" high with free standing wooden pillars and curved scroll ("swan's neck") tops;

Steeple or beehive shelf clocks, but *only* if the veneer is perfect, or nearly so. "These are plentiful with poor veneer. I want those in beautiful condition;"

Any American carved clocks. "I'm a pushover for clocks with carved columns or splats, eagles or fruit baskets;"

Clocks by *Eli Terry* or any of his sons;

Seth Thomas clocks;

French, German and **English clocks** from the 18th and 19th century. "Some excellent 20th century German clocks were made in Mission style, but no matter how good the clock, we don't buy 20th century," he cautions, so don't ask.

Coo-coo clocks if very old, very heavily carved, and in perfect condition. "I'm afraid I'll open a floodgate if I mention I'm interested in coo-coos, because there are so many junk ones around. I only want those that are very early, and very ornate...no souvenir clocks. Sending a photo a must."

Black Forest trumpeter clocks. These are chiming clocks, like coo-coos, but instead of a bird have a man who plays a tune on a trumpet. "These are valuable, and we'll travel to pick yours up if it's a nice one."

"We buy clocks with walnut or cherry cases. We buy spring driven clocks but especially like to find older weight driven clocks. We buy clocks with wooden works only if in running condition," they say, "but there are a few exceptions, so it's worth inquiring. We are *not* interested in oak clocks or metal figural clocks no matter who is depicted. We don't buy any 20th century clocks, oak gingerbread kitchen clocks, electric clocks, or Mission (Arts and Crafts) clocks. Nor do we buy *Lux* or *Keebler* novelty clocks with rolling eyes or swinging tails. We also do not buy plain ogee clocks (rectangular veneered clocks with fronts that look like picture frames). We almost never buy clocks that have undergone restoration or modification. We don't want to spend lots of time with the clocks. We prefer to buy them in nearly perfect condition."

"We think of ourselves as a clock adoption agency. We look for nice items in need of a good new home."

Old Timers
PO Box 392
Camp Hill, PA 17001
   (717) 761-1908

★ *Howard Miller* **clocks** from the 1950's and 60's. These are usually metal or metal and wood and marked on the back (and sometimes the front). A photograph or sketch is helpful.
> Frank Novak
> 7386 Beverly Blvd.
> Los Angeles, CA 90036
> > (213) 683-1963   Fax: (213) 683-1312

★ **Winking eye clocks.** "I'll buy any good specimens of these 19th century figural cast iron clocks which wink their eyes as the hands go around. Made in Connecticut during the 3rd quarter of the 19th century by *Bradley and Hubbard*, they bring $1,000 up in fine condition and paint. Take photos from more than one angle or phone me with the item in front of you."
> Gregory "Dr. Z" Zemenick
> 1350 Kirts #160
> Troy, MI 48084
> > (313) 642-8129 or (313) 244-9426

★ **Advertising clocks** made by *Baird.*
> Jerry Phelps
> 6013 Innes Trace Road
> Louisville, KY 40222
> > (502) 425-4765

★ **Novelty and animated clocks,** running or not. Want clocks with swinging cats' tails, rolling eyes, or other rhythmically moving parts, made by *Lux, Keebler*, and others.
> Ed Kazemekas
> 35 Riverview Circle
> Wolcott, CT 06716
> > (203) 879-1814

★ **Electric clocks covered with colored mirrors.** Wants 1930's clock brands like *GE, Telechron,* and *Seth Thomas* covered with blue, peach, or green mirrors as long as the mirrors are not cracked or damaged. It's OK if the clock doesn't work. Give the brand, model, dimensions, and the color of the glass.
> David Escoe
> PO Box 342
> Los Alamitos, CA 90720

Games, puzzles and toys

Games, puzzles, toys, and playthings of all types, from all periods, have value. Toy collecting has become particularly popular in the last decade. The increased competition, coupled with clever marketing by toy dealers, drove prices sharply upward in the late 1980's. The recent depression put a sharp halt to that trend. As always, premium pieces bring premium money.

Toy collectors love 19th century toys in original boxes, and frequently pay in excess of $5,000 for rare examples. Toys with moving parts from that period are particularly desirable. $15,000 and more has been paid for cast iron banks and toys, dolls, trucks, Teddy bears and even board games. Baby-boomer toys of the 1960's and 70's have taken the sharpest increase in value, and are expected to go higher.

Game collectors are more interested in the box than in its contents. Although having all the game pieces, boards, and instructions adds greatly to the value of a game, it is the colorful picture on the cover that makes a game collectible. The condition of the box is critical. Common games with names you recognize are not collectible, unless prototypes or hand made. Games based on movies and TV usually find ready buyers in the $20 to $100 range. Buyers for newer games are found in Pop Culture, pages 111-126.

Wooden, tin, and iron toys were usually painted. The amount of paint that still remains is vital information to a collector, as is any evidence that the toy might have been repainted. It is common practice to make an estimate expressed in percent terms of how much paint remains.

Toy banks, other than those marked BOOK OF KNOWLEDGE, are very desirable, particularly 19th century originals. These too were sold in boxes, the originals of which can add hundreds of dollars to the value. Colored paper advertising cards which depict banks sell for $300 to $1,000 each!

Cap guns have a dedicated following, and even minor differences in the castings, handles, and decoration can spark collector interest. Accurate descriptions can put extra money in your pocket.

Every toy vehicle made out of a material other than plastic will probably find a buyer. Although they are all popular, top dollar goes to the German wind-up cars and boats of the turn-of-the-century, with fine condition specimens bringing more than $10,000. Don't overlook any toy cars, however, even *Matchbox* and *Hot Wheels*. The traditionally most popular toy vehicle, the electric train, remains a favorite. One reader reported receiving $9,500 for his old train set, so they are obviously worth inquiry.

If you carefully read sections in *Where To Sell It!* about toys, dolls, games, and Pop Culture, you will become aware of a wide range of small and seemingly insignificant items sought by collectors. Printed and photographic information about those items is sought as well. If you have any of these items to sell, you should provide the potential buyer with a complete description, including the following information:

(1) What you have, including its size, color, and the material from which it is made;
(2) Names, dates, and numbers printed, embossed, stamped, or labeled on the item;
(3) Condition, including mention of any missing parts, pieces, or paint, or damage to what remains;
(4) Whether it has the box and/or instructions.

Don't forget your Self-Addressed Stamped Envelope.

GAMES & PUZZLES

★ **Card and board games.** A wide range of adult and children's games are wanted, especially games that are hand made, patriotic, or have unusual themes. Strategy games, domino sets, backgammon sets, cribbage boards, early *Monopoly* games, *Mah Jongg* **sets**, anagrams, and playing card decks will all be considered if they are in some way unusual. Pre-1946 items preferred. Best if complete with rules, all pieces, and original box. No *Pit, Rook, Authors, Flinch, Touring,* and other common card games are wanted except prototypes.
Dave Galt
302 West 78th Street
New York, NY 10024
(212) 769-2514

★ **Antique and collectible board and card games** made in the U.S. from 1840-1960's. Any game before 1860 is wanted, especially those made by *Ives, Crosby, Magnus,* or *Adams*, for which they will pay $500 and up. Other items of particular interest are baseball games before WWI, and games about TV shows, cartoon characters, space exploration and pop culture (including movies) of the 1930-1970's. They also buy **wooden jigsaw puzzles, blocks**, and **paper toys**. No chess, checkers, *Pit, Lotto, Rook, Flinch, Autobridge, Parcheesi, Touring,* variants of *Bingo*, TV "Game show" games, or "kiddie" games like *Chutes and Ladders*. Give name, condition, size, maker, copyright date, and the degree of completeness.
Dave Oglesby and Sue Stock
57 Lakeshore Drive
Marlborough, MA 01752
(508) 481-1087

★ **Jigsaw puzzles and board games with space theme** are bought. Only wants items from before 1966 in excellent condition. Puzzles may be jigsaw or frame type. Will pay $50 for *Lost in Space* puzzle. Pop culture, not real life space themes are wanted. Also buys greeting cards and phono record sleeves with space theme. Does not want items made after 1966, nor does he want things related to the real moon landing.
Don Sheldon
PO Box 3313
Trenton, NJ 08619
(609) 588-5403

★ **Games and puzzles with sexy or sentimental themes** dating from 1920-1959, such as pin-ups, children and animals, parents and children, patriotism, etc. Must be in the original box.
Charles Martignette
PO Box 293
Hallandale, FL 33009
(305) 454-3474

★ **Almost any complete playable game,** especially out-of-print titles by *Avalon Hill, 3M, SPI*, pre-1964 *Parker Bros.*, war games, sports games, political games, and TV related games. Include the name of the manufacturer and copyright date. Please thoroughly check the contents and note if anything, no matter how small, is missing. Describe how much wear shows on the box and pieces. Also buys **gaming magazines** such as *The General, Wargamer, The Dragon,* and *Games & Puzzles*. Please, no checkers, chess or common children's games like *Authors*.

> H.M. Levy
> PO Box 197-CC
> East Meadow, NY 11554
> (516) 485-0877

★ *Mah Jongg* **sets, racks, and accessories,** pre-1930. Tiles may be made of bone, bamboo, celluloid, jade, or ivory. Especially interested in jade, ivory, gold, or fine inlaid tiles and boxes. Pays $500-$1,000 and up. Does not buy partial sets unless unusual. *Mah Jongg* is also called *Ma Chuck, Pung Chow, Sparrows, Game of China,* etc. Buys *Mah Jongg* books and magazines. Also **domino sets** made of ivory or ebony and **ebony** *Pai Gow* **games**. For his offer, mail him two typical tiles (insured), a count of how many pieces you have, and a list of other items.

> Joe Scales
> 3827 Los Santos Drive
> Cameron Park, CA 95682
> (916) 677-0262

★ **Chess sets.** "I'll buy rare and unusual chess sets of all sorts, but primarily those with *themes* such as Disney, Watergate, etc. I like historical, literary, fictional, and mythological." If it's out of the ordinary in theme, design, material, or whatever, give him a call. He would especially like to find the 3-D chess set from *Star Trek* in the late 1960's. No plastic or "typical wooden sets," he warns, "I'm looking for works of art or imagination." Describe the board if one accompanies your set. Provide whatever background you can about the history of the board and pieces. Describe condition of both. Photo or photocopy, please.

> Dennis Horwitz
> 425 Short Trail
> Topanga, CA 90290
> (310) 455-4002

★ **Figural European chess sets** with playing pieces shaped like actual people or animals. Also antique chess boards. This 30 year veteran collector also wants porcelain or bronze figurines as well as paintings and other original **art depicting chess players.**

> David Hafler
> 11 Merion Road
> Merion Station, PA 19066
> (215) 839-7171

★ **Checkers ephemera,** primarily books about checkers or draughts, but also early handmade boards or anything unusual related to checkers. Give standard bibliographic information, and Don would like you to send a photocopy of any advertising in the book.
Don Deweber, Checker Book World
3520 Hillcrest #4
Dubuque, IA 52001

The games and puzzles in this section of *Where To Sell It!* are primarily board games, mechanical and jigsaw puzzles, and the largely outdoor game of marbles. The collectibles world thinks of them as related to toys. Pencil and paper puzzles, like rebuses and crosswords, are sought by a different type of collector and you will find those classified under Miscellaneous Paper on page 383.

★ **Mechanical and dexterity puzzles.** Wants all types of mechanical and dexterity puzzles. Not interested in jigsaw or paper and pencil puzzles. Please send a photocopy, sketch, or clear photo of your puzzle.
Cary Basse
6927 Forbes Ave.
Van Nuys, CA 91406
(818) 781-4856

★ **Mechanical puzzles of all types** including trick locks and matchsafes, "and all others." Also expresses some interest in advertising for trick locks and puzzles. A photocopy, photograph, or good sketch is appreciated. Dealers should price their goods, but he will help amateurs.
"Mr. Slocum"
PO Box 1635
Beverly Hills, CA 90213

MARBLES

★ **Marbles and marble-related toys.** Wants old marbles including clay, china and porcelain marbles decorated with flowers, people, animals or geometric designs. He also buys Indian swirls, German swirls, clam broth, sulfides and machine made marbles if before 1940. "I'll pay up to $2,000 for colored sulfide marbles with unusual objects or people in them and up to $1,000 for porcelain or china marbles decorated with flowers, ships, birds, or people and animals." He also wants, and will pay well for, early boxed sets of marbles made by *Christensen Agate Co., Peltier Marble Co.,* or *Akro Agate.* Toys related to marbles are also often of interest. He does not want *Chinese Checker* marbles and boards or any cat's-eye marbles. If you know your marble's history, tell him. Otherwise a good description should include what is on or in the marble and its diameter.

> Edwin Snyder
> PO Box 156
> Lancaster, KY 40444
> (606) 792-4816 eves

★ **Marbles and marble-related items.** "I'll buy marbles with pontil marks (from where they were hand-blown), toys or games using marbles, marble bags, tournament pins and medals, and boxes of marbles. Also pictures, magazine ads, and postcards which depict marble games." He does not buy beat-up or chipped marbles, machine made marbles, home-made games, or *Chinese Checkers.* When selling marbles, it is important to give the diameter as part of your description.

> Larry Svacina
> 2822 Tennyson
> Denver, CO 80212
> (303) 477-9203

★ **Better quality marbles.** Stan is the publisher of *Marble Mania Quarterly* and will make offers on marbles if you describe them well.

> Stanley Block
> PO Box 51
> Trumbull, CT 06611
> (203) 261-3223

★ **Marbles and marble related ephemera.** Will buy postcards, magazine covers, ads, trade cards, stories, calendars, or "anything depicting or written about kids playing marbles."

> William Nielsen
> 1379 Main Street
> Brewster, MA 02631
> (508) 896-7389

TOY BANKS

★ **Cast iron mechanical banks,** 1870-1920, **and Japanese tin battery operated banks,** 1946-1960. Include a bottom tracing. To sell a battery toy, indicate whether it works or not and if you still have the original box. Battery banks *must* be in near mint condition. No plastic banks.
> Rick Mihlheim
> PO Box 128
> Allegan, MI 49010
> (616) 673-4509

★ **Still banks made of cast iron or metal** with special emphasis on unusual or rare examples in excellent to near-mint condition. Letters should include an accurate description including an estimate of how much of the original paint is still there. Carefully measure the length, width, and height. Photos are appreciated. Private collector answers all letters which include SASE.
> Ralph Berman
> 3524 Largo Lane
> Annandale, VA 22003
> (703) 560-5439

★ **Mechanical banks made of cast iron, tin, or wood.** Especially any mechanical bank with its original box, packing, and receipt. Also buys painted and stenciled cast iron or tin still banks shaped like buildings. Will consider incomplete and non-working specimens, if old and genuine. No banks made after 1940, including those which say BOOK OF KNOWLEDGE on the bottom. Also buys trade cards, catalogs, and other advertising depicting mechanical banks. Send sharp photos of the bank from different angles, or telephone with the item in front of you. Greg is the former president of the club for bank collectors.
> Gregory "Dr. Z" Zemenick
> 1350 Kirts #160
> Troy, MI 48084
> (313) 642-8129 or (313) 244-9426

★ **Cast iron or tin banks, still or mechanical.** Also buys original boxes and color trade cards for mechanical banks. No banks after 1950. Indicate any repairs, repaints, and give the dimensions. Prefers you to set the price you want.
> Virginia Jensen
> c/o GI School
> 23270 East River Road
> Grosse Ile, MI 48138
> (313) 561-9259 eves

OPTICAL TOYS

★ **Fine old kaleidoscopes** made of wood and/or brass especially elaborate inlaid or complex instruments from the mid 19th century. No cardboard toys.
Lucille Malitz
Lucid Antiques
PO Box KH
Scarsdale, NY 10583
   (914) 636-3367

★ **High quality kaleidoscopes** from the 1800's, made of wood and/or brass by makers such as *Bush, Brewster, Carpenter,* or *Leach.* Prefer perfect original condition brass instruments in wooden cases with the Royal seal, but will consider less. He does not buy cardboard or other inexpensive kaleidoscopes. Nothing made in the 1900's. Include your phone number and time you're home so he can phone.
Martin Roenigk
Grand Illusions
26 Barton Hill
East Hampton, CT 06424
   (203) 267-8682

★ **Polyramapanoptique and megalethescopes.** If you have to ask what they are, you probably don't have one. The former are early 19th century cardboard or wooden boxes with flaps for slides, which permit viewing of hand painted or pin-pricked scenes. Megalethescopes, invented in 1860, are large wooden cabinets, often heavily carved, also devices for slides, usually seen as day and night views of the same scene in 3D. Lucile also buys and sells slides for these early optical toys.
Lucille Malitz
Lucid Antiques
PO Box KH
Scarsdale, NY 10583
   (914) 636-3367

EARLY TOYS

★ **Cast iron bell toys,** working or not. He will consider incomplete specimens of these early toys which move and ring a bell when pulled on a string. Send clear photos taken from more than one angle, or phone with the item in hand.
>Gregory "Dr. Z" Zemenick
>1350 Kirts #160
>Troy, MI 48084
>>(313) 642-8129 or (313) 244-9426

★ **Collections of fine tin and iron toys** are sought for cataloged specialty auctions by this well known New England auctioneer. No junk, reproductions or items made after 1940.
>James D. Julia Auctioneers
>PO Box 80
>Fairfield, ME 04937
>>(207) 453-7904 Fax: (207) 453-2502

★ Antique toys of many different types:
>**Mechanical banks,** pre-1920, made of tin or iron;
>Cast iron **bell toys,** circa 1890;
>**Figural clockwork toys,** in tin or iron, from the 1870's;
>**Political campaign toys** and banks;
>European **tin toys** and large boats;
>Colorful **paper on wood boats and trains** from the 1890's;
>Colorful **Victorian children's** games and **block sets;**
>**Hand painted tin clockwork toys.**

Not interested in anything after 1940, nor does he want banks marked BOOK OF KNOWLEDGE, repainted items, or things that have been dug up. Broken mechanical banks, or toys that are incomplete may be of minor interest. Give the size, condition of the metal, and the condition of the paint including fading. List all repairs and note if the item has been lacquered or refinished. This 15 year veteran insists you set the price you want for your items.
>Mark Suozzi
>PO Box 102
>Ashfield, MA 01330
>>(413) 628-3241

★ **Antique toys** in excellent condition, including cars, carousels, and character and comic wind-ups. German and American tin toys, penny toys, nested blocks, and pop-up books are all sought. Has no interest in dolls or trains. List manufacturer, size, and condition. Picture desirable.
>James Conley
>2758 Coventry Lane NW
>Canton, OH 44708
>>(216) 477-7725 or (216) 499-9283

★ **Sets of early wooden 9 pins or 10 pins bowling games.**
Craig Dinner
PO Box 4399
Sunnyside, NY 11104
(718) 729-3850

★ *Schoenhut* **circus animals, games and dolls.** "I'll pay $150+ for each glass-eyed animal in original or near original condition. Also want circus wagons, tents, and comic characters, but no pianos."
Harry McKeon, Jr.
18 Rose Lane
Flourtown, PA 19031
(215) 233-4094

★ **Old one of a kind kites from before 1940** especially those made by important inventors. Names on desirable kites include *Hargrave, Lecornu, Saconney, Conyne, Perkins, Bell,* and many others including *Barrage Kite, Target Kite,* and the *U.S. Weather Bureau.* Also wants prototype models of production kites. Also traditional kites of Europe, the Orient, Malaysia, or South America. If it's old, interesting, or unusual, she'd like to hear about it. As publisher of *Kite Lines,* Valerie says she can act as a contact person to help you sell your kite if it's something she doesn't want. Rare and important kites are scarce but the market is small. They bring from $100 to $500. Give the history of your kite if you can.
Valerie Govig, Kite Lines
PO Box 446
Randallstown, MD 21133
(410) 922-1212

★ **Any sand-operated self contained toys,** including the "not very old" enclosed boxes with figures set in motion by flipping over the box. Also **small toy scales** made of tin.
Donald Gorlick
PO Box 24541
Seattle, WA 98124
(206) 824-0508

★ **Yo-Yo items** including displays, boxes, pins, awards and patches.
John Fawcett
RR#2, 720 Middle Turnpike
Storrs, CT 06268

★ **Toys made by** *Fisher-Price.* Also **Raggedy Ann dolls.**
Pat Wagner
5492 Feltl Road
Minnetonka, MN 55343
(612) 442-4036

★ **Victorian toys:**   Jack-in-the-boxes, animals on rolling platforms, nine pins bowling games, and other traditional toys, especially those with nursery rhyme tie-ins. He does not want anything made after 1920. This 25 year veteran requests a photo or photocopy of what you'd like to sell. Prefers to find toys in like-new condition, because they are frequently used as part of Christmas theme displays.

    Dolph "Father Christmas" Gotelli
    PO Box 8009
    Sacramento, CA 95818
       (916) 456-9734

★ **Celluloid toys,** either wind-up or stationary are wanted. Advertises that she has a particular interest in jointed and non-jointed Teddy bears.

    Meredith Failla
    60 Babylon Ave.
    West Islip, NY 11795
       (516) 587-6977

★ *Erector* sets by *A.C. Gilbert.* Will buy complete sets, partial sets, manuals, signs, and sales catalogs. Give model numbers and dates whenever it's possible.

    Elmer Wagner
    256 South Pitt Street
    Carlisle, PA 17013
       (717) 243-3539

TOY SOLDIERS

★ **Toy soldiers of all type** including boxed sets of fine British soldiers and fine condition dime store soldiers. Make photocopies of your soldiers if you'd like a free appraisal and an offer to buy.

Dan Connolly, Toy Soldier Exchange
Number 3 Burlington Arcade
380 South Lake Ave.
Pasadena, CA 91101
(818) 356-9780 phone and fax

★ **Toy soldiers of all types** including boxed sets of fine British soldiers, dime store soldiers, 1930-50, made in the USA of painted (usually khaki) lead, and German composition soldiers of WWII. Make photocopies of your soldiers if you'd like a free appraisal.

Larry Bruch
PO Box 121
Mountain Top, PA 18707
(717) 474-9202

★ **Toy soldiers.**
Lt. Col. Wilfred Baumann
PO Box 319
Esperance, NY 12066
(518) 875-6753

★ **Repairable lead soldiers.** "I'll buy them if you have the broken pieces and you set the price wanted."

Ken Cross
6003 Putnam Ave.
Ridgewood, NY 11385

BB GUNS

★ **BB Guns.** Wants American made spring-air BB guns in excellent condition. Numerous brands are wanted, although *Daisy* guns are preferred from the Plymouth, MI, factory. Does not want recently made guns, or those that are damaged, broken or otherwise in less than very good condition. You must list everything that is broken or missing. Is the stock, forestock, or grip broken, cracked or worn? Describe the finish on all metal and wooden parts. Include all names, numbers and addresses found on the gun. Indicate whether it works or not.

James Buskirk, Toy Gun Collectors of America
312 Starling Way
Anaheim, CA 92807
(714) 998-9615

★ *Quackenbush* **air guns.** Send a complete description, including a sketch or photo. Will make offers, but appraisals are for a fee.

Charles Best
6288 South Pontiac
Englewood, CO 80111

CAP PISTOLS

★ **Cap pistols.** Especially interested in cast iron guns by *Kilgore, Stevens, Hubley* and *Kenton.* Premium paid for character guns such as the *Kilgore Long Tom, Big Horn, Roy Rogers, Lone Ranger* or *American,* the *Kenton Lawmaker,* the *Stevens Cowboy King,* or any of the many different models of *Gene Autry* guns made by *Kenton.* Also interested in the 1950's and 60's die cast guns. Buys any guns marked *Gene Autry, Roy Rogers, Dale Evans, Trigger, Lone Ranger, Tonto, Paladin, Alan Ladd, Hopalong Cassidy, Hoppy,* or *Shane.* Particularly seeks character guns made in Los Angeles by the *Schmidt Company* or by *LATCO.* Must give all identifying marks, numbers, etc., found on the guns and a complete accounting of damage or wear to the gun, finish, or handles (grips). Buys only guns in fine condition. Publishes the *Toy Gun Collectors Newsletter.*

James Buskirk, Toy Gun Collectors of America
312 Starling Way
Anaheim, CA 92807
(714) 998-9615

★ **Cap pistols made of cast iron,** especially animated guns from 1800's or guns featuring movie cowboys and other Pop Culture heroes before 1940. A magnet *must* stick to your gun or he's not interested.

George Fougere
67 East Street
North Grafton, MA 01536
(508) 839-2701

★ **Cap pistols.** "I'll buy cap guns, holsters and related items in good condition. I collect Western cap guns, and am not looking for new guns mint in their boxes, but rather for guns that have been played with but still work and look good. Price what you have or request my offer." Give material, maker, length, and model number of guns you'd like to sell. Welcomes letters from other collectors, as he buys, trades, and sells, and issues frequent catalogs, free if you send a long SASE.

Mark King
1504 Helena
Gallup, NM 878301

TOY MOTORS & ENGINES

★ **Early miniature outboard marine motors** used on model boats. Wants fuel type motors only. No electric motors or boats. Condition should be described carefully.

Sven Stau
PO Box 437
Buffalo, NY 14212
(716) 825-5448 or (716) 822-3120

★ **Toy outboard motors,** either battery or wind up, alone or mounted on toy boats. "I'll buy motors by *K&O Fleetline* between 1952-1962 with names of popular manufact'rers of real outboard motors." Will pay $75-$400 for your toy depending on the model. Describe both the decals and the color.

Jack Browning
214 16th Street NW
Roanoke, VA 24017
(703) 890-5083 eves

★ **Toys run by live steam or hot air** are sought, as are accessories and catalogs related to steam and hot air toys. "I'll pay from $100 to several thousand dollars for steam engines, or for boats, trucks, automobiles, trains or tractors run by live steam, whether American, English or German made. Collectible makers include *Weeden, Buckman, Union, Bing, Marklin, Carette* and others. I don't want modern steam toys made by *Wilesco, Mamod,* or *Jansen.*" Give dimensions and markings. Some *Marklin* power plants were nearly four feet tall, and can be worth as much as $10,000. "Usually I require a photo or two before I buy, since most people do not understand the technical aspects of steam toys."

Lowell Wagner
5492 Feltl Road
Minnetonka, MN 55343
(612) 442-4036 or (612) 933-2011

★ **Model airplane engines** made between 1930-1955 that used a miniature spark plug (often a *Champion*). These engines have a coil, condenser, batteries, and incorporate a movable timer for spark advancement. Later engines use a glow plug and do not require electrical support once running. "It is usually necessary to see the engine to assess its condition," so expect to ship yours prior to final sale.

Bruce Pike
Route 1 Box 291, Lot 92
Aliquippa, PA 15001
(412) 378-0449

TOY VEHICLES

★ **Metal vehicles and toys,** pre-1959, including cars, trucks, airplanes, trains, boats, and construction equipment:

Large steel toys by *Buddy-L, Sturditoy, Turner, Kingsbury, Sonny, Keystone,* and *Structo.* Will pay $800 for 14" *Ford Buddy-L* delivery truck;

Tootsietoys with white rubber tires or all metal wheels;

Old tin toy boats, the larger the better;

Children's pedal cars and trucks made before 1940;

Smith-Miller **or** *M-I-C* **trucks** made of steel in California between 1945 and 1957;

Tin windup automotive, aviation, or comic toys, U.S. or European, working or not. Will pay $2,500 for an 8" truck with "Aunt Eppie Hogg" in perfect condition;

Dinky toys, pre-1964, from England or France;

Any metal motorcycle 8" or longer, especially *Hubley Indian* delivery cycle worth $1,500 in original condition;

Japanese scale models of U.S. cars;

Cast iron toys by *Hubley, Arcade, Kilgore,* and *Williams.*

Plastic, rubber, or wooden vehicles are not wanted. Describe the condition carefully, paying particular attention to the quality of the paint and whether or not all the parts and pieces are present. Describe the condition of the wheels and tires. Dimensions are helpful.

Larry Bruch
PO Box 121
Mountaintop, PA 18707
(717) 474-9202 eves

★ **Metal vehicles** including:

Pedal cars and other vehicles;

Large steel toys by *Buddy-L, Turner, Sturditoy, Kingsbury, Sonny, Structo* and *Keystone;*

Small cast toys by *Dinky, Tootsietoy, Matchbox* and others;

Tin or steel toy boats;

Steel toys by *Tonka, MIC,* and others.

He also buys **plastic factory made dealer models** of new cars from the 1950's and 60's. Please send a photo and good description. Whether you are a dealer or an amateur, he wants you to price your goods as he does not make offers.

Calvin Chaussee
1530 Kenland Court
Colorado Springs, CO 80915

★ **Larger pressed steel toy cars and trucks** are wanted by this 10 year veteran collector-dealer. "I'll buy *Smith Miller, Doepke, Tonka, Buddy-L, Keystone, Arcade* and other makes of toy vehicles including construction types, boats, airplanes, and farm tractors." To sell your vehicles, tell him [1] the maker if you can, [2] what it looks like, including what type of vehicle it is, [3] how many you have, and [4] the condition of each. Make an estimate of what percentage of the original paint is left. "I prefer not to buy rusty or damaged vehicles, but this policy is not written in stone."

> Jay "The Chicago Kid" Robinson
> PO Box 529
> Deerfield, IL 60015
> (708) 945-8691 or 945-1965

★ **Pedal cars.** "I'll buy any pre-WWII pedal car, pedal plane or pedal truck, and will consider some from the mid-1950's. I'm a most generous buyer, as I buy to keep not to resell. Condition is not a problem. I'll even buy half a vehicle if that's all you have. Please send photos."

> Sandy Weltman
> 39 Branford Road
> Rochester, NY 14618
> (716) 442-8810

★ **Pedal cars.** "I'll buy pedal cars made after WWII in excellent original condition, and pedal cars made before the war in any condition. I will pay over $1,000 for the better examples." This relatively new collector also will buy any pedal car advertising, sales catalogs, and the like as well as photos of kids with their pedal cars. He does not want pedal cars with plastic wheel covers and/or plastic steering wheels, as they are considered too new by collectors. The *one* exception to that rule is the *Ford Mustang* pedal car which he does want. Give the name of the manufacturer and the length of the vehicle. "I will not purchase or make offers without a good clear color photo of both sides."

> Frank Martin
> 7669 Winterberry Drive
> Youngstown, OH 44512
> (216) 758-4470

★ **Hard rubber toys,** especially **vehicles**, motorcycles, trains, airplanes, ships, animals, **soldiers,** football and baseball players, especially by Rainbow Rubber Co. Hard rubber toys only. No vinyl. Hard rubber is painted. Vinyl is made in the color of the toy and is the same color throughout. Give the maker, size, colors, condition, and description of features. Also buys **toy vehicles of all sizes, from** *Dinky* **to pedal cars** if made before 1950. "Photos are best."

> Steve Kelley
> PO Box 695
> Desert Hot Springs, CA 92240
> (619) 329-3206

★ *Dinky* **toys** of all types except army vehicles. Also wants to buy all types of **toy motorcycles.**
Don Schneider
PO Box 1570
Merritt, BC
V0K 2B0 CANADA

★ **Toy motorcycles** made in the U.S., Japan, Germany, France, or England of tin, cast iron, hard plastic, or rubber that function by means of wind-up, friction, or batteries, especially by *I-Y*. Also other **vehicle and comic character toys** from Japan and Germany, especially those made by *Lehmann.*
Chris Savino
PO Box 419
Breesport, NY 14816
(607) 739-3106

★ **Toy farm tractors and equipment** from 1970 or older. "I'll buy the ones with real farm equipment company names like *John Deere, Farmall, Oliver, Ford, Allis-Chalmers* and the like, in plastic or metal, and will pay over $100 for some tractors. A *John Deere* Model 430 is worth $750+ in its original box and an *Oliver* Super 55 is worth $500+ in its box.   Also buys other scale model toys, like outboard motors, with tractor company names, and is interested in all scale *Caterpillar* **tractor and heavy equipment toys.** Does not want repros or anything made after 1975. Give the color, size, brand, model, condition, and the status of the original box.
Dave Nolt
PO Box 553
Gap, PA 17527
(717) 768-3554

★ **Toy firetrucks and fire related toys.** This veteran collector/dealer wants U.S. made fire toys built prior to 1960. Buys all types, all sizes, all styles as long as they are in good condition. Is particularly interested in finding *Ahrens Fox* and *Bulldog Macks* and other large steel firetruck toys, some of which can be worth $700 or more. Buys toy fire stations, firemen, and other toys and **games that are fire related.** Requests color photos, the price you'd like, and a statement of condition. Include your phone number. Will assist amateurs to set price. No Japanese tin toys or anything made after 1965.
Luke Casbar, Toys for Boys
22 Garden Street
Lodi, NJ 07644
(201) 478-5535

MODEL RACE CARS

★ **Model race cars from the 1940's,** that ran with model airplane engines. These engines used a miniature spark plug (often a *Champion*), and had a coil, condenser, batteries, and incorporated a movable timer for spark advancement. Later engines use a glow plug and do not require electrical support once running. The cars were operated with hand held wires. Describe the car and its condition, including the percentage of original paint. Indicate the brand name of the engine and whether it is complete. "It is usually necessary to see a car to assess its condition."

Bruce Pike
Route 1   Box 291, Lot 92
Aliquippa, PA 15001
(412) 378-0449

★ **Gas powered toy cars.**
Johnny Henard
820 Avery Dale Drive
Pacific, MO 63069

★ *Aurora* **and** *AFX* **electric race cars,** track, and accessories made after 1968.
T. Pat Jacobsen
437 Minton Court
Pleasant Hill, CA 94523
(510) 930-8531

★ *Atlas* **and** *Aurora* **electric race cars.** "No limit," he says, but emphasizes he wants to buy "complete collections." Like other pop culture collectors and dealers, he particularly wants items in complete sets and original boxes. Would love to find store displays and stock, but "will consider any *Atlas* and *Aurora* electric race cars you have." Photos are requested, but if you have a large collection for sale, you are encouraged to phone him. "I also collect colorful **hockey related games**, preferably complete in original box, but will consider incomplete sets if the boxes are good."

Joe Bodnarchuk
62 McKinley Ave.
Kenmore, NY 14217
(716) 873-0264 phone or fax

PLASTIC MODEL KITS

★ **Plastic model kits** especially from the 1950's made by *Monogram, Hawk , Aurora, Bachman, Comet, ITC, Frog, Allyn, Monogram, Revell, Strombecker,* and others. Models can be airliners, commercial ships, space, science fiction, TV, movie subjects, automobiles and figures. Also manufacturers catalogs and store display models. Kits must be complete and unbuilt, with minimal damage to the box. Sealed unopened kits are best. He offers to send a copy of the grading system used by kit collectors for an SASE. He'll pay $100 for a perfect condition *Athearn* gas-powered flying model of the *Convair XFY-1 Pogo.* Bob publishes *Vintage Plastic,* the journal for kit collectors and produces *The Model Club,* a public access TV show on model building.

> Bob Keller's Starline Hobbies
> PO Box 38
> Stanton, CA 90680
> (714) 826-5218 days

★ **Plastic model kits** of airplanes, tanks, ships, figures, cars, buildings, or what have you *if complete, unbuilt, and in original box.* Include the manufacturer and kit number. John publishes *Kit Collector's Clearinghouse,* a bimonthly newsletter for kit collectors and is the author of *Value Guide for Scale Model Plastic Kits,* available for $30, and other model books.

> John Burns
> 3213 Hardy Drive
> Edmond, OK 73013

★ **Plastic model car kits depicting antique cars.** Unbuilt kits from before 1970 only, please.

> Henry Winningham
> 3205 South Morgan Street
> Chicago, IL 60608
> (312) 847-1672

★ **Plastic 1/25th scale model car kits,** built or not. Also buys dealer promotional materials, model car books and magazines, if issued before 1975. Does not want anything currently available. Give the name of the maker and the model number on the box. If you have **dealer promotional models**, give the color, condition, and note whether the original box is present.

> Rick Hanson
> PO Box 161
> Newark, IL 60541
> (815) 695-5135

ELECTRIC TRAINS

★ **All types of old electric trains** including *Lionel, American Flyer, Ives, Marklin, Bing, Carette, Howard*, and other U.S. and foreign brands in "any amount, any condition, working or not." Is particularly interested in *Lionel* trains from the 40's and 50's, especially the pink *Lionel* trains made for girls. Give the number on the body of the engine, the color of the engines and cars, the condition, and whether or not you have the box. "I would be glad to help anybody interested in the hobby of collecting old toy trains."

Tom Ryan
234-04 Bay Ave.
Douglaston, NY 11363
(718) 423-3732

★ **Toy trains and accessories, U.S. or foreign, made between 1900 and 1970.** Will buy any maker and gauge except HO gauge trains. Items do not have to be in perfect condition to be considered. **Also buys train literature.** A wind-up *American Flyer* train with cars marked *Coca-Cola* is worth $350 in mint condition. This 40 year veteran will make offers only if you're serious about selling. Lazarus is past president of the Toy Train Operating Society and publisher of its attractive monthly newsletter. He will accept donations for the Society's exhibit at the California State Railroad Museum in Sacramento.

Hillel Don Lazarus
14547 Titus Street #207
Panorama City, CA 91402
(818) 762-3652 eves

DESCRIBING ELECTRIC TRAINS

When describing electric trains, give the brand name, any model numbers found on the engine, and a list of the cars. It's worth your time to indicate the color of each car, its purpose, and RR line name, since minor variations can affect value. If the car has been repainted or otherwise modified by someone other than the factory, make certain to note that fact. If you have the original box, describe its condition. Make a list of any accessories, noting the condition of the paint of each. Some buildings and other items have value in excess of $100.

★ **All makes of old toy trains except HO gauge and hand made scale models.** Buys *Lionel, American Flyer, Ives, Marx* and all foreign trains larger than HO. "I'll buy engines, cars, accessories, signals, and incomplete sets that are new, like new, used, and even incomplete but useful for parts, but no layouts, transformers, track, rusty junk, or other toys." This 37 year veteran hobby shop operator offers a very large price guide to trains for only $6.

Allison Cox
18025 8th Avenue N.W.
Seattle, WA 98177
(206) 546-2230

★ *Marklin* **and other European toy trains and metal toys.** "I'll buy trains powered by clockwork, electricity, or live steam. Other *Marklin* toys such as airplanes, boats, circus toys, and many others will also be considered for purchase. *Marklin* toys are generally marked with the company name, but others are marked with an entwined GM. "I want anything by *Marklin* before 1950 in decent condition." Also want *Bing, Schuco, Carlyle & Finch, Carette*, and *Bassett-Lowke* trains and metal toys in very good or better condition. "I will buy common items in excellent condition, but don't want repros, fakes, or toys with pieces missing. I'm a collector so prefer people not contact me unless they actually want to sell or trade what they have. I pay fair prices and am willing to travel to inspect collections." *Marklin* trains from the 1930's are worth from $500 to as much as $10,000 to Ron so check carefully.

Ron Wiener
Packard Bldg #1200
111 South 15th Street
Philadelphia, PA 19102
(215) 977-2266

★ **Toy trains in all gauges and types** are wanted, including electric, wind-up, floor type, etc. "Age is not the main consideration, but I do want items from before World War II. I like to buy large collections, but will buy smaller units, and consider properly priced junkers, but no reproductions." Wants to know the train's gauge, maker, condition, the number of pieces and the markings on each, and how many of the original boxes you have.

Jay "The Chicago Kid" Robinson
PO Box 529
Deerfield, IL 60015
(708) 945-8691 and (708) 945-1965

★ **HO trains and accessories,** preferably in running order, but "they don't have to be old." He also buys **HO railroad books and magazines**.
   Cliff Robnett
   7804 NW 27th
   Bethany, OK 73008
   (405) 787-6703

If toy trains interest you, consider joining the Toy Train Operating Society. Their Bulletin is one of the truly fine club publications. For information write to the Society at 25 W. Walnut St., Room 408, Pasadena, CA 91103. They'll send complete information and a sample of their Bulletin.

★ **Trains and other vehicles.** Will make an offer on trains in any gauge, especially HO, Standard, and O. He is also in the market for any fine old toys, but especially **steam engines, tin plate toys, and airplanes.** A color photo must accompany your description if you wish to sell to this long time dealer.
   Heinz Mueller, Continental Hobby
   PO Box 193
   Sheboygan, WI 53082
   (414) 693-3371

★ **Electric trains by *Marx*** with metal or plastic cars that have eight wheels. Especially wants complete sets in original boxes. "I'll pay $100 for *Marx* Pennsylvania RR car #53941. I also buy *American Flyer* standard (large) gauge freight cars, and prewar *American Flyer* three-rail trains and sets (1938-1942). Not interested in plastic engines numbered #400 or #490 or cars with only four wheels." When writing, give him all numbers you find on boxes or cars.
   Robert Owen
   PO Box 204
   Fairborn, OH 45324

Dolls

Doll collecting has become the second largest hobby in the United States with doll lovers spending one-half billion dollars annually. Collectors want all types from the high priced 19th century mechanicals and French fashion dolls which cost in the many thousands of dollars to modern plastic dolls worth a fraction as much. Because you are more likely to have the more modern dolls, a greater emphasis has been placed on them in this book.

Buyers of most dolls want the following information:

(1) Length of the doll, important because some dolls made in multiple sizes have different values;
(2) How big around the head is, important on old dolls. Use a seamstress's tape or string to measure;
(3) Material from which the head, hair, hands, feet and body are made. A doll's head, hands, and body may be made from different materials;
(4) Type and color of eyes (painted, button, glass) and whether or not they move;
(5) Whether the mouth is open and whether teeth (molded, painted, or attached) show;
(6) Marks incised into the scalp, neck, shoulders, or back of the doll;
(7) How the doll is dressed and whether the clothes seem to be original;
(8) Any chips, cracks, repainting, or other repairs.

When offering a doll for sale, a photo can be helpful, but you can often get better results faster, easier, and cheaper with a photocopy machine. Photocopies are particularly useful for showing how a doll is dressed.

If you have the original box for your doll, be certain to mention this fact as it may add as much as 50% to the doll's value. When describing modern dolls such as *Barbie* whose accessories are frequently marketed in plastic bubble packs mention packages that are unopened and unfaded as they are worth two or three times the value of loose items.

Include any information you can about the history of your doll. If your doll is a family heirloom and you have a photograph of an ancestor posed with the doll, tell the buyer. If you do not want to part with your photo, you might consider having a copy made for the doll's new owner. If that is expensive or inconvenient for you, consider using a photocopy machine as they usually make excellent reproductions of photographs. Most collectors would be happy to pay the costs of any picture you can provide.

Many readers do not want to sell their dolls, but are looking for information about their family heirloom. Information seekers usually want to be reassured by learning their emotional treasure has financial value as well. If you're not selling, make that clear up-front when you contact someone in *Where To Sell It!*

Researching dolls on your own can be frustrating. A specialized book such as *Barbie Rarities* by Florence Theriault is excellent, but at $45 is for the serious collector. For most other types of dolls, it is difficult to recommend any one single book certain to help you. Unfortunately, many guides are not readily available or are now out of print.

Most amateurs trying to research dolls are limited by what is available through their local public library. If you have 20th century dolls, books by Pat Smith may be of help. Ask the reference librarian to obtain these and other doll books through 'interloan' if you can't find what you need in your local branch.

ANTIQUE DOLLS

★ **Collections of early china headed dolls** are sought for cataloged specialty auctions by this well known New England auctioneer. No junk, reproductions, or dolls made after 1940.

James D. Julia Auctioneers
PO Box 80
Fairfield, ME 04937
(207) 453-7904 Fax: (207) 453-2502

★ **Antique and collectible dolls, primarily those with china heads.** "We are constantly looking for fine **antique** and older dolls for auction. If you are considering liquidating all or part of your collection, we can be of assistance. We are happy to visit with you to discuss packing, pricing, shipping, and selling dolls. We know how to make the sale easy, comfortable, private, and profitable for you." There is no obligation and all inquiries are handled personally and confidentially by Barbara. She does not want modern dolls made after 1940, broken dolls, plastic dolls, Japanese dolls, or other junk. Don't bother this lovely lady by fishing for free appraisals. Contact her when you're ready to sell.

Barbara Frasher's Doll Auctions
Route 1 Box 142
Oak Grove, MO 64075
(816) 625-3786

★ **Old dolls and their parts.** "I buy, both as a collector and as a dealer, a large variety of old dolls and their parts. I will also buy any **damaged dolls** if priced reasonably. I'm always looking for **accessories for old dolls,** such as shoes, clothing, wigs, purses, **doll carriages,** etc. I'm interested in old wooden creche-type jointed dolls for display at Christmas. Also any **cloth comic characters** such as Lulu, Tubby, Alvin, Nancy, or Sluggo and *old* **Raggedy Ann or Andy** dolls. I am most interested in adding to my collection of old German dolls, bisque snow babies, and **Buster Brown china dishes** but I have no interest at all in Japanese bisque or currently made dolls."

Patricia Snyder, My Dear Dolly
PO Box 303
Sparta, NJ 07871
(201) 729-8087

★ **Dolls and doll accessories.** This doll museum owner buys better and unusual dolls, both antique and modern. Also buys old cotton lace, costumes, trim and **material for dressing old dolls.** Also wants doll props like shoes, purses, combs, opera glasses, **furniture, buggies,** etc.

Madalaine Selfridge, Forgotten Magic
33710 Almond Street
Lake Elsinore, CA 92330
(909) 674-9221

★ **Dolls, doll parts, and doll clothes.** Buys old bisque and china heads even if the body or other parts are missing. Also wants to buy baby gowns, slips, bonnets, etc. "I do not make offers or bid against other collectors. You must price what you have."

Annie Nalewak, Shop 4
5515 South Loop, East Crestmont
Houston, TX 77033

ETHNIC DOLLS

★ **Realistic ethnic costume dolls,** 6"-14" tall, with nicely sculpted adult faces only. Faces may be composition, clay, wax, or wood but bodies can be of any materials. She only wants Asian, Mid-Eastern, and Eastern European dolls, especially representing peasants, dancers, musicians, and theatrical characters such as Japanese Kabuki dolls. No baby dolls, cute dolls, homemade dolls, or dolls from the United States, Western Europe, tropical Africa, or South America. Whether old or new, high quality is a must. If you wish to sell to her, a photograph is essential. She pays from $50 to $200 for dolls.

Karen Kuykendall
PO Box 845
Casa Grande, AZ 85222
(602) 836-2066

★ **Chinese Door of Hope dolls** sold by Christian missionaries to raise funds between 1909 and 1947. Also **china or bisque headed dolls** made before 1925. Will buy doll parts, bodies, heads, and old clothes, but will make no offers. Everyone must price their goods.

Marjorie Gewalt
94 East Parkfield Court
Racine, WI 53402
(414) 639-2346

★ *Skookum* **Indian dolls.** If you own an Indian doll wearing a colorful Indian pattern blanket, chances are it's a *Skookum*, and he buys perfect examples from the smallest sizes up to those five feet tall. Some dolls marked SKOOKUM and/or BULLY GOOD on the underside of the feet. He does not want *Skookums* with plastic parts. Please send a photo for offer.

Barry Friedman
22725 Garzota Drive
Valencia, CA 91355
(805) 296-2318

MODERN DOLLS

★ *Annalee Dolls.* Wants 1950's, 60's and 70's versions of these modern felt dolls with painted faces, most of which have internal wires for positioning arms and legs. All types considered, including human, animal, and holiday, especially those with embroidered tags. Tags, more than copyright dates, are indicators of when a doll was made, although early dolls didn't always have tags, and doll owners often cut them off. Dating dolls by their tags is a job for experts, and never foolproof, as many different tags appear on the oldest dolls. Some *Annalee Dolls* were custom made, some limited production, and others factory made in fairly large quantities, so in most cases Sue will need to talk to you or inspect the doll before giving an offer. If you are certain your doll was made between 1950 and 1975 and not later, you may ship it for a check, but only if certain. Dolls tend to be worth $20 to $150 with a few very special ones worth more. "I'll analyze your doll and will always give you a fair price." Pictures are helpful, but "I need to know what the doll is (human or animal) and what it's doing and how it's dressed. I also need to know the height of the doll, as they come in many different sizes. Condition is important in determining price. If you think you have an early *Annalee Doll*, I'd really like you to call with the doll in front of you. Before you call, please make a careful inspection for moth and silverfish damage in the form of holes, pock-marks, etc., and for any signs of fading in the doll or costume. Also I want to know if there is evidence of glue on either of the doll's hands" Sue is willing to train pickers who regularly shop at yard sales and flea markets.

Sue Coffee
10 Saunders Hollow Road
Old Lyme, CT 06371
(203) 434-5641

★ *Barbie* **dolls.** Wants to buy all *Barbie* dolls, fashions and accessories, 1958-1972. "Anything *Barbie* related," she says, especially prototypes, gift sets, lunch boxes, watches, ponytails, color magics, *American Girls*, and the rest of *Barbie*'s family, including Ken (introduced in 1961), Midge (1963), Rickey (1963), Skooter (1963), Skipper (1963), Allan (1965), Julie (1966), Tutti, Todd, Stacey, Casey, Francie, and Twiggy. Watch for Christie, the Black *Barbie*, among many others. Will pay $1,000 for a mint in box airplane and $500 for a MIB *Barbie* boat. She does buy porcelain and international *Barbies* too. It's worth your time to look for early *Barbie* dolls, especially for clothes and accessories in original boxes, because some were made for a very short time, or sold in very limited markets. Some inside tips: Sleep eyes were introduced in 1964. If the knees bend, the doll was made after 1965. Rooted eyelashes come into use in 1966, talking *Barbie* family in 1968. The dolls that are easy to pose, and those with growing hair are both products of the 1970's, and too late to interest most *Barbie* collectors. To describe a *Barbie*, you must give the name of the doll, hair color, lip color and condition. "Please," she asks, "do not send or write about *Barbies* because they say 1966 on their back. Today's dolls still say 1966 on them." Marl offers an important clue about how to tell if your *Barbie* is old. "If it does not say JAPAN on the buttocks, I don't want it. Today's dolls say HONG-KONG, MALAYSIA, PHILLIPINES, OR TAIWAN on their behinds. Even CANADA turns up on a few dolls." Marl buys dolls for her personal collection and for resale.

>   Marl Davidson, WTS
>   5707 39th Street Circle East
>   Bradenton, FL 34203
>   (813) 751-6275

★ *Cabbage Patch Kids.* There is not much premium paid for *Cabbage Patch* dolls; most sell slightly above or below their original issue price. A few rare dolls can bring $150 and up. Identifying them can be tricky and not for amateurs. To discover whether you have a rare doll means providing a great deal of information:

  (1) Head mold number (from 1 to 45) impressed on the back of the neck; some dolls don't have a mold number;

  (2) Hair style and color; colors are generally beige (champagne or wheat), lemon yellow blond, gold or mustard, red orange, dark brown, and rust red brown;

  (3) Eye color;

  (4) Whether or not it has freckles;

  (5) Pull down the diaper and find the body tag, usually stitched into the doll's lower left hip; in a circle on that tag is a letter or combination of letters (UT/P/OK/PMI/IC/KT are typical) that tells what factory made the doll; you must include this information when you write;

  (6) On the lower buttock is usually found a signature and sometimes a very tiny date; give the <u>color</u> of the signature (black, forest green, turquoise, etc.) and the date if you can read it;

  (7) With the above info, send a color picture.

None of these characteristics by itself means a doll is rare; it is the combination of particular sex, hair color and style, eyes, mold number, factory mark, freckles, signature color, etc., that makes a doll desirable. Sometimes an outfit can be worth more than the doll if it is a rare or hard-to-find outfit on a mundane doll. A good many cabbage patchers are not "box fanatics" and do not believe that the box adds any value. If you're unwilling to take your doll out of the box, then you can't give the information needed (you can open the box from the end and untwist the wire holding the doll in place). BJ, who writes a fun monthly column on *Cabbage Patch* dolls for *Collector's Companion & Exchange*, is not a buyer of *Cabbage Patch* dolls except for a select few for her own collection, but can in many cases refer you to someone who is *if you provide sufficient information and include a stamped self-addressed envelope.*

>   B.J. Resue
>   130 Lori Lane
>   Broomall, PA 19008

★ *Nancy Ann Storybook Dolls* were created by actress Nancy Ann Abbott, who began by dressing dolls in movie costumes for her co-stars in the mid 1930's. These early dolls were bisque (unglazed china) made in Japan, and usually marked with a sticker reading NANCY ANN DRESSED DOLL. Early dolls are marked JAPAN 1146 or 1148. Other companies used the same doll so it's the outfit that distinguishes a Nancy Ann doll. Just prior to WWII she began using 3.5" to 7" high china dolls with movable arms and legs. After 1942, dolls had what collectors call "frozen legs." For a while in the mid to late 1940's, *Nancy Anns* were the number one seller in the girls' toy market, and produced in very large quantities. In 1947 they introduced plastic arms while she used up supplies of bisque bodies, then converted to all plastic bodies, the earliest of which were painted to look like bisque. In 1949, a doll was introduced with eyes that opened and shut. Many different series were created:

Famous pairs, such as Hansel and Gretel, the Twin Sisters, and Jack and Jill, all of which are desirable.

Nursery rhymes, days of the week, and months of the year, the most common of her dolls.

Margie Ann is same doll but dressed as little girls in suits.

Audrey Ann is one particular doll, a little larger than the others (5.75"), wearing an organdy dress and white boots. It's hard to find.

Geraldine Ann was a gift set, #400, based on her movie days. It came with eight outfits and a "movie set" with a director's chair, lights, etc. It is fragile and very desirable today.

Judy Ann was marketed for a while, but a copyright conflict prevented use of the name. Dolls marked JUDY ANN/USA are very scarce.

Muffie and Debbie, 8" and 10" hard plastic dolls, were the tops of the line, and came with many matching outfits.

Nancy Ann made a great many other dolls too, and most are common. Values range from $20 to $175 with a few over $500. Dolls must be individually evaluated, however, because there are so many different costumes. The Days of the Week series was sold for a dozen years, with new costumes each year, almost 100 different dolls in one series! In general, the frozen leg and plastic dolls are less valuable, but boy [male] dolls are rare and desirable in any form as is furniture made in the *Nancy Ann* factory, recognizable only by the fabric. The bed, sofa, chairs, bassinet, dressing table, ottoman and chaise lounge often bring $100+. Even the *McCalls* pattern (#811) for making the cardboard and cloth furniture at home can be worth a good $50+ to you! All *Nancy Ann* dolls have a hat or ribbon in their hair. A missing hat reduces the value of a doll by more than half, and "you can't put just any old ribbon in the hair. Hers were special imports." To sell a *Nancy Ann*, you must tell whether it's plastic or bisque, has moving or frozen legs, has eyes that move or not (and their color), and the height. Make a photocopy of the doll which shows the dress. If you have the original box, copy that too, since some boxes are more valuable than others.

Elaine M. Pardee
PO Box 6108
Santa Rosa, CA 95406
(707) 538-3655   Fax: (707) 537-0604

★ **Modern collectible fashion dolls** including a range of scarce collectible modern dolls:

Nancy Ann Storybook Dolls, particularly the Black *Nancy Ann Dolls*, Topsy and Mammy, and the brown skin *Nancy Anns* with Indian Sari clothes, in either bisque or plastic. Wants others as well, but notes, "Once *Nancy Anns* are played with, or the hair is messed up, or they're a little dirty, many collectors pass them up. At one time, this factory produced 8,000 dolls a day, so most *Nancy Anns* need to be in unused condition to interest collectors."

Miss Revlons were fashion dolls made by Ideal Toy Company in the 1950's. "These were the modern woman of the 50's," complete with girdles and nylons, little high heels, and pierced ears with pearls.

Ideal **fashion dolls** from the 1950's, such as *Miss Clairol, Toni* and *Bonnie Braids*. Ideal Toy Company dolls are usually marked on their head with the company name, the earliest with the name enclosed in a diamond.

Hollywood **dolls**, in either bisque or hard plastic. "The costume's the thing," she says. During the 1940's and 50's, more *Hollywood* dolls were produced than any other company, but without their costumes, these are relatively undistinguished, and are modestly prices. They are often, but not always, marked HOLLYWOOD on their backs, between their shoulder blades. Look for boxes covered with Hollywood stars as it's their most distinguishing characteristic.

If you have a perfect condition doll, especially one with its original box, give length, description, and tell whether clothes are original. A photocopy is helpful.

Sharon Vohs-Mohammed
PO Box 2891
Glen Ellyn, IL 60138
(708) 858-1852

★ *Vogue Ginny* **dolls** are among many sought by this active dealer. She also buys *Kathe Kruse, Chase, Madame Alexanders, Izannah Walker,* and *Steiff* character and animal dolls. She also buys **early cloth dolls**, and will consider a wide range of good looking **fine condition dolls** in papier maché, wood, china, or bisque, including expensive French fashion dolls, character dolls, and what have you. Also has some interest in **doll houses, and Teddy bears** as well. Describe what you have thoroughly, following directions at the beginning of this chapter.

Valerie Makseyn
61 6th Street
Cambridge, MA 02141
(617) 576-0796

★ *Madame Alexander* **dolls of the 1950's.** Beatrice Alexander began making dolls in 1923. Early dolls were cloth, then composition. In 1948 she adapted WWII plastic technology to make dolls that were both sturdy and beautiful. These uniquely 1950's Alexanders were made of hard plastic, jointed at neck, shoulders and hips, and often knees, elbows, and even ankles! In the early 1960's, these hard plastic dolls gave way to squeezable vinyl dolls with rooted hair. Lia wants to buy **hard plastic dolls with wigs glued on,** as long as they are in good condition with original clothes. There are a few basic styles of hard plastic dolls that she wants:

> Dolls that are 14", 18", 21" or 25" high;
> Any 8" dolls (called *Alexanderkins*);
> *Cissy,* a 21" fashion doll, and its 9" high counterpart, *Cissette;*
> *Lissy,* 11" tall, and 16" high *Elise.*

Wants all sizes, from 8" to 21", but they must be in good condition with original clothes. As with many other types of dolls, the costume makes the doll. The same doll might have 80 or more different costumes, and a variety of hair. "Some that don't look too exciting may actually be rare and valuable because they didn't sell and were only offered for a short time." Many, but not all, *Madame Alexander* dolls are marked on the backs of their heads or across their shoulders. Marks include MME ALEXANDER, ALEXANDER, or ALEX. Other Alexander dolls were not marked, and only a tag attached to the clothing stated who or what the doll represented. The 1950's dolls she seeks were generally tagged and marked. To sell your doll, give her the information on the clothing tag, a description of the costume, and a statement of condition. Note whether you have the original box. Have the doll in hand if you call. Lia says, "I will consider older composition or cloth *Alexander* dolls, but only if in mint perfect condition. They don't have to be in the original box, but must be like new."

Lia Sargent
74 The Oaks
Roslyn Estates, NY 11576
(800) 421-9912 Fax: (516) 621-7517

★ *Renwall* **plastic dolls and furnitures.** *Renwall* made hard plastic jointed dolls ranging in height from a few inches to a foot. They are embossed "Renwall USA" and with a number. In addition to *Renwall* dolls, she is also interested in other kinds of **hard plastic dolls and furniture that were made by** *Ideal* **and** *Acme*. No foreign plastic furniture or anything with broken or missing parts or costume.

Judaline McNece
11270 Sirius Way
Mira Loma, CA 91752

DOLL HOUSES

★ **Doll houses and miniatures,** especially *Schoenhut* and *Bliss* houses for which he will pay $500-$1,500. "We are one of the oldest and most experienced companies in the doll house and miniatures industry," Bob says, "and we will consider buying anything in miniatures that is old and in good condition." Their catalog of new doll house parts is fascinating, and well worth the $5.50 charge.

Robert Dankanics, The Dollhouse Factory
PO Box 456
Lebanon, NJ 08833
(908) 236-6404

★ **Doll houses and furniture circa 1900,** but *only* wooden houses covered with colorfully lithographed paper, especially made by *Bliss*.

Jerry Phelps
6013 Innes Trace Road
Louisville, KY 40222

TEDDY BEARS

★ **Teddy bears that are fully jointed with glass or shoebutton eyes.** Wants pre-1920 *Steiff* bears in any condition and will pay $1,000+ for those larger than 20" long. Not interested in any non-jointed bears or bears made after 1940. Also Teddy bear books, postcards, photos, trays, etc. Polly also buys **stuffed animal toys on cast iron wheels**.

Polly Zarneski
5803 North Fleming
Spokane, WA 99205
(509) 327-7622

★ **Mohair Teddy bears with long arms and big feet** made between 1903-1915 are wanted in all sizes as long as they are fully jointed. Also wants perfume and compact bears in various colors and any unusual mohair Teddy or Teddy related items. Also looking for early *Steiff* **cats and dogs** with printed ear buttons. Also wants **Billy Possum stuffed dolls with shoebutton eyes,** President Taft's answer to Roosevelt's Teddies. All Billy Possum related items are also wanted including doll dishes and silverware, banks, and postcards. Mimi wants us to assure you that your dolls are going to a "loving home, not a dealer."

Mimi Hiscox
12291 St. Mark
Garden Grove, CA 92645
(310) 598-5450

Pop Culture

Pop Culture was once defined as "the fun stuff in life," a definition that's hard to beat.

When people talk about collecting Pop Culture, they mean the products and advertising associated with all forms of entertainment, movies, radio, television, popular music, magic, cartoon and comic characters, celebrities, and personalities.   Pop Culture is Superman, Little Lulu, and Donald Duck. Pop Culture is Tom Mix, Milton Berle, and Star Wars. It's Elvis, P.T. Barnum, and Charlie Chaplin. It's Godzilla!

Pop Culture also embraces advertising characters. A recent poll discovered more 7-year-olds recognized *Mr. Clean* than Santa Claus, qualifying that bald giant to join Pop Culture superstars like *Aunt Jemima, Speedy Alka-Seltzer, The Campbell Soup Kids,* and *Reddy Kilowat* as collector favorites.

It's not surprising these Pop icons have value. It's *how much* value that can shock you. With many pieces of fine 19th century porcelain selling for $250, it surprises folks to learn someone would pay $1,000 for a cardboard cereal box from the 1940's. Nowhere is the law of supply and demand more evident than in the world of Pop Culture.

The age of $1,000 *G.I.Joe* dolls is here now! Pop Culture is hot. I encourage you to cash in on this trend instead of throwing these things away. Like the section on Household items, this Pop Culture section is jammed with items you are likely to own.

How do you recognize Pop Culture items? Collectors and dealers in Pop Culture tend to want rare, brightly colored items in original boxes and mint condition. Many of the Pop Culture buyers are dealers who seek a wide range of items. They tend to pay very well for them.

The best way for you to prepare yourself to cash in is to read all the Pop Culture entries as well as those in the closely related Entertainment section in *Where To Sell It!* and see what's hot.

To sell Pop Culture toys and other items, you should provide the following information:

(1) What it is, its size, color, and the material from which it is made;
(2) All names, dates, and numbers embossed, incised, or labeled on the item;
(3) An accurate statement of condition, noting missing parts, pieces, or paint. Be certain to describe all repairs or repainting;
(4) Mention whether the original box, packaging and instructions are included and in good condition.

Some buyers want additional information. Vehicle and other toy buyers want the size, color, and the material from which the tires and wheels are made.

Good close-up photos are important since a great many vehicles, dolls, robots, and other Pop Culture toys and games are worth $100+ and a surprising number bring $1,000 or more. Buyers want to see what you are offering, as the condition affects value greatly.

POP CULTURE

★ **Americana and Pop Culture of all sorts** is wanted by Ted Hake the longest established mail dealer and auctioneer of pop collectibles. The wide range of items Ted buys includes:
Political and other pin back buttons;
Premiums from radio, TV or cereal;
Disney characters pre 1970;
Animation art from Disney and other cartoons;
Battery or wind up toys especially those related to Pop Culture characters from comics and movies;
Television related toys, games, lunch boxes, etc., from 1950's and 60's;
Singing cowboys and other western film heroes memorabilia;
Robots and space toys;
U.S. Space Program items;
Elvis Presley pre-death items;
Beatles and other famous rock and roll personalities;
Movie posters, lobby cards, etc.;
Toys of the 1960's like *GI Joe, Capt. Action, Batman*, etc.
"I'll buy or auction just about any item related to a famous character or personality." Ted wants to know the material your item is made from, its size, any dates you can provide, and general condition. Firm offers are made only after inspection of your item. Hake has written four books on pin back buttons which are the basic reference works in the field. No reproductions are wanted, nor are political items after 1968.
Ted Hake, Hake's Americana
PO Box 1444
York, PA 17405
(717) 848-1333 days

★ **All comic character toys and collectibles from the 1930's and 40's,** made of any material from cardboard to cast iron, especially Disneyana, radio premiums, and all **children's play suits** from western heroes to sailor suits. No Halloween costumes. There are also many pieces of **comic character related sheet music** Ralph is seeking.
Ralph Eodice, Nevermore
161 Valley Road
Clifton, NJ 07013
(201) 742-8278

★ **Comic character pin back buttons,** 1896-1966, from the earliest *Yellow Kid* to all comic strip and comic book characters since then. This *Star Trek* actor (Chekov) will pay as much as $500 for rare buttons like the *Flash Gordon* Movie Club or *Washington Herald Mickey Mouse*. Ask and he'll send an illustrated wants list. Include your phone number.
Walter Koenig
PO Box 4395
North Hollywood, CA 91607

★ **Pop Culture toys** related to radio, television or movie characters and superheroes including :
> **Western movie/TV toys**, wristwatches, and premiums from
>> Roy Rogers, Gene Autry, *Lone Ranger, Red Ryder,*
>> *Hopalong Cassidy,* Tom Mix, and other riders of the range;
> **Western style cap guns** of metal;
> **Disney and other comic character toys**;
> **Doll houses** of tin in fine condition and *Renwall* plastic
>> doll houses and accessories;
> **Toy vehicles** by *Smith Miller, Tonka, Doepke, Dinky, Renwall*
>> (plastic), *Auburn* (rubber), *Arcade, Marx*, and *Wyandotte*;
> **G.I. Joe** dolls, accessories, pre-1970, in the 12" size;
> **Toys advertising** nationally known products.

Condition is critical and only excellent condition items are wanted. Items in original box always preferred. Descriptions should include dimensions. Photo helpful. "Generous prices paid, but all offers contingent on personal inspection." Will answer all inquiries that have SASE. Calls welcome.
> William Hamburg
> PO Box 1305
> Woodland Hills, CA 91365
> (818) 346-9884

★ **Items depicting pre-1960 comic characters, superheroes, fictional detectives, movie heroes** and villains are sought by this well known mail order dealer of fine collectibles:
> **Toys and pin back buttons**;
> **TV games, premiums, and ephemera**;
> **Radio and cereal premiums**;
> **Buttons from various radio "clubs"** worth up to $500;
> **Movie Posters** from serials, cartoons, and adventure movies;
> **Store stand-up figural displays**;
> **Memorabilia associated with heroic characters** such as
>> *Tarzan, Batman, Superman, Flash Gordon,* etc.

"I do not want 1970's *Batman*, modern *Dick Tracy,* beat up lobby cards, coverless comics, or other junk...just rare, fine condition collectibles, please. I want a very wide range of Pop Culture toys and pay more than anyone for the top range items." He warns, "I pay more! If you want to sell to me it has to be on my terms. You must write first, providing a full description of the item and its condition." If Rex is interested he will request that you ship for inspection. Rex pays postage both ways on items he does not buy. "I have bought and sold this way for 20 years," he adds, pointing out numerous awards he has won for dealer integrity. Rex does not want *Hopalong Cassidy* and

"There are so many repros and fakes now that I will no longer buy something sight unseen. Rings worth 2¢ and rings worth $1,500 can look quite similar to the inexperienced seller."

other 1950's cowboys, nor does he buy lunchboxes, common items, or anything damaged. Do not contact him with anything except perfect rare items. If you have something really good, "call between 10 and 10."
Rex Miller
Route 1   Box 457-D
East Prairie, MO 63845
(314) 649-5048

★ **Pop Culture treasures,** especially made of paper, including:
Comic books, 1890's-1980's, but only hero comics after 1963;
Sunday comics from the 1890's to 1959;
Original comic strip art;
Walt Disney books and anything else before 1960;
Big Little Books, 1933-1950;
Movie magazines 1920-1945;
Television collectibles 1948-1970;
Radio and cereal premiums and giveaways pre-1960;
Song magazines, 1929-1959, like *Hit Parader* and *400 Songs;*
Popular music magazines 1920-1959 including *Downbeat* and
    Billboard;
Pulp magazines, 1930-49, except love, Westerns, and crime.
Wants nothing in poor condition. Ken has been in business 25 years, and pays Americans in U.S. dollars and drafts for quick payment.
Ken Mitchell
710 Concacher Drive
Willowdale, Ontario M2M 3N6 CANADA
(416) 222-5808

★ **Radio premiums from children's adventure programs** such as *The Lone Ranger, Jack Armstrong, Tom Mix, Sky King, Sgt. Preston, The Shadow, Doc Savage, Buck Rogers, Dick Tracy, Radio Orphan Annie*, etc. Also **cereal boxes offering premiums** from the 30's through the 60's. Tom buys **superhero action figures, space adventure items, and Disney**. He wrote the four volume book on Disney collectibles and will buy *anything* **related to Disney** that is not pictured in one of his price guides, especially *Mickey Mous*e items from the 1930's including *Mickey* with teeth, celluloid *Mickey*, wood and bisque *Mickeys* and any Disney wind-up toy. He also wants Disney Studio Xmas cards, **character watches** and odd Popular Culture items in original boxes. Tom prefers items to be priced, and makes offers only on items he can see in person.

"I will not jeopardize my reputation by underpaying and making someone mad. Sellers must understand how much even small blemishes reduce an item's value."

Tom Tumbusch
3300 Encrete Lane
Dayton, OH 45439
(513) 294-2250

★ **Robots and space toys** made of tin before 1965, either wind-up or battery operated are wanted. "I'll pay $2,000 for *Mr. Atomic* and $750 for the *Robby Space Patrol* vehicle. Condition is important with these toys, so I'll pay an extra 10% for any toy in its original box." Also buys tin wind-up **comic character toys** made in the USA or Europe, whether working or not, and any **Disney toys** especially celluloid toys from the 1930's. **Santa Claus toys** are also of interest.

Larry Bruch
PO Box 121
Mountaintop, PA 18707
   (717) 474-9202 eves

★ **Comic, cartoon, and other Pop Culture items** such as:
   Original animation and comic strip art from before 1970;
   Watches and clocks but only if pre-1978 and in original box;
   Empty boxes for toys, watches, and models;
   Cereal, gum, candy and food wrappers and boxes, some of
      which, like the *Kix* atom bomb box are worth $1,000+;
   Premiums from radio and TV shows, comic books or cereal,
      1920-70's; pays $5,000+ for *Superman of America* member
      rings or *Superman* secret compartment rings, and $1,000+
      for *Superman* and *Captain Marvel* wooden statues;
   Monster toys, games and masks, especially masks made by
      Don Post;
   1960's TV characters such as *Munsters, Addams Family,*
      Jetsons, Flintstones, Lost in Space, Batman and the like;
   PEZ **candy dispensers**, premiums and store displays; pays
      $400+ for *Make-A-Face* dispenser if unopened;
   Children's books (coloring, sticker, paper doll, cut-out, pop-up)
      if near mint condition only. $2,500+ for *Mickey Mouse*
      or *Wizard of Oz* Waddle Books;
   Celluloid, battery, wind-up and friction toys, especially
      Disney and *Popeye*; pays $10,000+ for German *Mickey* and
      Minnie on a motorcycle or celluloid *Horace Horsecollar*
      pulling *Mickey* in a cart;
   Captain Action **and** *G.I. Joe* **dolls** with painted hair, but only if
      still in their original boxes.

Condition is crucial. Make certain to note all damage and if there are missing parts. Make certain to mention if item is in its original box or wrapper since they can be "worth more than the item they held." Photos are "very helpful." Does not buy reproductions.

David Welch
PO Box 714
Murphysboro, IL 62966
   (618) 687-2282

★ **Pop Culture toys,** including
    Older **comic books**;
    Marilyn Monroe memorabilia;
    Elvis memorabilia;
    Disney paper collectibles;
    Non-sports cards;
    Western collectibles from B movies.
This well known magazine collector/dealer has expanded into the above related ephemera. Please describe what you have fully. Items are purchased for resale.
    Stan Gold
    7042 Dartbrook
    Dallas, TX 75240

★ **Disneyana from before 1946,** especially:
    Mickey or *Donald* painted **plaster lamps**;
    Waddle Books from the 1930's;
    Animation cels from before 1960;
    Mickey, Minnie, Donald costume dolls;
    Vernon Kilns ceramic statues;
    Tin or celluloid toys of Disney characters;
    Wood or porcelain figurines;
    Original art for WWII combat insignia.
Art from the 1950's is of interest, but nothing newer. Include dimensions, color, maker's markings, condition (mention all damage or missing parts). Dennis will make offers for items "only when I'm holding it in my hand," preferring you to set the price. Include your phone number when you write.
    Dennis Books, Comic Characters
    PO Box 99142
    Seattle, WA 98199
        (206) 283-0532

★ **Wind-up and battery operated toys** made in Germany, Japan, or the U.S., including comic characters, carnival items like merry-go-rounds, airplanes (no jets), and space toys. "I'll pay over $1,000 for *Mr. Atomic* robot or *Mickey the Magician*, two battery toys." He doesn't want common items like the Charlie Weaver bartender toy, plastic toys, wind-up dogs, toy trains, dolls, items with missing parts, or toys made in the third world. Tell this toy consultant and restorer the condition of the item and box, and whether there is any restoration or repainting.
    Don Hultzman
    5026 Sleepy Hollow Road
    Medina, OH 44256
        (216) 225-2668

★ *Marx* **playsets and plastic figures** from the 1950's to early 1970's. These toys came with metal buildings and loads of plastic people and accessories. Particularly desirable are boxed sets of *Gunsmoke, Wells Fargo, The Civil War, Disneyland, The Untouchables, Alaska, Ben Hur, Johnny Ringo,* and the *Revolutionary War.* Some of these, if clean and complete in the original box, can be worth several hundred dollars. Rare individual parts can sometimes be worth that much. Condition is extremely important. Figures from one inch to six inches tall that were not sold in boxed sets are are also wanted.
> David Welch
> PO Box 714
> Murphysboro, IL 62966
> (618) 687-2282

★ **Action figures** such as *G.I. Joe, Masters of the Universe, Ninja Turtles,* and various other super heroes. "I prefer to buy ones that are still in their original blister pack on a card."
> Ken Clee
> PO Box 11412
> Philadelphia, PA 19111
> (215) 722-1979

★ *G.I. Joe* **action figures.** "I'll buy figures, uniforms, vehicles and accessories...anything in good condition whether boxed, carded or loose." Especially seeks store displays and stock, dolls, novelties, puzzles, games, vehicles, and carded stock but will buy nearly anything. Purchases both for his personal collection and for resale.
> Joe Bodnarchuk
> 62 McKinley Avenue
> Kenmore, NY 14217
> (716) 873-0264 phone and fax

★ **Action figures** by *Marx,* 1965 to 1976. These 8" and 12" fully jointed figures had solid color plastic bodies and soft flesh colored heads and hands. They were made as cowboys, Vikings, and knights and came with soft plastic accessories. "I will buy large or small lots of these figures in any condition, whole or in parts, if they are reasonaly priced. Horses must be complete. I am particularly interested in finding the *Noble Knight and Horse* in black armor." Also buys some *Star Wars* action figures, in or out of their original package, as long as they are complete. When describing your item, tell the color of the plastic. "Price sought is helpful," but not necessary.
> Arnie Starkey, Starkey Art
> 11054 Otsego Street #5
> North Hollywood, CA 91601

★ **Toy robots from 1950-1972.** Wants *Mr. Atomic, Robby the Robot,* and the *Robby Space Patrol vehicle* among others. Especially in original boxes! Also buys other **German and Japanese wind-up, friction, and battery operated toys**, vehicles, and comic characters.
    Chris Savino
    PO Box 419
    Breesport, NY 14816
       (607) 739-3106

★ **Toy robots and *Erector* sets** are sometimes purchased by this specialist in toy vehicles.
    Jay "The Chicago Kid" Robinson
    PO Box 529
    Deerfield, IL 60015
       (708) 945-8691   or   (708) 945-1965

★ **Comic character items from the 1920's and 30's** are wanted, especially Disney but also *Betty Boop, KoKo the Clown, Felix the Cat, Maggie and Jiggs, Mutt & Jeff, Krazy Kat and Ignatz, Little Nemo, Barney Google,* and more. Wants figurines, masks, toys, premiums, posters, dolls, pins, original art, lamps, radios, store displays, etc.
    John Fawcett
    Route 2   720 Middle Turnpike
    Storrs, CT 06268

★ *Yellow Kid* **character items.** Wants tins, buttons, dolls, paper items, "anything."
    Craig Koste
    Route 2   Box 194
    Morrisonville, NY 12962
       (518) 643-8173

★ *Yellow Kid* **memorabilia.** Wants tins, toys, buttons, postcards, advertisements, "and anything else with the Kid on it."
    William Nielsen
    1379 Main Street
    Brewster, MA 02631
       (508) 896-7389

★ *Mutt & Jeff* **collectibles** are sought, including books, comic books, figurines and dolls. "Thoroughly describe what you have, please."
    Larry Whitfield
    PO Box 1330
    Duvall, WA 98019
       (206) 788-1523

★ **Radio show giveaways,** membership cards, pins, photos, games, rings, toys, etc. from *Lone Ranger,* Tom Mix, *Sky King, Capt. Midnight, Charlie McCarthy*, Gene Autry, etc.
John Fawcett
Route 2   720 Middle Turnpike
Storrs, CT 06268

★ **Radio show giveaways** such as rings, badges, decoders, etc. Wants *Captain Midnight, Superman, Little Orphan Annie, Buck Rogers, Howdy Doody, The Shadow, Sgt. Preston, Doc Savage, Sky King*, and other characters. Also buys the manuals from old radio, TV and cereal advertising campaigns. "Please advise what you have and what you want for it, or ship for offer."
Alan Levine
292 Glenwood Ave. or PO Box 1577
Bloomfield, NJ 07003
(201) 743-5288

★ **Jimmie Allen radio show giveaways** from the 1930's. "I will pay $100 each for certain Jimmie Allen wings and premium prices for other items." Since dozens of different types of wings, membership cards, and certificates were given away, it is important to make a photocopy and indicate which sponsor's name is printed on the item. Manuals, model kits, I.D. bracelets, and "other rare and/or unusual Jimmie Allen premiums" are sought. Include your phone number when you write.
Jack Deveny
6805 Cheyenne Trail
Edina, MN 55435
(612) 941-2457

★ **Cereal boxes with advertisements for giveaways or** the premiums themselves, if before 1970. Jerry also buys radio, TV, and movie cowboy and space premiums and pre-1960 *CrackerJack* **boxes, premiums, and signs.** Send for his wants list of other Pop Culture ephemera. No *Orphan Annie* decoders or manuals. Does not make offers.
Jerry Doxey
HCR#1, Box 343
Sciota, PA 18354
(717) 992-7477

★ **Cereal boxes depicting comic characters or giveaways.** Wants 1930-1959 boxes and the premiums they offered. A series of 1940's *Cheerios* boxes featuring Disney characters is particularly desirable as is the 1946 Atom Bomb ring box of *Kix*.
John Fawcett
Route 2   720 Middle Turnpike
Storrs, CT 06268

★ **Monster items** of all types including:
Gum cards, display boxes and wrappers such as *Mars Attack,*
Outer Limits, Terror Tales, Spook Stories, Monster Flip
Movies, and *Flash Gordon*;
Plastic model kits of Frankenstein's monster, wolfman,
mummy, *King Kong, Rodan, The Munsters,* and so on,
whether built or unbuilt. Will even purchase some broken
models for parts, and pay up to $50 for some empty boxes;
Toys and games, puzzles, novelties, and the like that feature any
movie, TV, or comic book monsters or creatures. Will pay
$75 for the board game, *Outer Limits*;
Halloween masks of monsters, especially masks by Don Post;
Comic books by *Zenith, E.C.* and other 10¢ publishers of
monster titles;
Magazines and record albums, especially *Famous Monsters,*
Castle of Frankenstein, World Famous Creatures, Monster
Parade and similar titles.
"I welcome any calls or letters, and am always happy to talk with anyone
who has monster items." If you write, include where you got the item.
Don't forget your phone number.
Joe Warchol
5345 North Canfield
Chicago, IL 60656
(708) 843-2442 days or (312) 774-1628 eves

★ **Model kits of human, monster, comic, or science fiction
characters** are sought. Kits were produced by *Aurora, Hawk, Revell,*
MPC, Multiple, and *Lindbergh.* Any kits containing figures (not cars
and boats) may be of interest as long as it is unbuilt in its original box.
Will also buy empty boxes, factory promos, store displays and
advertising and manufacturer's catalogs. A few items, like *Godzilla's*
Go-Cart, can bring as much as $1,000.
David Welch
PO Box 714
Murphysboro, IL 62966
(618) 687-2282

★ **Children's cartoon and comic character books** such as *Big Little*
Books, Pop-Up Books, Fast Actions, Fawcett Dime Action Books,
Cupples and Leon, and other early comic reprint books from 1910's,
20's, and 30's. Also **coloring books**, *Whitman* hard cover children's
books with dust jackets, *Whitman Penny Books, Nickel Books, Buddy*
Books, and any similar books published by *Salsfield, Mclaughlin, Lynn*
Publications, Engel Van Wiseman, etc. "Let me know what you have
and what you want for it, or ship for immediate offer."
Alan Levine
PO Box 1577
Bloomfield, NJ 07003
(201) 743-5288

★ **TV related memorabilia.** "I'll buy toys, puzzles, games, lunchboxes, etc., but specialize in all types of records and fan magazines associated with television." Wants records in all speeds, adult and children's, serious or funny, as long as it is related to television. Also TV fan type magazines like *TV-Radio Mirror, TV Fan, TV Carnival, TV Western* and the like as well as paperback books spun off from TV series. Items from before 1970 only, please. Examine your fan magazines carefully and note if they have had pictures clipped. No movie fan mags. When describing, give the date, volume and issue number and condition of magazines. Record info should include title, label, condition, and whether or not it has a sleeve.

> Ross Hartsough
> 98 Bryn Mawr Road
> Winnipeg, ON R3T 3P5 CANADA
> (204) 269-1022

★ **Television private detective and spy memorabilia.** Wants to buy games, puzzles, toys, books, photos, gum cards, wrappers, dolls, model kits, autographs, comic books, and just about everything else you can think of from shows like *77 Sunset Strip, Dragnet, Surfside 6, Peter Gunn, I Spy, The Man from U.N.C.L.E., The Wild Wild West, Secret Agent, Hawaiian Eye, Adventures in Paradise, The Untouchables* and others. This relatively new collector dealer says he's interested in everything in good condition. Include photocopy or good description as condition is very important. Describe the package if you still have it.

> Gary Pimenta
> 64 Lakeside Drive
> Tiverton, RI 02878

★ *Gilligan's Island* **collectibles.** "I'll buy or trade for all *Gilligan's Island* TV show items, including cast photos and videos of episodes." Especially interested in the 1965 *Gilligan's Island* bubblegum cards and the box they came in. Will also pay for video recordings of the cartoons *The New Adventures of Gilligan* or *Gilligan's Planet.* His club also produces a newsletter with classified ads for people who want to buy, sell, or trade *Gilligan* ephemera.

> Bob Rankin
> Original Gilligan's Island Fan Club
> PO Box 25311
> Salt Lake City, UT 84125

★ *Howdy Doody* **memorabilia** is wanted, including all items related to any character on the show. Especially seeks items in original boxes. Runs *Howdy* auctions, "so will buy anything in fine condition."

> John Andrea
> 51122 Mill Run
> Grander, IN 46530
>   (219) 272-2337   Fax: (219) 271-1146

★ **Tom Mix collectibles** including *Shredded Ralston* cereal boxes from the 1930's and 40's with Tom Mix markings, arcade and gum cards, postcards, unusual photos, feature films, short subjects, various radio premiums, and the 1930's Tom Mix *Ingersoll* pocket watch. This 40 year veteran is author of *The Tom Mix Book*, available from him for $24.95. Note that he does not want lobby cards, movie posters, newly made items, common photos, *Big Little Books,* clothing, video tapes or any material that is not in good condition. He insists that sellers price what they have.

Merle "Bud" Norris
1324 North Hague Ave.
Columbus, OH 43204
(614) 274-4646

★ *Hopalong Cassidy* **collectibles.** Offer any in good condition.
Ron Pieczkowski
1707 Orange Hill Drive
Brandon, FL 33510

★ *Lone Ranger* **items.** Wants a wide range of 1930-59 items including cereal boxes, dolls, games, posters, premiums, gun sets, carnival plaster figures, books with dust jackets, autographs, and other items.
John Fawcett
RR #2, 720 Middle Turnpike
Storrs, CT 06268

★ *Superman* **items.** Buys all rare or unusual *Superman* items, particularly dating from 1938 to 1966, but "I purchase interesting items from all years." Seeks toys, figurines, puzzles, watches, games, buttons, advertising, etc. "Please write me about any good *Superman* item because I buy duplicates and quantity." No comic books, except free premiums. No homemade items. Give a complete description, including *every* defect, and include its color, manufacturer, copyright date and country of origin. Photo or photocopy is appreciated. Danny has collected *Superman* for 30 years and is co-author of *The Adventures of Superman Collecting.*
Danny Fuchs
209-80 18th Ave.
Bayside, NY 11360
(718) 225-9030

★ *Captain Marvel, Captain Marvel Jr.,* **and** *Mary Marvel* **memorabilia** including toys, buttons, posters, comic books, mechanical items, and statues produced between 1940-1953. Also items related to similar *Fawcett Comics* characters.
Michael Gronsky
9833 Meadowcroft Lane
Gaithersburg, MD 20879
(301) 926-1049

★ *Dick Tracy, Sparkle Plenty* and *Bonny Braids* **collectibles.** "I'm buying premiums, toys, books, paper, figures...anything!"
Larry Doucet
2351 Sultana Drive
Yorktown Heights, NY 10598

★ *James Bond 007,* **and Ian Fleming memorabilia** including first edition hard and soft cover books, magazines with articles about Bond, movie posters, record albums, toys, dolls, plastic model kits, beer cans, clothing, games, comic books, and much more. Especially wants books autographed by Fleming, the British 1st edition of *Casino Royale,* and one of the signed and numbered limited editions of *On Her Majesty's Secret Service.* Give standard bibliographic information on any books, paying attention to the condition of the dust jacket (or the covers on paperbacks). On other items, indicate whether you have the original packaging for the item or not, and if you do, describe its condition as well as that of the item itself. He does not want *Saturday Evening Post, Life* or *Look* magazines. Neither does he want *Signet* paperbacks after 1961 or U.S. Book Club editions.
Gary Pimenta
64 Lakeside Drive
Tiverton, RI 02878

★ *Tarzan* **and Edgar Rice Burroughs memorabilia** including books, magazines, and collectibles. This enormous library collection still seeks items, such as the 1915 edition of *Return of Tarzan* with a dust jacket for which they'll pay over $1,000. Also seeking early *Tarzan* movies, foreign editions, Armed Services Editions and many smaller items associated with Burroughs or any of his characters. George advises, "Don't waste your time if your items aren't in fine to mint condition, including dust jackets." Please describe what you have carefully, give a guarantee, and tell us what form you'd like payment.
George McWhorter
Burroughs Memorial Collection
University of Louisville
Louisville, KY 40292
(502) 588-8729

★ *Tarzan* **books, comics and memorabilia.**
Jim Gerlach
2206 Greenbrier
Irving, TX 75060
(214) 790-0922

★ *Flintstones* **and** *Bedrock.* "Anything!" says this avid collector.
Troy Holck
16513 Horton
Stilwell, KS 66085

★ *Peanuts* **cartoon character toys and memorabilia** of all types and characters including advertising, music boxes, ceramics, jewelry, etc., as long as it is marked UNITED FEATURES SYNDICATE and in fine condition. Especially wants a musical ice bucket and the *Ansi* and *Schmidt* music boxes made of wood. Not interested in *Avon*, squeak toys, or other common items, though. A picture is appreciated. This top collector is author of the price guide to *Peanuts* collectibles; send her $12 if you want one. She reminds you not to assume the © date is the date the item was produced. "It's not," she says.

Andrea Podley
Peanuts Collector Club
539 Sudden Valley
Bellingham, WA 98226

★ *Snoopy* **and** *Peanuts* **toys and memorabilia** such as ceramics, music boxes, advertising, pins, buttons, books, magazines, toys. Especially wants a *Snoopy Says See and Say* game, *Charlie Brown's Talking Book*, and wooden *Snoopy* music boxes, pianos, etc. Boxes are needed for many of his toys, so don't throw one away. All items *must* be marked UNITED FEATURES SYNDICATE or UFS. Freddi co-authored the price guide to *Peanuts* collectibles, and says, about *Peanuts* items, "If I don't have it, I want it."

Freddi Margolin
12 Lawrence Lane
Bay Shore, NY 11706
(516) 666-6861

★ *Uncle Wiggily* **items** including books, toys, Sunday comics, puzzles, mugs, dishes, games, and "all other memorabilia." Especially wants *Uncle Wiggily's* hollow stump bungalow and stand-up figures, *Put-Together* puzzles, *Marx Crazy Car* wind-up toy, and a decorated tin *Uncle Wiggily* drinking cup.

Martin McCaw
1124 School Avenue
Walla Walla, WA 99362
(509) 525-6257

★ *Uncle Wiggily* **items** including toys, paper dolls, 1st edition books, comics, dishes, etc.

Audrey Buffington
2 Old Farm Road
Wayland, MA 01778

★ *Smokey the Bear* **ephemera.**

Thomas McKinnon
PO Box 86
Wagram, NC 28396

★ *Alice In Wonderland* **books and memorabilia** including films, figurines, tins, toys, games, puzzles, posters, greeting cards, dolls, etc. Especially wants a *Beswick* china figurine of the Cheshire Cat, but encourages all inquiries. Also wants other Lewis Carroll items, including **books, letters, and personal articles associated with Carroll**. No books published by *Whitman* or illustrated by John Tenniel but would love the Alice published by *Appleton* in 1866, worth at least $1,000!
> Joel Birenbaum
> 2486 Brunswick Circle #A1
> Woodridge, IL 60517
> (312) 968-0664

★ *Alice In Wonderland* **memorabilia** including dolls, figurines, tins, cookie jars, coffee mugs, and "anything else" is wanted, especially editions of **books in obscure languages**, or editions with lesser known illustrators like Allen, Adams, Appleton, McEune, Norfield, or Sinclair. Alice encourages you to "quote all Alice items."
> Alice Berkey
> 127 Alleyne Drive
> Pittsburgh, PA 15215
> (412) 782-2686

★ **Comic character children's lunch boxes,** both metal and vinyl, from 1970 or before. Must have pictures depicting space, cartoon, TV, sports, western, or other kid-related themes. Condition is very important. Boxes and bottles should look as if they were only slightly used, with no rust, bad rubbing, dents, serious scratches, or names written on the outside of the box. The most sought after boxes bring over $100.
> David Welch
> PO Box 714
> Murphysboro, IL 62966
> (618) 687-2282

★ **Children's lunch boxes,** metal or vinyl, with space, sports, cartoon, rock and roll or other themes, from the U.S. or Canada, 1950-to the mid 1970's. Mention whether *Thermos* bottle is present.
> Allen Woodall
> PO Box 1640
> Columbus, GA 31994
> (800) 445-4106   or   (706) 596-5100

★ **Hula dancer dolls,** figures, lamps, etc., with real grass skirts. Describe height, pose, condition, or send a photo or sketch.
> Meredith Whipple, c/o Rick Ralston, Inc.
> 99-969 Iwaena Street
> Aiea, HI 96701
> (808) 486-1243   Fax: (808) 486-1276

Comic Books and Art

Comic strips and books, the ultimate in Pop Culture, have been around since the turn-of-the-century, but didn't reach top popularity until the Depression of the 1930's and the ensuing two decades.

Approximately 17,000 comic book titles have been published, but only about 300 of these have serious collector interest. Age has little to do with the value of comic books, and almost all of them, 1930's and 40's included, sell for $10 or less.

The popularity of the artist who drew the comic has more to do with value than any other characteristic. Other factors influencing comic book value are the popularity of the character, the popularity of the publisher (the best are *Marvel, DC,* and *E.C.*), the historical significance of the series or specific issue, the condition of the comic, and the availability of the title in light of current demand.

Death issues of comics are usually popular. Spiderman's girlfriend was killed in issue 121, making it four times as valuable as issue 120. The first appearance of popular characters or the appearance of one popular character in another's magazine can also influence value, as evidenced by the $50,000 figures now being touted for the first appearance of Superman.

Comic collectors are among the nation's fussiest folks. Every tiny crease, tear, wrinkle, misprint, and off-center or rusty staple affects the value of comic books. Severe grading standards are suggested in comic book price guides, and collectors tend to follow them fairly closely.

If you have large numbers of comics for sale, you may enjoy reading Overstreet's *The Comic Book Price Guide*, the reference used by nearly all collectors and dealers. You can purchase the latest edition at bookstores or mail order dealers ($15-20) or borrow it from your public library.

The Comic Book Price Guide contains current "prices" for nearly every American comic book. You will also find pages of ads from comic dealers. Whether you find your buyer in *Where To Sell It!* or in Overstreet's guide, expect they will pay you from 30% to 70% of prices quoted in Overstreet's book, although that range varies according to the dealer's finances, customer wants, and that month's market. As a general rule, the more valuable the comic you are selling, the higher percentage of the value listed in Overstreet's guide. Dealers are not interested in lots of inexpensive comic books. Like dealers in most collectibles in the 1990's, they know that top items move quickly. Low priced items don't sell. Badly worn comics, even rare titles and issues, are difficult to sell.

Collectors and dealers will usually request that you send your comics for inspection prior to payment since the value of comics is so tightly linked to condition. Ask your post office for "return receipt requested" which costs about one dollar. Always include a list of what you are sending and keep a copy of the list for yourself. Cautious sellers photocopy the covers of what they send, since the creases on the cover are like a finger-print and can identify your comic should it become
necessary.

Selling comic art is no different than selling any other paper goods. Make a clear photocopy of what you have and send it to one of the potential buyers along with your Self-Addressed Stamped Envelope.

COMIC BOOKS

★ **Comic books,** 1935-1970, especially superhero, Western, science-fiction, humor and funny animal, and movie or TV related. Particularly looking for comics published by the following companies: E.C., Dell, Marvel & DC [before 1970], Fawcett, Fiction House, Quality, and Harvey. Also buys **Classics Illustrated comic books,** both originals and reprints. The comics most wanted are "Timely Titles" including *Captain America, Marvel Mystery, Mystic, All Winners, Human Torch, Sub-Mariner, USA,* and *Young Allies.* He will pay up to $1,000 for early issues of *Marvel Mystery.* He does not want any comics newer than 1970 or any comics without covers, no matter how old or rare they may be. When writing or calling, give the title, publisher, and issue number (usually found on the cover, inside front cover, or first page). Describe condition including cover gloss, creases, stains, tears, tape, and damage to the spine. Note loose or missing pages, bends, and folds, as well as browning of the pages. All inquiries answered if you include an SASE.
> Joe Hill, Phoenix Enterprises
> RD #1   Box 423
> Erin, NY 14838
>   (607) 796-2547 eves

★ **All 10¢ comic books,** for which he claims to have "unlimited funds" to pay 50% to 100% of price guide figures. Send a list of titles and issue numbers with a brief description of condition. No comics which sold for more than a dime originally. Also **comic strip original art** for daily or Sunday strips. This chain of comic book stores has six Illinois outlets.
> Gary Colabuono, Moondog's
> 1201 Oakton Street #1
> Elk Grove Village, IL 60007
>   (708) 806-6060 or (800) 344-6060

★ **Comic books** from the 1940's, 50's and 60's with the work of the "EC gang" of Johnny Craig, Reed Crandall, Jack Davis, Wally Wood, George Evans, Al Feldstein, Frank Frazetta, Basil Wolverton, Graham Ingels, Bernie Krigstein, and Harvey Kurtzman. "I'm also a big fan of the comic book artists Simon & Kirby, especially their post war work. Other illustrators whose work I want to buy include Matt Baker, Steve Ditko, Will Eisner, Lou Fine, Bob Powell, Alex Raymond and Alex Schomburg." Does not want EC's, but does want all other comic book appearances of these artists. Geoff deals in movie memorabilia. Send $2 each for his long catalogs of **inexpensive movie memorabilia for sale** in the bad girl, Western, and science fiction/ horror genres.
> Geoffrey Mahfuz
> PO Box 171
> Dracut, MA 01826
>   (508) 452-2768

★ **All comic books in fine condition 1900 to 1969** are wanted by this active Canadian dealer. He also buys *Big Little Books* and *Better Little Books* from 1932 to 1950. He has no interest in anything brittle or damaged. Pays in U.S. dollars and bank drafts.

> Ken Mitchell
> 710 Concacher Drive
> Willowdale, Ontario
> M2M 3N6 CANADA

★ **Comic books** from before 1968 are wanted, as are *Better Little Books* and *Big Little Books*. Hugh has been buying and selling comic books for twenty years.

> Hugh O'Kennon
> 2204 Haviland Drive
> Richmond, VA 23229
> (804) 270-2465

FLIP BOOKS

★ **Flip books** from any period, in any style or size. These are small booklets whose pictures move like an animated motion picture when the pages are flipped. Wants all kinds of flip books, including cartoons, photos of real people or animals, "how to" instructions, product advertising, sexy, or artistic abstractions. Especially seeking two rare hardcover books from the 1920's, *Santa Claus Play Pictures* and *Mother Goose Play Pictures*, which had pages to be cut out and assembled into flip books, and would pay $200 for them. He is not interested in the *Big Little Books* which sometimes had flip illustrations in the upper corner, nor does he want the recent reproductions by *Merrimack* or *Shackman & Co*. A photocopy of the cover is suggested, along with a brief description of the action. Give the dimensions, whether the book is color or black and white, identify whether it contains cartoons or photos, and describe the condition.

> Jeff Jurich
> 1220 Hudson Street
> Denver, CO 80220

SUNDAY COMIC PAGES

★ **Full color comic sections from Sunday newspapers,** 1900-1940 in good or better condition. Value depends on what comics you have, the completeness of the run, the newspaper, and the condition. Write or phone giving the city, newspaper, date, number of pages, and list the major comics included. Free appraisals.
> Al Felden
> 8945 Fairfield Street
> Philadelphia, PA 19152
> (215) 677-0657

★ **Sunday comic sections,** 1930-60. Prefers to purchase runs of several years. "A few odd sections are not needed." He especially wants the color comics from the Saturday issues of the Chicago or the NY *Journal American*, from 1934 to 1964.
> Claude Held
> PO Box 515
> Buffalo, NY 14225

★ **Sunday and daily adventure comic strips, 1930-60** such as *Tarzan, Prince Valiant, Flash Gordon, Terry and the Pirates, Steve Canyon, Casey Ruggles, Captain Easy,* and *Dick Tracy.* No single daily panels, humor strips or torn items. He is particularly interested in long complete runs of these adventure strips.
> Carl Horak
> 1319 108th Ave.
> SW Calgary, Alberta
> T2W 0C6 CANADA

★ **All Sunday comic sections in fine condition** from 1929 to 1959 *but nothing brittle or damaged.* Pays in U.S. dollars and bank drafts.
> Ken Mitchell
> 710 Concacher Drive
> Willowdale, Ontario
> M2M 3N6 CANADA

ORIGINAL COMIC ART

★ **Original artwork for comic strips and cartoons, 1920-1950,** especially animation cels from Disney and Warner Bros, for which this 25 year veteran has paid as much as $12,000. Jerry also buys original art from comic strips and magazine cartoons. Information he wants includes title, artist, description, the year, and any documentation you might have. In your description of condition, note any yellowing, folds, tears, cracked or missing paint, paste overs, etc. He does not want reproductions from newspapers or magazines, nor does he buy posters or prints of any type. Museum Graphics publishes a bimonthly newsletter and price list, available for $2 a year.

    Jerry Muller, Museum Graphics
    PO Box 10743
    Costa Mesa, CA 92627
      (714) 540-0808

Most comic art sells for $50 to $2,000, but certain Disney pieces have been known to sell for more than $50,000. Value depends upon the age, artist, subject matter. and condition. The work of Carl Barks, a prime mover at the Disney Studios, is particularly popular as is the work of Walt Kelly and a few others who bring premium prices.

★ **Comic strip art by any noted cartoonist.** Dennis issues an illustrated annual catalog which you may write for.

    Dennis Books, Comic Character Shop
    PO Box 99142
    Seattle, WA 98199
      (206) 283-0532 eves

★ **Original art used in creating comic books and strips.** Please make a photocopy of what you have.

    Charles Martignette
    PO Box 293
    Hallandale, FL 33009
      (305) 454-3474

★ **Original comic book or comic strip art.** This well-known Canadian Pop Culture dealer pays in U.S. dollars and bank drafts.

    Ken Mitchell
    710 Concacher Drive
    Willowdale, Ontario
    M2M 3N6 CANADA

Entertainment memorabilia

Nearly everything associated with the entertainment industry is worth money to someone.

Movie related items are the most popular entertainment collectible, but the category also includes legitimate stage, magic shows, Disneyland, world's fair souvenirs, and items related to other places and entertainment events. The distinctions between Pop Culture and Entertainment are arbitrary, so when selling an entertainment collectible, also try Pop Culture buyers on pages 111-126, and check the index of things you can sell, pages 451-479.

Entertainment items with bright colors, good graphic images, and important stars usually sell best. Some buyers are serious historians, eager to buy entertainment advertising, catalogs, and other paper that will help their research.

Movie memorabilia makes up the largest category of Entertainment collectibles. Though valuable movie items continue to surface, and to get a lot of publicity from the media when they do, most star photos and production stills from films bring a few dollars at most. Many movie star autographs and signed photos are not genuine, but signed by secretaries or machines. Real signatures on hand-written letters and on scripts are of much more interest to collectors.

A few stars, notably James Dean and Marilyn Monroe, are hot and genuine autographed photos can be worth $1,000 or more. If you have movie star autographs, find additional buyers in the Autograph section, pages 386-389.

Posters from popular stars and important or cult films can bring hundreds of dollars. Check for additional movie poster buyers in the section on Posters on page 390.

Follow general guidelines for describing, including the dimensions, colors, all markings, and an accurate statement of condition. Whenever possible send photocopies.

Because they are such large fields on their own, music-related collectibles, instruments, and music itself (in recorded or printed form) are often sought by one set of folks, while another is out chasing photos and other hype and ephemera associated with pop music.

Radio and television sets are popular with a different breed of collector than the "Entertainment ephemera" collector. Set collectors will often collect ephemera as decorative items called "go-withs" to enhance the display of their sets.

Items sought by more than one type of collector are called "cross-over collectibles" and are most common in areas like Pop Culture, Entertainment, Vices, Advertising, and Photographs. A signed photograph of Marilyn Monroe would find buyers in many categories. Cross-over items are often evaluated very differently (hence, priced differently) by the two types of collectors.

Go-withs are photos, catalogs, premiums, signs, and advertising related to a collector's main specialty. A photo of the interior of a radio store in 1923 would be a fine go-with for a radio collector. That some photo would also be of interest to a collector of photos of store interiors, or to a collector of something else pictured in the store. Many entertainment collectibles make attractive go-withs, so consider all possibilities when looking for a buyer.

MOVIE MEMORABILIA

★ **Kinetoscopes and peep machines from old arcades and amuse-ment parks.** He does not buy a great many machines, but is instead selectively looking for a few fine examples with historical or intrinsic value. "Amateurs can't tell one machine from another. An expert should look at all old arcade machines." Pays $7,500 for an Edison Kinetoscope from 1894. He suggests you shoot a roll of high speed 35mm film, covering all aspects of whatever machine you wish to sell. Send him the roll and he'll process it and reimburse you for your film. That's a good deal so it's not fair to waste his time with junk or late model machines. "It is very important for me to know where you got your machine." Richard is author of numerous books on slot machines, trade stimulators, pinball and arcade machines and is the historical editor of *The Coin Slot*, the quarterly magazine for people who collect coin operated machines.

Richard Bueschel
414 North Prospect Manor Ave.
Mt. Prospect, IL 60056
(708) 253-0791

★ **Professional motion picture cameras from the silent era,** 1900-1927, especially with wooden bodies and hand cranks, although some desirable cameras have metal bodies and electric motors. They range in size from small hand held to as large as suitcases. When describing, pay particular attention to the size, finish, and whether the film magazine is square or round, inside or outside the camera. There are a number of cameras that are worth more than $1,000 to him, including the *Bell & Howell #2709* and machines by *Mitchell* or *Gaumont*. He does not want home movie or 16mm cameras, nor does he want motion picture projectors. Wes is a member of numerous clubs devoted to film, and is publisher of *Sixteen Frames*, a quarterly bulletin for collectors of early cine equipment.

Wes Lambert
1568 Dapple Ave.
Camarillo, CA 93010
(805) 482-5331

★ **Anything depicting silent movie stars** including coming attraction slides, posters, lobby cards, figurines, sheet music, pin back buttons, paper dolls, plates, especially a *Star Players* photo plate of Bryant Washburn and anything featuring *Our Gang* or Jackie Coogan. Nothing from the talkies or from later stars. No autographs or photographs from any period are wanted.

Richard Davis
9500 Old Georgetown Road
Bethesda, MD 20814
(301) 530-5904

★ **Movie ephemera** including posters, lobby cards, **souvenir booklets**, and standees, both American and European. "I guarantee a fast decision and faster check."
>George Theofilis, Miscellaneous Man
>PO Box 1776
>New Freedom, PA 17349
>(717) 235-4766 days   Fax: (717) 235-2853

★ **Movie memorabilia,** including lobby cards (especially from B movies 1930-1960), theater souvenirs, tickets, programs, photos of theaters, and materials sent by studios to theater owners. Also wants **magazines** such as *Motion Picture Herald, Box Office, The Exhibitor*, and others aimed at theater owners and will buy them in any condition. This 20 year veteran collector does not buy items made after 1960.
>Chris Smith
>26 Ridge Ave.
>Aston, PA 19014
>(215) 485-0814

★ **Paper movie ephemera,** 1925-1950, including movie heralds, posters, sheet music, photographs, and studio disks of film music. Wants **studio disks**, 78rpm for studio use only. Interested in **movie magazines**, 1930-1944, and in trade journals sent to theater owners.
>Buddy McDaniel
>2802 West 18th Street
>Wichita, KS 67203
>(316) 942-3561

★ **Original studio production movie scripts** with original binders or covers when possible. "I am not interested in photocopies, TV scripts, or unproduced scripts unless the latter are by very important writers." When describing your script, indicate the name of the author, whether the script has its cover, what draft (or the date), whether all pages are present, and whether there are notations.
>Grayson Cook
>367 West Avenue 42
>Los Angeles, CA 90065
>(213) 227-8899

★ **B Western cowboy star memorabilia** from *Hopalong Cassidy*, Tom Mix, Ken Maynard, Roy Rogers, Tex Ritter and especially Gene Autry. "I'll buy buttons, photos, games, toy guns, radio giveaways, autographs, and most anything else that has to do with these stars." Dennis is interested only in B westerns, not the epics. He has only minor interest in paper items, and does not buy "damaged or overpriced goods."
>Dennis Schulte
>8th Avenue NW
>Waukon, IA 52172
>(319) 568-3628 before 10 p.m.

★ *Gone With The Wind* **items** associated with the film or the book such as tickets, posters, autographed books, magazines, scarfs, buttons, handkerchiefs, candy boxes, dress patterns, hair nets, bow ties, lockets and you name it. "I'd love to find a ticket to the premier," he says. He expects you to price what you have. No offers.

> Robert Buchanan
> 277 West 22nd Street #2B
> New York, NY 10011
> (212) 989-3917

★ *Gone with the Wind* **memorabilia from 1939 only** including jewelry, games, posters, music, paper dolls, press books, and the like. No reproductions, story books, fakes, copies, or junk. NO OFFERS.

> Frank Garcia
> 13701 SW 66th Street #B-301
> Miami, FL 33183

★ *Gone With The Wind* **items** associated with the film, the book, or its author. Wants book and Mitchell related items 1936-1965, foreign language editions of the book, movie scripts, movie posters, banners, props from the film, and all the promotional items such as dolls, games, scarfs, book ends, figurines, jewelry, nail polish, paint books, paper dolls, and more. Nothing printed after 1965. Herb has joined the ranks of collectors who will no longer do free appraisals or make offers.

> Herb Bridges
> PO Box 192
> Sharpsburg, GA 30277
> (706) 253-4934

★ *Wizard of Oz* **memorabilia** from 1900 to the present, with particular emphasis on the 1900-1939 period. Is especially interested in movie items from 1939, especially the August issue of *Movie Life*. Also pin back buttons picturing *Oz* characters. He requires sellers to price, but says "I am open to and willing to consider all offers." Like most collectors, he says, "I am very particular about condition," so make certain you describe it completely. Tell him how much you want for shipping as well. Remember to price your goods.

> Jay Scarfone
> 6 Westmont
> Hershey, PA 17033
> (717) 533-5806

★ **Cartoon posters from silent movies.** "I buy posters featuring cartoon characters like *Felix the Cat*, *Out of the Inkwell*, and other silent films, but will consider other silent movie posters as well."

> Richard Davis
> 9500 Old Georgetown Road
> Bethesda, MD 20814
> (301) 530-5904

★ **Comedy movie posters (and a few others).** Dennis wants original posters from movies by The Marx Brothers, W.C. Fields, The Three Stooges, Laurel and Hardy, Buster Keaton, Charlie Chaplin, and Woody Allen. He also wants movie material from specific films: *Psycho, Bedtime for Bonzo, 2001: A Space Odyssey, Some Like It Hot, Midnight Cowboy, Clockwork Orange,* and *The Kid From Cleveland.* Prefers American posters but will consider foreign editions. When describing posters, mention folds, tears, and stains, whether rolled or linen backed, and if it is an original release poster. A photo is desirable.

> Dennis Horwitz
> 425 Short Trail
> Topanga, CA 90290
> (310) 455-4002

★ **Movie memorabilia** including autographs of stars, promotional stills, lobby cards, and posters. This dealer is primarily interested in buying in bulk rather than in buying single items from private parties, unless, of course, the items were unusually good. Everything is purchased for resale.

> Ralph Bowman's Paper Gallery
> 5349 Wheaton Street
> La Mesa, CA 91942
> (619) 462-6268

★ **Movie memorabilia.** Buys posters, lobby cards, pressbooks, heralds, fan photos and other memorabilia from 1898 to 1970. Also movie **magazines** before 1950. "Please let me know what you have and what you want for it, or just ship for my immediate offer."

> Alan Levine
> 292 Glenwood Ave. or PO Box 1577
> Bloomfield, NJ 07003
> (201) 743-5288

★ **Movie memorabilia** 1920-59, including posters of all sizes, inserts, and lobby cards. Also wants movie **autographs** and **magazines**. Stars of particular interest include Jean Harlow, Marlene Dietrich, Bette Davis, Errol Flynn, James Cagney, Humphrey Bogart, James Dean, and Marilyn Monroe. Condition of material is important. Include your phone number.

> Gary Vaughn
> PO Box 954
> Clarksville, TN 37041
> (615) 552-7852 eves

★ *101 Dalmations* **related items** such as games, etc. "A photocopy would be nice. Describe condition honestly," and give the year you bought it, if you can remember.

> Michael Dyer
> 230 Eldon Drive NW
> Warren, OH 44483

★ **Movie posters, lobby cards, and still photos** pre-1950 especially from major stars like Jean Harlow, Boris Karloff, Laurel and Hardy, etc. All types of films (comedies, Westerns, Sci-fi, etc.) are wanted. No reprints, reissues, or magazine ads. Will buy 1950's posters from **Marilyn Monroe, James Dean, and John Wayne movies** only. Prefers to buy in quantity. Give title of movie, releasing company, the major stars, size, and the condition of your posters.
> Gene Arnold
> 2234 South Blvd.
> Houston, TX 77098
> (713) 528-1880

★ **Shirley Temple** items are "always wanted" by this specialty collector.
> Rita Dubas
> 8811 Colonial Road
> Brooklyn, NY 11209

★ **Shirley Temple memorabilia** especially sheet music and "unusual stuff" including paper dolls and jewelry. Pays $50 for early press books featuring Shirley.
> Frank Garcia
> 13701 SW 66th Street #B-301
> Miami, FL 33183

★ **8x10 studio glosses of sexy starlets** and actresses, 1920-1990.
> Charles Martignette
> PO Box 293
> Hallandale, FL 33009
> (305) 454-3474

★ **Jeanette MacDonald and Nelson Eddy memorabilia.** Wants scrapbooks and original material. Send description and asking price.
> IBT Hanson
> PO Box 1222
> Edgewood, MD 21040

★ **Humphrey Bogart and Woody Allen memorabilia.** "I want anything of interest about these two personalities." Among special wants, he lists film or video copies of early Bogart films: *Broadway's Like That, A Devil with Women, Body and Soul, Bad Sister, A Holy Terror* and *Women of all Nations.*
> Dennis Horwitz
> 425 Short Trail
> Topanga, CA 90290

★ **Three Stooges and other comedy team memorabilia.** Frank buys and sells.
> Frank Reighter
> 10220 Calera Road
> Philadelphia, PA 19114
> (215) 637-5744

★ **James Dean memorabilia** including books, magazines, photos, records, sheet music, lobby cards, film programs, posters, scrapbooks, plates, novelties, etc. Description should include the item's size, year, condition, and how much you want for it.
> David Loehr
> GPO Box 7961
> New York, NY 10116

★ **Marilyn Monroe and other sex symbol movie star memorabilia.** He not only wants Marilyn, but also will buy ephemera related to Jayne Mansfield, Mamie Van Doren, Diana Dors, Anita Ekberg, and Brigitte Bardot. He asks that you quote prices for any pre-1962 items, including U.S. and foreign magazine covers, in excellent condition.
> John Van Doren
> 60 Wagner Road
> Stockton, NJ 08559
> (609) 397-4803

★ **Marilyn Monroe.** Wants "anything and everything" U.S. and foreign including lobby cards, press books, sound track albums, collector plates, dolls, and the like. Will buy magazines with Marilyn on the cover if they are uncut condition. He does not want scrapbooks, new posters, or new pictures. Photocopies are helpful.
> Clark Kidder
> 1582 West County Highway "N"
> Milton, WI 53563
> (608) 868-2376

★ *Castle* **newsreels,** from 1937 to 1975, sound or silent, 16mm or 8mm, as long as they are complete. No shortened 50' or 100' versions are wanted. Will also buy selected titles of *Castle* space and moon flight films, and 200' or longer 8mm comedies by Laurel and Hardy or *Our Gang* if made before 1935. Please list film number if possible.
> Art Natale
> Newsreels
> 278 North 11th Street
> Prospect Park, NJ 07508

AMUSEMENT PARKS

★ **Amusement park memorabilia:** catalogs, brochures, photos, tickets, stationery, sheet music, letterheads, pennants, tokens, advertisements, books, postcards, and anything else.
Jim Abbate
1005 Hyde Park Lane
Naperville, IL 60565

★ **Roller coaster and amusement park memorabilia** including official or amateur photos, prints, blueprints, postcards, souvenirs, home movies, and *anything* else, no matter how small or odd that is remotely related to roller coasters or amusement parks. This long time collector has ridden 230 different roller coasters, once for 9 hours!
Thomas Keefe
PO Box 464
Tinley Park, IL 60477

★ **Ferris Wheel memorabilia** related to the Columbian Expo (1893) and the St. Louis World's Fair (1904), including folders, guide books, photos of the wheel (even in the background), sheet music, drawings, newspaper or diary accounts of first time riders. He will pay $1,500 for blueprints of the wheel.
Richard Bueschel
414 North Prospect Manor Ave.
Mt. Prospect, IL 60056

★ **Carnival, motordrome, and amusement park ephemera** is sought. Will purchase posters, handbills, route arrows, ride catalogs, show and fair promotional material, letterhead, contracts, and "anything else" but "I don't want circus material," he emphasizes.
David Gaylin
PO Box 9686
Baltimore, MD 21237

OTHER AMUSEMENTS

★ **Circus ephemera.** "I'll buy anything directly related to circuses, especially Barnum & Bailey, but other tented shows as well. I want posters, programs, photos, route books, etc."
Al Mordas
66 Surrey Drive
Bristol, CT 06010

★ **Chalk carnival prizes**, especially cartoon and movie characters or figures marked *Jenkins, Rainwater, Venice Dolls*, or *Gittins*. No animals except movie or comic characters. The earliest figures were not painted on the back and have a pink cast to the plaster. When describing what you have, mention whether or not is has glitter highlights. His *The Carnival Chalk Prize*, a 250 page illustrated guide is available for $15.

    Thomas Morris
    PO Box 8307
    Medford, OR 97504
    (503) 779-3164

★ **Mardi Gras souvenirs, tokens, and other ephemera** are wanted, especially pre-1900 ball invitations and colorful Carnival Bulletins originally printed in local newspapers. Hardy and his wife are always looking for photographs, postcards, early magazine articles, and other items from before 1940 which they can reproduce in their annual *Mardi Gras Guide*. Please inquire about all illustrated items and this prominent New Orleans collector will help you with pricing.

    Arthur Hardy
    PO Box 19500
    New Orleans, LA 70179
    (504) 488-2326

★ **National Orange Show, San Bernardino, CA,** 1911-1920, souvenirs and paper ephemera.

    Gary Crabtree
    PO Box 3843
    San Bernardino, CA 92413

★ **Carnegie Hall memorabilia.** Seeking relics of its own past, the Carnegie Hall Corporation wants especially to find programs and stagebills from 1892-98, 1929-31 and 1944-45. Also photos of the building in construction, or any interior shots of performers or speakers on stage. Also recordings, films and posters of events as well as any historical records. Interested in ephemera from any type of performances.

    Gino Francesconi, Archivist
    Carnegie Hall Corporation
    881 Seventh Ave.
    New York, NY 10019
    (212) 903-9629

DISNEYLAND

★ **Disneyland souvenirs.** Dean will buy all types including ceramic figurines, guidebooks, maps, buttons, pins, coins, postcards, employee materials, etc. All items should be marked DISNEYLAND. Also will buy *Disneykins*, tiny one to two inch high plastic figurines of Disney characters sold by *Marx* in the 1950's and 60's. Also will buy anything related to *Tinker Belle*. Special wants include Disneyland items from 1955-59, a *Tinker Belle* glow-in-the-dark wand, and Walt Disney's autograph. Everything must be in mint to near mint condition. Items may be sent on approval or described in writing if you want an offer.

    Dean Mancina
    PO Box 2274
    Seal Beach, CA 90740
       (310) 431-5671

★ **Disneyland souvenirs and memorabilia** "from the California Park" before 1980. Wants maps, guidebooks, tickets, food wrappers, brochures, parking tickets, special event programs, posters, passes, postcards, and what have you. Especially wants a *Marx Playset* of Disneyland. Linda has been to Disneyland more than once a month for thirty years! Nothing from Florida's Disney World is wanted.

    Linda Cervon
    10074 Ashland Street
    Ventura, CA 93004
       (805) 659-4405

★ **Disneyland and Disney World souvenirs.** Wants licensed, marked items only.

    Mike Dyer
    230 Eldon Drive NW
    Warren, OH 44483

MAGIC APPARATUS & EPHEMERA

★ **Magic apparatus of all sorts** including all paraphernalia and props, escape devices, tokens, programs, books, and other ephemera. Has a particular interest in pre-1900 posters, original photos of Houdini, and a complete set of Houdini letters, one on each of his twelve letterheads (worth $5,000 if you have it). A complete set of *Thayer Manufacturing's* wooden turned devices (1910-20) is worth $12,000 to some lucky seller. No items after 1950, newspaper clippings, radio premiums, or pulp books issued by *Wehman Bros.* An illustrated catalog of magic books and devices is available for $5 from this veteran collector dealer.

> Mario Carrandi, Jr.
> 122 Monroe Ave.
> Belle Mead, NJ 08502
> (201) 874-0630

★ **Magic memorabilia.** "I'll buy old original magic posters and lithographs, old magic playbills, programs, old magicians photos, letters, autographs, old original magic books, old magic sets, and all advertising and promotional materials to do with magic and magicians. I am especially interested in any old **Houdini memorabilia** including original old posters, playbills, programs, photos, letters, etc." Your description should include the item's approximate age, and notation of any chips, tears, stains, foxing, or other damage.

> Joseph Gargano
> PO Box 170 or   124 North Beverwyck Road
> Lake Hiawatha, NJ 07034
> (201) 538-2501 eves

★ **Harry Houdini memorabilia** including book, magazine and news-paper articles, photos, handbills, pamphlets, autographs, posters, personal apparatus and personal belongings. Anything relating to Houdini will probably be of interest. He especially wants to find a voice recording of Houdini or copies of any of his silent movies (including home movies) except *The Man From Beyond*. If you are offering personal apparatus or effects you must explain why you know it is from Houdini. You may price or he will make offer. Provide standard bibliographic information when offering books. Art is a 15 year veteran collector and happy to provide free appraisals and make offers.

> Arthur Moses
> 3512 Wosley
> Ft. Worth, TX 76133
> (817) 294-2494

★ **Magic posters and memorabilia** including posters, books, lithographs, autographed photos and letters, and **children's magic sets**, particularly *Mysto*. Ken buys items from the famous and not so famous, including Kellar, Thurston, Blackstone, Nicola, Raymond, Germain, and especially Houdini. Prices offered will depend on the rarity and condition of what you have, so it is often necessary to inspect your item before a final offer can be made. Ken promises prompt response to any item you offer that is of interest.

> Ken Trombly
> 5131 Massachusetts Ave.
> Bethesda, MD 20816
> (800) 673-8158 or (301) 320-2360   Fax: (202) 457-0343

★ **Harry Houdini memorabilia** of all types, including apparatus, posters, letters and books.

> Joe and Pamela Tanner
> Tanner Escapes
> PO Box 349
> Great Falls, MT 59403

STAGE & THEATER MEMORABILIA

★ **Minstrel memorabilia of all sorts.** "I'll buy playbills, autographs, letters written by minstrels, news clippings, postcards, posters, radio and TV programs, rare book and magazine articles, recordings, and miscellaneous artifacts. I'm particularly interested in Bert Williams, **Al Jolson, Eddie Cantor**, Sophie Tucker, and Jimmy Durante." He can send you a lengthy multi-part wants list which details books, TV shows, movies, phonograph records and other items he seeks. If you have *anything* related to minstrels or minstrel shows, give Norm a call. Norm recreates minstrel shows and is a serious historian of this entertainment profession.

> Norman Conrad
> PO Box 184
> East Walpole, MA 02032
> (508) 668-6926 eves

★ **Ventriloquist's dummies,** ephemera, photos and other items related to early ventriloquism.

> Vent Haven Museum
> 33 West Maple Ave.
> Ft. Mitchell, KY 41011
> (606) 341-0461

★ **Theater programs and souvenirs** especially items related to an anniversary such as 50th performance, 100th performance, etc. Wants pre-1920 items mostly.

> D. IBT Eliot
> 400 West 43rd Street #25-T
> New York, NY 10036
>   (212) 563-5444

★ **Theatrical memorabilia related to Charles Hoyt,** whose plays always started with "A" as in *A Rag Baby, A Midnight Bell*, etc. Will buy posters, playbills, souvenirs, etc., as well as theatrical magazines and other items dating 1884 to 1901.

> Cliff Hoyt
> PO Box 3
> Buckeyestown, MD 21717

★ **Theatrical lighting from the gaslight era.** "I'll buy anything you have dealing with theatrical lighting, particularly gas and limelighting. I want spotlights themselves, stage lights, footlights, parts, manuals, patents, and catalogs. I will even buy photocopies of documents related to the history of their development and use." A good description includes how complete the item is, any maker's information, and a good sketch or photo. No magic lantern or cinema projectors as a rule but Lindsay will buy projector literature that has information about limelight that he can use in his research. "I would be grateful if people set the price they want." Lindsay would pay as much as $400 for a perfect condition complete spotlight from the mid 1800's.

> Lindsay Lambert
> 324-B Somerset Street West
> Ottawa, ON
> K2P 0J9, CANADA
>   (613) 232-7797

WORLD'S FAIR EPHEMERA

★ **1851 Crystal Palace memorabilia** including books, engravings, stereo cards, photos, newspapers, tickets, guidebooks, awards, and various artifacts made of paper, glass, porcelain, metal, or something else. Ron wants **all material on the building's history (1851-1937)**, but is especially interested in the early years.

> Ronald Lowden, Jr.
> 314 Chestnut Ave.
> Narberth, PA 19072
>   (215) 667-0257

★ **International expositions and fairs, 1851-1940.** The library buys print and photographic materials including reports from various governmental and official bodies relating to the construction, exhibits, awards, and demolition of expositions. Also interested in letters, sheet music, tickets, passes, award medals, maps, and photos (both commercial and non commercial). The library does not collect exposition artifacts or souvenirs. "Purchase offers are made based on the value to the collection rather than on any other consideration."

> Ron Mahoney, Head of Special Collections
> Madden Library
> Calif. State University
> Fresno, CA 93740
>   (209) 294-2595

★ **World's Fair ephemera from before 1935.** "I'll buy tickets, official and unofficial stationery, postcard sets, badges, pin back buttons, tokens, medals, elongated coins, toys, and souvenirs. Please write or ship for offer." Hartzog does not buy single items after 1935 except unusual items. Newer pieces are wanted only in large collections. Rich runs numerous auctions and invites your consignments.

> Rich Hartzog
> PO Box 4143 BFT
> Rockford, IL 61110
>   (815) 226-0771

★ **1895 Atlanta Cotton States Exposition** memorabilia, especially medals, tokens, and postcards. Also **agriculture medals from Georgia state fairs**.

> R.W. Colbert
> 4156 Livsey Road
> Tucker, GA 30084

★ **1876 Centennial** collectibles such as tokens, books, textiles, trade cards, tickets, posters, broadsides, pamphlets, medals, plates, and all other souvenirs of the exposition. Describe fully, noting all damage. Will make offers only on items he requests you send on approval.

> Russell Mascieri
> 6 Florence Ave.
> Marlton, NJ 08053
> (609) 985-7711 Fax: (609) 985-8513

★ **1904 World's Fair in St. Louis** and other U.S. expositions from 1876 to 1939. Especially wants *Ingersoll* souvenir watches, clocks, banks, lamps, steins, lithopanes, hold to light postcards, large china souvenirs picturing fair scenes, ribbons, badges from judges and officials, full sets of stereo cards, photographs, complete decks of playing cards, and more. Only "very rare and unusual items from fairs after 1939."

> Doug Woollard, Jr.
> 11614 Old St. Charles Road
> Bridgeton, MO 63044
> (314) 739-4662

★ **World's Fair ephemera from 1904 or before** including china, wood, metal, textiles, paper, souvenirs, and glass. "Any and all items from a fair from 1851 to 1904 will be considered," although he has a particular interest in 1851, 1876, 1893, 1901, and 1904 fairs. A photo is requested, especially of any possibly expensive items. He requests you indicate the price you'd like for your item, although he will make offers on "things genuinely for sale."

> Andy Rudoff
> PO Box 111
> Oceanport, NJ 07757
> (908) 542-3712

★ **1907 Jamestown Exposition memorabilia** of all types is sought, except "no postcards, please."

> W.T. Atkinson, Jr.
> 1217 Bayside Circle West
> Wilmington, NC 28405

★ **1909 Alaska-Yukon-Pacific Exposition** in Seattle. "Postcards and memorabilia."

> W. E. Nickell
> 102 People's Wharf
> Juneau, AK 99801
> (907) 586-1733

★ **Trylon and perisphere at the 1939-40 NY World's Fair** pictured on paper items is sought by this major NY stamp dealer, in business for 50 years. Send a photocopy of what you have.
>   Harvey Dolin
>   5 Beekman Street #406
>   New York, NY 10038

★ **1964 New York World's Fair.** Especially want fabrics, jewelry, toys, and unusual items.
>   Dave Oglesby
>   57 Lakeshore Drive
>   Marlborough, MA 01752

★ **Paper ephemera from any World's Fair before WWII** including award and attendance certificates, honorable mention diplomas, passes, admission or concession tickets, invitations, stationery, employee badges, and playing cards.
>   William Lipsky
>   1800 Market Street #260
>   San Francisco, CA 94102
>   (415) 821-6017

★ **Atlanta Cotton States Exposition memorabilia,** including paper such as postcards and envelopes.
>   Gordon Mc Henry
>   PO Box 1117
>   Osprey, FL 34229
>   Fax: (813) 966-4568

★ **World's Fair memorabilia suitable for resale or auction.** All fairs before 1940 are wanted, especially very early ones. Rex is one of the larger mail order dealer/auctioneers in the country. He offers a large quarterly auction catalog, and constantly needs new quality items. No items valued under $20 are wanted, but "the very rare always is!"
>   Rex Stark, Americana
>   49 Wethersfield Road
>   Bellingham, MA 02019
>   (508) 966-0994

Radios and TV sets

Valuable radios and television sets are difficult for the typical person to recognize. Radios they could sell for thousands of dollars are thrown away by people who keep other radios worth $10 because they "looked valuable."

The folks who buy old radios and televisions like to know the brand name, model name and number and its cosmetic condition (what does the radio *look* like?). Describe whether it is scratched, faded, dented, chipped, cracked, or the paint or veneer is peeling. Examine the chassis carefully for missing parts or damage. If the chassis has blank spots where a tube or component might have originally been, tell the potential buyer.

Radios and television sets are among those few collectible items that do not have to be in perfect condition to find a buyer. Certainly, the better the condition, the better the price, but scarce radios and television sets will sell in almost any condition, because parts are always in demand by people who enjoy rebuilding them.

Do not test old equipment. Plugging it in may cause damage because insulation around wires deteriorates, resulting in short circuits or fire. Buyers will arrange for packing and shipping of these bulky yet fragile items.

Two buyers, Don Patterson and Gary Schneider, produce magazines which contain advertising and information about radios and radio collecting.

RADIOS

★ **Radios of many types** including crystal sets, battery operated of the 1920's, wireless sets and parts, WWI military radios, unusual cathedral radios by *Grebe* or *Ozarka*, grandfather clock style, odd shapes, and all luxury models like *Zenith* Stratosphere (pays $6,000+). Other names and models to watch for are *Marconi, De Forest, Leutz, Wireless Specialty, EICO, Norden Hauck, E.H. Scott, Grebe*, and *RCA Radiolas VI* and *VII.* Also novelty radios like *Snow White and the Seven Dwarfs, Peter Pan,* or *Mickey Mouse.* In addition, he likes radio dealer indoor and outdoor **advertising signs,** point of purchase displays, brochures, instruction books, and service manuals. Not interested in plastic radios of any kind. Don is editor of the monthly *Radio Age* for collectors of vintage electronics. Don is a collector rather than a dealer but will consider buying large collections.

> Donald Patterson
> 636 Cambridge Road
> Augusta, GA 30909
> (706) 738-7227

★ **Radios of many types 1905-40,** including crystal sets, wireless receivers and transmitters, battery operated radios 1914-1928, and small electric table models 1928-35. Buys radios in wood, metal, or plastic cabinets. Especially interested in large collections of usable speakers, **tubes and parts** for radios from this period. No large console models of the 30's except those with chrome plated interiors. Also radio **magazines, catalogs, service manuals, sales literature, and advertising,** pre-1935, including novelties and radio dealer **promotional items** such as banks, toys, pin back buttons, games, postcards, and dealer promotional items. Gary publishes *Antique Radio Classified*, a monthly digest for electronic collectors.

> Gary Schneider
> 14310 Ordner Drive
> Strongsville, OH 44136
> (216) 582-3094

★ **Old radios, tubes, test equipment, open frame motors, generators** and other electrical apparatus, switch board meters, knife switches, **neon signs, fans,** Tesla coils, **quack medical devices,** and **electric trains** and accessories, as well as early books on radio and electrical theory and practice. Give info from the item's ID plate. Include a sketch or photo.

> Hank Andreoni
> 504 West 6th
> Beaumont, CA 92223
> (909) 849-7539

★ **Antique radios.** Wants horn speakers, crystal sets, *Atwater Kent* breadboards, *Radiola, Kennedy, Federal,* the older and the more primitive the better, working or not. Also buys, **art deco and novelty radios of the 1930's** and **WWI wireless communications equipment** from ships, planes, and ground forces, either complete or for parts (worth from $200-$3,000 and up). Especially looking for old U.S. Navy equipment with CN prefixes. Also **pre-World War II television sets** and sports transmitting equipment. No floor model radios.

> Mel Rosenthal
> 507 South Maryland Ave.
> Wilmington, DE 19804
> (302) 322-8944

★ **Wireless, crystal sets, and battery radios** from before 1930 such as *Atwater Kent, Crosley, Amrad, Deforest, Federal, Grebe, Kennedy, Firth, Paragon, Marconi, R.C.A.,* and *Zenith.* Also early vacuum tubes with brass or *Bakelite* base. Also *Jenkins* **scanning disc television**. Also all wireless and radio books and magazines printed before 1930. Also radio advertising, parts, relays, ear phones, horn speakers, amplifiers, batteries, meters, etc. Will pay $500 for a *Marconi CA294,* $600 for a *Marconi 106,* $800+ for a *Pacific Wireless Specialty* audio receiver, and some others to $2,000. "I do not want anything made after 1940, floor model radios, or transistor radios."

> David Shanks
> 115 Baldwin Street
> Bloomfield, NJ 07003
> (201) 748-8820

★ **Unusual radios from the 1930's and 40's,** "the more odd looking the better." Look for sets shaped like baseballs, bottles, ships, horses, *Mickey Mouse* or *Charlie McCarthy.* Mirrored radios in blue, peach or silver, can be worth from $1,000 to $15,000 (for a floor model *Sparton Nocturne,* model 1186). *RCA* radios made in black painted wood with chrome trim are worth between $500 and $5,000. Table top radios made of celluloid, *Catalin,* or colored *Bakelite* radios are $200 to $10,000. Look for *Air King, Fada, Garod, Emerson, Motorola, Kadette,* and more. Will buy floor model radios only if they are unusually shaped or colored. Will also buy novelty transistor radios shaped like hands, bottles, animals, or advertising items. "If you send a photo and a SASE, we'll try to help you sell your radio if we don't want it!"

> Harry Poster
> PO Box 1883
> South Hackensack, NJ 07606
> (201) 794-9606 weekdays before 7 p.m.

★ **Plastic radios** from the 1930's and 40's. Brand names to look for include *Detrola, DeWald, Addison, Crosley, Emerson, Espey, Fada, Garod, Halson, Kadette, Motorola, RCA, Sentinel, Sparton, Air King, Arvin* and others. Will also buy odd or novelty radios, including any radio with mirrors. Radios need not work but the condition of the cabinet must be excellent. If in doubt, call him. Whether you write or call, give the brand name, model number, color, measurements, and a description of condition. No stereos, phonographs, or clock radios.

 Jeff Viola
 475-B Eltone Road
 Jackson, NJ 08527
  (908) 928-0666 or (201) 902-3313

★ **Mirrored glass radios.** "I'm especially fond of green mirrored glass radios and forever trying to acquire *Sparton* floor model mirrored glass radios (model 1186). I pay through the nose if I have to." That translates to as much as $35,000 for a perfect condition peach colored glass and up to $30,000 for a perfect blue glass radio. Glass covered radios do not have to work and the glass may be cracked as "I don't turn down mirrored glass radios offered to me." He claims to outbid anybody, and points out that he will either come pick up any radio or have it professionally moved so you don't have to worry about shipping. He also buys **colorful plastic radios** of the 1930's and 40's. He prefers you to price but will make offers if you seriously intend to sell.

 Ed Sage
 PO Box 1234
 Benicia, CA 94510
  (707) 746-5659

★ **Radio manuals, handbooks, and sales literature** pre-1970.
 Alan C. King
 PO Box 86
 Radnor, OH 43066

★ **Radios with wood cabinets.** Give make and model number, condition, and price. Does not make offers.
 Alvin Heckard
 Route 1 Box 88
 Lewistown, PA 17044
  (717) 248-7071

★ **Microphones,** 1940-1960, but only the short stand-up desk type mics used by broadcasters and radio stations. Especially wants to find microphones with the station or network letters still attached.

> Charles Martignette
> PO Box 293
> Hallandale, FL 33009
> (305) 454-3474

HI-FI EQUIPMENT

★ **Early tube high fidelity equipment** 1947-1960 especially monaural but also some early stereo from companies such as *Dynaco, Marantz, Fisher, McIntosh, Scott, Eico, Altec Lansing, JBL*, etc. Most makes and models are wanted, working or not, complete or for parts, as well as tubes, loudspeakers, schematics, manuals and **hi-fi magazines**. Of special interest are all early *McIntosh* amps. Nothing after 1970, "but I'll buy a wide range of things relating to early audio, from broadcast equipment to home systems."

> Jack Smith
> 288 Winter Street
> North Andover, MA 01845
> (508) 686-7250

★ **Early tube high fidelity equipment** including stereo and mono amplifiers, pre-amps, tuners (especially *McIntosh, Marantz, Western Electric* and *Quad*), large old speakers (especially *Altec, JBL, Tannoy, Western Electric,* and *Jensen*). Also buys old radios, vacuum tubes, home made amplifiers and kits (*UTC, Dynaco,* and *Heath*), movie theater sound equipment (including amps, speakers, and microphones), **antique electrical, electronic, telephonic, and telegraphic items**. Also wants old **hi-fi magazines**, books, and other literature. He does not want "department store console stereos, television tubes, or any TV's after 1955." When you write or call, give the manufacturer's name, model number, electrical condition, cosmetic condition, and tell whether any of the original literature is included.

> Vernon Vogt
> 330 SW 43rd Street #247
> Renton, WA 98055
> (206) 251-5420 ext 247

TELEVISION SETS

★ **Television sets made before 1941** are sought by Chase, one of the country's biggest buyers of memorabilia from TV's earliest years. "Mechanical TV's are often mistaken for early electronic junk," he cautions, "so look for 12" metal disks containing tiny holes that spin in front of a neon glow lamp. These early TV's drew their sound from radio sets, and most had no cabinets. Look for names like *Daven, Insuline, ICA, Jenkins, See-All, Western Television,* and *Shortwave Television.* The electronic era sets from 1938-41 used picture tubes and were often combined in consoles with radios. One popular early style was the 'mirror in the lid' which reflected the picture from a vertical picture tube. Brands to look for include *Andrea, GE, Philco, RCA, Stewart-Warner,* and *Westinghouse.* Minimum value for an early set is $500 with many of them a great deal more. A 1939 *Zenith* television would be worth about $10,000 to me, regardless of condition," says Chase. He will also buy selected sets made from 1941-1948 which can be recognized by having a Channel 1. He will also buy early giant screen 30" sets made by *Dumont* and *CBS-Columbia's* sets with a spinning color wheel. Readers are encouraged to send for his large and informative wants list. Interested only in the items mentioned above. Please don't offer other things.

>Arnold Chase
>9 Rushleigh Road
>West Hartford, CT 06117
> (203) 521-5280

★ **Early television items.** "If it's from before 1950 and it's related to television, let me know what you have."

>Gary Schneider
>14310 Ordner Drive
>Strongsville, OH 44136
> (216) 582-3094

★ **Television sets** with a reflective mirror in the lid and other small screen television sets such as the *RCA TRK-9* or *TRK-12* ($2,000+ each), and the *GE HM 171* (worth $750). Don is only interested in TV sets dating from before 1940.

>Donald Patterson
>636 Cambridge Road
>Augusta, GA 30909
> (706) 738-7227

★ **Early television sets.** "I'll buy old or unusual TV's, and will pay more than $2,000 for any TV sold before 1942, including mechanical scanners such as *Baird, Western, Empire, Pilot, ICA* and others. Also interested in mirror-in-lid sets by *Pilot, Andrea, Philco, RCA, GE, Garod,* and *Zenith.* Also buy *Fada* and *Meissner* 5" kit televisions. An *RCA TRK-5, TRK-9,* or *TT-5* will bring $3,000+ each. I pay $50 to $500 for unusual 1940's TV's with 3", 7", and 10" picture tubes. Also buys early 1950 color TV's with 16" or smaller picture tubes, and color wheels, and color adapters. Will also buy unusually shaped transistor TV's such as the *Sony 8-301W, Panasonic TR-005* (flying saucer), *JVC Video-sphere* (ball). I am willing to buy an entire TV shop, attic, or estate to get one TV I want." Harry is willing to travel. He publishes an illustrated price guide to vintage TV's and radios, available for $16.

Harry Poster
PO Box 1883
South Hackensack, NJ 07606
   (201) 794-9606 weekdays before 7 p.m.

WHERE TO FIND EARLY TV'S

Cities where you are most likely to find early TV's are those cities where TV began: Los Angeles, New York, Chicago, Philadelphia, and Schenectady. We're a mobile society and they could turn up anywhere, however.

★ **Television literature,** including books, catalogs, and company pamphlets (whether internal or intended for the public) from before 1940.

Harold Layer
San Francisco State University-AV
1600 Holloway Ave.
San Francisco, CA 94132

Music

Music collectibles fall into five broad categories, each sought by a different group of collectors.

(1) Musical instruments are prized, especially fine quality guitars, violins, and unusual instruments of all types. To sell any instrument, you need to state the maker and the model (if possible), a description of the type and quality of finish, and an indication of its condition. Include mention of all cracks, dents, and the like. If some thing seems unusual to you, make a sketch or include a photo. If you have a piano or organ to sell, unless it's a concert grade *Steinway*, there is no national market and it is usually best to offer it for sale in a local classified ad.

(2) Phonograph records are seldom exceptionally valuable, with most records still selling for $5 to $10 retail. Few records bring over $100, but some rock and roll records, some country songs, even a few 33 rpm show tune albums are considered scarce! Don't let the fact your records are worth only a dollar or two discourage you. Records come in piles, and can add up! Record buyers want to know the title, artist, record label, and catalog number (there's one on every record). Don't forget this latter information since records, like books, have editions, and one can be a lot more valuable than another. Note the condition of the record, the record jacket, and the paper sleeve. Mention any tears, scuffs, owner's names, cracks, chips, or scratches on the record or the cover. Damaged records are seldom worth your time.

(3) Sheet music collectors, in general, are more concerned with the picture on the cover than with the musical content. As a result, classical music and school

scores are seldom of interest. In their drive to amass the fascinating pictorial covers, sheet music buffs have become among the world's fussiest collectors regarding condition. To bring more than a few pennies, perhaps to be sellable at all, music must be in exceptionally fine condition, free of significant tears, writing, or other damage. When trying to sell a few pieces of sheet music, a photocopy is perhaps the best strategy, but with large quantities, follow the suggestions of buyer Wayland Bunnell, giving quantity, general condition, number of songs in each of the two sheet music sizes, and the percentage of the pile that are movie, show, and pop tunes.

(4) Memorabilia collectors interested in music, musicians and singers are like other Pop Culture collectors. Although some seek personal items, and obscure information, *rare* and *colorful* remain the two operative words when buyers describe what they want. Condition remains critical. Buyers of music books and songsters tend to be historians seeking the old , rare, and fine condition only.

(5) Mechanical music refers to phonographs, record players, player pianos, music boxes, and other devices which play music by mechanical means. Some collectors of old cylinder records also collect the machines on which to play them, but for the most part, these collectors do not compete with record, sheet music, or other instrument collectors. Describing what you have is usually a matter of taking a good photograph, listing all the information on the maker's ID plate, and describing the condition.

Buyers of juke boxes, which are a form of mechanical music, are part of the "Coin-Op" world and are listed in that section of *Where To Sell It!* on pages 178 and 179.

STRINGED MUSICAL INSTRUMENTS

★ **American guitars, banjos, and mandolins** made by the following: *C.F. Martin, Gibson, Fender* (older models only), *Dobro, National, D'Angelico, B&D (Bacon & Day), Epiphone* (older), *Paramount, Vega, Fairbanks, SS Stewart, Washburn, Lyon & Healy, Stromberg, Gretsch,* and *Rickenbacker.* "If you have fine condition instruments for sale by these makers *only* you may call us collect for an offer. Have your instrument in your hand. Be prepared to answer specific questions about condition, originality, serial number, color, and the type of case it has. Without this information, we cannot provide meaningful evaluation. *Serious sellers only may call collect.* All others are welcome to call for advice or information." Among instruments Jay would most like to find are the *Martin* D-45 with abalone inlay, the electric *Gibson* Les Paul Standard made in 1958-59, and *Gibson* Mastertone banjos made during the late 1930's. Dates and models are very important. "Another model made at the same time might be worth only 1/20 as much. Original condition matters a lot." Offers an interesting catalog of high quality new and used instruments. Wants list available.

> Stan Jay, Mandolin Bros.
> 629 Forest Ave.
> Staten Island, NY 10310
> (718) 981-3226

★ **Fretted stringed musical instruments** such as banjos, guitars, mandolins, ukuleles, and the like. "A *Martin* D-45 guitar made prior to 1942 could be worth as much as $20,000," so instruments are worth selling properly. Also **related memorabilia** such as manufacturer's catalogs, old photos of guitar shops and players, accessories, etc. State the preservation of your instrument. Examine carefully for repairs. Look for any signs that it might not be original. Mention the type of case. Offers a monthly 8 page catalog of new and used instruments for $4 per year.

> Stan Werbin, Elderly Instruments
> PO Box 14210
> Lansing, MI 48901
> (517) 372-7890 days

★ **Most string, wood, and brass musical instruments** are of interest for trade or resale. "I'll buy **any museum quality instrument.**" For his own collection he wants instruments that are rare, very old, pretty, unique, or hand crafted. He especially wants trumpets or cornets that have extra keys, fewer keys, or keys that are in unusual positions or shapes. Also **instruments of other cultures** including African, Asian, Pacific, etc., but no pianos or organs. A photo should go with a complete description, including all labels or markings.

> Sid Glickman
> 42 Butterwood Lane East
> Irvington, NY 10533
> (914) 591-5371

★ **Stringed musical instruments** including banjos, electric and acoustic guitars, mandolins, ukes, and violins. No ukelins or Mandolin-Harps, please. He'll buy banjos by *Fairbanks, Cole, Vega, Stewart, Epiphone, Stromberg, Gibson, Leedy, Ludwig, Baystate, Haynes, Lyon & Healy, Bacon, B&D, Studio King, Recording King,* or *Paramount.* Will buy the following brands of guitar in any condition: *D'Angelico, Gibson, Martin, Epiphone, Fender, Gretsch,* and *Rickenbacker.* "There are lots of guitars purchased for $100-$300 in the 1950's that are worth five to ten times as much today. I'll pay $1,500+ for a *Gretsch* White Falcon guitar, $2,000+ for a *Gretsch Chet Atkins*, $5,000+ for a *Gibson Flying V* electric guitar, and up to $10,000 for a mint *Gibson* Les Paul with the sunburst finish. We will consider **all violins** from any country, especially carved or inlaid, no matter what its country of origin." Photos of the front and back of any instrument are requested.
   Steve Senerchia, The Music Man
   91 Tillinghast Ave.
   Warwick, RI 02886
      (800) OLD ONES   Fax: (401) 823-1612

★ **French and Italian violins, violas, and cellos.** "I'll pay high prices for high grade quality instruments, both commercial and hand-made from anywhere in the world, but especially France and Italy. I don't want children's or school violins nor any imitations of Stradivarius, Guarnerius, or other masters." Describe the label inside the instrument. Appraisal services available.
   Robert Portukalian's Violin Shop
   1279 North Main Street
   Providence, RI 02904
      (401) 521-5145

STRADIVARIUS VIOLINS

Many readers own violins with labels proclaiming them to be made by Stradivarius in the 1700's. These are usually cottage industry pieces made in Germany at the turn of the 19th century for Sears Roebuck, who sold them for $9 in their catalog. A few, although not genuine Strads, are quality instruments and can command good prices.

★ **High quality Italian violins and some of their imitators** are the prime interest of this 18 year veteran West coast dealer. Cremona school violins, 1650-1750, can be worth from $2,500 to $100,000 or more, but many copies exist. Jones will consider better French instruments and your fake "Stradivarius" violins. Most of the "Strads" were cottage industry instruments or made in German factories between 1850 and 1920, and originally sold by *Sears Roebuck* for $9. They seldom bring over $100, but a few more valuable "fake Strads" were made by fine craftsman who affixed the Stradivarius label in an effort to sell the instrument. Others were high quality reproductions of the master's work, deliberately copied in homage to his craftsmanship. Many other **guitars, banjos, basses, violas, and mandolins** can be fairly valuable to Jones if you have one of better quality. It takes years of handling violins to be able to recognize originals or instruments of value. For this reason "it is difficult to buy through the mail, but not impossible." The reputation of the maker and the condition of the instrument are crucial in determining value. To sell a stringed instrument, you must describe all damage, the type and quality of finish, the bow, and give every word on the label. In many cases, he will request seeing the instrument before making a final offer. No Oriental instruments are wanted.

    David N. Jones' Violin Shop
    3411 Ray Street
    San Diego, CA 92104
    (619) 584-1505

OTHER MUSICAL INSTRUMENTS

★ **Rare and unusual musical instruments** including harps, bagpipes, hurdi-gurdies, wooden flutes, concertinas, ethnic instruments, and all manner of brass and woodwinds, stringed instruments, and others. No keyboards. Mickie repairs instruments and will purchase good ones in "any restorable condition." Can make arrangements for consignment selling of instruments he doesn't wish to buy. This 20 year veteran conducts annual seminars on musical instrument history and performance and is available for insurance appraisals and offers. An extensive illustrated catalog may be ordered for $3.

    Mickie Zekley
    Lark in the Morning
    PO Box 1176
    Mendocino, CA 95460
    (707) 964-5569

★ **Drums and drum catalogs** from the early 1900's to 1970. Buys sets or single tom toms, bass drums, or snare drums, and buys uncracked **cymbals marked K.ZILDJIAN** but not those made by A.ZILDJIAN. "To save everyone effort, a thorough and complete inspection of your instrument should be done before contacting us. Check and note modifications and/or damage of any kind including scratches, cracks, peeling, bulging, holes drilled, warps of rims and shells, rust, pitting, stains, or discoloration." Information needed to evaluate your drum(s): the brand name, shape and color of the ID emblem, the diameter of the head(s), the depth of each drum's shell (not including the rims), and the color and type of finish of the drum(s) on both the outside and inside. Does not buy drums or drum catalogs produced after 1970, exotic or ethnic drums, or parade basses. He requests "serious inquiries only, please. Kindly keep in mind that we do not offer appraisals or estimates by mail or phone. If you have no idea of the value of your item(s), I'll give you a retail price range that your item sells for in the vintage drum market and then request you quote me your wholesale asking price. I'm willing to educate sellers so they can make an informed decision and determine a fair price, keeping in mind that we must often recondition items, resell them, and make a profit." One of the world's largest dealers in collectible drums, Vintage Drum Center publishes a quarterly catalog, available to drum buyers on request.

"If you are a sincere seller interested in selling your item specifically to us, we would like to hear from you. If you are planning on selling your drums to another party, please do not call us."

> Ned Ingberman
> Vintage Drum Center
> Route 1, 95-B
> Libertyville, IA 52567
> (800) 729-3111 ext 5 (buy or sell)   Fax: (515) 693-3101

★ **Saxophones made by *Selmer***, especially in the early 1930's in Paris, but also other models as late as 1980. Serial numbers are found on the neck and on the back bottom, and must match. Look for serial numbers 60,000 through 89,000 on tenor saxes and numbers 50,000 through 120,000 on alto saxes, as they are the most desirable. Other serial numbers will be considered, however. Original finish, even if worn, is preferable to refinished instruments. Large dents and heavy scratches will take away some value. "Write or call collect if you want to sell an instrument described above." Other brands of sax considered by this nationally known specialist.

> Ed Hakal
> 10126 Signal Butte Circle
> Sun City, AZ 85373
> (602) 972-3091 evenings

★ **Brass musical instruments,** especially the unusual and obsolete. He wants "to know about all your old brass instruments since they all look the same to the untrained." Among other instruments, he especially wants a B-flat cornet with the bell pointing over the shoulder and a Schreiber horn with a straight up bell. He is attempting to assemble a representative collection of the hundreds of different brass instruments. Also interested in **band related memorabilia** such as photos of bands or individual musicians holding instruments, band programs, **catalogs** of instruments, mouthpieces, decorative or unusual **wooden music stands,** and old-style **conducting batons.** Also interested in your coffin shaped wooden instrument cases. If you regularly sell musical instruments, get his informative illustrated wants list.

Jonathan Korzun
1201 Williamson Road
North Brunswick, NJ 08902
(201) 297-0308 eves

★ **Cigar box musical instruments.** Any type musical instrument made out of a cigar box is wanted, as long as it's in fine condition. When describing what you have, please include any of the instrument's history you know. Mention whether strings, pegs, bow and carry bag are present, the type and condition of finish, and any applied or painted decorations. Photo helpful. "Unless your instrument is very unusual, I am interested in purchasing only good condition instruments. I'm not keen on the idea of going into the restoration business."

Tony Hyman
PO Box 3028
Pismo Beach, CA 93448
(805) 773-6777 Fax: (805) 773-0117

★ **Jew's harps** (also called jaw harps, juice harps), especially those that are hand-forged or made of ivory, bone, silver, or gold. They must be in good condition, complete with the tongue ("twanger"). "I'll buy Jew's harp cases in any material and want literature, instruction books, etc., and would love to find instruments composed of several harps joined together."

Leonard Fox
2965 Marlin Road, Box 729
Bryn Athyn, PA 19009

PHONOGRAPH RECORDS

★   **Rare 78 rpm records and phonograph cylinders.** Among his particular wants are:

> Jazz, blues, cajun and country 1925-1935;
> Rock & Roll, 1948-1960;
> Records before 1903 (often 7" diameter with no paper labels);
> Speeches by historical figures;
> **Picture records** (transparent records with a picture visible under the grooves);
> Advertising, promotional, and special purpose records, some of which are made of thin cardboard *[don't play them!]*;
> Unusual sizes and shapes of records;
> Classical and operatic records made before 1908, especially disks smaller than 10";
> **Long play 78's**, marked "longer playing," "five minute record," or some such;
> Puzzle, or multi-track, records;
> Rare labels, of which he can supply you a long list, including names like *Black Patti, KKK, Sunshine, Marconi, Vitaphone,* and many more.

He urges you to read Les Dock's *The American Premium Record Guide* and to make a list of any records you have that catalog for more than $15 in that publication. You can also use his wants list to help you decide which disks are worth listing. Include the label, number, artist, and any noticeable defects. "If you have a large collection so that making a list would be impractical, call me and we can discuss the possibility of evaluating your collection in person." A wants list is available if you send a long SASE. He does not want big bands, Hawaiian, popular songs, religious music, album sets, country music after WWII, home recordings, or later opera and classical, nor does he want 45's or LP records of any type music. "Just the early cylinders and 78's," says this well known auctioneer.

"Records in mint condition are preferred by collectors, but a few rare early ones have never been found in perfect condition. If it lists for more than $15 in Les Docks' guidebook, some collectors may want it even if it looks beat up."

> Kurt Nauck
> Vintage Records
> 6323 Inway
> Spring, TX 77389
>   (713) 370-7899

★ **78 rpm recordings, 1900-1940,** including popular, classical, jazz, country and Western, and personality. Also catalogs and **sheet music** in those areas of interest. David especially likes to buy entire collections and will travel anywhere in the East.

> David Alan Reiss
> 3920 Eve Drive
> Seaford, NY 11783
> (516) 785-8336

★ **Jazz, blues, big band, hillbilly, rock and roll, rhythm and blues, rockabilly, and celebrity records** in 78rpm, 45rpm and LP's.
Jazz and dance bands from the 1920's and 30's;
Jug and washboard bands;
Radio transcription disks;
Anything recorded on the following labels: *Autograph, Black Patti,* and 50 other labels (send for a list);
Records which are marked "Fox Trot," "Stomp," or "For Dancing."
He buys many rare, obscure, and unpopular records, but does not want easy listening, hit records, or pop singing stars like Al Jolson and Bing Crosby. If you have 78's to sell, send $2 for the *Shellac Shack's Wants List,* a 72 page book listing the prices they pay for thousands of records. Les is author of *American Premium Record Guide,* the basic reference book on phonograph records, available for $26 postpaid from him.

> Les Docks
> The Shellac Shack
> PO Box 691035
> San Antonio, TX 78269
> (210) 492-6021

★ **Pop American 78 rpm records, 1888-1949,** especially in quantity. Pays 10¢ to $1 apiece, less if records are not in fine condition. Buys disks, cylinders, and sapphire ball recordings at higher prices. Likes to find pre-1960 versions of *Froggy Went a Courtin',* especially the *Victor* black label version from 1926, worth $100 to him in fine condition. Some interest in **sheet music for pop music and songs** from 1890-1925.

> Ron Graham
> 8167 Park Ave.
> Forestville, CA 95436
> (707) 887-2856

★ **78 rpm *Columbia* Grand Opera Series** 10" one-sided records. Also buys *Mercury* **records' "Living Presence Series" LP's** in stereo. Does not want damaged items or reissues. Include the label and catalog number when you write.

> John Widmar
> 3829 8th Ave.
> Kenosha, WI 53140
> (414) 654-6802

★ **Recorded music.** "I'll buy collections of all 45's, used CD's, and record albums, but I don't buy 78's or any classical music or other instrumentals. Be specific in your descriptions, including label and catalog number. Seller must price."
Otti Schmitt, Finders-Keepers Collectibles
7724 Hayfield Road
Alexandria, VA 22310
(703) 550-1454

★ **Transcription discs of old radio programs** such as *Suspense, Jack Benny, Lux Radio Theater, Bing Crosby*, newscasts, the big bands, dramas, mysteries, kids shows, "and most other categories." Discs are typically 16" and aluminum based, but may also be 10" or 12" and can be found single and double sided. Glass disks from WWII years are extremely fragile and desirable. Larry is not interested in dubs or copies of originals, nor does he want disks of advertising, public service spots, or promotions. "Not interested in most library type disks but will consider if asking price is low." Prefers not to make offers.
Larry Kiner
PO Box 724
Redmond, WA 98073

★ **Bobby Breen phonograph records and song sheets** dating from the late 1930's.
Ralph Eodice
161 Valley Road
Clifton, NJ 07013

★ **Jazz LP's from the 1950's and 60's.** Also buys "all kinds of **jazz literature and magazines**, any years, and some other materials associated with jazz." No 45's or 78's. No music other than jazz. No records with poor condition covers. Please include your phone number.
Gary Alderman
PO Box 9164
Madison, WI 53715
(608) 274-3527   Fax: (608) 277-1999

★ **Rhythm and Blues or Rock and Roll 45's from the 1950's.** Wants original recordings of groups like the *Flamingos, Robins, Wrens, Penguins*, etc. Will buy any 45's from race labels such as *Chance, Red Robin, Blue Lake, Harlem, Grand, Rockin, After Hours, Aladdin, Parrot, Flip, Allen, Rhythm, Club 51,* and *Swingtime.* No records that are reissues, bootlegged, or damaged. When writing, give the label, catalog number and condition.
John Widmar
3829 8th Ave.
Kenosha, WI 53140
(414) 654-6802

★ *Vogue* **78 rpm picture records.** Will pay $500 for *Rum and Coca Cola*. Records must be clean and in excellent condition. Long SASE brings a list of other records John wants to buy.

> John Widmar
> 3829 8th Ave.
> Kenosha, WI 53140
> (414) 654-6802

★ **Rock and roll, rhythm and blues, and country music records.** Wants 45 and 33 rpm, especially:

> 45's with picture sleeves;
> Odd ball items;
> Disc jockey radio promos;
> Rock, blues, or country sheet music;
> Rock, blues, or country magazines.

Nothing having to do with classical, big band, opera, or polka music is wanted at all, no matter how old or interesting.

> Cliff Robnett
> 7804 NW 27th
> Bethany, OK 73008
> (405) 787-6703

★ **45 rpm records in quantity** in unplayed or nearly unused condition. Looking for store stock or radio station collections, but will also buy small collections if they contain desirable records. Nothing worn or scratched. "Phone if you think you have what I'm looking for."

> Ken Clee
> PO Box 11412
> Philadelphia, PA 19111
> (215) 722-1979

SHEET MUSIC

★ **Old popular sheet music** from 1820-1970, with pictorial covers, especially music or songs from movies, shows, WWI or WWII. Wants ragtime, blues, Negro, ethnic music, and particularly likes covers with baseball, cartoons, fire, aviation, and automobile songs especially with illustrations by Homer or Nathaniel Currier. No classical or religious. **Also buys *Downbeat, Metronome, Billboard* and movie magazines.**

> Beverly Hamer
> PO Box 75
> East Derry, NH 03041
> (603) 432-3528

★ **Sheet music** in small or large collections or accumulations. Primary interest is in popular music of the 20th century (1890-1970). Movie and show tunes are of primary interest, but "also any music that falls into any of the main collectible categories, like presidential, political, patriotic, war, transportation, cartoon, baseball, *Coca-Cola,* advertising, historical, Black related, and anything else that has interesting cover art." Particularly likes to find music published by the *ET Paull Music Company*, and will pay between $10 and $300, depending upon the title and condition. **Does not want to buy classical music or sheet music designed for teaching.**

"Please don't describe sheet music as 'good for its age.' That means fair or poor condition. In the world of sheet music 'Excellent' and 'mint' are terms reserved for music that has almost never seen the light of day, music store stock, or publisher's remainder."

"If the person wants to sell the music as a lot, I need to know quantity, condition, and the rough percentage of movie, show, and pop tunes. I also want to know the percentage of large format (11" x 14") and small format (9" x 12") music."

> Wayland Bunnell
> Clean Sheets
> 199 Tarrytown Road
> Manchester, NH 03103
> (603) 668-5466

★ **Bound volumes of sheet music from before 1900.** Pays $1 or more per title for illustrated ones. Those by rare publishers bring more. Prefers to buy bound books of sheet music with no music titles removed.
> Jim Presgraves
> Bookworm & Silverfish
> PO Box 639
> Wytheville, VA 24382
> (703) 686-5813

★ **Sheet music about WWI and WWII,** but only in very good to mint condition. Also wants sheet music with pictures of Frank Sinatra or Presidents of the U.S. Also buys **music by Charles K. Harris and Irving Berlin.**
> Herman Rush
> 10773 Ojai-Santa Paula Road
> Ojai, CA 93023

★ **Sheet music illustrated by E.H. Pfeiffer.** They are signed in a variety of ways including EHP, Fifer, Pfeiffer Illustrating Co., and Pfeiffer Publishing Co. She can provide you with a lengthy wants list. Also buys other items illustrated by Pfeiffer. Please describe carefully, noting all tears, creases, stains, tape, etc.
> Ann Pfeiffer Latella
> 70 Mariposa Drive
> Rochester, NY 14624
> (716) 247-2823

All collectors are fussy about condition. Sheet music collectors are among the most fussy. Don't waste their time and yours by offering items in poor condition. They won't want them!

MUSIC, MUSICIANS & SINGERS

★ **Song books and song broadsides:**
Songsters (books) from between 1700 and 1900, either British
or American in paper, leather, or hard covers, including
political candidate song books, temperance song collections,
medicine company advertising song books, and vaudeville
performer songsters, as well as circus promotional songsters;
Song broadsides and ballad sheets, 1500-1900, American and
British;
Hillbilly or Country and Western song folios before 1946;
Song books of occupational groups, miners, sailors,
lumberjacks, etc;
Regional American folk song collections from any period;
British and Irish folk song collections.
This is a fairly restrictive list of books of collected songs. Ken is a
prominent authority, author, and producer in the world of folk music and
has no interest in common items or things not on this list. Full biblio-
graphic information is required. **Please do not inquire about collections
of sheet music or religious song books.**
Kenneth Goldstein
4840 Cedar Ave.
Philadelphia, PA 19143
(215) 476-5857

SELLING MUSIC BOOKS

To sell a music book, you must provide what the book
world calls Standard Bibliographic Information:
Title as it reads on the title page, not the spine;
Author;
Publisher and place of publication;
Date of copyright and of publication (list all);
Number of pages and illustrations;
Give the condition of the binding, spine, pages, and
the dust jacket. Note bookplates, writing, and other
damage to the book. A photocopy of the title page
will save you lots of writing. If your old music book contains musical notations, make certain to photocopy a
sample if the notes are not standard shapes.

★ **Song books with oddly shaped notes.** "I'll pay $25 and up for singing school books with oblong, triangular, rectangular, pictorial or other shaped notes, especially those published before 1860, in good condition. Authors of popular versions of these books include Funk, Carden, Davisson, Swan, and others."

> Jim Presgraves
> PO Box 639
> Wytheville, VA 24382
> (703) 686-5813

★ **Paper ephemera associated with the history of pianos** including advertising signs, posters, catalogs, photos of factory and store interiors, models of pianos and mechanisms, tools used by piano tuners and builders, and piano trade publications. He is not interested in magazine ads. Your description should include size and condition as well as noting the materials from which it is made. Photo or photocopy helpful to this 20 year piano tuner. "The history of pianos and of their manufacture fascinates me." **He does not want to buy your piano. No exceptions!**

> Phillip Jamison III
> 17 Sharon Alley
> West Chester, PA 19382
> (215) 696-8449

★ **Concert Band memorabilia** from the **John Philip Sousa**, Patrick Sarsfield Gilmore, and Arthur Pryor era. "I'll buy posters, programs, autographs, photographs, letterhead, uniforms, books, sheet music, diaries and musical instruments that can be authenticated as having been used in the bands mentioned." Also wants advertising items with Sousa's picture on it such as cigar labels, tobacco cans, shot guns, *Victor* records, music cylinders, etc. Would like to find autographed copies of Sousa's various books. Condition is very important. Sheet music should not be trimmed or repaired, post cards should not have damaged corners. Send a good description or a photocopy. He does not want anything related to these men that was printed after their death: Gilmore died in 1892, Sousa in 1932, Pryor in 1942.

> Barry Furrer
> 491 Valley Road
> Gillette, NJ 07933

★ **Big Band memorabilia from the 1930's and 40's** especially of Glenn Miller or Bunny Berigan. John buys phonograph records, home recordings, tapes of concerts or radio performances, transcription disks, autographs, photographs, newspaper articles, magazine articles, movie short subjects, home movies, posters, and sheet music if it has to do with big bands. This 30 year veteran collector will negotiate an item's value.

> John Mickolas
> 172 Liberty Street
> Trenton, NJ 08611
> (609) 599-9672

★   **Music related photos, concert programs, and autographs.** Please give the title, date, and other information. Photocopies are very helpful.
> Steve Jabloner
> 7380 Adrian Drive #23
> Rohnert Park, CA 94928
> (707) 795-3081

★   **Eubie Blake or Sissle & Blake memorabilia** and records, especially a 10" recording called *Jammin' at Rudi's*.
> Steven Ramm
> 420 Fitzwater Street
> Philadelphia, PA 19147

★   **Al Jolson and his brother Harry.** "I have an extensive collection of items and music sheets, so I'm really interested only in very rare or unusual items and novelty song sheets. I certainly don't need well known songs or any more recordings of *Mammy*."
> J. Markowitz
> 964 Hillside Blvd.
> New Hyde Park, NY 11040

★   **Elvis Presley memorabilia** dating from before his death, including all marked E.P. ENTER 1956, such as lipsticks, skirts, perfume, gloves, and anything else out of the ordinary. He also buys posters and promotional items from Elvis movies, records, and appearances. He'd especially like to find a plastic guitar with pictures on it, and issues of 1950's magazines such as *Dig* and *Teen Stories* with all Elvis features. Autographs are always wanted. No records except promotional copies.
> Robert Urmanic
> Bob's Nostalgia
> 199 Brookvalley Drive
> Elyria, OH 44035
> (216) 365-3550

★   **Janet Lynn memorabilia.** "I buy photos, articles, and books, from 1970 to the present," says this fan. Photocopies are helpful.
> Alberic Gerard
> PO Box 97
> Lafayette, OR 97127

★ **Rock and roll memorabilia** is wanted, including the **Beatles, Kiss, The Monkees and other headliners**. Autographs of rock singers and musicians are especially desired. He does not purchase rock and roll records unless you have studio dubs or tapes or radio station promotional copies. No other exceptions.

> Robert Urmanic
> Bob's Nostalgia
> 199 Brookvalley Drive
> Elyria, OH 44035
> (216) 365-3550

★ **Beatles memorabilia** from before their 1970 breakup. Everything is wanted, including games, toys, dolls, posters, movie related items, candid photos, concert posters and programs, tickets, and ads for merchandise or concerts. Would love any Beatles toy musical instruments picturing the group, and will pay from $200-$500 for Beatles bongos or banjo. Buys common items as long as they are old and original. Wants to know where you got your item, and requests your phone number.

> Jeff Augsburger
> 507 Normal Ave.
> Normal, IL 61761
> (309) 452-9376

★ **Beatles memorabilia** of all sorts including toys, dolls, games, tickets, cartoon kit, model kits, *Yellow Submarine*, Halloween costumes, wallpaper, talcum powder, shampoo, ice cream wrappers, blankets, jewelry, china, toy musical instruments, fan club items, etc., especially items sealed in their original factory cartons. Rick is also looking for hard-to-find Beatles albums such as *Beatles vs the 4 Seasons* or *Yesterday & Today* with the butcher block cover. "I'll pay $800 for a Beatles record player in mint condition, and up to $500 for an unopened bottle of pomade, and $250 for a *Kaboodle Kit* in new condition." Rick also buys **The Monkees ephemera** of all types.

> Rick Rann
> PO Box 877
> Oak Park, IL 60303
> (708) 442-7907

MECHANICAL MUSIC

★ **Any pre-1930 device that plays music mechanically** including disk and cylinder music boxes, clocks and watches that play tunes, disk players, automata dolls, player organs, monkey organs, nickelodeons, horn phonographs in any condition from perfect to incomplete. Especially a barrel operated monkey organ with pipes ($2,000-$4,000), large disc music boxes that play more than one disc at a time ($10-$12,000), and cylinder music boxes with more than 175 teeth, and early musical watches. No player pianos are wanted, but most other mechanical music brings $300 up. Give measurements of any disk or cylinder. Please include your phone number with correspondence.

> Martin Roenigk, Grand Illusions
> 26 Barton Hill
> East Hampton, CT 06424
> (203) 267-8682

★ **Anything that makes music automatically or mechanically** such as phonographs, music boxes, **player pianos**, nickelodeons, organettes, and others. Also the records, discs, rolls, cobs, and anything else that plays these instruments. Also any catalog, magazine, bulletin, book, literature or advertising pertaining to these items.

> Violet and Seymour Altman, Vi & Si's
> 8970 Main Street
> Clarence, NY 14031
> (716) 634-4488

★ **Musical instruments "that play themselves"** by motor, springs, pneumatics or other means: **music boxes**, roller organs, cylinder music boxes, musical bird cages, nickelodeons, and organettes. Will buy rough condition items for parts or repair. Also musical disks, cylinders, piano rolls, old photos, postcards or paper ephemera depicting anything in mechanical music. Doug does not make offers.

> Doug Negus, Phonograph Phunatic
> 215 Mason Street
> Sutherland, IA 51058
> (712) 446-2270

★ **Music boxes.** "I'll buy *Regina* automatic changers, *Orchestrions* by *Seeburg* and others, Band organs by *Wurlitzer* and others. The larger the better! I'll make immediate decisions and immediate payment. Give me a call if you have one of these for sale."

> Q. David Bowers
> PO Box 1224
> Wolfeboro, NH 03894
> (603) 569-5095 weekdays

★ **Phonographs, music boxes, and related ephemera.** Would like to hear from you regarding all disc and cylinder phonographs with outside horns, especially those with wooden horns. Also floor model wind-up phonographs in deluxe or fancy cabinets. Also antique disc or cylinder music boxes, especially those that sit on the floor. Will pay from $200 to $10,000, depending on type, style, and condition. "I am also interested in purchasing old record catalogs, posters, metal signs, *Victor* dogs, needle tins, and the like. Phonograph related paper items before 1910 are especially desirable, particularly **items associated with Thomas Edison**. Send descriptions and photocopies.

> Kurt Nauck, Vintage Records
> 6323 Inway
> Spring, TX 77389
>   (713) 370 7899 phone or fax

★ **Antique music boxes and phonographs.** Want all types, 1850-1920, including cylinder, disc, paper roll, and cob organs. Brands like *Regina, Mira, Stella, Symphonian,* and *Kalliope* are sought. Especially interested in a *Regina Changer,* a 15 1/2 inch upright music box which changes automatically. He'd pay $12,000 for a nice one. He wants to know the brand, model, size, and condition. Pictures are most helpful. Is not interested in "late miniature music boxes."

> Chet Ramsay
> Route 1 Box 383
> Coatesville, PA 19320
>   (215) 384-0514

★ **Music cylinders.** The following cylinders (early phonograph recordings) are wanted by a well known music auctioneer:

> Cylinders colored brown, pink, purple, white or orange;
> Cylinders 6" long or 5" in diameter;
> Blue cylinders numbered 5000 to 5750;
> Cylinders with historical content.
> Operatic cylinders;

It is a plus if the cylinders are in their original boxes, but it is not necessary. Cylinders can bring from $5 to $200 each, depending on the size, color, and condition. List the title, artist, catalog number, color, length and diameter, and note whether you have the box. If your collection is very large, so listing is impractical, phone him to make other arrangements.

"Cylinders break or scratch easily. Avoid touching the surface. Do not play them, even if you think you have the right equipment."

> Kurt Nauck
> Vintage Records
> 6323 Inway
> Spring, TX 77389
>   (713) 370 7899 phone or fax

★ **Phonographs and related memorabilia** from before 1930 including cylinder and disc records, catalogs, needle tins, postcards, stereoviews depicting phonographs, toy phonographs, signs and other advertising except magazine ads. Also buys cylinder records of speeches by Taft, Teddy Roosevelt, and other famous people, for which he pays $10-$50. Also all material related to Thomas Edison. List make, model, and condition. Include label, artist, and title of records. SASE for offer.
> Steven Ramm
> 420 Fitzwater Street
> Philadelphia, PA 19147
> (215) 922-7050

★ **Horn phonographs in any condition.** Will buy parts from machines made by the following companies: *Berliner Gramophone, National Gramophone, Universal Talking Machine*, or *Zonophone*.
> Charlie Stewart
> 900 Grandview Ave.
> Reno, NV 89503
> (702) 747-1439 days

★ **Phonographs with outside horns,** complete or for parts. No Victrolas. Alvin doesn't want to be bothered unless you're serious about selling. Does not make offers.
> Alvin Heckard
> RD 1, Box 88
> Lewistown, PA 17044
> (717) 248-7071

★ *RCA* or *Capehart* **radio-phonographs that automatically flip records over** to play the other side. Pays $500-$700 for these large complicated machines from the 1930's. "If your machine weighs less than 75 pounds, I'm probably not interested." Take a photo of the record changing mechanism or give him a call.
> Joseph Weber
> 604 Centre Street
> Ashland, PA 17921
> (717) 875-4401 from 3 to 5 p.m.

★ **Catalogs, repair manuals, and advertising for phonograph records and piano rolls** published by record and piano roll companies, 1890 to 1960. Prefers to buy collections or very early pieces. No records, magazine ads, or damaged items. Tim is past president of the Association for Recorded Sound Collections, a national club for recording historians.
> Tim Brooks
> Box 41 Glenville Station
> Greenwich, CT 06831

Coin-operated machines

"Coin-ops" is what collectors call slot machines, jukeboxes, arcade games, trade stimulators (games you play for product prizes), kinetoscopes (early flip-card "movie" machines), and other machines which are put into play by dropping a coin into a slot.

If you give the make, model, and serial number, most dealers will know exactly what machine you mean. You can find this information on an identification plate along with the address of the manufacturer, patent dates, and (sometimes) the operating instructions.

When writing about a coin-op, indicate whether it works and whether parts are missing or broken. Coin-ops are among those few collectibles which do not need to be in perfect condition to sell readily. Most collectors and dealers restore them. It is important, however, when describing pinball machines, to note how much paint is peeling off the back board illustration.

Almost all collectors want a photo of older items, especially pinball and arcade games, vending machines, and trade stimulators since unfamiliar models turn up regularly. When taking photos of pinball machines, include the play field in one photo and back glass (the vertical pictorial area) in another.

Because the machines are large, heavy, and valuable, buyers will assist in making shipping arrangements.

COIN-OPERATED MACHINES

★ **Coin-op machines** especially early wood cabinet and cast iron machines 1885-1912, very rare pinball machines, kinetoscopes, and 1888-1905 peep machines. Offers $20,000 for the *Fey* 1906 Liberty Bell slot machine but has only minor interest in most other slots. Pays $7,500 for an *Edison* Kinetoscope from 1894. Particularly interested in paper ephemera about coin-ops including catalogs, advertising, letterheads, and anything else historical. Also photos of store or saloon interiors which depict machines. Also *The Coin Machine Journal, Automatic Age, Automatic World, Spinning Reels, The Billboard* (pre-1932), and other trade magazines devoted to coin-op machines. Bueschel is an editor of the quarterly *The Coin Slot* and responsible for dozens of guides to coin-ops. Since thousands of dollars are involved, he wants you to shoot a roll of 35mm film of details of your coin-op and ship the undeveloped roll to him. He'll reimburse. You *must* tell him where you got your machines.

> Richard Bueschel
> 414 North Prospect Manor Ave.
> Mt. Prospect, IL 60056
> (708) 253-0791

★ **Coin-op machines** including jukeboxes, nickelodeons, arcade devices such as diggers and claws, view machines, coin-op fans and radios, and **vending machines** for gum, condoms, etc. Has particular interest in **slot machines** and **gambling devices that pay cash** rewards. These have a minimum value of $500 with the more unusual machines bringing considerably more. Pre-1910 gambling machines made on the West coast are very desirable. Also **paper ephemera** about coin-op machines including catalogs, brochures, advertising, and anything historical. No pinball, video, or service machines like washers.

> Fred Ryan, Slot Closet
> PO Box 83135
> Portland, OR 97203
> (503) 286-3597

★ **Coin-op machines** especially pre-1940 slots and jukeboxes. No solid state pinball machines. Ted publishes the monthly *Coin Machine Trader* devoted to ads and information about coin-ops.

> Ted Salveson
> PO Box 602
> Huron, SD 57350
> (605) 352-3870

★ **Coin-op machines** including 78 rpm *Wurlitzer* jukeboxes from 1938-48, **penny arcade machines** from before 1920, **vending machines** from before 1910, and all **slot machines**.

> Martin Roenigk, Grand Illusions
> 26 Barton Hill
> East Hampton, CT 06424

★ *Gottlieb* **pinball machines,** 1948-58. Machines before 1948 don't have flippers and are not of interest. He explains that most of the games from before 1956 have wooden cabinets, trim, and legs; after 1956, they're metal. Will buy *Gottlieb* machines in any mechanical condition, but the back glass must be present and in good condition with little or no chipping, cracking, or paint flaking. Normal wear on the playing surface is expected, but severely damaged play fields make a game uncollectible. Damaged machines have some value for parts, but it's a fraction of what games in fine condition command. Pays $500 for *Gin Rummy* or *Mystic Marvel* games by *Gottlieb*. "I will consider games by other manufacturers, but only if they are in very good condition. No games which have revolving reels to record scores or that have metal cabinets. If you are in doubt, call and I will try my best to identify your game. When you describe your machine, pay attention to cosmetics, missing bumper caps, light shields missing, cracks, etc." He prefers amateurs to set the price wanted, but he will make offers, but only if you are serious about selling.

Gordon Hasse, Jr.
PO Box 1543 Grand Central Station
New York, NY 10163
(212) 996-3825 eves

★ **Table model jukeboxes.** He will buy *all* pre-1960 jukeboxes if you live close enough for him to pick them up. Only buys the small ones if they have to be shipped. Also jukebox literature, advertising and parts. If you live far enough away that your machine must be shipped, he only wants the small ones. He doesn't want to ship the larger machines.

Alvin Heckard
Route 1 Box 88
Lewistown, PA 17044
(717) 248-7071

★ *Wurlitzer* and *Rock Ola* **jukeboxes,** working or not, especially *Wurlitzer* model 42 (worth up to $1,800) and model numbers 500 or above (which begin at $450 for a #500 and can go to nearly $12,000 for a nice condition model #950). Also **all slot machines, in any condition**, complete or not, working or not. All but the most common working machines will bring $500, many over $1,000. He advertises widely that $50,000 is waiting for the finder of a working *Fey* Liberty Bell slot machine. Will pick up machines anywhere in the U.S.

Frank Zygmunt
Antique Slot Machine Co.
PO Box 542
Westmont, IL 60559
(708) 985-2742   Fax: (708) 985-5151

★ *Wurlitzer* **jukeboxes** with model numbers lower than 500. These 1930's machines predate the "plastic-and-bright-lights era" favored by most collectors. Also *Capehart* **radio-phonographs** and **jukeboxes from the 1930's that flip records over.** Pays $500-$700 for *Wurlitzer 416* or *Capehart C20-30*. He'll buy these in any condition, but condition does affect value. Will pick up anything east of the Mississippi and arrange for shipments in the West.
>Joseph Weber
>604 Centre Street
>Ashland, PA 17921
>(717) 875-4401 between 3 and 5 p.m.

★ *Wurlitzer* **jukeboxes** from the 1940's. Also **paper ephemera, service manuals, and advertising related to jukeboxes** of all types. Rick publishes the monthly *Jukebox Collector Newsletter* and is author of three books about jukeboxes, including *A Complete Identification Guide to the Wurlitzer Jukebox* available from him for $15.
>Rick Botts
>2545 SE 60th Court
>Des Moines, IA 50317
>(515) 265-8324

★ **All types of coin-operated machines,** especially unusual ones.
>Marvin Yagoda
>28585 South Harwich Drive
>Farmington Hills, MI 48018
>(313) 851-8158

★ **Penny arcade games** such as grip tests, target games, kicker and catcher, Pike's Peak, and the like. Prefers penny machines.
>James Conley
>2405 Brentwood Road NW
>Canton, OH 44708
>(216) 477-7725

★ **Pinball machines and coin-op kiddie ride animals** pre-1965.
>Don Olson
>PO Box 245
>Humboldt, IA 50548

★ **Coin-operated scales** in any condition and quantity are sought by this 10 year veteran collector/dealer who also buys scale parts, literature, advertising, and "anything else" related to coin-op scales. Provide the brand name, model, serial number and condition. Note whether the scale in complete. He does not want scales that were not coin-operated.
>Bill Berning
>PO Box 41414
>Chicago, IL 60641
>(708) 587-1839

WHERE TO SELL IT!

Sports ephemera

Sports collectibles are another form of Pop Culture, but they rate their own section by the sheer magnitude of the hobby, ranking among the five most popular forms of collecting in America today.

Balls, gloves, bats, uniforms, championship belts, trophies, medals, photos, programs, virtually anything associated with sports is collectible.   Value typically depends more on the names of the players or team involved than in the artistry or rarity of the individual item.

Championship anything brings top prices, with Baseball Hall of Fame player relics the most sought after of all sports collectibles. Recently one of my radio listeners found a Hall of Fame player's uniform worth over $150,000!

Baseball may be the king of collectible sports, but golf and fishing continue their meteoric rise in popularity and value of the last few years.   Readers have discovered how easily fishing tackle that had been gathering dust in the garage for years can be turned into cash. Small plugs (wooden and metal baits) purchased in the 1920's and 30's for pennies are worth hundreds of dollars today. Some *boxes* they originally came in are worth $50!

Duck decoys deserve even more care. The largest price paid for a decoy is over $300,000 and good wooden birds routinely sell in the $500 to $3,000 range!   A top decoy buyer says there are $10,000,000 in decoys waiting to be found in the basements and barns of Connecticut, Massachusetts and Maine alone!

Decoys bring these small fortunes because they are considered to be "folk art." Baseball collectibles bring high prices because there are so many collectors, and the law of supply and demand pushes the prices up, much as is beginning to happen with fishing tackle. In other sports (and in minor league baseball), the competition is not as fierce, and prices remain generally reasonable. For example, the top price for a baseball card is over $400,000 with dozens bringing more than $500. The most valuable basketball and football cards are only about $300.

Sports and non-sports gum cards must be evaluated by an expert. A mistake can cost you $1,000 or more. Right now, most baseball player cards from the 1950's and 60's are not hot, although some experts say now is a good time to cash in your cards from that period. They fear the influx of counterfeit cards will lead to a collapse of the market and a sharp drop in values. It's happened in other hobbies!

When you are selling sports collectibles, the importance of condition varies. Card collectors require near perfection while collectors of other baseball items treasure cracked game bats and scuffed balls and gloves, a sign they were used by their heroes.

To sell sports collectibles, you should provide the following information:

(1) What it is, its size, color, and the material from which it is made;
(2) All names, dates, and numbers embossed, incised, labeled or decaled on the item;
(3) An accurate statement of condition, noting missing parts, pieces, or paint.
(4) Mention whether the original box, packaging and instructions are included and in good condition.

Since many sports collectibles are paper, remember that a photocopy machine is a seller's best friend!

SPORTS EQUIPMENT & EPHEMERA

★ **Sports memorabilia of all types, especially from baseball,** but also **football, boxing, hockey,** and others. Bill buys and sells:
Baseball bats and autographed balls;
Paper ephemera such as programs, contracts, scorecards, tickets,
photographs, postcards, sheet music, and the like;
Major league **uniforms and shoes**;
Gum cards;
Pin back buttons, films, books, and advertising featuring sports.
"I'll buy just about anything related to professional sports." Kenrich Co.,
one of the country's largest mail order sports dealers, has 23 years' experience buying and selling sports ephemera by mail.
Bill Colby, Kenrich Co.
9418-T Las Tunas Drive
Temple City, CA 91780
(818) 286-3888 Fax: (818) 286-6035

★ **Baseball, football, basketball, and Olympic memorabilia** is wanted including items such as:
Uniforms, trophies, and medals from famous athletes;
Baseball gum cards pre-1920;
Sports photographs, but only cabinet size;
Posters and advertising pieces related to sports, pre-1930;
World Series (1903-11), all star game programs, and press pins;
Black baseball bats;
Autographed material from important dead players;
Song sheets, games, and toys related to sports pre-1920.
"Unique and unusual" sports equipment and other material especially related to Hall of Fame baseball players from the 1920's and 1930's is sought. All items must be old, rare, and original.
Joel Platt, Sports Immortals Museum
807 Liberty Ave.
Pittsburgh, PA 15222
(412) 232-3008

★ **Baseball, football, and boxing memorabilia** especially autographs of dead Hall-of-Famers and other important players. Wants yearbooks of New York sports teams and programs from championship events in all three sports. Will buy tickets, pins, and advertising items which mention players or teams, but **not interested in baseball or other sports cards.**
"Sellers should be willing to send the item to me, or a good photo or photocopy for inspection."
Richard Simon Sports, Inc. #TH
215 East 80th Street
New York, NY 10021
(212) 988-1349

★ **Baseball, football, and boxing memorabilia** including:
   Gum and tobacco cards;
   Paper ephemera such as World Series programs, books from
       before 1920, display posters, baseball score-cards pre-1900,
       baseball guides pre-1920, and early ads featuring baseball;
   Baseball equipment from before 1920;
   Uniforms from any sport before 1960;
   Football guides and equipment, pre-1930;
   Boxing ephemera, but only those dealing with James J. Corbett,
       Jim Jeffries, and John L. Sullivan.
"Premium prices paid for 19th century baseball items." This 30 year
veteran collector offers $1,500 for an *Allen & Ginter* poster depicting
1890's baseball cards, but does not want or buy *anything* after 1970.
   John Buonaguidi
   540 Reeside Ave.
   Monterey, CA 93940
   (408) 375-7345

★ **Baseball memorabilia,** especially from before 1948. Wants gum
and tobacco cards and silks picturing baseball players, postcards, photos,
games, programs, yearbooks, guides, advertising, fans, sheet music and
autographs from dead Hall-of-Fame players. This 25 year advanced collector-dealer does not buy anything after 1960. Be as accurate as possible with descriptions and include your phone number with your letter.
Photocopies are helpful.
   William Mastro
   25 Brook Lane
   Palos Park, IL 60464
   (708) 361-2117

★ **Early sports memorabilia.** "I'll buy sports ephemera, 1860-1970.
I'm mainly interested in early baseball items such as pins, postcards,
silks, leathers, advertising, and autographs, but will also buy paper and
other ephemera from **boxing and football**." Describe the condition and
indicate the price you have in mind.
   Steve Applebaum
   10636 Wilshire Blvd. #204
   Los Angeles, CA 90024
   (310) 475-3861

★ **Babe Ruth material.** Send photocopy to this major Eastern stamp
and ephemera dealer.
   Harvey Dolin & Company
   5 Beekman Street #406
   New York, NY 10038
   (212) 267-0216

★ **Philadelphia Phillies memorabilia,** especially pre-1920 programs.
Gary Gatanis
3283-B Cardiff Court
Toledo, OH 43606

★ **Baseball memorabilia from the Pacific Coast League** and selected other minor leagues. Most items wanted date from the 1940's and early 50's and include programs, selected team and League year books, *P.C.L. Baseball News,* postcards of ball parks, 1947 *Signal Oil* cards, and team photos. No cards from *Mothers Cookies, Union Oil, Remar,* or 1948 *Signal Gasoline.* Also buys programs and other ephemera associated with the **non-baseball use of Gilmore Field, Gilmore Stadium and Pan Pacific auditorium.**
Jerry Mezerow
442 Via Porto Ave.
Anaheim, CA 92806
(714) 630-6198

★ **Negro League memorabilia** including bats, autographed balls, gloves and uniforms. "Anything in good condition will be considered."
Robert Faro
PO Box 11286
Boulder, CO 80301

★ **Notre Dame football programs and other memorabilia** from pre-1960, especially Knute Rockne and George Gipp autographs and other items. Other Notre Dame sports items will be considered.
Michael Tiltges
2040 185th Street
Lansing, IL 60438
(312) 895-3222

★ **Canadian sports memorabilia.** "I'll buy all items associated with **Canadian hockey** teams and players before 1960, **Canadian lacrosse** teams and players, and **Canadian basketball** teams and players. I'm particularly looking for game schedules and calendars, programs, autographed photos, gum cards, etc. If practical, a clear photocopy is best. Small items can be sent on approval as I will always refund postage."
Michael Rice
PO Box 286
Saanichton, BC
V0S 1M0, CANADA
(604) 652-9047 eves

★ **Old sports equipment** that is suitable for restaurant, theme, model home, and other decorative purposes, including:

Balls from various sports including pre-1950 leather footballs, baseballs, soccer balls, and basketballs. Looking for moderately priced old leather balls from before 1940 suitable for decorator items. Not interested in balls autographed by famous persons.

Wooden skis and bamboo poles. Brand name doesn't matter, and neither do bindings, as long as they are all wood and in reasonably good condition;

Leather football helmets;

Lacrosse equipment such as sticks, balls, and leather knee pads;

Snow shoes, which are preferred intact with original gut, but empty frames in fine condition will be considered;

Croquet mallets or complete boxed sets if old and if the paint is in good condition;

Cricket bats and balls;

Riding equipment including tall boots, leather whips, velveteen riding hats, English style ladies' side saddles;

Wicker creels and inexpensive bamboo fishing poles, nets, etc.

All items should be pre-1940 and be fairly well cared for. Please give a general description of what you have, or telephone with the item in hand. "I am seeking low-end items suitable for decorating theme restaurants, not fine expensive antiques. If what you have is very valuable, take it somewhere else. If you find that it isn't valuable, but you want it preserved, offer it to me."

Joan Brady
834 Central Ave.
Pawtucket, RI 02861
(401) 725-5753

★ **Sports equipment:** bats, gloves, catcher's gear, and football stuff. "I'm ready to make offers."

David Bushing
342 North Third
Libertyville, IL 60048
(708) 816-6847

★ **Bodybuilding ephemera.** "I'll buy anything before 1975 related to strength, body building, physical culture, weight lifting, strongmen, etc. I buy books, magazines, training courses, photos, catalogs, programs, posters, letters, figurines, trophies, medals, certificates and videos. I'd like anything by *Milo Publishing Company*, George Jowett, or Eugen Sandow. I am not interested in magazines after 1970, nor do I want anything that is currently in print. Please describe what you have, give its date and condition, and your price."
William Moore, Joe Weider Fan Club
PO Box 732
Tuscaloosa, AL 35402

★ **Strongmen, weightlifters, and bodybuilders.** "I'll buy magazines, photos, books, posters, sculpture, and equipment related to these fields."
David Chapman
656 32nd Ave. East
Seattle, WA 98112
(206) 329-7573

★ **Ephemera related to Frank Gotch,** a turn of the century wrestling champion. He wants posters, postcards, books, photographs, etc.
Don Olson
PO Box 245
Humboldt, IA 50548

★ **Tennis memorabilia** such as trophies, figurines, art, postcards, cartoons, tableware, trade cards, lighters, first day covers, and all sorts of other little tennis-related knickknacks from before 1940. He does *not* want to buy rackets, photos, newspaper clippings, books, autographs, or programs, but "I'll buy any quantity of other reasonably priced items if they send a photo or photocopy and price what they have."
Sheldon Katz
211 Roanoke Ave.
Riverhead, NY 11901
(516) 369-1100

★ **Running memorabilia.** "I'll buy medals, ribbons, trophies, cards, annuals, magazines, programs, and books related to running, track & field, road races, and the Olympics." Not interested in items since 1960, but will consider reproductions of some posters and other printed material. Tell what you have and its condition. Ed is president of the Motor City Striders, has been director of numerous races, and writes for various running magazines.
Ed Kozloff
10144 Lincoln
Huntington Woods, MI 48070
(313) 544-9099

★ **Ice skating memorabilia** including early skates, skater's lanterns, Ice Show programs, and related books, magazines, postcards, photos and autographs. Send details and price you want.

Keith Pendell
1230 North Cypress
La Habra, CA 90631

★ **Roller skating memorabilia.**

Frank Zottoli
PO Box 241
Holden, MA 01520

★ **Surfboards and surfing related items,** from before 1970, such as magazines, posters, stickers, patches, etc. Wants round nosed pre-1970 longboards over 9' long, but will consider "transitional" boards from 1967-1971, if unusual in some way. Not interested in pointed nose boards. Wants to know the make and size of the board, shape, material, age, condition, and by whom it was used. Make certain to describe the fin. If you have a foam board, note the number, material, and thickness of the stringers. Would love to find a board ridden and signed by the legendary Duke Kahanamoku.

Wayne Babcock
4846 Carpenteria Ave.
Carpenteria, CA 93013
(805) 684-8148 days or (805) 684-0195 eves

★ **Pool tables** and other ephemera related to pool or billiards. Wants cased custom cues, catalogs, advertising, and other items.

Time After Time
North Ridge Plaza
5 Padanaram Road
Danbury, CT 06810
(203) 743-2801

★ **Pool and billiard memorabilia.** Wants interesting and unusual items associated with pool such as light fixtures, cue sticks and racks. Also buys catalogs, advertising, prints and other related items.

Dilworth Billiards
300 East Tremont
Charlotte, NC 28203

★ **Croquet ephemera.** Will buy distinctive full size mallets, pegs, wickets, table or parlor sets, books pamphlets, catalogs, photos of people playing croquet, jewelry, and other items related to the game. Please send photocopies or photos, along with your description of condition. Prefers that you price what you have if possible.

Allen Scheuch
356 W. 20th Street
New York, NY 10011

★ **Recreational and competitive horseback riding.** Wants ephemera related to Morgan horses, Arabians, saddlebred horses, polo ponies, side-saddles, and Lippizzaners. Buys books, catalogs, prints, and tack. She would especially like to find books by or illustrated by Paul Brown and George Ford Morris.
>
> Barbara Cole, October Farm
> Route 2   Box 183-C
> Raleigh, NC 27610

★ **Rugby and soccer memorabilia** wanted for resale. Can be either U.S. or foreign. Wants prints, cigarette cards, stamps, postcards, and paper ephemera. Also buys large items like coin operated games and strength machines with soccer or rugby themes.
>
> Matt Godek
> PO Box 565
> Merrifield, VA 22116

★ *Flexible Flyer* **sledding.** Wants "anything" having to do with *Flexible Flyer* sleds, including membership cards, models, pins, advertising, company literature, and rare sleds. Thorough description, with a photocopy or photograph, is helpful.
>
> Joan Palicia
> 15 Canton Road
> Wayne, NY 07470
>   (201) 831-0527

★ **Loving cup trophies** from before 1950. May be awarded for sports, beauty, service, heroism, or anything else as long as they have handles on each side and are 8" high or taller. No other style of trophy is wanted, nor is anything dating after 1950.
>
> Joan Brady
> 834 Central Ave.
> Pawtucket, RI 02861
>   (401) 725-5753

★ **Pennants** of all types, sports, events, tourist spots, universities, etc. Particularly interested in larger quantities of older ones. Depending on quantity, condition, size, age and rarity he pays from $1-$5 each. Doesn't want tears, moth holes, fading, cracked or missing lettering, and has no interest in pennants "made of a stiff felt-like material." Usually not interested in pennants that are printed in neon or fluorescent colors, as they are newer. Please send a photo or photocopy.
>
> Curtis Sharp
> 232 South Reeves
> Beverly Hills, CA 90212

BASEBALL & OTHER GUM CARDS

★ **Baseball and all other sports and non-sports cards** from gum, tobacco, dairy, candy and other sources. This major sports card dealer especially wants baseball cards pre-1930. Also buys **wrappers** from pre-1970 sports and non-sports gum packs.
> Bill Colby, Kenrich Co.
> 9418-T Las Tunas Drive
> Temple City, CA 91780
> (818) 286-3888

★ **Baseball and other sports cards** from gum, cigarettes, or candy. Also buys all yearbooks, programs, press pins, ticket stubs, autographs. "To a lesser degree" he also buys **basketball, football, and hockey items,** especially cards 1930-1959. Give condition details.
> Robert Sevchuk
> 70 Jerusalem Ave.
> Hicksville, NY 11801
> (516) 822-4089

★ **Non-sports gum cards** from candy, tobacco, and other sources from before 1975. Wants *Horrors of War, Dark Shadows, Hogans Heroes, Lost in Space, Mars Attack,* etc. Also seeks unopened boxes, wrappers, original artwork, and advertising, especially for test issues of *Hee Haw, The Waltons, Green Acres* etc. "I'll pay $1,000 for the set of *Horrors of War.*" Items must be in excellent to mint condition with no creases and fairly sharp corners. Roxanne offers a catalog of cards for sale.
> Roxanne Toser
> 4019 Green Street
> Harrisburg, PA 17110
> (717) 238-1936

★ **Non-sports gum cards from 1930-49.** This *Star Trek* star wants only cards featuring pirates, WWII, Indians, cowboys, and comic strip characters. Cards must be in fine condition.
> Walter Koenig
> PO Box 4395
> North Hollywood, CA 91607

GUM AND TOBACCO CARDS

Bubble gum sports and non-sports cards of today were previously packed in tobacco, candy and cookies as early as the 1880's. Thousands of non-sports card sets depicting every imaginable topic from animals to zeppelins exist. You can expect to get from 10¢ to $10 for most cards. 19th century cards often bring more.

WHERE TO SELL IT!

BOBBING HEAD DOLLS

★ **Bobbing head sports and non-sports dolls of all types,** especially composition/papier maché dolls from the 1960's. Wants all types of dolls from all sports, but especially miniature bobbing heads about 4" tall and real player dolls. When you write, give the color of the base.
> Dale Jerkins
> 1647 Elbur Ave.
> Lakewood, OH 44107
> (216) 226-7349

★ **Bobbing head sports and non-sports dolls,** Japanese ceramic or composition models only, no plastic dolls or dolls made in Taiwan or Korea. Indicate team or character portrayed. Also give the size, color, and shape of the base. Will pay $150 for any Blackface bobbing baseball doll in perfect condition and $600 for a perfect Roberto Clemente. Also wants **sports and non-sports plastic statues by Hartland.** Will pay between $100 and $700 for excellent and complete statues, depending on the character.
> Chip Norris
> PO Box 235
> Leonardtown, MD 20650
> (301) 475-2951

★ **Bobbing head and nodder dolls.** Prefer people or famous characters. Special wants include the *Pillsbury Doughboy, Elsie* the *Borden's* cow, *Popeye,* Presidents Eisenhower and Kennedy, *Maynard Krebs, Minnie Mouse, Porky Pig,* and *Elmer Fudd.* Also want double nodder salt and pepper shakers, nodder ashtrays and other unusual nodders.
> Roxanne Toser
> 4019 Green Street
> Harrisburg, PA 17110
> (717) 238-1936

BOBBING HEAD DOLLS

Bobbing head dolls are in the Sports chapter because the most valuable nodders are baseball and football figures. Rising prices for these odd sports souvenirs led to increased attention to all these kitschy collectibles, now considered among Pop Culture icons. When you describe a nodder for sale, give the height of the figure and the colors of the clothing, hat (helmet) and base.

GOLF EQUIPMENT & EPHEMERA

★ **Golf memorabilia** from before 1930, especially:
Wooden shaft golf clubs that are in some way unusual;
Books, magazines, and **catalogs** related to pre-1930 golf;
China and **pottery** with a golf motif by *Royal Doulton, Lenox,*
and other fine makers;
Golf balls and golf ball molds from before 1900;
Miscellaneous items related to "the knickers era."
This 35 year veteran collector does not want common wooden shaft clubs or common golf bags, nor does he buy trinkets, ashtrays, petty jewelry or reproductions. Frank prefers you set the price you want, but will make offers on rare items.
Frank Zadra
Route 3 Box 3318
Spooner, WI 54801
(715) 635-2791

★ **Golf memorabilia** of all sorts, including:
Wooden shaft clubs and early **golf balls**;
Books, magazines and **catalogs** related to pre-1940 golf;
Paintings, prints and **photos** with a golf motif;
Golf **trophies**;
Paper ephemera, scorecards, tournament programs, catalogs, etc.;
Miscellany, such as statues, and ashtrays.
"If it has a golf motif, I'm interested, and will pay premium prices for premium pieces." Does appraisals for a fee. Accepts select high quality items on consignment for sale or auction.
Richard Regan
3 Highview Terrace
Bridgewater, MA 02324
(508) 826-3537 or (508) 279-1296 eves

★ **Old golf books, magazines, and ephemera.** No paperback reprints or magazines published after 1950.
George Lewis, Golfiana
PO Box 291
Mamaroneck, NY 10543

★ **Golf award medals from before WWII** and other pre-1930 golf ephemera. "If it's early and in good condition, ship it insured for my top offer." Items are purchased outright or, if you prefer, taken on consignment for his international auctions.
Rich Hartzog
PO Box 4143 BFT
Rockford, IL 61110
(815) 226-0771 Fax: (815) 397-7662

BOXING MEMORABILIA

★ **Boxing memorabilia of all types.** "I'm the world's largest dealer in boxing memorabilia. I sell to boxing collectors all over the United States and Canada. As a result, I need to continually replenish stock, which means I am always willing to buy, sell, or trade." Please send a photograph or photocopy of what you have.
>   Jerome Shochet
>   6144 Oakland Mills Road
>   Sykesville, MD 21784
>   (410) 795-5879

★ **Boxing memorabilia of all types.** Private collector who operates a gym seeks posters, programs, tickets, films, photographs, books and magazines about boxing, boxing awards, medals, belts and trophies from any level, Golden Glove to World Championship. "If you have single items or a large collection, whether it's from the earliest days or the present champs, I'd like to hear about it."
>   Fredrick Ryan
>   PO Box 83135
>   Portland, OR 97203
>   (503) 286-3597

★ **Boxing photos and autographs** from before 1920. Please photocopy what you have.
>   Johnny Spellman
>   10806 North Lamar
>   Austin, TX 78753
>   (512) 836-2889 days or (512) 258-6910

★ **Championship boxing belts** and robes, plus **song sheets, games, and toys** related to boxing from before 1920. This giant sports museum buys only quality unusual items that are old, rare, and original.
>   Joel Platt
>   Sports Immortals Museum
>   807 Liberty Ave.
>   Pittsburgh, PA 15222
>   (412) 232-3008

AUTO RACING EPHEMERA

★ **Auto racing memorabilia.** If it's related to auto racing, and in good condition, George will probably want it. He'll buy one piece or a large collection of anything or everything associated with auto racing: awards, arm bands, dash plaques, entry forms, flags, goggles, helmets, magazines, models (built or unbuilt), movies, photographs, paintings, passes, postcards, posters, rule books, toys, board games, trophies, uniforms, and "any and all items that are auto racing related." If you know any history of the item, let him know when describing what you have and its condition. This ex race driver has been collecting 25 years and is willing to travel "a reasonable distance" to buy collections.
>George Koyt
>8 Lenora Ave.
>Morrisville, PA 19067

★ **Indianapolis 500** pit badges from before 1952 are wanted, as are race tickets from before 1950, racing programs from before 1941, and all rings or trophies, any year. Jerry will pay $300 for a 1946 pit badge.
>Jerry Butak
>242 West Adams
>Villa Park, IL 60181
>(312) 834-3729

★ **Auto racing ephemera,** including books, programs, posters, and what have you are purchased by this giant dealer in automobile parts, manuals, advertising, and ephemera.
>Walter Miller
>6710 Brooklawn Pkwy
>Syracuse, NY 13211
>(315) 432-8282

★ **Auto racing before 1916,** especially items associated with the Vanderbilt Cup races or with the Long Island Motor Parkway.
>George Spruce
>33 Washington Street
>Sayville, NY 11782
>(516) 563-4211

HORSE RACING MEMORABILIA

★ **Thoroughbred racing** memorabilia including:
Racing and breeding books;
Prints and **photographs**;
Trophies;
Paintings and **prints**;
Paper ephemera including programs, posters, trade and tobacco cards, postcards, games, and anything unusual;
Kentucky Derby programs, glasses and anything unusual.
Phar Lap memorabilia, especially a program from his 1932 race at Caliente.
All material from all racing thoroughbreds will be considered. Not interested in anything having to do with harness horses or harness racing.
Gary Medeiros
1319 Sayre Street
San Leandro, CA 94579
(510) 351-6193

★ **Dan Patch memorabilia,** especially Dan Patch mechanical postcard. Also wants pre-1950 **Kentucky Derby programs** and **drinking glasses** featuring horse racing. He will consider other **horse racing programs** from the turn of the century.
Gary Gatanis
3283-B Cardiff Court
Toledo, OH 43606

★ **Trotters, pacers, and harness horse memorabilia.** This former horse trainer wants advertising signs, county fair posters, tins, buttons, and other ephemera depicting famous trotters and pacers. He generally wants depictions of horses in harness or with their record winning time. The item he'd most like to find? A *Dan Patch* coffee container. Please describe thoroughly what you have, including an accurate description of condition. A photocopy is appreciated.
Donald Ackerman
33 Kossuth Street
Wallington, NJ 07057

HUNTING & FISHING ITEMS

★ **Hunting and fishing ephemera** including catalogs, posters, calendars, pin back buttons, trade cards, and **envelopes** decorated with advertising from before 1940. He is also interested in possibly buying any fishing and hunting images from before 1900, including prints, original art, and illustrated books. He will make offers, but only after personally inspecting what you have for sale.

> Russell Mascieri
> 6 Florence Ave.
> Marlton, NJ 08053
> (609) 985-7711   Fax: (609) 985-8513

★ **Fishing tackle from before 1945** including wooden lures (especially with glass eyes or made of hollow metal), high quality fresh or salt water reels, fine cased bamboo rods, and tackle boxes. "Most people can't tell good stuff from bad. I'll check it all for you," says this veteran collector. List all brand names and numbers and make photocopies of lures. Collect calls will be accepted if you have a collection of old items for sale.

> Rick Edmisten
> PO Box 686
> North Hollywood, CA 91603
> (818) 763-9406

★ **Antique fishing tackle** including bait and fly reels, bamboo fly and bait casting rods, willow creels, wooden nets, fishing lures (especially those with glass eyes), and early tackle boxes made of leather. Wants to find brass *Snyder* bait casting reels from early 1800's. Also buys **fishing equipment catalogs and books**. Not interested in anything made in the last 25 years.

> Robert Whitaker
> 2810 East Desert Cove Ave.
> Phoenix, AZ 85028
> (602) 992-7304

★ **Old fishing lures,** especially *Heddon 7500* vamps, *Heddon 100* and *150* minnows, and all frog shaped lures. Also **odd fish scalers**. When writing, include a photocopy of your lures, and indicate their color. Please include your phone number if you'd like a quick response.

> Thomas McKinnon
> PO Box 86
> Wagram, NC 28396
> (919) 369-2367

★ **Antique and classic fishing tackle** and ephemera from before 1940.
Among items the Corwins want to buy are:
> **Old wood or metal lures** in good condition; metal lures must be
> marked with the name of the maker or patent information,
> but wooden lures need not be marked; do not want plastic
> lures or lures in poor condition;
>
> **Reels of all types**, especially higher quality or with unusual
> features; some broken or damaged reels will be considered;
> do not want reels by *Penn, Ocean City, True Temper,* or
> *Lawrence* nor do they want spinning reels or spin casting
> reels unless very unusual;
>
> **Bamboo rods**; do not want metal rods, fiberglass rods, or any
> rods in poor condition;
>
> **Fishing paraphernalia,** creels, tackle boxes and tools;
> do not want lead sinkers;
>
> Early **fishing licenses**;
>
> **Paintings and prints** related to fishing, including calendars,
> advertising, and **cigarette cards**; no damaged artwork.

"We will deal with experts or with novice sellers. We make offers when
necessary, but prefer folks to set their own prices. You may call, *not
collect*, between 9am and 10pm. When writing, include a photocopy or
photograph. Please always include your phone number. Do not ship
anything without our permission first." They do not want anything made
in the Orient or made after 1940.

> Ed and Carolyn Corwin
> All-Safe Storage
> 200 State Road 206 East
> St. Augustine, FL 32086
>   (904) 797-6464 days   (904) 692-2037 eves

★ **Antique and modern fishing tackle** is wanted by an "avid
fisherman" who buys quality bamboo fly rods, wooden lures with glass
eyes, old tackle boxes, large ocean reels, and early tackle catalogs.

> Lee Pattison
> 113 North 4th Street
> Olean, NY 14760
>   (716) 373-3098

★ **Traps, set guns, alarm guns, trapping and fur company items**
such as posters, calendars, catalogs, advertising, and related memorabilia
from before 1940. Does not want paper items that have been trimmed.

> Ron Willoughby
> 1072 Route 171
> Woodstock, CT 06281
>   (203) 974-1226

DUCK & OTHER DECOYS

★ **Early decoys of all types** are wanted by this well known auctioneer, noted for his record setting decoy sales. Many duck decoys have value in excess of $1,000 so you are encouraged to send a good photograph along with a tracing or sketch of any markings or signatures on the bottom. Julia's Auction service does not handle decoys made after 1940. One of Jim's assistants adds. "There are an estimated $10,000,000 in duck decoys sitting in barns, basements, and garages in Massachusetts, Connecticut and Maine alone!"   Good decoys from the Mid-Atlantic, Midwest, and South are also sought.

James D. Julia Auctions
PO Box 830
Fairfield, ME 04937
(207) 453-7904   Fax: (207) 453-2502

★ **Wooden decoys and calls** for ducks, geese, crows, and fish. Buys ice fishing decoys, wooden plugs, and early reels made by *Meek, Talbot, Milan*, or *KY Bluegrass* (for which he will pay $100 up). Joe quotes prices of $200+ paid for better duck calls. Also buys various signs that are related to hunting or fishing. He suggests you send photos, but may require you to send the item for inspection before he purchases it.

Joe Tonelli
PO Box 130
Spring Valley, IL 61362

★ **Wooden decoys of all types** including duck, swan, goose, crow, owl, shorebirds, and fish. Only old wooden items are wanted, but will consider items in any condition. You must include photos.

Art Pietraszewski, Jr.
60 Grant Street
Depew, NY 14043
(716) 681-2339

★ **Old duck, crow, and goose calls and decoys.** "I'll buy wooden decoys and calls in any quantity." Send a note or call with the description and the price you'd like.

Jack Morris
821 Sandy Ridge
Doylestown, PA 18901
(215) 348-9561

The "Vices"

Nearly everything associated with alcohol, tobacco, sex, and gambling is collected.

These vice-related collectibles are a form of Pop Culture with advertising and packaging prominent among wants you'll read about in this section. Although some newer items are hotly collected, vice collectors prize 19th century items and pay premium prices for brightly colored items to decorate their walls. Among vice collectors are a few who seek photos, catalogs, and scraps of historical information. Because there is less competition for historical ephemera, prices tend to remain modest.

To sell, you should provide the following information:

(1) Size, color, and the material from which it is made;
(2) Names, dates, and numbers on the item;
(3) Statement of condition, noting missing chips, cracks, and missing parts, pieces, or paint.

When you offer paper goods, photocopy what you have to offer. Each buyer's entry indicates whether there is other information needed.

Pre-1920 beer trays and signs command prices in the hundreds, and even thousands of dollars, so handle them carefully. Even a small amount of damage is costly. The hot item among new beer collectibles is *Budweiser* mugs, with scarcer versions selling for hundreds of dollars. Beer steins have been collected for a century, and are still popular. The retail price of steins run from $300 to $800. Appraisals are easy to get, so why take chances?

The biggest money in whiskey collectibles goes for tin signs, but bottles with labels embedded in the glass are worth $150 and up.

More than 90 different forms of tobacco collectibles are sought, with values ranging from a few cents for cigar bands to thousands of dollars paid for rare tin signs and cans. One of the world's finest meerschaum pipes recently brought $3,500 at a Missouri house auction. "I was delighted," said the buyer, "as I came prepared to spend $25,000."

Collecting wooden pipes is one of the faster growing hobbies. Don't throw out (or pass by) briar pipes without looking for brands such as *Dunhill, Barling,* or *Caminetto.* Worth $25 to $100 to collectors, they can still be bought for pennies at yard sales and second hand stores.

Cigar box collectors pay from $5 to $150 each for fine condition pre-1920 boxes with interesting labels. Cigar bands, on the other hand, are a dime or less apiece. Cigarette packages dating after WWI generally bring only $5 to $10 each, about the same price as paid for cigarette ads featuring endorsements by doctors and movie stars. Prices for tobacco collectibles have been curiously stagnant, but look for cigarette lighters and ashtrays to increase in value in coming years. Matchcovers and match boxes will always remain moderately priced.

With sex taboos in our society relaxing, the collecting of erotica has come out of the closet, thus making it more competitive. If you throw away "dirty stuff," you could be tossing out substantial cash. Although magazines bring 25¢ to $2 each, early photographs and postcards with explicit pictures can be worth $10 to $50 or more each.

Gambling collectors want items from the 19th century and pay very well for them. The value of newer items remains relatively low.

BEER COLLECTIBLES

★ **Anything with the name of a beer on it.** It's called *breweriana*, and includes glasses, coasters, trays, calendars, label collections, signs, mugs, and anything else used to promote beer. Lynn particularly wants tin signs and other display advertising from the turn of the century. Lynn operates an auction service exclusively devoted to items associated with the golden brew. No *Billy Beer* or *J.R. Beer*.

> Lynn Geyer
> 300 Trail Ridge
> Silver City, NM 88061
> (505) 538-2341

★ **Beer cans** from before 1950. This 18 year veteran beer collector also wants other beer advertising signs, trays, coasters, and bottles. He is particularly interested in cans for the seven brands of the Los Angeles *Monarch Brewing Company* (five of which will bring you over $1,000 each if you can find them). Make certain to describe condition carefully. No *Billy Beer, J.R. Beer*, or cans with pull tab tops.

> Mike Miller
> PO Box 1275
> La Canada, CA 91012
> (800) 882-2337

★ **Beer and soda cans from small regional companies** before 1965. Prefers cone top cans but also buys flat top cans, brewery advertising, signs, trays, statues and glasses from the same period. Especially likes to find items from the *Manhattan Brewing Company* owned by Al Capone and the *Grace Bros. Brewing Company* in California. Prices on cans from these two companies tend to start at $500. No rusty cans are wanted by this 10 year veteran collector/dealer, but "some light spotting and aging is natural. I do require cans be sent before a final purchase offer is made because condition so greatly affects the value and I need to examine cans closely."

> Tony Steffens
> 1115 Cedar Ave.
> Elgin, IL 60120
> (800) 443-8712   Fax: (708) 742-5778

★ **Beer uniform sew-on patches from anywhere in the world.** Jim wants any sewn patch: arm, cap, shirt, all ages, all sizes, all breweries. He isn't interested in beer club patches. Please describe condition noting whether it is used or unused, clean or not, and indicate whether it is a "second" or has been cut from a larger patch. Photocopy helpful.

> Jim O'Brien
> PO Box 885
> Sugar Grove, IL 60554

★ **Beer bottles with painted labels.** American breweries only. Most of these are 6, 7 or 8 oz., but some older ones from the 1930's are 12 oz. There are a few, very desirable, larger bottles with painted labels. He is particularly interested in finding New York bottles, especially from Buffalo, Rochester, Utica, Syracuse, Troy, Tonawanda, and New York City. Describe the condition of the paint and whether there are neck chips. No soft drink bottles, please, even if bottled in breweries.

> Jim O'Brien
> PO Box 885
> Sugar Grove, IL 60554

★ *Hamm's* **brewery memorabilia** including advertising, packaging and bottles, souvenirs, foam scrapers, coasters, bottle caps, kegs, glasses, signs and so on, for all of *Hamm's* brands. These include *Buckhorn, Velvet Glove, Matterhorn, Burgie, Right Time, Old Bru*, and *Waldech*. When selling glasses or cans, it is important to include *all* writing that appears on the object. Pete wants everything he doesn't already have and says the areas around Houston, Los Angeles, San Francisco, Baltimore, and St. Paul "are particularly saturated with *Hamm's* breweriana."

> Peter Nowicki
> 1531 39th Ave.
> San Francisco, CA 94122
> (415) 566-7506

★ **Beer mugs and steins** made in the 1970's and 80's by the *Ceramate Brazil Company*. "I'll buy both the lidded and unlidded varieties of such favorites as *Budman, Busch Gardens, Clydesdales, Olympics*, etc."

> Tony Steffens
> 1115 Cedar Ave
> Elgin, IL 60120
> (800) 443-8712   Fax: (708) 742-5778

★ **New Jersey breweriana** from the 1930's or older including signs, calendars, trays, tap knobs and inserts, coasters, labels, cans and books. "I would buy some collections of general breweriana if they contained some NJ items I want." He warns amateurs not to guess at age of items, that it's better to ask and urges you not to "buy breweriana items with the thought of reselling them to make money, since the chances are you won't." This 17 year veteran collector requests that you make it clear whether you are seeking information or have the item for sale.

> Paul Brady
> PO Box 811
> Newton, NJ 07860
> (201) 383-7204

★ **Near beer advertising from the days of prohibition in Chicago** and items related to Chicago pre-prohibition beers and breweries like *Budweiser, Schlitz, Blatz, Old Milwaukee, Atlas, Keely, Schoenhoffen, Sieben's,* and *Manhattan.* Wants signs, beer barrels, bottles, etc.
Michael Graham, Roaring 20's
345 Cleveland Ave.
Libertyville, IL 60048
(708) 362-4808 days

★ **Any coasters with advertising, especially for beer.** Interested *only* in U.S. coasters. "Send any quantity for my fair offer by return check."
Art Landino
88 Centerbrook Road
Hamden, CT 06518

★ **Pottery ginger beer bottles** and associated paper ephemera. Sven has an illustrated wants list of these bottles, some of which can be worth $150. He is author of *The Illustrated Stone Ginger Beer,* a limited edition available from him for $13.
Sven Stau
PO Box 437
Buffalo, NY 14212
(716) 825-5448 or (716) 822-3120

★ **American and foreign miniature beer bottles** especially pre-prohibition 1880-1920. The earliest are about 5" tall, filled with beer, and have a cork stopper. These are desirable if they have complete labels or the bottles are embossed. Post-prohibition bottles are smaller and of interest only if all labels are complete and in good condition. Foreign bottles must be in mint condition to be of interest. Also bottle openers with handles in the shape of mini beer bottles, wood or metal. There is a small group of post prohibition mini beers which can be worth to $100 each. They include *Old Glory, Royal Pilsen, Wagner, Spearman, Ambrosia, Nectar, Frederick's 4 Crown, Citizens, Manro, Atlantic, Pennsy* and others. Alex will pay top price for sets of mini bottles in their original box. Condition of the label is crucial so describe every scratch or discoloration. Measure exact height. Also buys bottle shaped bottle openers. No Taiwan bottles.
Alexander Mullin
915 Lincoln Ave.
Springfield, PA 19064

★ *Anheuser Busch* **advertising and ephemera** from pre-prohibition.
Vern Bauckman
2219 Old Bridge Road
Woodbridge, VA 22192
(703) 590-2988 eves

★ *Budweiser* **ceramic beer steins.** "I'll buy, for top dollar, any of the early Grant's Farms steins, and various *Bud* steins from 1975 and 1976. Steins are for my personal collection and must be in mint condition."
Joseph Venanzi
46 Wolfpack Road
Trenton, NJ 08619
(609) 586-3414

★ *Dixie* **beer and** *Lexington Brewery* **ephemera** including openers, trays, fobs, mirrors, letterheads, and what have you.
Thom Thompson
1389 Alexandra Drive, #5
Lexington, KY 40504

BEER STEINS

★ **Antique beer steins of all types,** from $10 to $10,000 as long as it was made before WWII. This active collector/dealer will buy one or a large collection. A photo is helpful, as are all markings, measurements, and a description of what is portrayed. Don't forget to note the condition of both the stein and lid. He offers free appraisals with no obligation and, if you telephone him with your stein in your hand, he can usually tell you its wholesale and retail value over the phone. He holds regular stein auctions, writes articles and is available to give talks.
Les Paul
568 County Isle
Alameda, CA 94501
(510) 523-7480 Fax: (510) 523-8755

★ **Steins.** "I buy etched and print *Mettlachs*, colored glass steins with pewter casings/lids or fine enameling, milk glass, early blue-gray *Westerwald*, faience, figural steins or plain gray steins with painted decorations of brewery logos, any *Muenchen*, and anything unusual. All must have lids and be before 1920. I do not want gaudy low relief pottery souvenir steins either cream colored or gray-blue." Photo is essential, as is a complete description including any cracks, hairlines, dents, chips, or color wear. Lottie is a collector and prolific writer about steins.
Lottie Lopez
PO Box 885
Santa Paula, CA 93060

★ **Steins** including fine early *Mettlach*, regimental, faience, stoneware, glass, porcelain, occupational, *Royal Vienna, Meissin*, or wooden. Gary has written five books on steins; his *The Beer Stein Book* is $42 postpaid.
Gary Kirsner
PO Box 8807
Coral Springs, FL 33075

WHISKEY COLLECTIBLES

★ **Ceramic** *Jim Beam* **type figural liquor bottles.** The bottle *must* have its original stopper. Your description should include the brand name, the figure, all marks on the bottom, the dimensions, and all colors. Fred offers a price guide to 1,500+ figural bottles for only $3.
> Fred Runkewich
> PO Box 1423
> Cheyenne, WY 82003
> (307) 632-1462

★ *Jack Daniels, Green River Whiskey,* **and** *Lem Motlow* memorabilia including crockery jugs, embossed bottles, cork screws, shot glasses, lighters, and old paper advertising. Only older items are wanted.
> Don Cauwels
> 3947 Old South Road
> Murfreesboro, TN 37129
> (615) 896-3614

★ *Green River Whiskey* **advertising and other memorabilia,** including paper, signs, display bottles, watch fobs, "giveaways," counter displays, and company receipts, letterheads, etc. Will pay $150-$250 for warehouse receipts or shot glasses. Clear pencil rubbings of advertising coins is a must, as many types exist. No *Green River* soft drink, please.
> Elijah Singley
> 2301 Noble Ave.
> Springfield, IL 62704
> (217) 546-5143 eves

★ *Dewar's* **scotch figural liquor bottles made by** *Royal Doulton.* Called *KingsWare* by *Doulton* collectors, more than 100 different figural bottles were commissioned in the 1920's and 30's. These distinctive brown-glazed bottles feature various literary characters and English historical figures. He pays $300+ each, says this veteran *Royal Doulton* dealer, as long as the figure is not chipped or cracked. If you wish to sell yours, telephone with the item in front of you.
> Ed Pascoe, Pascoe & Co.
> 545 Michigan Ave.
> Miami Beach, FL 33139
> (800) 872-0195   Fax: (305) 532-8543

★ **Whiskey miniatures.** Buys pre-1960 miniature American whiskeys and will pay "top dollar for rare brands." Used since 1875, he buys them all. Mike likes the post-prohibition ones best for his personal collection.
> Mike Olson, MELO
> 309 Knopp Valley
> Winona, MN 55987
> (507) 454-1499

★ **Pub jugs (whiskey pitchers).** They are made in glass, pottery, pewter, and plastic, but "I'm buying only the pottery (ceramic) ones, and pay from $5 to $20 for pitchers I can use." Will make offers if you give an accurate description, including the exact height, shape, color and all the information on the pitcher. "I don't buy jugs with chips or cracks." But he'd love to find copies of a magazine called *The Pub Jug*.

    Victor Case
    200 SE "B" Street
    Bentonville, AR 72712
       (501) 273-7276

★ **Liquor advertising pitchers and ashtrays.** "I'll buy liquor advertising pitchers and ashtrays that are unusual and in excellent condition. I don't want the more common ones but if you are unsure of what you have, please send a sketch or photo. The mark on the bottom and the liquor company advertising are important for identification, as is the color. I don't want any glass pitchers or glass ashtrays, only pottery, china or porcelain."

    Robert & Susan Cox
    800 Murray Drive
    El Cajon, CA 92020
       (619) 447-0800 days

★ **Swizzle sticks** and picks made of any material, as long as the stick has a three dimensional or cut-out design, either letters, people, buildings, etc. Collections of at least 100 sticks are preferred. Sticks *must* advertise a product, place, or service. Generally pays a dime each.

    Edy Chandler
    PO Box 20664
    Houston, TX 77225
       (713) 531-9615 eves

★ **Cocktail shakers** from before 1960 are wanted, especially unusual, chrome, etc. "I buy and sell so contact me with any fine condition, complete shakers and shaker sets you have."

    Stephen Visakay
    PO Box 1517
    West Caldwell, NJ 07007
       (914) 352-5640

WINE & WINE LABELS

★ **Wine.** Old and rare vintages will be purchased by this well known wine dealer but only if you can guarantee the wine has been properly stored, under cool conditions away from light. The fill level and color of a wine need to be inspected prior to purchase. There must be no signs of leakage. Single bottles of rare wines are sometimes purchased, but cases or entire cellars are preferred. Single bottles of pre-prohibition wine found in walls or trunks are purchased for curiosity but are seldom worth more than a few dollars. Free appraisals are available if you supply him with brand name, type of wine, any dates, and what you know of the wine's history.

    Rene Rondeau
    Draper & Esquin Wine Merchants
    655 Davis Street
    San Francisco, CA 94111
    Fax: (415) 397-1851

★ **Wine bottles with embossed oval or circular seals on the shoulder** of the bottle marked with the name and vintage, especially fine wineries and vintages. "The more crude the bottle, the better." No beer, whiskey, or wine bottles that do not have shoulder ovals. Also **pre-WWII paper wine labels** especially 19th century European and pre-prohibition California companies. This expert wine dealer prefers loose labels but will buy important ones still on the bottle. Rene notes that "values are still relatively low for most labels, but they are appreciated as additions to my collection."

    Rene Rondeau
    120 Harbor Drive
    Corte Madera, CA 94925

CORKSCREWS & WINE EPHEMERA

★ **Corkscrews and wine-related artifacts** from before WWII. Buys **wine tasters**, wine funnels, **silver and porcelain wine labels,** silver coolers, coasters, **decanter wagons**, and the like. Will also buy unusual drinking vessels, but **does not want to buy** glassware or cut glass decanters. Corenman is a leading buyer of corkscrews from the 18th and 19th centuries who is seeking mechanical types, bar mounted types, and those with ivory, silver, bone, or pearl handles. Modern post war types are not needed, nor does he want anything that is broken, missing parts, or has repairs. This 25 year veteran expert offers a catalog and wants list. Include your phone number.

    Aaron Corenman
    PO Box 747
    Los Altos, CA 94023
    (415) 948-6174

★ **Corkscrews and wine related items.** Collects hand held and bar mounted corkscrews that are unusual in some way. Also wants wine related items such as wine tasters, **pre-1930 bottles, silver or ceramic bottle labels,** bottle cradles and **buckets,** etc. "I have little interest in paper labels." Make a photocopy of smaller items if possible. Describe the others. "I will answer all letters," says Joe.

 Joe Young
 PO Box 587
 Elgin, IL 60123
  (708) 695-0108

SALOONS

★ **Everything associated with saloons and speakeasies** including **photos of interiors** and exteriors, advertising, saloon equipment catalogs, letterheads, etc. Also trade magazines such as *the National Police Gazette* pre-1919, *Fair Play, Brewers Gazette,* and others.

 Richard Bueschel
 414 North Prospect Manor Ave.
 Mt. Prospect, IL 60065
  (708) 253-0791 eves

★ **Prohibition artifacts of all kinds,** 1919-1933, related to gangster activity in Chicago and environs. Seeks relics from famous speakeasies such as *Colosimo's Cafe, Four Deuces, Red Lantern, Pony Inn, Cotton Club,* and *The Green Mill.* Also pamphlets, posters, and the like from the **Anti-Saloon League, WCTU, the Prohibition Party** and other groups for or against prohibition.

 Michael Graham's Roaring 20's
 345 Cleveland Ave.
 Libertyville, IL 60048
  (708) 362-8531 eves

ANTIQUE & BRIAR PIPES

★ **Antique pipes** including carved meerschaums, opium pipes, water pipes, porcelain figural pipes, early bas-relief and high-relief wood pipes, and selected clays. Ben is a specialist in the literature of tobacco, and buys **books, magazines and pamphlets** on all aspects of tobacco culture and use, in any language, from any period. If you are seeking literature on tobacco, he has the world's largest selection of books on that topic.

> Ben Rapaport, Antiquarian Tobacciana
> 11505 Turnbridge Lane
> Reston, VA 22094
> (703) 435-8133 eves

★ **Antique smoking pipes and pipe parts.** Also buys books and other publications on pipes, tobacco, and related items. Primary interest is in meerschaums, but also buys other antique pipes, especially porcelains, and any historical or unusual items including pipes from any culture. Will purchase complete collections as well as individual pipes. Not interested in damaged pipes or reproductions. Give size (length and width), condition, and all other information you can provide.

> Frank Burla
> 23 West 311 Wedgwood
> Naperville, IL 60540
> (708) 961-0156

★ **Antique meerschaum pipes, carved briar, and fine English briars** by *Charitan, Barling*, or *Frieborg & Treyer.* This 25 year collector also buys **American Indian pipes.**

> Lee Pattison
> 113 North 4th Street
> Olean, NY 14760
> (716) 373-3098

★ **Clay pipes and clay pipe ephemera.** Especially wants figurals, faces, or political clay pipes. Prefers American pipes, but buys others. This author-historian also buys **pipe molds, presses, or anything else involved in the making of clay pipes**. Also wants billheads, letterheads, checks, catalogs, and other advertising before 1950 for any clay pipe maker. Has a particular interest in William Kelman, a Baltimore pipe manufacturer. Generally not interested in plain white clay pipes with no markings or decoration. Please make a photocopy of your items, indicating any markings, and tell what you know about its origin or background. Paul has produced a giant limited edition book on 19th century pipe patents which he sells for $55, and a large reproduction of an 1892 tobacconists' wholesale catalog for $45.

> S. Paul Jung, Jr.
> PO Box 817
> Bel Air, MD 21014
> (401) 676-2194

★ **Name brand "pre-smoked" (used) briar pipes.** Especially wants *Dunhill, Charatan, Barling, Castello* and other top European brands from 1900-1990. Among special wants, Barry lists *Barling* pipes with bent stems in any finish. When describing a pipe, include the brand name, its dimensions, shape, finish and all stampings on the pipe. If you are not familiar with standard pipe shapes, make a photocopy of the pipe and list everything written on the pipe's shank. Barry does not buy antique pipes, meerschaums, or tobacciana. Barry is a popular dealer who produces 6-8 color sales catalogs a year of used briar pipes.

Barry Levin, Levin Pipes International
Route 1   Box 83
Craftsbury, VT 05826
(802) 586-7744

★ **High grade briar pipes.** Brand names of interest include *Dunhill, Charatan, Barling, Comoy, Castello, Caminetto, Sasieni, Preben Holm,* and *Peterson.* "I'll buy them smoked or new, as long as they are in good looking condition, with no uneven surfaces on the rim, no tooth holes in the stem, etc." Wants collections of pipes, but will buy singles. He especially wants *Dunhills* with "ODA" or "ODB" and patent dates marked on the stem and *Peterson* pipes with IRISH FREE STATE or ERIE on the shank. Please, no "drug store pipes" like *Medico, Yellow Bole,* or *Dr. Grabow.* When offering pipes for sale, mention any writing on the pipe and its condition. There are dozens of standard pipe shapes, so if you don't know them, send a photocopy of your pipe.

Marty Pulvers, Sherlock's Haven
4 Embarcadero Center
San Francisco, CA 94111
(415) 362-1405   or   (415) 965-4773

★ **Hookah (water) pipes.** "I'll buy one hose or multiple hose Hookahs made of brass, ivory, or other materials. I'm seeking antique pipes, not head shop items, common glass bongs, and other drug paraphernalia. Please send a picture and information about the pipe's background. Dealers should price your goods but I will make offers for amateurs."

Mark Rivkind
363 Bailey Court
Palm Harbor, FL 34684
(813) 787-1169

IF YOU GO TO YARD SALES LOOKING FOR PROFIT...

Good quality used briar pipes bring from $15 to $150 each and are often found for pennies. As a general rule, only a handful of brands are resellable, with *Dunhill* the favorite.

★ **All high grade tobacco related collectibles:** "We'll consider purchasing tobacco jars, tobacco tins, cigar labels, catalogs, books about tobacco, cigar boxes, posters, advertising, and other tobacco related ephemera. We prefer collections, but buy individual items if value or collectible interest is sufficiently high. We buy for resale. SASE required for an answer; we regret sometimes unavoidably long delays in response. We have no interest in poor condition items, drug store pipes, pipe racks, common tins, magazine ads, flat 50 cigarette tins, cigarette packages after WWII, things covered with cigar bands, or cigar boxes dating after 1940. *The Lucky Strike Story* from 1939 is also common."

> Tobacciana Resources
> 2141 Shoreline Drive
> Shell Beach, CA 93449

★ **Smoking accessories and other objects marked** *Dunhill* including **pipes**, cigarette holders, cigarette **lighters**, pens, etc. This disabled combat vet says, "I prefer items to be sent to me for my offer. I will refund shipping costs if my purchase price is rejected. But I would like to stress *that I do not need common items, junk, or damaged goods.* I buy only for my own collection and will pay fair prices."

> C. Ray Erler
> Box 140 Miles Run Road
> Spring Creek, PA 16436
> (814) 563-7287

★ **Humidors** made of fine glass, china, or copper. Please send a photo of what you have.

> Lee Pattison
> 113 North 4th Street
> Olean, NY 14760
> (716) 373-3098

★ **Metal tobacco jars from before 1900.** This 10 year veteran collector is interested in unusual good condition tobacco jars made of pewter, iron, lead, bronze, brass or silver. No tin cans or ceramics. He requires a clear photograph and a statement of condition. He is available to make appraisals but wants you to price your item. Some research may be in order since these can be in the multiple hundreds of dollars.

> Arthur Anthony, Mystic Valley Foundry
> 14 Horace Street
> Somerville, MA 02143
> (617) 547-1819 weekdays

★ **Snuff boxes** of all types, including early American, Civil War period, and Oriental.

> Eli Hecht
> 19 Evelyn Lane
> Syosset, NY 11791

TOBACCO ADVERTISING

★ **Tin tobacco tags** and tag collections are bought, sold, and traded by this very active collector, who offers a free "suggestion sheet for new collectors" that will teach you all about tin tobacco tags. He also has the remaining stock of Gary Schild's basic book on tobacco tags, and is happy to sell you one for only $10.
>Lee "Tagger Lee" Jacobs
>PO Box 3098
>Colorado Springs, CO 80934

★ **Tin tobacco cans** from before 1940. Wants mint or very fine condition smoking tobacco, chewing tobacco and cigar items only. Save time and effort by sending a photocopy of the top and front of your tin along with a description of the colors and condition. SASE is a must. If you regularly pick or deal, he will send you an informative flyer listing some tins to look for. **Brands not wanted include** *Bond Street, Briggs, Buckingham, Bugle, Dial, Dills Best, Edgeworth, George Washington, Half & Half, Hickory, Holiday, John Middleton, Kentucky Club, Model, Philip Morris, Prince Albert, Red Jacket, Revelations, Sir Walter Raleigh, Stag, Target, Tuxedo, Twin Oaks, Union Leader, Velvet,* and *Willoughby Taylor.* "Flat fifty" cigarette tins such as *Lucky Strike* and *Chesterfield* have no value.
>Tony Hyman
>PO Box 3028
>Pismo Beach, CA 93448
>   (805) 773-6777   Fax: (805) 773-0177

★ *Mail Pouch Tobacco.* "I'll buy anything and everything, in any size and in any condition."
>Mike Boggs
>4022 Farnham
>Dayton, OH 45420
>   (513) 252-4839 eves

★ *Seal of North Carolina* smoking and chewing tobacco advertising. Does not want tin cans, only lithographed ads. Fine condition a must. Photos appreciated.
>Lisa Van Hook
>PO Box 13256
>El Cajon, CA 92022

CIGAR EPHEMERA

★ **Cigar industry ephemera** including boxes, labels, advertising, photographs, counter top lighters, **cigar store figures**, and everything else related to cigar making, selling, and smoking before WWII. Especially want trade directories (1865-1940), books which list cigar and tobacco factories. Want all materials relevant to the **Cigar Maker's International Union** or to **Samuel Gompers**, former CMIU officer. Condition is important. Please photocopy the inside lid. Pays from $5 to $50+ for cigar boxes, with top boxes bringing $400. Send a long SASE for informative priced wants list (which includes a useful list of common boxes). Tony's *Handbook of Cigar Boxes* is available with *Price Guide* for $17. He says, "I have very little interest in bands or items covered with cigar bands, so pay very little for them."
> Tony Hyman
> PO Box 3028
> Pismo Beach, CA 93448
>   (805) 773-6777   Fax: (805) 773-0177

★ **Cigar boxes.** "I'll buy common cardboard and wooden cigar boxes from the 1950's and 60's and 70's. I'm looking for clean usable boxes, not collectibles, and pay from 50¢ to $3 each. Send a self-addressed stamped envelope with a description of the boxes and the numbers involved. It's helpful when you give dimensions."
> Judith Garlinger
> 14225 Garden Road
> Poway, CA 92064
>   (619) 679-9552

★ **Cigar bands** pre-1941 especially older European and Cuban bands or bands with pictures of people, animals, places, etc. No common, current, or damaged bands. Not interested in incomplete sets or large accumulations of similar bands. "I will accept receipt of the bands by mail for an appraisal with an option to purchase. It is next to impossible for a seller to list all the required data. I will not make an offer without actually seeing your bands," says this 40 year veteran.
> Paul Krantz
> 356 Delaware Avenue NE
> Massillon, OH 44646
>   (216) 833-5429

★ **Cigar bands.** Small or moderate collections of inexpensive bands are wanted by a relatively new collector. Your help in developing a collection is appreciated.
> Margo Toth, c/o Up Down Tobacco Shop
> 1550 North Wells Street
> Chicago, IL 60610
>   (312) 337-8505

★ **Cigar band collections** especially U.S. bands prior to 1920. Good or mint condition, only.
Joseph Hruby
1511 Lyndhurst Road
Lyndhurst, OH 44124
(216) 449-0977

★ **Cigar store Indians.** Wants full size wooden or metal figures, especially Punch. Take photos from more than one angle, or phone with the item in front of you.
Gregory "Dr. Z" Zemenick
1350 Kirts #160
Troy, MI 48084
(313) 642-8129 or (313) 244-9426

CIGARETTE PACKS & EPHEMERA

★ **Cigarette packs, tins, and cardboard boxes** from obsolete U.S. brands of cigarettes. No cards, premiums, silks, flat 50's tins, or cigar or tobacco items. Give the series number found on the tax stamp. Dick is president of the Cigarette Pack Collector's Association and editor of *Brandstand*, a monthly newsletter for cigarette pack collectors.
Richard Elliott
61 Searle Street
Georgetown, MA 01833
(508) 352-7377

★ **Cigarette packs of discontinued brands.** Wants U.S. brands only, but will buy tins, boxes, and labels as well as packs.
David Brame
5405 Vicksburg Lane
Durham, NC 27712

★ *Lucky Strike* **collectibles of any kind.** "I'll buy bridge hand cards, celebrity ads, pre-1930 magazine ads, and LS/MFT marked items."
John Van Alstyne
466 South Goodman Street
Rochester, NY 14607

★ *Philip Morris* **ephemera** prior to 1955, including cigarette packs, tins, advertising, signs, stand-ups, matches, buttons, and what have you. This beginning collector does not want reprints, and expects you to price what you wish to sell.
Stuart Morrell
8925 Laureate Lane
Richmond, VA 23236

LIGHTERS & ASHTRAYS

★ **Cigarette lighters.** This lighter historian buys old or new lighters, as well as books, catalogs, brochures, pictures, advertising, parts lists, instruction sheets, boxes, counter displays, etc. Will pay cash, trade for other lighters, or borrow for research. "All material is guaranteed safe return." Send a photocopy of what you have. Jack offers an interesting illustrated catalog of lighters for sale if you send $3.

> Jack Seiderman
> 1631 NW 114th Ave.
> Pembroke Pines, FL 33026
>   (305) 438-0928 phone and fax

★ **Cigarette lighters.** Wants to buy a wide range of quality lighters, including those made by *Ronson, Dunhill, Evans, Thorens, Negbaur, Demley, Touchtip, Art Metal Works, Parker, Cartier, Tiffany,* and *Silent Flame.* He wants cigarette case-lighter combinations, figural lighters, lighters in watches, and other oddities. Buys pocket and table models. Will consider all lighters made from any precious metals: gold, sterling silver or platinum. Send a photocopy or photograph to sell your lighter.

> Richard Weinstein, Authorized Repair Service
> 30 West 57th Street
> New York, NY 10019
>   (212) 541-5618

★ *Zippo* **lighters,** especially with Navy and Marine Corps insignia, including ships, squadrons, submarines, etc. Will buy some imitation *Zippo* lighters from military units. Lighters with ZIPPO in block letters and "PAT.2032695" or PAT.2517191" are desirable as well as outside hinge or square cornered *Zippos* even if plain. Personalized lighters with names or dates or places or unusual decoration are sought, especially those decorated on both front and back. Please send a photocopy of your lighter. "We actively buy all quality lighters and lighter combinations. Our lighter museum is open to the public."

> Jeff Mogilner, Racine & Laramine, Ltd.
> 2737 San Diego Ave.
> San Diego, CA 92110
>   (619) 291-7833   Fax: (619) 297-6653

★ **Ashtrays,** but *only* those in the shape of a person, animal, or thing, such as airplanes, frogs, etc., especially when combined with lighters or cigar cutters. No ordinary glass hotel or bar advertising ashtrays. Most are $5 to $15, but we have paid $100+ for unusual pieces. Send a clear photo or a good sketch. Tire ashtrays are fairly common. Ship yours (if it has the original glass) and we'll pay at least $5 each (more if it's one we need) plus reimburse your postage. Sorry, but no SASE, no answer.

> Tobacciana Resources
> 2141 Shoreline Drive #2
> Shell Beach, CA 93449

TOBACCO & OTHER INSERT CARDS

★ **Cigar and cigarette silks and flannels** and items such as pillows and quilts that have been made from them are wanted by this prestigious quilt dealer. "No junk," she emphasizes, since everything is for sale in her shop. Please take a photograph or make a photocopy of your item. List how many flags and silks and their approximate size.

> Margaret Cavigga
> 8648 Melrose Ave.
> Los Angeles, CA 90069
> (310) 659-3020

★ **Cigarette and other insert cards.** Wants 19th century U.S. cigarette insert cards, especially the *State Seal* series from *August Beck Tobacco* and the *Wellstood Etchings* from *Wm. Kimball*. This 50 year veteran also wants cards from **Brooke-Bond Tea Company, Van Houten Cocoa,** and the **Liebig Meat Extract Company.** He will consider *Liebig* cards in any language, especially menu and calendar cards. Give quantities, and send a photocopy showing samples of the front and back of the cards you have for sale.

> Ron Stevenson
> 4920 Armoury Street
> Niagara Falls, ON
> L2E 1T1 CANADA
> (416) 358-5497

★ **Felts and silks of national flags.** Will pay 10¢ to $1 each depending on rarity.

> Jon Radel
> PO Box 2276
> Reston, VA 22090

★ **Cigarette cards, silks, leathers, and pins** in fine condition. Is particularly interested in the very early U.S. cards. Will also buy some **cigar and cigarette flannels**, except flags. Also buys some **gum, candy,** and other tobacco insert cards, primarily from pre-1920 U.S., but will buy some foreign cards and albums at a lesser price. No silks or flannels that have been sewn together, but will consider other tobacco related items. Will not make offers to dealers.

> Charles Reuter
> 6 Joy Ave.
> Mount Joy, PA 17552

★ **Cigarette and tobacco insert cards and other tobacco related paper.** Wants 19th and early 20th century U.S. **tobacco and cigarette insert cards**, tobacco advertising trade cards, banners, counter stand-ups, hangers, posters, **albums**, giveaways, premiums, and cigarette slide packs. Will pay $25 each and up for many early American trade cards, and $700 for the Marquis of Lorne card issued in 1879. He does not want cigar bands, cigar labels, tobacco caddy labels, reproductions or reprints, matchbooks, badly damaged items, or British or other foreign items. Give the size (vertical then horizontal), the maker, and condition. A photocopy is a good idea. Items must be in at least very good condition.

"I buy only cards that contain one of the following words printed on the card: tobacco, cigarette, cigarros, smoking, cut plug, chewing, long cut, fine cut, scrap cut or navy cut."

    Peter Gilleeny
    36115-76 Rose Drive
    Fruitland Park, FL 34731
       (904) 728-4819

★ **Cigarette and tobacco insert cards, silks, and leathers.** Wants 19th century U.S. items primarily, such as cards by *Allen & Ginter*, but buys many 20th century pieces. Also buys **tobacco advertising trade cards** and tobacco related **match covers.** "Please describe and price, or send on approval. I pay all postage expenses and respond within 48 hours of receipt of your cards. Condition is important as I do not collect trimmed cards, badly creased or otherwise battered items." Does not want flannel flags (often erroneously called "felts").

    William Nielsen
    PO Box 1379
    Brewster, MA 02631
       (508) 896-7389

MATCHCOVERS & BOXES

★ **Matchcover collections,** match boxes, salesman's sample books, pamphlets, and other match industry ephemera. Send brief description and SASE to this active officer in national collecting clubs.

> Bill Retskin
> 16 Forest View Drive
> Asheville, NC 28804
> (704) 254-4487

★ **Paper matchcover collections.** Dave is a long time collector of matchcovers and past president of the Sierra Diablo Club. He collects many different types of matchcovers and buys accumulations and collections. Individual covers are not worth much, but collections of pre-WWII covers are worth your while. Dave is happy to hear from folks with questions or collections.

> David Hampton
> Creekside Mobile Home Park #31
> 16425 Dam Road
> Clearlake, CA 95422
> (707) 995-1411

★ **Matchcovers and match boxes,** foreign or domestic. "I don't want damaged covers generally, but will consider those with *minor* damage if they're from the early 1930's or before." Wants to know approximately how many covers or boxes you have, whether they are U.S. or foreign, whether they are used or unused, whether the covers are in an album or loose, and whether the matches are present. John is Secretary of the Rathkamp Matchcover Society.

> John Williams
> 1359 Surrey Road TH
> Vandalia, OH 45377
> (513) 890-8684

SELLING MATCHCOVERS

Matchcovers are considered "damaged" if they are torn or dirty, or if their striker has been cut off. Collectors do not want your matchcovers if they have been glued, taped, or stapled into a book.

★ **Matchcovers and match boxes.** Wants interesting singles or entire estates. Hiller is a West Coast auctioneer who can handle large collections. The ideal condition for matchcovers is unused, open, with the staples carefully removed. No "grocery store" covers, "Thank You's," or covers not identified as to origin (like *Holiday Inn* covers that don't give a location). His favorite find would be a matchcover from the Lindbergh welcome home dinner, worth in excess of $100.

> Robert Hiller
> 2501 West Sunflower #H5
> Santa Ana, CA 92704
>   (714) 540-8220

★ **Match books and boxes.** "We'll buy match books and boxes if the covers are in good condition and the matches are intact. Please send a photocopy along with your asking price."

> Robert and Susan Cox
> 800 Murray Drive
> El Cajon, CA 92020
>   (619) 447-0800 days

MATCH SAFES

★ **Match safes.** Buys small pocket match safes if they are in unusual shapes or if they advertise tobacco products or outlets. Photocopy what you have, rather than take photographs which show the lighter as a small blur. Prefers you to price your safe(s), understanding that almost all are worth under $100 to him, and ordinary silver match safes that are not figural will only bring $10 to $20 or so depending on the pattern.

> Tony Hyman
> PO Box 3028
> Pismo Beach, CA 93448

★ **Match safes.** "I'll buy figural, fancy, and unusual match safes and related items such as catalogs, advertisements, and ephemera prior to 1915. I'll take one or a collection, but interested in quality items only. I want a detailed description, including the type of material and size, and condition. Asking price helpful. Photograph or photocopy." Nothing later than 1915.

> George Sparacio
> PO Box 791
> Malaga, NJ 08344
>   (609) 694-4167 eves

★ **Wall model match safes made of cast iron.** No others.

> George Fougere
> 67 East Street
> North Grafton, MA 01536
>   (508) 839-2701

EROTICA & GIRLIE MAGAZINES

★ **Erotic art in all forms and formats** including statues, paintings, prints, post cards, photography, and three dimensional objects of all kinds from the days of the Roman empire up to the present. Especially seeks Oriental and European erotic bisque or porcelain figures, revolving lamps from the 50's with pin-up shades, arcade "peep" machines, and photos of all types. Also **original art for pin-up calendars** or illustrations 1920-1970, especially work by **Alberto Vargas** and **George Petty**, but other artists are wanted including Earl Moran, Gil Elvgren, Zoe Mozert, Armstrong, Alk Buell, Al Moore and others. Also Vargas *Esquire* calendars and prints, other calendar pin-ups, and some homemade erotica, including obscene letters written by private parties. Describe condition. A photograph or photocopy is suggested. Include your phone number when you write.

> Charles Martignette
> PO Box 293
> Hallandale, FL 33009
> (305) 454-3474

★ **Erotica of all types, all languages, all eras**, including girlie and pornographic magazines, hard and soft cover books, sex newspapers, typescripts and mimeos, sex comics, original erotic art, films, photos, statuary, and sexually explicit objects of all types.

> C.J. Scheiner
> 275 Linden Blvd. # B2
> Brooklyn, NY 11226
> (718) 469-1089

★ **Erotica of all types,** including nude photos and photo books, original art and paintings, Oriental or European, and three dimensional materials of all sorts.

> Ivan Gilbert, Miran Art & Books
> 2824 Elm Ave.
> Columbus, OH 43209
> (614) 236-0002

★ **Sexy books and magazines of all types,** old or new. "We will buy any sized quantities of all types of girlie magazines including newsstand titles, nudist, hardcore, softcore, and foreign. Will also buy boxes of real photos, picture pages from magazines and books, videos, calendars, and cards." Does not want regular monthly issues of *Playboy* after 1964, *Penthouse* after 1971, or any issues of *Playgirl*. The owner writes, "I'm picky about condition, but will pay freight both ways if you send good items." He will consider sexually oriented photo, movie, motorcycle and fashion magazines.

> The Antiquarian Bookstore
> 1070 Lafayette Road
> Portsmouth, NH 03801

★ **Girlie magazines published by** *Parliament* from the 1950's, 60's, and 70's. Also *Playboy* from the 1950's only. Buys related girlie material, calendars, and paperbacks, but nothing from the 1980's. Fine condition items only. For $3 Warren offers an extensive catalog of girlie magazines for sale.

Warren Nussbaum
29-10 137th Street
Flushing, NY 11354
(718) 886-0558

★ **Girlie magazines published by** *Parliament, Nuance, Marquis* **and** *Briarwood* from 1970 to late 80's. Will pay $1 or $2 each for complete copies or ones with a page or two missing (unsalable elsewhere). Will consider similar "under the counter" publications from the 1970's and pay 25¢ to $1 each. Pays more if cover price $10 or more. "No need to write or call. No embarrassment. Simply ship one or a hundred for immediate cash. OK to ship via Post Office 'Special 4th Class Book Rate' and I'll reimburse." No *Playboy, Oui, Hustler, Penthouse,* or *Gallery.*

Hank Anthony Magazines
PO Box 3001
Shell Beach, CA 93448

★ **Autographed** *Playboy* **playmate ephemera** including covers, gatefolds, and partial pages, but the photo must be from the magazine. Items may be dedicated ("To Bill," etc.) or not, but those without dedications are preferred, and bring from $20 to $50. Autographs of other women (actresses, models, celebrities) who have appeared in *Playboy* will be considered but only if they have signed the cover or photo spread in which they appear. Photocopy what you have.

David Kueragas, McTieg Books
1943 Timberland
Clarks Summit, PA 18411
(717) 587-3429

★ *Playboy* **jigsaw puzzles** and other *Playboy* ephemera is wanted, but only a select list of items: puzzles (preferably in their original unopened boxes), posters, playing cards, square yellow ashtrays, foreign issues of the magazine, and "unique novelties." No orange ashtrays, glasses, mugs, or calendars later than 1960, and "I do not want copies of the U.S. edition of *Playboy* magazine except for issues #1, #2, or #3."

David Kueragas, McTieg Books
1943 Timberland
Clarks Summit, PA 18411
(717) 587-3429

★ **Alberto Vargas illustrations,** 1918-1960. "I'll buy magazine covers, Zigfield Follies posters, and other Vargas art depicting nudes, but only his work before he began drawing for *Playboy*." He does not want *Esquire* calendars unless they have their original jackets and is not interested in any of Vargas's *Playboy* art.

    David Kueragas, McTieg Books
    1943 Timberland
    Clarks Summit, PA 18411
        (717) 587-3429

★ **Prostitution in the U.S.** and around the world. He buys a wide variety of ephemera from anywhere, but is particularly interested in Nevada. What have you?

    Douglas McDonald
    PO Box 20443
    Reno, NV 89515

★ **Burlesque, strippers, and sexy dances.** Buys photos, posters, signs and any unusual items related to these skinful arts. Likes to find 3-D picture books and unusual pictorial items, especially art originals..

    Charles Martignette
    PO Box 293
    Hallandale, FL 33009
        (305) 454-3474

★ **Condom (prophylactic)** and **feminine hygiene** vending equipment, fine condition condom tins (the older and more colorful the better), and advertising relating to condoms or prophylactics, especially before 1960. Will buy single items or large lots.

    Mr. Condom
    1725 Lincoln Ave.
    Dubuque, IA 52001
        (319) 556-3633

GAMBLING & CARD PLAYING

★ **Clay, ivory, or mother-of-pearl gambling chips** and selected other memorabilia. No plain, paper, or interlocking chips. Send a sample, rubbing or photocopy. Tell how many chips of each color. Dale wrote *Antique Gambling Chips*, available with a price guide for $20.

> Dale Seymour, Past Pleasures
> PO Box 50863
> Palo Alto, CA 94303

★ **Poker chips and other gambling markers** made of ivory or mother-of-pearl with scrimshawed designs. Designs can be numbers, animals, birds, or other patterns and figures. Prices start at $10 and up. Especially desired are chips or markers inscribed with the words DEALER, YOUR DEAL, or picturing an Indian or a deer. These are worth $300 up depending on size, condition, and design. Does not want chips made of plastic, paper, clay, metal, rubber, or any mass production process. Send a photocopy of the chips you have to sell. If the chips are in a rack, describe the rack and indicate whether any chips appear to be missing. Note any maker's name. Strongly warns, "Do not clean your chips! Send a photocopy of your chip[s] because I must give instructions how to pack these for shipment, as quality chips are very fragile."

> Bryan Eggers
> PO Box 3491
> Westlake Village, CA 91359
>   (805) 373-1586

★ **Antique decks of playing cards** are wanted, complete with joker and box or wrapper. Wants decks before 1930, identifiable because they are 2 1/2" wide (with no box) and 2 5/8" wide if boxed. Robert is the founder of a club for antique playing card collectors, and wants new complete decks with those dimensions, but "might be interested" in open decks. Make a photocopy of the back of one card and the face of the Joker and the Ace of spades.

> Robert Harrison
> 582 Woodlawn Ave.
> Glencoe, IL 60022
>   (708) 835-0842

★ **Unusual playing cards, poker chips, and gambling devices and memorabilia.** All early **books and paper ephemera** about cards or gambling are wanted but no coin operated machines. He asks you to photocopy the Joker and the Ace of spades, and indicate whether the box is present. "Bridge size cards with picture backs are usually worthless" to this 25 year dealer who offers an illustrated catalog of playing cards.

> Gene Hochman
> 10086-B Andrea Lane
> Boynton Beach, FL 33437

★ **Anything concerning playing cards and card games.** Unusual playing cards including transformation cards, non-standard decks, and decks with a different picture on the face of each card. Also single cards in quantity with colorful backs and unusual Jokers, Aces or court cards. Also **books, magazines**, and other items on the games of contract bridge, auction bridge, and whist. Will consider early or limited edition books on other card games as well as plates, figurines, and other artwork depicting card playing. Will pay $100 up for *Royal Bayreuth* china in the pattern called "Devil and the Cards." Photocopies almost essential. Include an SASE to get an answer.
> Bill Sachen
> 927 Grand Ave.
> Waukegan, IL 60085
> (708) 662-7204

★ **Bingo cages** and other interesting and early items or ephemera related to the game of bingo. When describing, include everything written on the item. For paper items, make a photocopy. No children's games. Also interested in gambling equipment, pre-1940 **slot machines**, and mechanical **punchboards**. A photo is required of all gambling items.
> Roger Snowden
> PO Box 527
> Vashon, WA 98070
> (800) 327-6437 or (206) 463-5656

★ **Bridge tallies.** Please send a photocopy of any early bridge tallies.
> Fran Van Vynckt
> 7412 Monroe Ave.
> Hammond, IN 46324

★ **All types of lottery tickets** from the 1600's to the present, from any country. 18th and 19th century tickets are worth $3-$5 up depending on the country and age. Modern scratch off tickets newer than 1964 normally bring 5¢ each, but smaller less populated states and smaller games fetch more. Complete sets or series are desirable and also worth more. Non-negotiable "sample void" scratch off tickets issued to teach people how to play games are of particular interest. Condition is important; bends, tears or damage make 20th century tickets worthless. Photocopy preferred.
> Karen Lea Rose
> 4420 Wisconsin Ave.
> Tampa, FL 33616

★ **Scratch off type lottery tickets.** "I'll buy instant rub-off lottery tickets from the 1970's and 1980's."
> Bill Pasquino
> 1824 Lyndon Ave.
> Lancaster, PA 17602

Americana

When you think of "America," what images come to mind? Flags, politicians and elections, fireworks, cowboys, Indians, Boy Scouts, church? Or are your thoughts of more personal remembrances? Collectors call these memories of our country, "Americana."

These relics are uniquely American, widely collected, and with a good chance of raising money for you.

It seems appropriate to follow the "Vices" with a section on religious collectibles, traditionally ignored by collectors. If the idea that the vices are so collectible is offensive, take heart. Recent interest in Russian icons and Latin Santos is causing some people to reexamine other religious items as collectibles. This book store edition of my Where To Sell series has the most buyers of religious items ever. Values of most religious items remain modest, except for artistic pieces made from precious metals or gemstones, but collectors help to preserve these sacred treasures, and see they get proper care and respect.

Cowboy artifacts and the old West is one focus of this section. The collectors and dealers in this field are usually fans of the old West, interested in what cowboys wore and how they lived, and glad to preserve Western artifacts. A set of fancy California made spurs brought $5,000 recently, so it sounds like time to check your tack room.

Movie cowboys are also popular. Hoppy, Roy, Gene, Lash, the Lone Ranger and all the other kings of the range during the 1930's, 40's and 50's are eagerly sought by collectors, but you'll find their buyers listed with Pop Culture. Be sure to look, since Hoppy lunch boxes bring over $100, and they're not the most valuable of the items.

If you own any authentic American Indian items purchased prior to 1940, caution is in order. Tourist trade pottery is of little interest, but all other Indian items require expert examination. Over the years, values have steadily increased with dramatic prices paid for pre-1910 American Indian art, now popular nationwide. A grandfather's trunk held a bonanza of nearly $500,000 worth of Indian clothing for an Eastern couple... because they sold it the right buyers. And to think, they came close to selling it for $500! Even simple Items like arrowheads require an expert's eye to filter "buck stuff" from that worth $100. A cigar box full of arrowheads rescued from the city dump brought an Ohio teen a cool $10,000. If your arrowhead collection was assembled before WWII, the odds are 50-50 you'll have some pieces worth $20 each or more. Good photos are almost essential when selling Indian goods.

Most Scouting items are fairly inexpensive, a few dollars or so, but very early or very rare Scouting badges and medals are highly prized, with a few top national jamboree items bringing $500 to $1,000. Rummaging in those old trunks and closets could turn up a gem or two as well. Photocopies are appreciated by most buyers.

Whether gleaning your own stuff or shopping for profit, watch for anything old from our nation's heritage. You won't find these items often at house sales, but I know of a valuable Indian rug from the mid 19th century that sold for $5 at New York farmhouse. Hundreds of newspapers have carried the story of a helpful neighbor who was given a wooden "letter opener" as a thank you by a neighbor she had helped. It turned out to be an $18,000 Indian dagger.

There's still plenty of good stuff to be found by you!

RELIGIOUS ITEMS

★ **Crucifixes, medals, Stars of David, and other symbols from any religion.** Wants a wide variety of items...interesting, unusual, precious, sentimental...anything you want preserved or displayed. Donated crosses and other items are preserved with your family name or other identification of your choice. Religious items don't bring much money, but this avid collector is looking for all the religious artifacts he can find and afford. He buys postcards decorated with crosses. He's looking for an "angel" to subsidize a museum of religious artifacts and symbols. Send a stamped self-addressed envelope if you'd like an offer, response to a donation, an answer to a question regarding crosses, or simply more information about his goals.

Ernie Reda
3997 Latimer Ave.
San Jose, CA 95130

★ **Catholic First Communion books.** "I'll buy small celluloid, mother-of-pearl, or ivory First Communion books and Catholic missals from the late 1800's to 1950, although the earlier ones are preferred. As long as the condition is near mint, will buy them in any language. Send photo and description with your asking price."

Monica Murphy, Savannah's Antiques
1419 Fern
New Orleans, LA 70118
(504) 866-2221

★ **Catholic holy cards (religious cards) from pre-1940.** Holy cards are small decorated cards similar to trade cards, depicting various religious figures and events, usually beautifully printed. Wants steel engravings and other quality pieces "the older the better." Hand made ones particularly sought. "I do take donations of cards and don't resell. Some of my best cards came from seniors who treasured them for ages." Photocopy what you have. If you have large lots of pre-1940 cards, you may ship on approval without calling first.

"People give cards to me because they know I'll preserve and take care of them, and give them the proper respect."

Mary Jo O'Neil
618 Riversedge Court
Mishawaka, IN 46544
(219) 259-0357

★ **Catholic art calendars, 1938-1969.** "Over $100 paid for certain issues. No *Messenger* calendars, please." SASE for more information.

Joe Speciale
2353 Pruneridge Avenue #2
Santa Clara, CA 95050

★ **Catholic religious paper** such as **holy cards**, prayer cards, Infant of Prague materials, and illustrated **prayer books**, religious school books, and visual aids, as long as they are before 1963. He does not want Bibles, postcards, items not made of paper, items dating from after 1963, or paper goods that are not illustrated. Please, no Old Testament pictures or stories. Give the age, description, publisher, and condition. A photocopy is helpful.

  Joe Flynn, Wah To Wah Park
  PO Box 1473
  Greenwood Lake, NY 10925
  (914) 477-9373

★ **Jewish ephemera** including business-related items such as signs, advertising, letterheads, and the like, but also photos, family documents, books, cookbooks, tins, bottles, postcards, Judaica, *chatchkelas*, and what have you. Also interested in **anti-Semetic material**. Please send a photocopy of what you have.

  Peter Schweitzer
  5 East 22nd Street Apt. 21-A
  New York, NY 10010
  (212) 677-6939

★ **Israel, Palestine, and the Holocaust.** What have you? It could be worth your time to make an inquiry.

  Harvey Dolin
  5 Beekman Street #406
  New York, NY 10038

★ **New Testaments** before 1820 in any language printed anywhere in the world. They may be in any condition. Also interested in any and all **books with the words "Holy Spirit" in the title.** "You may ship for an offer and I will respond within three days."

  Miles Eisele
  4417 Chase Park Court
  Annandale, VA 22003
  (703) 642-6639

★ **Sacred books, including Bibles before 1800, Books of Common Prayer, The Koran**, and other unusual, beautiful or early sacred book.

  Ron Lieberman, Family Album
  Route 1 Box 42
  Glen Rock, PA 17327
  (717) 235-2134

★ **Paper ephemera about Mormons,** pre-1900.

  Warren Anderson
  PO Box 100
  Cedar City, UT 84720

★ **Russian religious icons,** especially those with silver covers. Also **enameled bronze crosses** (wall size), icon lamps (*lampadki*) especially with "cut to clear" glass, and other pre-revolutionary religious items. Prices depend upon rarity, authenticity, and condition. Wants a full description but a good clean color photo is probably necessary. Phone to discuss your piece; he'll probably request that you ship for inspection and will tell you how to best ship. What you know of the item's history could be important.
> David Speck
> 35 Franklin Street
> Auburn, NY 13021
>   (315) 252-8566 eves

★ **Shaker artifacts and ephemera.** "I specialize in Shaker books, pamphlets, photographs, and ephemera. I also buy and sell small Shaker artifacts such as bottles, sewing boxes, baskets, seed boxes, and the like. Four times a year, I publish a catalog of Shaker items for sale. If you have something to sell me, generally all I need is a photo or photocopy to come to a decision."
> Scott DeWolfe
> PO Box 1283
> Saco, ME 04072
>   (207) 282-4773

★ **Watchtower Society publications and ephemera** including *Golden Age, Consolation,* and *Awake* magazines, *Millennial Dawn* books, *Watchtower* books before 1927, items related to **Pastor Russell**, and any pre-1940 Jehovah's Witness literature.
> Mike Castro
> PO Box 2817
> Providence, RI 02907

★ **Phrenology items** including heads showing trait lines, or numbered zones on the head, posters, and wall hangings. No books.
> Donald Gorlick
> PO Box 24541
> Seattle, WA 98124
>   (206) 824-0508

★ **Mystical arts, crystal balls, tarot cards,** and ephemera related to astrology, spiritualism, pyramids, palmistry, Yoga, numerology, psychic research, Atlantis, Tibet, UFO's and the like.
> Dennis Whelan
> PO Box 170
> Lakeview, AR 72642

INDIAN ARTIFACTS

★ **Antique American Indian and Eskimo items.** "I'll buy quality items made by Indians and Eskimos: baskets, bead work, quill work, pottery, clothing, weapons, old Navajo rugs, and blankets. If you've got a 16 foot long birch bark canoe I'll buy that too. I don't buy any Indian jewelry, books, or modern items purchased ten years ago at a trading post on the Interstate." A photo is a must, and please list dimensions and any flaws the piece has in your first letter. Dealers price your goods as he makes offers to amateur sellers only. Answers inquiries promptly.

> Barry Friedman
> 22725 Garzota Drive
> Valencia, CA 91355
> (805) 296-2318

★ **Indian artifacts** including arrowheads, stone axes, celts, pipes, flint, ceremonial pieces, bannerstones, birdstones, baskets, beaded items, pottery, rugs, blankets, masks, wooden bowls, and any other Indian related items. He will pay high prices ($500-$1,000) for ancient birdstones he can use for his own collection. Please list what you have and make a drawing or photocopy, giving all measurements. Include your home and work phone numbers. This 40 year veteran holds four to six auctions a year of Indian artifacts and is always in the market for good items.

> Jan Sorgenfrei
> 10040 State Road 224 West
> Findlay, OH 45840
> (419) 422-8531 days and (419) 384-3730 eves

★ **Museum quality American Indian relics.** "I'll buy fine baskets, pre-1900 Plains bead work, quill work, weapons, Southwestern pots, pre-1950 jewelry, Kachinas, Navajo blankets and rugs, Northwest Coast masks and carvings, Eskimo objects, old photos of Indians, and more. Some of these items can be worth $10,000 or more." Dan does not want anything modern, small pots, or reproductions of early work.

> Daniel Brown
> PO Box 149
> Davenport, CA 95017
> (408) 426-0134

★ **Hopi and Zuni Pueblo Kachina dolls.** "I especially want those made between 1900 and 1940. Other Indian items, dance wands, costume parts, pottery, baskets, and jewelry from Southwest Indians are also of interest." Kachina dolls can range in value from $100 to $5,000 or more, but there are many fake Kachinas. "An expert can tell the difference." He'll need a photo and all background information.

> John C. Hill
> 6990 East Main
> Scottsdale, AZ 85251
> (602) 946-2910

★ **Indian baskets, pottery and other art** are wanted by this nationally known folk art expert.
Louis Picek
PO Box 340
West Branch, IA 52358

★ **Indian stone animal effigy pipes.** He has no interest in reproductions, but says he'll to pay from $100 to as much as $10,000 for well documented pipes. Photos are advisable.
Mel Rosenthal
507 South Maryland Ave.
Wilmington, DE 19804

★ **North and South American Indian rugs** and weavings are sought by this major rug dealer. Color photo and dimensions, please.
Renate Halpern, Halpern Galleries
325 East 79th Street
New York, NY 10021

★ **American Indian and Eskimo,** including art, rugs, crafts, baskets, pottery, weapons, and clothing, especially old beaded buckskin moccasins. The museum does not buy modern Indian items. Prefers a color photo be sent with your inquiry. Prefers you price what you have to sell, but "our appraiser will suggest a value after examination."
Lynn Munger, Potawatomi Museum
PO Box 631
Fremont, IN 46737
(219) 833-4700

★ **Indian totems and carvings** from before 1950, including good quality items made for the tourist trade. Please provide a physical description, noting all obvious signs of damage. If you know the history of the ownership of the item, please give that information as well. Photos are helpful.
Edwin Snyder
PO Box 156
Lancaster, KY 40444
(606) 792-4816 eves

COWBOY ARTIFACTS

★ **Cowboy equipment and regalia** including:
    Spurs of all type except English and new military. Especially wants unusual spurs that are silver and maker marked;
    Cuffs made of leather, chaps, hats, scarves, and fancy boots;
    Western saddles, pre-1920, all types if maker marked, including black military McClellan saddles;
    Saddle bags with maker's marks;
    Riatas, quirts, and **bridles** that are marked, tooled, or carved;
    Horse bits more than 50 years old with silver mounts or inlay; some plain and/or foreign bought; inquire about any old bit;
    Prison made spurs, horse bits, quirts, belts, and lead ropes;
    Catalogs for saddle makers pre-1936;
    Photographs of old cowboy scenes;
    Advertising related to the frontier, especially watch fobs;
    Movie posters of cowboy movies;
    Books by Will James.
Especially wants marked spurs authenticated as having been made for some well known personality. Does not want anything made in the last 25 years or made in the Far East. In your description, make certain to describe all marks. Give dimensions and mention all damage or repairs. He prefers if you set the price, but will make offers to amateur sellers. No guns! Will buy single items or collections for resale.
    Lee Jacobs
    PO Box 3098
    Colorado Springs, CO 80934
        (719) 473-7101

★ **Cowboy clothing, gear, artifacts** and **ephemera.** Wants everything associated with both working cowboys and badmen and peace officers: clothing, trail maps and brand books, wanted posters, "historically important letters," photos of cowboys, badmen, and peace officers. Has strong interest in **Samuel Colt, Sam Houston** and **Benito Juarez.**
    Johnny Spellman
    10806 North Lamar
    Austin, TX 78753
        (512) 836-2889 days or (512) 258-6910 eves

★ **Antique cowboy regalia** such as chaps, holsters, belts, badges, saddles, hats, boots, and lassos. Also buys *Colt* and *Winchester* guns and rifles pre-1900. No reproductions or fakes. Wants to know where you got your item(s). You must include photo and your asking price, and will be expected to ship for inspection. He does not make offers.
    Pierre Bovis
    The Az-Tex Cowboy Trading Co.
    PO Box 460
    Tombstone, AZ 85638
        (602) 457-3359

POLITICS & POLITICAL SYMBOLS

★ **Presidential campaign memorabilia made of paper or cloth,** from any campaign before 1976. *All* candidates are wanted including third party or those who lost in primaries, but **Lincoln** is a particular favorite. Small paper items from the 19th century are generally worth from $5-$15 and include pamphlets, posters, tickets, sample ballots, and cards of any kind. Cloth items such as bandanas, flags, ties, ribbons, and handkerchiefs are wanted, as long as they were used in a presidential campaign. He'll pay $75-$250 for bandanas picturing candidates. He does not buy buttons, bumper stickers, or daily newspapers, and prefers to buy piles of paper rather than single pieces, unless the items are early or unusual. When writing to him, indicate the candidate, the year (if you know), the size, any slogans or messages, and what's pictured.

Charles Hatfield
1411 South State Street
Springfield, IL 62704

★ **Election memorabilia of all types, 1780-1960,** for resale, especially higher quality items (not paper). Wants china, ribbons, plates, mirrors, clocks, boxes, glass, paintings, textiles, etc., that are **political or patriotic in content.** "I'll pay from $500-$5,000 for small historical medallions with pewter rims and lithographed portraits of military and political figures." Rex is not interested in doing free appraisals. Please don't contact him unless you want to *sell.*

Rex Stark, Auctioneer
49 Wethersfield Road
Bellingham, MA 02019
(508) 966-0994

★ **Presidential memorabilia** including glass, china, campaign buttons and ribbons, posters, **White House gift items,** inauguration medals, invitations, Xmas cards, etc. Will pay $4,000 for a mint condition Theodore Roosevelt inaugural medal. Author of *Collectors Guide to Presidential Inaugural Medals and Memorabilia* available for $8.95.

H. Joseph Levine
6550-I Little River Turnpike
Alexandria, VA 22312
(703) 354-5454

★ **Political buttons, tokens, and ribbons from any election before 1925.** From before 1910, he will buy tokens, medals, ribbons, glass, china, paper, canes, figures, silks, etc. The only buttons after 1925 that he wants are those that catalog for more than $20 in Ted Hake's book on political buttons. Consignments to his auction are invited.

Rich Hartzog, World Exonumia
PO Box 4143 BFT
Rockford, IL 61110
(815) 226-0771

★ **Political campaign items of all kinds.** "I'll buy buttons, badges, ribbons, banners, tintypes, portrait flags, and three dimensional objects. Unless unusual, generally not interested in items later than the election of 1960, with top priority given to better 19th century items, especially those associated with **Abraham Lincoln** and his contemporaries in the Civil War period." This 25 year veteran dealer /collector is not interested in buttons later than 1960 or in commemorative items that were not actually issued as part of a campaign. The one exception is **political quilt**s, which he does buy. A photocopy or photo is of "great help."

> Cary Demont
> PO Box 19312
> Minneapolis, MN 55419
> (612) 922-1617

★ **Presidential political items of all sorts.** Will buy buttons, banners, ribbons, and paper material, especially from the candidates of the 1920's, Coolidge, Davis, Harding, LaFollette, Cox, Hoover, Smith, and Debs, with a strong interest in **Calvin Coolidge**. Please don't send him any *Kleenex* buttons, other reproductions, or anything in poor condition. This well known collector and dealer has been active for nearly 30 years. He requests a photocopy and thorough description. The price you'd like is appreciated but "will make offer if you have no idea of an item's value."

> Larry L. Krug, Americana Resources
> 18222 Flower Hill Way #299
> Gaithersburg, MD 20879
> (301) 926-8663

★ **Victoria Woodhull memorabilia.** Anything in any condition is wanted about this spiritualist, feminist, and Presidential candidate, from 1865 to her leaving for England in 1877. Wants portraits, photos, programs, flyers, handbills, booklets, personal effects, and any newspaper or magazine stories by or about her that were written prior to 1900. Materials from **her 1872 Presidential campaign for the Equal Rights Party** are especially sought.

> Ronald Lowden, Jr.
> 314 Chestnut Ave.
> Narberth, PA 19072
> (215) 667-0257 anytime

★ **Women's suffrage and political campaign** items, especially 19th century buttons, ribbons, posters, and pennants.

> Ken Florey
> 153 Haverford
> Hamden, CT 06517
> (203) 248-1233

★ **Abraham Lincoln presidential campaign memorabilia** including items related to his various opponents: Douglas, Bell, Breckinridge, McClellan, and Jefferson Davis. Will buy flags, banners, posters, broadsides, tokens, ribbons, and photographic badges. A photographic Lincoln/Johnson badge would be worth "several thousand dollars" to this 27 year veteran collector/dealer. He does not want books, memorial items or commemoratives of any sort. "I'll only buy items issued during an election or for Lincoln's two inaugurations." He wants a photocopy or photo, or a sketch with dimensions and information about material, inscriptions, and all defects. "I require to see the item before I buy it."
> Donald Ackerman
> 33 Kossuth Street
> Wallington, NJ 07057

★ **William Jennings Bryan memorabilia** including campaign items, letters, banners, autographs, newspapers, photos, items owned by him, etc. Also books by or about Bryan.
> Francis Moul, Wordsmith Books & Art
> PO Box 81066
> Lincoln, NE 68501
> (402) 477-2665

★ **William Jennings Bryan and Tom Dewey memorabilia.**
> Rich Hartzog, World Exonumia
> Box 4143 BFT
> Rockford, IL 61110
> (815) 226-0771

★ **Personal and other memorabilia related to Harding, Coolidge, Hoover, FDR** and **Al Smith**. Documentation will be requested.
> Michael Graham's Roaring 20's
> 345 Cleveland Ave.
> Libertyville, IL 60048
> (708) 362-4808 days

★ **Illinois and Chicago politicians of the 1920's.** Wants posters, pamphlets, photographs, and buttons from Chicago politicians of the prohibition era such as Mayors William Thompson, William Dever, and Anton Cermak. Also Illinois Governor Len Small, US Senator Charles Deneen, and Cook County States Attorney Robert Crowe. Especially wants items related to prohibition and gangsters. If offering personal items, documentation will be requested.
> Michael Graham's Roaring 20's
> 345 Cleveland Ave.
> Libertyville, IL 60048
> (708) 362-4808 days

★ **Richard M. Nixon collectibles.** "I'll buy campaign collectibles, anti-Nixon items, and Watergate related ephemera including, but not limited to, buttons, jewelry, textiles, glassware, medals, coins, games, novelties, pens & pencils, pocket knives, keychains, stamps, stickers, caricatures, matchbooks, postcards, puzzles, headgear…almost anything picturing or referring to Nixon." He does not want magazines, posters, bumper stickers, and newspapers. He is interested in Nixon's entire history as a public figure. Please send a "crisp photocopy or photo of the item along with a description of all flaws such as foxing, chips, scratches, fading, etc." Include the price you'd like (although he will make offers to amateurs) and an SASE if you want photos returned. His book on Nixon collectibles may be ordered for $60 postpaid.

    Eldon Almquist
    975 Maunawili Circle
    Kailua, HI 96734
      (808) 262-9837 eves

★ **Gubernatorial (governor) or U.S. Senate race political buttons.** "I'll pay $25-$50 each for those I can use. Please send a photocopy or good description."

    Dave Quintin
    PO Box 800861
    Dallas, TX 75380

★ **Tennessee political campaigns.** "I'll buy buttons, posters, post-cards, and other souvenirs of Tennessee political campaigns, especially for governor." Also buys U.S. presidential campaign items. Send photo-copies and an SASE, please.

    Peggy Dillard
    PO Box 210904
    Nashville, TN 37221
      (615) 646-1605

★ **North and South Carolina political buttons and ephemera** with a special interest in locating items from Taft's 1909 visit to Charlotte. Asks that you photocopy and describe all defects.

    Lew Powell
    700 East Park Ave.
    Charlotte, NC 28203
      (704) 358-5229 or (704) 334-0902

★ **Canadian election memorabilia,** pin back buttons and badges from political campaigns before 1965, especially material on John MacDonald and Wilfred Laurier. Small items may be sent on approval. If Mike does not buy them, he will reimburse your postage.

    Michael Rice
    PO Box 286
    Saanichton, BC
    V0S 1M0 CANADA

★ **American flags.** "I'll buy cloth hand held size (smaller than 3') American flags with 47 stars, 43 stars, and all others with less than 39 stars. I especially want unusual star patterns and flags with advertising printed on them. Larger ones will be considered. Description should include the size, condition, and star pattern. No repros or pictures of flags."
Mark Sutton
2035 St. Andrews Circle
Carmel, IN 46032
   (317) 844-5648

★ **Flags.** Wants European, African, and all other obsolete foreign or domestic flags. Also buys some current U.S. state flags and all city flags. "I will consider just about any real flag, military, yachting, naval, or other, as long as it is priced appropriately, but I don't want 48 star flags or decorative banners and other tricolor bunting." Although rare flags exist, most flags bring $5 to $100. To sell your flag, provide dimensions, a guess at the material, any info about the flag's history, photo or sketch. As a point of interest, he notes, "Family oral history to the contrary, 13 star flags seldom date from the Revolution. Most were Centennial souvenirs dating from 1876, or they were Naval flags."
Jon Radel
PO Box 2276
Reston, VA 22090

★ **Statue of Liberty.** Wants French bronzes of the statue, books from before 1890, advertising items depicting or satirizing the statue, tin signs or containers, bottles, thimbles, lamps, medals and tokens, and other 19th century items related to Liberty or sculptor **Auguste Bartholdi**. Wants U.S. Committee 6" or 12" pot metal models sold to raise money for the pedestal and will pay $300 to $1,000. Wants early ones only. Photo or photocopy requested. Not interested in postcards or centennial items.
Mike Brooks
7335 Skyline
Oakland, CA 94611
   (510) 339-1751

★ **Statue of Liberty items.** What have you? Send a photo or photocopy of what you have to this well known stamp dealer.
Harvey Dolin & Company
5 Beekman Street #406
New York, NY 10038

★ **White House memorabilia** including china, dinnerware, silverware, jewelry, and anything else that authentically came from the White House, including pieces of the building itself.
Paul Hartunian
127-B East Bradford Ave.
Cedar Grove, NJ 07009
   (201) 857-7275

BOY SCOUT MEMORABILIA

★ **Boy Scout memorabilia and patches,** especially World Jamboree items pre-1951, National Jamboree patches pre-1940, Order of the Arrow items pre-1940 and anything "old and rare." Pays $1,000 each for 1924 World Jamboree patch or Lodge 219 Order of the Arrow pocket flap. Other World and National events can be worth $100 each. Ron has a reputation for paying very well for Scouting items, and encourages you to "comparison shop for prices before you sell."
>Ron Aldridge
>14908 Knollview
>Dallas, TX 75248
>(214) 239-3574

★ **Boy Scout, Girl Scout** and **Lone Scout items**, especially early:
>**Uniforms, badges**, and **pins**. Patches with WWW from Order of the Arrow lodges, and badges from Senior Scout & Explorer groups particularly needed;
>**Rank and Honor medals**: lifesaving medals, medals for war service, Eagle and Golden Eaglet medals, Ace, Ranger, Silver, and Quartermaster medals, and World Jamboree medals. Note: some medals are worth $500+;
>Soft and composition **Girl Scout dolls** of various sizes if reasonably complete. *Kenner Steve Scout* dolls from 1975, if mint in original box. All *Steve Scout* accessories, such as a summer uniform;
>**Scout toys and games**, including figures, board games, etc.;
>Scout table model *Bakelite* radios from the late 1930's, in various colors;
>Official **books and other literature** including manuals and magazines before 1930, merit badge pamphlets and Cub Scout literature from before 1940, and "all Air Scout stuff;"
>**Historical items** related to founders of Scouting, including Baden-Powell, Juliette Low, Seton, Beard, West, Boyce, and Robinson.

When you are offering things to him for sale, he reminds "a photocopy is worth 1,000 words."
>Cal Holden
>257 Church Street
>Doylestown, OH 44230
>(216) 658-2793

★ **Boy Scout memorabilia** from before 1960. "I will buy both official and semi-official items, including toys, card games, pins, patches and uniforms, especially National and International events. Handbooks before 1940 are wanted as are books by Baden-Powell, J. West, E.T. Seton, Dan Beard and other Scouting authors." Sayers wrote *Value Guide to Scouting Collectables*. Sayers buys outright or sells on consignment.
Rolland Sayers
PO Box 629
Brevand, NC 28712

★ **Boy Scout items of all sorts** including toys, posters, photos, badges, Order of the Arrow, and magazines. Wanted books include the *Boy Scout Handbook* pre-1940, *Patrol Leader Handbook* pre-1945, and many other pre-1945 fiction and non-fiction Scouting books including *Every Boy's Library* with original dust jackets. Buys adult, Cub, and Air Scout uniforms pre-1940 and all pins and medals before 1960. Offers up to $750 for a 1924 World Jamboree patch. He is also interested in hearing from you about any items from the founders of Scouting.
Doug Bearce
PO Box 4742
Salem, OR 97302
(503) 399-9872

★ **Boy Scout items,** patches, pins, medals, Jamboree souvenirs, neckerchiefs with patches, Eagle awards, and Order of the Arrow patches (marked O.A., Lodge, or W.W.W.). "I'll pay from $1 to $100 for most items, though some very scarce items may bring $1,000 or more. I need a photocopy, although you may send what you have for sale to me and if we can't agree on a fair price, I will return and pay shipping costs both ways." He does not want handbooks printed after 1915, first aid kits, neckerchief slides, belt buckles, knapsacks, tents, or camping gear.
Greg Souchik
PO Box 133
Custer City, PA 16725
(814) 362-2642 Fax: (814) 362-7356

★ **Scouting coins, medallions, wooden nickels** and other exonumia (coins that aren't money). He even buys Scouting paper money! These have been issued by Troops and events all over the world. Rudy's $10 book, *Scouting Exonumia* is the guide used by collectors everywhere. For a free appraisal, describe (or make a rubbing or photocopy of) both sides of the coin. Tell the material from which it's made. Give the diameter. If you know the country and date, tell him.
Rudy Dioszegi
3307 126th Street East
Burnsville, MN 55337
(612) 890-6336 Fax: (612) 882-8332

GIRL SCOUT MEMORABILIA

★ **Girl Scout memorabilia.** "Try me for anything that says or means Girl Scout, including calendars, magazines, story books, sheet music, records, song books, membership cards, Senior Round-Up items, badge sashes, loose badges, pins, postcards, first day covers, etc." She especially wants very old items, such as 1913 blue uniforms, 1914 khaki uniform with bugle and drums, 1916 uniform with bloomers, pre-1920 adult uniforms, Mariner and Wing Scout items, Senior Girl Scout items, all pre-1938 items, World's Fair items, war time items, and pre-1945 items from Camp Edith Macy, Our Chalet, and Our Ark. Tell her what you have, and its date if possible. Make certain to note condition and whether anything is missing. Asking price is appreciated. Since she will buy so many different items, it is important to note she does not want the following: handbooks from after 1918, 1940's green covert uniform, 1960's green cotton or Dacron Brownie and Intermediate uniforms, 1960's forest green two piece senior uniform, 1970's or 80's uniforms, any mess kits, canteens, back packs, sleeping bags, and other big camping gear after 1925.
>   Phyllis Palm
>   PO Box 5272
>   Mt. Carmel, CT 06518

★ **Girl Scout memorabilia.** Wants to buy pre-1960 catalogs, post-cards, magazines, uniforms, handbooks 1912-1920, equipment, and other items. Send a list of what you have along with a photo or photocopy. Do not send items without prior arrangement.
>   Jerry King
>   8429 Katy Freeway
>   Houston, TX 77024
>   (713) 465-2500

★ **Girl Scout memorabilia.** Wants to buy items from before 1963 only. Handbooks must be before 1920 to be of interest.
>   Mary Degenhardt
>   85-37 109th Street
>   Richmond Hill, NY 11418
>   (718) 847-6518

IMMIGRATION EPHEMERA

★ **Immigration memorabilia.** "I'll buy documents, photos, passports, pre-1920 naturalization certificates, books, postcards, and other material related to immigrants, Immigrant Aid Societies, Immigrant Social and Political Clubs, Ellis Island, Castle Garden, and ethnic festivals before 1950." Also Immigration and Naturalization Service forms and documents from before 1930. Photocopy please.
　K. Sheeran
　PO Box 520251
　Miami, FL 33152

★ **Immigrant and ethnic stereotypes** of Jews, Orientals, Scandinavians, French, Poles, Russians, and other immigrants printed before 1920. Wants stereotypes on prints, photos, valentines, postcards, magazines, posters, sheet music, trade cards, and what have you. Wants Blacks only if shown with immigrant characters. Subject matter can include life in their country of origin, arrival, settlement, assimilation, etc. Not interested in reproductions, native costume, *Harper's Weekly* material, or general articles on immigration. Prefers photocopy of priced items. Don't send unsolicited material, please.
　John and Selma Appel
　219 Oakland Drive
　East Lansing, MI 48823
　　(517) 337-1859

★ **Chinese immigration memorabilia.** Wants anything to do with Chinese movements to U.S. prior to 1950, including items related to Chinese laundries, and Chinese social and political clubs.
　K. Sheeran
　PO Box 520251
　Miami, FL 33152

KU KLUX KLAN EPHEMERA

★ **Ku Klux Klan** paper, documents, photos, and small items.
　Steve DeGenaro
　PO Box 5662
　Youngstown, OH 44504

★ **Items related to Ku Klux Klan activity in the U.S.,** especially the Midwest, during the 1920's.
　Michael Graham's Roaring 20's
　345 Cleveland Ave.
　Libertyville, IL 60048

BLACK & NEGRO MEMORABILIA

★ **Black memorabilia** that is **exaggerated, comic, insulting** or **derogatory** made between 1800 and 1960. Images of mammies, chefs, *Uncle Tom*, picaninnies, *Aunt Jemima*, butlers, *Topsy*, and other Pop Culture portrayals are wanted in almost any form:

> **Folk art** and primitives including rag dolls, whirligigs, etc.;
>
> **Figural kitchen items,** tea pots, pitchers, sugar bowls, etc., especially large faced items and Black cookie jars;
>
> **Mammy and chef salt shakers** with matching stove grease jars and mammy tea pots with wire handles;
>
> **Ceramic jugs** by *Weller*;
>
> **Plastic cookie jars**, sugar bowls, syrup jugs, etc., from *F&F Die Works* or marked LUZIANNE;
>
> **Humidors and bisque figurines** from Europe or Japan;
>
> **Papier maché**, composition and glass **figurals** such as candy containers and Xmas ornaments depicting Blacks;
>
> **Advertising** on paper or tin, trade cards, die-cuts, packaging, and cereal boxes such as *Cream of Wheat* and *Korn Kinks,* and all *Aunt Jemima* products and ads;
>
> **Games of all types**, card and board, which feature Blacks even if pieces are missing.

Needs a detailed description of colors, size, condition, place of origin or manufacturer's name. Clear close up photo or photocopy is strongly urged. Describe all damage, chips, stains, tears, faded spots, repairs, or missing pieces. Wants to know the color of skin and expression on face. Prefers black to brown. On pottery pieces, describe whether surface is shiny or matte (flat).

> Mary Anne Enriquez
> 716 West 17th Place Rear
> Chicago, IL 60616
> (312) 243-3425

★ **All items depicting Blacks** in a manner that is exaggerated, comic, or patronizing including dolls, folk art, sewing items, walking sticks, miniature bronzes, jewelry, paintings, valentines, playing cards, games, children's books, cookie jars, string holders, small advertising items, souvenir spoons, Golliwogs, linens, jigsaw puzzles, candy containers, Christmas ornaments, and items associated with the Our Gang Comedy's Farina. No postcards, sheet music, trade cards, photos, outhouse figures, ads, large signs, damaged items, or reproductions. This active dealer/collector does not make offers.

> Jan Thalberg
> 23 Mountain View Drive
> Weston, CT 06883
> (203) 227-8175

★ **Black memorabilia** that is stereotyped or comic including cookie jars, older dolls, toys, kitchen items, prints, Black folk art, *Uncle Remus*, advertising items, *Aunt Jemima*, *Cream of Wheat*, *Amos 'n Andy*, and "all items relating to Blacks in America. Buys one piece or a collection."
   Judy Posner
   PO Box 273 W
   Effort, PA 18330
      (717) 629-6583 anytime

★ **Black memorabilia** that is comic or exaggerated manner including cookie jars, plates, lamps, clocks, salt and pepper shakers, table cloths, towels, plaster or ceramic items, and other household items depicting Blacks. "I also buy advertising pieces of all kinds that depict a Black person, including whiskey ads, *Aunt Jemima* items, *Cream of Wheat* packs, *Uncle Ben's Rice* memorabilia, etc."
   Diane Cauwels
   3947 Old South Road
   Murfreesboro, TN 37129
      (615) 896-3614

★ **Black memorabilia** that is stereotyped or comic including cookie jar chefs, string holders, teapots, toys, advertisements, sugar and creamer, "one piece or a whole collection." Will pay from $100 to $4,000 for useful items, but no outhouses, sheet music, postcards, or trade cards.
   Mike Kranz
   659 Oneil Road
   Hudson, WI 54016
      (715) 386-7333

★ **Popular portrayals of Black dancers** on sheet music, figurines, postcards, etc. Wants dancers doing the cake walk, jitterbug and the like.
   William Sommer
   9 West 10th Street
   New York, NY 10011
      (212) 260-0999

★ **Malcolm X ephemera** such as letters, copies of speeches, autographs, and personal items. Photocopy what you have to offer.
   Eric Mizrahi
   11 Forest Ave.
   Framingham, MA 01701

★ **Racism and the civil rights movement.** "I'll buy buttons, posters, and other ephemeral items having to do with Martin Luther King, but no newspapers, magazines, or damaged items."
   Peggy Dillard
   PO Box 210904
   Nashville, TN 37221
      (615) 646-1605

SOCIALISM & UNIONISM

★ **Socialism and Communism in the U.S. before 1940.** "I'll buy anything pre-1940: books, magazines, leaflets, brochures, buttons, postcards, pennants, etc., that were produced by radical groups such as the Communist Party, Socialist Party, I.W.W. (Industrial Workers of the World), Socialist Labor Party, etc. Would especially like to find the magazines *Masses, New Masses,* and *International Socialist Review.*" Mike will purchase items written in Yiddish, Italian, and other foreign languages, but "I'm really not too interested in material not written in the U.S.A." What does Mike consider important? "Condition! Condition! Condition!"

>   Michael Stephens
>   2310 Valley Street
>   Berkeley, CA 94702
>   (510) 843-2780

★ **Labor union and Socialist material.** "I'll buy just about everything relating to organized labor, unions, and working people" including dues buttons and books, pins, convention and parade ribbons and badges, photographs of workers or unions, programs, contracts, labor trade cards, union magazines, books, and most any type of labor collectibles. "I'd like to find items about labor leaders, and the old and unusual from groups like The Knights of Labor, I.W.W., Railroad Brotherhood, AFL, and CIO. I'll consider anything but am most interested in learning about items before 1960."

>   Scott Molloy
>   550 Usquepaugh Road
>   West Kingston, RI 02892
>   (401) 792-2239 or (401) 782-3614

★ **Cigar Maker's Union and Samuel Gompers.** "I'd like to know about anything from the Cigar Maker's Union or any of its top officers, including stamps, pamphlets, regulations, photographs, and letterhead." Does anyone have a letter by Samuel Gompers on CMIU stationery? Or a copy of the papers that dissolved the Union? Please include photocopies and price or ask for offer.

>   Tony Hyman
>   PO Box 3028
>   Pismo Beach, CA 93448
>   (805) 773-6777 Fax: (805) 773-0117

MISCELLANEOUS HISTORIC EPHEMERA

★ **Atomic bombs, nuclear war, and the anti-nuclear movement** from the 1950's to mid 60's. Wants all information, official and anti-bomb, including stuff on CONELRAD, civil defense, government pamphlets on atomic survival, books, comic books, and anything else from that period on atomic bombs and survival, including postcards of the bomb tests. Would love to find a copy of the book *How to Build an Atomic Bomb in Your Kitchen* by Bob Bale. Also "funky" atomic bomb stuff from the 1950's and mid 60's.

Edy Chandler
PO Box 20664
Houston, TX 77225
(713) 531-9615 eves

★ **Radical movements' paper ephemera** from Tories of the American Revolution, the social and political radicals of the 1800's, the labor unionists, women's suffrage, etc., right down to and including the Black activists, Peace movement, and other "hippies" of the 1960's. Wants letters, documents, posters, broadsides, books, and pamphlets.

Ivan Gilbert, Miran Arts & Books
2824 Elm Ave.
Columbus, OH 43209
(614) 236-0002

★ **British Royalty.** Buys souvenirs, tins, plates, mugs, medals, busts, postcards and programs from various ceremonies and events involving British royalty from Queen Victoria to Queen Elizabeth Reign. Also wants commemorative souvenirs from special events involving Prince Charles and Princess Diana. Wants pictorial items. Audrey is the author of *British Royal Commemoratives*, available from her for $25.

Audrey Zeder
6755 Coralite T
Long Beach, CA 90808
(310) 421-0881

★ **All fraternal order** materials that are small and flat, such as coins, tokens, medals, badges and ribbons. Especially interested in Masonic chapter pennies and hand engraved badges of precious metal. Will consider larger BPOE items or unusual fraternal items. If what you have is pre-1930, simply ship it to him for an offer. Hartzog will send you a check for the lot. He claims to pay higher prices than anyone else.

Rich Hartzog
PO Box 4143 BFT
Rockford, IL 61110

★ **Mafia or organized crime items** including books, magazines, photographs, autographs, videotapes, recordings, documents, government reports, and any other memorabilia or artifacts. "I'd love to find a cigar box from the *Yale Cigar Co.* of New York and a poster from the Italian American Civil Rights League meeting of June 28th, 1971." Wants nothing fictional.

> Ron Ridenour
> PO Box 357
> Moorpark, CA 93020

★ **Spy material.** Will consider anything you have related to real spies, from any country, any period: documents, signatures, photos, etc.

> Keith Melton
> PO Box 5755
> Bossier City, LA 71171
> (318) 747-9616

★ **Slave tags.** These small metal tags worn by slaves to indicate their status or occupation. Pays $200-$600 and up for tags reading SERVANT, PORTER, MECHANIC, SEAMSTRESS, FISHERMAN, FRUITERER, etc. Some rare types, dates, styles, or occupations can bring $1,500 or more. Call collect or ship insured for his offer. *Do not* clean the tags.

> Rich Hartzog
> Box 4143 BFT
> Rockford, IL 61110
> (815) 226-0771   Fax: (815) 397-7662

★ **Everything about the homeless children who sold newspapers to survive** in 19th century N.Y.C. and elsewhere. "I buy photographs, paintings, statues, prints, badges, passes, magazine articles, and newspaper accounts pertaining to them, Printing House Square, Newspaper Row, or Father John C. Drumgoole, founder of Mount Loretto, the largest child care facility in the U.S. at the time." Also material about **Charles Loring Brace and the Children's Aid Society**, especially about their orphan trains to the West.

> Peter Eckel
> 1335 Grant Ave.
> South Plainfield, NJ 07080
> (908) 757-0748

★ **Anything pertaining to statues of newsboys around the U.S.** including souvenir figurines, advertising for the figurines, and photos of any statue of a newsboy. Replicas of the statues bring $50+.

> Gary Leveille
> PO Box 562
> Great Barrington, MA 01239

EPHEMERA OF FAMOUS PEOPLE

★ **Samuel Gompers ephemera** from before 1886 is sought, particularly items related to his career as a cigar maker or a NYC union officer, but please inquire about *any* Gompers item.
Tony Hyman
PO Box 3028
Pismo Beach, CA 93448

★ **Lillie Langtry memorabilia** including postcards, photos, cigarette cards and silks, trade cards, letters, programs, posters, tickets, costume or set sketches, and cosmetics issued under her name. Also seeks a wine label or bottle produced on Langtry Farms, 1889-1906, worth up to $500 if you can find one for him. Langtry was also known as Langtree, the Jersey Lily, Lady Lillie de Bathe, Mrs. Jersey, and Emilie Charlotte Le Breton. In addition to his interest in Mrs. Langtry, he also wants material on **Edward Langtry** and **Freddie Gebhard(t)**.
Orville Magoon
PO Box 279
Middletown, CA 95461
(707) 987-2385 days

★ **Carrie Nation memorabilia** including vinegar bottles in her caricature, souvenir hatchet pins, photos, tickets to lectures, *The Hatchet*, newspaper articles about her, and *anything* else. You find it and you've got a buyer here if it's in any decent condition at all.
Steve Chyrchel
Route #2 Box 362
Eureka Springs, AR 72632
(501) 253-9244

★ **John"Johnny Appleseed" Chapman memorabilia** including books and personal items. He's looking for artifacts from the real Johnny Appleseed, not the Disney cartoon character.
Frederic Janson, Pomona Book Exchange
Rockton PO, Ontario
L0R 1X0 CANADA

★ **Commodore Matthew Perry material** including autographs, letters, and manuscripts, especially any artifacts or documents related to his expedition to Japan.
Jerrold Stanoff, Rare Oriental Book Co.
PO Box 1599
Aptos, CA 95003
(408) 724-4911 Fax: (408) 761-1350

★ **Frank Lloyd Wright material** including drawings, furniture, letters, photographs, books, smaller publications, and other ephemera.
> J.B. Muns' Fine Arts Books
> 1162 Shattuck Ave.
> Berkeley, CA 94707
> (510) 525-2420

★ **Stalin, Hitler, and Mussolini** items, especially those from the 1920's and 1930's are bought. Wants documented personal effects, autographs, letters, photos and some magazine and newspaper accounts.
> Michael Graham
> 345 Cleveland Ave.
> Libertyville, IL 60048
> (312) 362-4808 days

★ **Personal effects from Al Capone** and **other Chicago prohibition era figures,** both good guys and bad guys, including gangsters, police chiefs, State attorneys, FBI men, Elliott Ness, etc. Particularly interested in Capone and will pay from $50 to $1,000, depending on what you have, its condition, and its documentation. If offering personal items such as clothing, guns, jewelry, letters, etc., you should phone him.
> Michael Graham
> 345 Cleveland Ave.
> Libertyville, IL 60048
> (708) 362-4808 days

★ **Richard Halliburton ephemera** including books, films, photos, manuscripts and personal effects of this 1920's-30's author/adventurer. He wants signed first edition books, some foreign editions, and anything associated with the 1933 Halliburton film *India Speaks*. Selected items from the 1949 release are also wanted. Also news clippings and magazine articles by or about Halliburton. Also personal items from his home in Laguna Beach or anything related to the U.S. Navy ship *Richard Halliburton*. Also wants items relating to his associate **Paul Mooney.**
> Michael Blankenship
> 5320 Spencer Drive SW
> Roanoke, VA 24018
> (703) 989-0402 eves

★ **L. Ron Hubbard collectibles** such as books, photos, documents, pulp magazines, and other ephemera. She does not want ratty condition pulp magazines or books reprinted after 1960 unless autographed. Photocopy small items and send standard bibliographic information on books. Some autographed books are worth as much as $5,000 each to her.
> Karen Jentzsch Barta
> 1216 North Geneva Street
> Glendale, CA 91207
> (818) 243-0125   Fax: (818) 507-5702

★ **Things by, about, or related to author John Steinbeck** including signed limited editions, first editions, first printings by subsequent publishers, appearances in anthologies, spoken word records and tapes, film and theater memorabilia, and things owned by him. Does not want book club editions, items in poor condition, or fakes. If a book had a dust jacket, slipcase, box, or wrap-around as originally issued, then these items should still be present. Be specific about what you have for sale, giving complete bibliographic information and a full description.

    James Dourgarian, Bookman
    1595-A Third Avenue
    Walnut Creek, CA 94596
      (510) 935-5033

★ **Jack London memorabilia, books** and **personal effects.**
    Russ Kingman, Jack London Bookstore
    PO Box 337
    Glen Ellen, CA 95442
      (707) 996-2888

★ **Queen Victoria.** Buys a variety of small items associated with the Monarch and her era. "Anything" might be of interest, except furniture.
    J. Markowitz
    964 Hillside Blvd.
    New Hyde Park, NY 11040

★ **Sherlock Holmes** items, particularly the rare and unusual. Wants pre-1930 books, early magazines, games, pamphlets, non-book three dimensional items, and "curious items." If items are very rare, they may date after 1930 and still be of interest. John is a Baker Street Irregular, owns 12,000 Holmes items, and is well known as a Holmes authority.
    John Bennett Shaw
    1917 Fort Union Drive
    Santa Fe, NM 87501
      (505) 982-2947

★ **Sherlock Holmes.** Wants "anything related to Sherlock Holmes or **Sir Arthur Conan Doyle**" including figurines, drawings, autographs, posters, photos, etc. He wants books, but only first editions. Also wants ephemera from **actors who have played Holmes** including Nigel Bruce, Basil Rathbone and William Gillette.
    Robert Hess
    559 Potter Blvd.
    Brightwaters, NY 11718
      (516) 665-8365

WEIRD & MORBID THINGS

★ **Anything odd, unusual** or **morbid,** especially:
> **Two headed calves** and other **freak animals,** natural or man-made, alive or mounted and preserved;
> **Mummies, skeletons** and **human skulls;**
> **Shrunken heads** and other **headhunter** and **cannibal items;**
> **Funeral equipment,** coffins, embalming kits, and **tombstones;**
> **Torture** and **execution devices** and photos of executions;
> **Mounted reptiles, trophy heads** and **uncommon animals;**
> **Man-made mermaids** (up to $300);
> **Medicine show** photos and literature;
> **Tattoo equipment,** tattoo photos, and tattooed skin;
> **Voodoo** and **black magic** ephemera;
> **Flea Circus** props and photos;
> **Reward posters** and crime photos;
> **Human oddity** photos and artifacts.

For 50+ years, this wheel chair bound vet has been buying odd, unusual, and bizarre items for public exhibit in his traveling and stationary museums. He does not buy furniture, clothing, plates, or jewelry. If you have something you think he might want, send a photo, a description, a statement of condition, and your lowest price. When driving through Wilson, NC, you'll find The Palace of Wonders on Route 4.
> Harvey Lee Boswell's Palace of Wonders
> PO Box 446
> Elm City, NC 27822

★ **Skulls, skeletons, tusks, teeth, fossils, shrunken heads** and **mounted insects.** This relatively new dealer does not make offers.
> Ronald Cauble, The Bone Room
> 5495-C Claremont
> Oakland, CA 94618
> (510) 652-4286

★ **Animal trophies and skulls.** Please give your phone number with your description.
> David Boone's Trading Company
> 562 Coyote Road
> Brinnon, WA 98320
> (206) 796-4330 Fax: (206) 796-4511

★ **Steer horns, cow skulls with big horns, mounted steer heads, and old buffalo horns.** "I want the real thing, and do not want horns wrapped with the wide, tooled, tapered leather center, nor those wrapped in vinyl and rope." Send photo or sketch with dimensions.
> Alan Rogers
> 1012 Shady Drive
> Gladstone, MO 64118
> (816) 436-9008

COLLECTIBLES OF DEATH

★ **Funeral ephemera.** "I'll buy things having to do with funerals such as funeral parlor advertising, mirrors, ribbons, trays, badges, and other items issued by funeral parlors. I am not interested in caskets, funeral or embalming equipment, or cemeteries."
> Rich Hartzog, World Exonumia
> PO Box 4143 BFT
> Rockford, IL 61110
> (815) 226-0771   Fax: (815) 397-7662

★ **Cemetery ephemera.** "I'll buy books, maps, magazines, photos, catalogs, deeds, etc., related to the cemetery business, especially:
> Cemetery advertising from before 1920;
> Maps and deeds of cemeteries, before 1900;
> Sales catalogs for mausoleums, before 1940;
> Photos and real photo postcards of mausoleums;
> Magazines like *The Cemetery Beautiful*;
> Burial society certificates, before 1940.
Since these are paper items, include a photocopy and describe condition. "Do not confuse cemeteries with funerals. I am interested in land, monuments, memorials, vaults, and mausoleums, not funerals and embalming. The only funeral item I want is *The American Funeral Gazette* from the early 1880's." Not interested in colored photo postcards of famous tombs or cemeteries.
> Steve Spevak
> PO Box 3173
> Winchester, VA 22601

★ **Human hair mourning pieces.** Human hair jewelry with black "beads" worked in, or human hair woven into wreathes, mounted in frames with photos worked in. Also buys **wicker or wooden caskets**. "Wicker ones were used for display of bodies at wakes and funerals. The bodies were removed and buried in plain pine boxes. Want wooden caskets that are dove-tailed, made of odd woods, tapered, or with face plates." Describe as best as you can, giving dimensions. Interested in buying of **photos of caskets** with bodies on display.
> Steve DeGenaro
> PO Box 5662
> Youngstown, OH 44504

★ **Human hair wreaths.** This serious collector wants to buy wreaths made of human hair, either framed or unframed. Send photograph and or a good description with your asking price.
> Monica Murphy, Savannah's Antiques
> 1419 Fern
> New Orleans, LA 70118

ROCKS, FOSSILS & CAVES

★ **Meteorites.** Many types exist, and he wants them all, rough or smooth, large or small. Look for rocks that are especially heavy, or with signs of melting or with rust. A freshly fallen meteorite often has a thin black skin, called "fusion crust." If you have a rock that attracts a magnet, you may have a meteorite. "A strong magnet on a string will swing towards all meteorites, which makes this one of the best preliminary tests. Other excellent field tests for meteorites include checking for rust, and filing off a tiny corner to look inside for bright metal or metal flakes. If you think you have found a meteorite, please send a small, dime-sized piece for me to examine along with a description and photo of the enjire specimen. If you wish to have the sample returned to you, you must enclose return postage. All non-meteorite samples without return postage are added to the pile outside the back door. If I suspect your sample is a meteorite, I will contact you, so be sure to enclose your name, address and phone number along with all samples." Rare forms of meteorites can be surprisingly valuable.
   Robert Haag
   PO Box 27527
   Tucson, AZ 85726
      (602) 882-8804   Fax: (602) 743-7225

★ **Rock, mineral, and fossil collections** are wanted, as are samples of gold, silver, and copper, particularly samples associated with Western mining. Pays in any form you prefer.
   David Crawford
   1308 Halsted Road
   Rockford, IL 61103
      (815) 637-6720

★ **Cave or cavern memorabilia** before 1950, including books, magazine articles, pamphlets, prints, postcards, etc. "Any items that would make a contribution to the history of a particular cave or area such as journal entries, deeds, wills, maps, tickets, and advertising, are of interest." Common souvenirs and chrome postcards are not desired.
   Jack Speece
   711 East Atlantic Ave.
   Altoona, PA 16602
      (814) 946-3155 eves

★ **Caves or cavern memorabilia of all sorts.** "I'll buy anything old or unusual pertaining to caves or caverns worldwide" including photos, brochures, postcards, souvenirs, silver spoons, plates, etc. Does not want anything after 1940, and prefers items from before 1900.
   Gordon Smith
   PO Box 217
   Marengo, IN 47140
      (812) 945-5721

Transportation and work related collectibles

If it rolls, floats, flies or travels in any way imaginable it probably has the attention of collectors. Everything related to the history and use of transportation is popular as are the artifacts and tools of the business, trades, and professions of the past.

The physical artifacts of just about any 19th or early 20th century enterprise will find a buyer. As is the case with most collectible items, it is difficult for you to assess the value or importance of what you own. Using the experts and buyers in *Where To Sell It!* will solve that problem for you.

When sorting through old things, yours or someone else's, pay particular attention to paper items, catalogs, flyers and company brochures about any business or mode of travel. Letters about experiences aboard trains, planes, ships and automobiles are also wanted, as are photographs and records. Collectors gladly buy products, advertising signs, business records, letters, bills, posters, store displays, and the like. The fact that many of these items are quite difficult to find does not necessarily make them valuable, although large illustrated company catalogs from the turn of the century usually sell for more than $100 and signs made of tin often bring $500+.

Collectors also buy tools, uniforms, instruments, signs, badges, emblems, and other three-dimensional items characteristic of any industry. The goal of serious collectors is to learn about the manufacture and marketing of items which interest them today. In some industries, it can be difficult to find information about what took place 30 years ago. You can imagine how hard it is to obtain information from before the turn of the century! Although these items may not have large monetary value, the information they contain may be useful, so you are encouraged to take the time to sell even the less expensive items.

If you own old records regarding transportation or any other business or profession in the United States or Canada, and you feel it is too much effort to sell what you have, you are encouraged to give the items away to one of the historian minded collectors so the information is not lost.

To sell your transportation, business, or profession related item, your description should include:

(1) What it is you wish to sell;
(2) What material(s) it is made from;
(3) Its size, shape, and color (especially colors of glass);
(4) Markings embossed (raised) or incised (stamped in);
(5) Information contained on an ID plate;
(6) Accurate information regarding condition.

License plate collectors want to know the origin, date, license number, and how many chips, cracks or bends it shows. Set the copy machine to legal size, lay the plate gently on the glass, and make a photocopy. Plates may be washed in mild soap and water, not abrasives!

The history and artifacts of some industries is being preserved by fewer than a half dozen people. In some cases, *Where to Sell It!* will put you in touch with the *only* person in the country willing to buy what you have!

SHIPS & THE SEA EPHEMERA

★ **Fine marine antiques of all types** including but not limited to:
  Paintings and **prints of boats**, ships and the sea, 1700-1900;
  Navigational instruments from the 19th century, sextants,
    telescopes on tripods, marine clocks, compasses, etc.
  Photographs of **whaling**, yachting, ship launchings, and
    identified parts in the 19th or early 20th century;
  Journals, logs and **out-of-print books** about whaling, **yachting**,
    clippers, "but only in resellable condition;"
  Wood carvings such as figureheads, pilot house eagles,
    name boards, and tail boards;
  Scrimshaw teeth and sailor's whimsies, inlaid boxes, **crimpers**,
    bone swifts, and tools, but only genuine quality old pieces;
  Paper and other ephemera including deck plans, broadsides,
    ship's china...anything rare, interesting and in fine condition;
  Artifacts related to **lighthouses** and the **Life Saving Service.**
Generally buys only 19th century items. He does not want fakes, altered
items, modern scrimshaw, boxed compasses, or ship's telegraphs unless
they are small, very early, or historically important. Description should
include dimensions, note of repairs or restoration, history and price ("if
you can"). He specializes in forming and liquidating collections and issues interesting catalogs of items for sale.
  Andrew Jacobson's Marine Antiques
  PO Box 2155
  South Hamilton, MA 01982
    (508) 468-6276

★ **Model sailboats.** "I'll buy wooden models that are at least 18"
long, made of wood, with rigged canvas sails. May be up to 8' high. I
prefer them to have stands. I'm looking for their decorative value so am
not particularly looking for famous boats, ship builder's models, and
other high ticket items. Send a picture of what you have, please."
Should be in fine or readily restorable condition.
  Joan Brady
  834 Central Ave.
  Pawtucket, RI 02861
    (401) 725-5753

★ **Nautical instruments** by American and foreign makers including
brass sextants, wood octants, spyglasses, pocket sundials, cased naviga-
ting devices, as well as map drawing tools. Must be made before 1890.
  Jonathan Thomas, Scientific Americana
  1208 Main Street North
  Southbury, CT 06488
    (203) 263-2233

★ **Ship models,** particularly identified 19th century American, English, or French vessels. "I also deal in 20th century high quality models of all types: sail, steam, liners, yachts, and **pond models.**" Also buys **builder's half models**, including 19th century American or British hulls, exceptional 20th century hulls, and all yacht models. Does not want reproductions, or items which have been heavily "restored" or otherwise altered. Please give the dimensions, age, condition, history, and price. "If you want an appraisal, I must examine the object personally, and there is a fee, although I will give 'ball park' verbal estimates on routine items, with the understanding there is no legal responsibility or liability."

    Andrew Jacobson's Marine Antiques
    PO Box 2155
    South Hamilton, MA 01982
      (508) 468-6276

★ **Steamship memorabilia** including china, silver, ashtrays, whistles, locks, lanterns, badges, signs, uniforms and caps, calendars, posters, route maps, and numerous similar items. **Does not want** paper ephemera after 1910, low value paper goods, fake or altered items or big heavy tools. Nor does he buy items that are shabby or missing important parts.

    Scott Arden
    20457 Highway 126
    Noti, OR 97461
      (503) 935-1619 from 9 to 9 Pacific time

★ **Ocean liner memorabilia** from all companies especially paper items such as deck plans, menus, booklets, and passenger lists from *Cunard, French, German, White Star, Italian, Canadian, Dutch,* and all others. "We do not buy reproductions or items that are strictly 'travel' interest, such as brochures describing Paris. You are invited to send items on approval as we cannot make offers based only on your description."

    Alan Taksler, New Steamship Consultants
    PO Box 30088
    Mesa, AZ 85275

★ **Ocean liner memorabilia,** deck plans, postcards, paintings, posters, and anything relating to passenger ship travel especially from "disaster ships" such as the *Titanic* or *Andrea Doria.* After 1945, only maiden voyage items wanted. Ken produces a large illustrated catalog for $15.

    Ken Schultz
    PO Box M-753
    Hoboken, NJ 07030
      (201) 656-0966

★ **Alaskan steamship ephemera** such as photos, postcards, letterheads from the *Alaskan Steamship Company* and others.

    Nick Nickell
    102 People's Wharf
    Juneau, AK 99801

★ **Canadian steamship ephemera** before 1950 such as deck plans, calendars, stock certificates, bonds, fancy letterheads, envelopes, etc. Seeks *Canadian Pacific* steamships, *BC Coast* steamships, and others.
> Michael Rice
> PO Box 286
> Saanichton, BC   V0S 1M0   CANADA

★ **Steamship ephemera collections** dating pre-1960, including menus, programs, deck plans, posters, etc., from either American or European lines. Promises a quick answer to all inquiries.
> George Theofilies, The Miscellaneous Man
> PO Box 1776
> New Freedom, PA   17349
> (717) 235-4766 days   Fax: (717) 235-2853

★ **Great Lakes ships and shipping.** "I'll buy photos, documents, fiction and non fiction books, technical and statistical reports, anything old, new, or historic having to do with Great Lakes shipping."
> James Baumhofer
> PO Box 65493
> St. Paul, MN 55165
> (612) 698-7151

★ **Wooden motor boat memorabilia** especially items related to Gar Wood, the man and his boats, 1923-47. Also *Chris Craft, Hacker, Old Town*, and others. Buys sales literature, catalogs, magazines, etc.
> Tony Mollica
> PO Box 6003
> Syracuse, NY 13217
> (315) 433-2643 days

★ **Outboard motors.** "I'll buy outboard motors, boat and sales literature, and engine manuals from before 1940. Also **boating magazines**, nautical books, and other ephemera including information about marine engines, outboard motors, yachts, canoes, treasure hunting, Arctic voyages, and boat building." Nothing after 1940 please. When describing outboard motors, give serial number and tell whether the engine is frozen or turns over. Offers wants list and catalog of items for sale.
> Robert Glick, Columbia Trading Co.
> 504 Main Street
> West Barnstable, MA 02668
> Fax: (508) 362-3551

★ **Lighthouses, U.S. Coast Guard**, and **sea rescue services**, pre-1940.
> Robert Glick, Columbia Trading Co.
> 504 Main Street
> West Barnstable, MA 02668

RAILROAD MEMORABILIA

★ **Almost anything related to American railroads** especially dining car china, silverware, glass, marked lanterns, and marked brass locks. Pays $20-85 for sugar tongs or spoons marked with railroad names. Make certain your description includes dimensions and all marks and logos. Rick does not want date nails, books, or model trains. This 25 year veteran says he'll be helpful and answer questions from amateurs with or without things to sell.

> Richard Wright, West Coast Rick's
> PO Box 8051
> Rowland Heights, CA 91748
> (714) 681-4647

★ **Railroad items** including dining car china, silverware, lanterns and lamps, stock certificates, engine builder's plates, ticket dating machines, depot signs, advertising, postcards of depots, brochures and timetables pre-1940, historical documents, hat and cap badges, wax seals, Express Company signs, annual passes from before 1920, and books, manuals, and guides. Nothing newer than 1959, no letters, receipts, or minor paper. This 30 year veteran requests your phone number.

> Fred Arone, The Depot Attic
> 377 Ashford Ave.
> Dobbs Ferry, NY 10522
> (914) 693-1832

★ **Railroad and Express Company memorabilia** including dining car china, silverware, ashtrays, playing cards, paperweights, brass lamps and lanterns (including unmarked ones), locks, badges, switch keys, builder plates, steam whistles, caps pre-1960, uniforms pre-1920, railroad pocket watches if in perfect condition, pre-1916 timetables, posters, and calendars. Also *RR Cyclopedia*, dictionaries or other reference books published by *RY Gazette, Simmons-Boardman, Moody,* or *Poors* pre-1950. No large tools, large oil cans, spikes, low value paper, junky or damaged items, or material other than U.S. or Canadian. No "overly cleaned" or replated items. This 15 year veteran dealer carries an extensive list of items for sale so always needs new merchandise.

> Scott Arden
> 20457 Highway 126
> Noti, OR 97461
> (503) 935-1619 from 9 to 9 Pacific time

★ **Canadian railroad memorabilia** from before 1950, especially *White Pass and Yukon Railway, Grand Trunk Railway,* and *Canadian Pacific,* among others.

> Michael Rice
> PO Box 286
> Saanichton, BC V0S 1M0 CANADA
> (604) 652-9047 eves

★ **Railroad dining car memorabilia** including china, silver, glass-ware, menus, and anything else. Items without markings as to the rail-road are "worthless" to him.
Charles Goodman
636 West Grant Ave.
Charleston, IL 61920
(217) 345-6771

★ **Railroad memorabilia** such as dishes, silver, lanterns, keys, locks, books, etc. "I'll pay at least $300 for the 10 1/2" china plates used on the trains." Especially interested in items from Southern roads. Also wants **pre-1930 postcards** showing exteriors of small town depots or trains, and cards of any era showing depot or train interiors. Does not make offers, but claims to be "willing to pay your price." Include your phone.
Les Winn
PO Box 80641
Chamblee, GA 30366
(404) 458-6194 eves

★ **Chesapeake & Ohio Railroad memorabilia** of all sorts, as long as it features the two cats, "Chessie" and "Peake." A photocopy or photo is appreciated. No repros. SASE please.
Charles Worman
PO Box 33584 (AMC)
Dayton, OH 45433
(513) 429-1808 eves

★ **Memorabilia from Arkansas railways** including *Eureka Springs Railway, St. Louis and North Arkansas Railroad, Missouri and Arkansas Railroad*, and the *Missouri and North Arkansas Railroad*. "I'll buy ad-vertising, passes, china and silver, photos, switch locks and keys, lan-terns, tickets, bills of lading, stock certificates, etc."
Steve Chyrchel
Route #2 Box 362
Eureka Springs, AR 72632
(501) 253-9244

★ **Railroad date nails and other small railroad items** such as lanterns, locks, and keys. Will buy almost any date nails (nails about 4" long with a date on the head). If you describe the shape of the head, the number, and whether it is incised or raised, he says he's glad to tell you what you have. Dick is a collector with limited storage so is interested only in small fine items.
Dick Gartin
619 Adams
Duncanville, TX 75137
(214) 296-8742 anytime

★ **Date nails** used by railroads, telephone, telegraph, and power companies to record when their ties or poles were placed in service. Most, but not all, have either round or square heads and have numbers (or other symbols) either raised or indented on the head. Nails may be steel, copper, or aluminum. Although there are many common nails, there are also nails worth $50 up so describe what you have and Jerry will make an offer. Jerry is editor of *Nailer News* a brief bimonthly newsletter for nail collectors.

> Jerry Waits
> 501 West Horton
> Brenham, TX 77833
>   (409) 830-1495

★ **Railroad books** of all types, fiction, biographies, histories, etc. Seeks *Poor's Manual of Railroads*, pre-1920. **Also other items, especially from Colorado and New Jersey,** such as pre-1920 annual passes, **uniform buttons,** pins, and brass padlocks with raised letters. Especially wants anything from Central RR of NJ (*The Blue Comet*).

> Dan Allen
> PO Box 917
> Marlton, NJ 08053
>   (609) 953-1387 eves

AIRPLANE & AIRLINE ITEMS

★ **Antique airplane memorabilia** including entire airplanes, parts, early flight equipment, books, magazines, photos, etc., are sought by the 6,000 members of The Antique Airplane Association. Write what you have for sale in the way of early air memorabilia, and President Taylor will forward your letter to a member who is looking for what you have to sell. The Association is the parent organization of the Air-power Museum and Bob is empowered to accept tax deductible donations of significant and interesting items from the history of air flight.

> Bob Taylor
> Antique Airplane Association
> PO Box 172
> Ottumwa, IA 52501
>   (515) 938-2773 days

★ **All early airplane memorabilia** including propellers, instruments, badges, flight awards, tools, manuals, emblems, accessories, checks, bonds, and virtually any good quality early item.

> Joseph Russell
> 455 Ollie Street
> Cottage Grove, WI 53527
>   (608) 839-4736 eves

★ *Pan Am's China Clipper* **and all Chinese airline memorabilia,** **1925-45,** including caps, uniforms, medals, photos, diaries, badges, posters, and what have you.
> Gene Christian
> 3849 Bailey Ave.
> Bronx, NY 10463
> (212) 548-0243

★ *Ford* **tri-motor airplane memorabilia.** "Will pay $100 for Ford Airplane Co. employee badge."
> Tim O'Callaghan
> 46878 Betty Hill
> Plymouth, MI 49170
> (313) 459-4636

★ **Wooden airplane propellers.**
> Charles Martignette
> PO Box 293
> Hallandale, FL 33009
> (305) 454-3474

★ **Helicopter items** including objects of all sort, toys, printed items, art depicting helicopters, and "anything else" in any age or condition. "I'll consider anything helicopter related."
> Rick Bohr
> 12865 NE 85th Street #239
> Kirkland, WA 98033
> (206) 828-9417

★ **Commercial aviation memorabilia, American or foreign, 1919-50** including books, letters, magazines, photographs, and miscellaneous small artifacts. Especially interested in uncommon items. No books on how to fly, radio, or navigation. Book club editions or defective books are not wanted.
> Ron Mahoney, Air Age Book Co
> PO Box 40
> Tollhouse, CA 93667
> (209) 855-8993

★ **Commercial airline memorabilia** including pilot and stewardess wings and hat emblems, display models, anniversary pins, playing cards, **postcards**, buttons, flight schedules, kiddie wings, and almost anything else old and unusual from the airlines. Especially ephemera from *Northeast Airlines, Delta, Chicago and Southern* and *Western Airlines.*
> John Joiner
> 245 Ashland Trail
> Tyrone, GA 30290
> (404) 487-3732

★ **Airline models from travel agencies.** Buys all types of planes, from 1920 to 1990. Photo best.
Charles Martignette
PO Box 293
Hallandale, FL 33009

★ **Airline pilot and stewardess wings and hat badges** pre-1970. Also stewardess uniforms pre-1965 *if they are complete.* Looking for pilot and stewardess wings from the 1940's and 50's from airlines such as *Mohawk Airlines, Northeast Airlines, Inland Airlines, Pioneer Air Lines, Empire Airlines, Colonial Airlines, Chicago and Southern Airlines, Mid-Continent Airlines,* others. Also **metal desk models of airliners** (travel agent type) from 1940-70. No military items. Photocopies helpful.
Charles Quarles
204 Reservation Drive
Spindale, NC 28160
(704) 245-7803 eves

★ **Desk display models of aircraft** and **weapon products** from various manufacturers such as *Convair, General Dynamics, Douglass, Lockheed,* and others. Models created by Topping are preferred but all considered. All models should have their original stands.
Bob Keller, Starline Hobbies
PO Box 38
Stanton, CA 90680
(714) 826-5218 days

★ **China and silverplate** used by any airline.
Les Winn
PO Box 80641
Chamblee, GA 30366
(404) 458-6194 eves

★ **Zeppelin, blimp** and **dirigible memorabilia** including anything shaped like, or about, the giant gas bags such as photos, paper ephemera, postcards, china marked "LZ," stereocards, timetables, books, souvenirs, stamps and covers, training films, toys, games, and Christmas ornaments. Especially wants pieces and parts of zeppelins. No repros, repainted or restored items, homemades, or fakes. "I am a historian not a dealer."
Zeppelin
PO Box 2502
Cinnaminson, NJ 08077
(609) 829-3959

★ **Aviation magazines, pilot's handbooks**, and **overhaul manuals** dating from before 1970.
Alan C. King
PO Box 86
Radnor, OH 43066

SPACE MEMORABILIA

★ **Memorabilia of all early rocket research** including "newsletters, journals, books, magazines, reports, studies, correspondence, blueprints, drawings, photographs, films, and any other documentation from France, Germany, UK, USSR or the US regarding speculation, research, development and implementation conducted by any amateur, military, or civilian group or any individual pertaining to rockets, missiles and space travel, 1900-1960." He especially wants "any material from WWII pertaining to work done at Peenemunde, Germany, by Wernher Von Braun, which led to the V-2 and rocket weapons. Also any material having to do with Robert H. Goddard and the experiments he conducted in Worcester, MA, and Roswell, NM, during the 1920's through 1940's." He is not interested in science fiction or Pop Culture figures like *Buck Rogers* but does want speculative articles that are scholarly or serious.

> Randy Liebermann
> 4 Lafayette Station
> Fredericksburg, VA 22401

★ **Space shot memorabilia** including souvenirs such as magazines, buttons, autographs, etc. Especially wants "internal" souvenirs such as special medallions, mission patches, models, etc., produced for people directly involved with some space "event" such as a launching or completion of construction. Also internal documents such as manuals, flight plans, charts, and so on. Also hardware, pieces of spacecraft, and other items discarded as part of mission preparation or completion. Also video tapes of launchings or reports from space. Does not want recent items which NASA still sells such as slide sets, T-shirts, etc.

> Mike Smithwick
> 25215 La Loma Drive
> Los Altos Hills, CA 94022
> (408) 244-8987 eves

★ **NASA and space program items,** including anything produced or distributed by NASA, authentic patches, manuals, medallions, space shuttle tile samples, pieces of spacecraft or spacecraft construction materials, and items owned or carried into space by astronauts.

> Paul Hartunian
> 127B East Bradford Ave.
> Cedar Grove, NJ 07009
> (201) 857-7275

★ **Space age memorabilia** including souvenirs issued to commemorate various launchings, U.S. or Soviet. Buys glasses, coasters, ashtrays, cards, plates, jewelry, and trinkets as well as books, magazines, and albums of newspaper clippings. He requests you price what you have.

> Barry Burros
> 160 East 48th Street
> New York, NY 10017

BICYCLES & EPHEMERA

★ **Bicycles and bicycle memorabilia,** generally before 1900, although some items are wanted to 1930. Wants all material about high wheelers and velocipedes ("bone shakers") including posters, advertising, trophies, photos, prints, toys and other representations or depictions, especially ephemera created by the *Pope Mfg. Company.* He does not want anything related to balloon tire bicycles.
> Pryor Dodge
> Box 71 Prince Street Station
> New York, NY 10012
> (212) 966-1026

★ **League of American Wheelman memorabilia** is sought by this expert 20 year veteran collector who buys pins, medals, ribbons, magazines, etc., from 1880-1955. You might try him for general **early bicycle memorabilia** as well. Not interested in anything after 1955.
> Walley Francis
> PO Box 6941
> Syracuse, NY 13217
> (315) 478-5671

★ **Bicycling before 1910,** with an emphasis on **League of American Wheelmen (LAW)** memorabilia. Artifacts include medals, pins, awards, ribbons, photos, and figurines made of glass, porcelain, silver, etc. Small items or large. Especially interested in items depicting high wheelers or from the high wheeler era.
> Charlie Stewart
> 900 Grandview Ave.
> Reno, NV 89503
> (702) 747-1439 mornings

★ **Bicycle memorabilia** including paper ephemera, sales literature, catalogs, advertising, and small objects such as pins, medals, and give-away trinkets. Jay specializes in mail order sales of transportation memorabilia of all types and always needs good fresh new stock. He accepts boxes of good clean items sent on approval and "makes immediate offers."
> Jay Ketelle
> 3721 Farwell
> Amarillo, TX 79109
> (806) 355-3456

★ **Balloon tire bicycles** made between 1934-1960 in new or mint condition only, especially *Schwinn, Shelby, Monarch, Columbia,* or *Elgin* (Sears Roebuck). Please include a photo.
> Gus Garton, Garton's Auto
> 5th & Vine
> Millville, NJ 08332

★ **Balloon tire bicycles** from the 1930's to 1960 are wanted. The most desired are boys' bikes with tanks, lights, horns, springs, and other accessories. "The more gaudy features, the better." Look for brands like *Schwinn, Road Master, Shelby, Evinrude, Elgin, Hiawatha* and *Western Flyer.* Will buy in any condition, but the value is determined by condition and accessories. Mike also buys parts, signs, shop fixtures, and literature relevant to this period of bicycles. No racing bikes, middleweights with 26 x 1.75 tires, or plain bikes. Photographs and a complete description are important to accurately estimate value.

"Collectible bikes usually have tires sized: 26x1.125, 24x2.125 or 28x1.5 and are especially desirable if colored red or blue."

Michael Brown
260 19th Avenue North
Clinton, IA 52732
(800) 383-0049

★ *Whizzers* **and balloon tire bicycles** are wanted. *Whizzers* are motor driven bicycles, some of which were factory built, others made from kits with a belt drive attached to the rear wheel. If you're selling a *Whizzer*, include the serial number as part of your description, which ideally should include a sharp photo of the vehicle. The bicycles he wants have tires sized 20, 24, or 26" x 2.125". Especially looking for a 1933 *Schwinn Aerocycle* or a 1938-39 *Shelby Speedline Airflow.* "The longer and weirder the bicycle's tanks are, the more I want them." Also buys **signs and shop fixtures**, including old brake parts cabinets, literature, and advertising. He does not want middleweight bikes with 1.75" tires or plain bikes with no tanks. Send a photo and complete description.

Alan Kinsey
318 NE Grant
Ankeny, IA 50021
(515) 964-5472

★ **Bicycle license tags,** often called "sidepath licenses," from any state as long as they are from before 1930. Value ranges from $5-40 depending on the age and place of issue.

James Case
Route #1   Box 68   Crane Road
Lindley, NY 14858

MOTORCYCLES & EPHEMERA

★ **Motorcycle memorabilia** including awards, pins, clothing, signs, postcards, trade cards, racing trophies and memorabilia, motorcycle **toys**, and any unusual items. Chris also buys complete **American motorcycles** and **racing cycles** from before 1950.

> Chris Savino
> PO Box 419
> Breesport, NY 14816
> (607) 739-3106

★ **Motorcycle memorabilia** including advertising, giveaway trinkets, watch fobs, and other items. Both foreign and domestic, pre-1960. "I will accept boxes sent to me on approval and will make immediate offers to buy." Promises to reimburse your postage if his offer not accepted.

> Jay Ketelle
> 3721 Farwell
> Amarillo, TX 79109
> (806) 355-3456

★ **American motorcycles and motorcycle parts.** Give marks and numbers when appropriate in your description. "I pay all shipping costs. I'm in the parts business and will travel to pick up large lots."

> Robert Fay
> Star Route Box AF
> Whitmore, CA 96096
> (916) 472-3132

★ **Motorcycles and motorcycle ephemera** from before 1920. Wants advertising, factory sales catalogs, manuals, magazines, pins, fobs, trophies, medals, and related items.

> Herb Glass
> Route #1 Box 506-A
> Pine Bush, NY 12566
> (914) 361-3657

★ *Can-Am* **motorcycle parts and ephemera** including *Rotax* motor, brochures, decals, gloves, leathers, goggles, and anything else marked CAN-AM. This motorcycle is made by *Bombardier* of Canada.

> Don Schneider
> PO Box 1570
> Merritt, BC V0K 2B0 CANADA

★ *Cushman* **motor scooters** and related ephemera, especially signs and sales literature. Also **pre-1965 motorcycle** photos, postcards, sales literature, manuals, and magazines.

> Don Olson
> PO Box 245
> Humboldt, IA 50548

PUBLIC TRANSPORTATION EPHEMERA

★ **Horsedrawn streetcars and pre-1920 electric railways.** "I'll buy bells marked with the name of a streetcar line, car gongs, car maker's plates, wall mounted and hand held fare registers, signs reading HAVE FARE READY or PAY AT REAR, hat badges, motorman's and conductor's certificates, fare tokens, and photos of early cars.
> Jonathan Thomas, Trolley Fare
> 1208 Main Street North
> Southbury, CT 06488
> (203) 263-2233

★ **Memorabilia from buses, taxis, hearses, ambulances, and any other public conveyance** before 1960 including emblems, badges, licenses, license plates, advertising, promotional giveaway trinkets, operator's manuals, sales literature, etc. May be foreign or U.S. as long as they are old, genuine, and small. Will accept items sent on approval.
> Jay Ketelle
> 3721 Farwell
> Amarillo, TX 79109
> (806) 355-3456

★ **Bus, trolley, and streetcar memorabilia** pre-1940 including photos, artifacts, driver's badges, caps, bus emblems, route maps, and advertising. Has particular interest in Florida companies but says "I will consider any items if the seller describes them well and attaches a price."
> Sam LaRoue
> 5980 SW 35th Street
> Miami, FL 33155
> (305) 347-7466

★ *Greyhound* and *Trailways* **bus memorabilia.** Wants wide range of items, such as cap badges, driver awards, etc., but mostly interested in toy *Greyhound* and *Trailways* busses, and *Greyvan Moving* truck toys. Prefers a picture or photocopy. No magazine ads, timetables, postcards or posters, but he does want internal company data like garage locations, driver assignments, and organizational directories.
> Eugene Farha
> PO Box 633
> Cedar Grove, WV 25039
> (304) 340-3201

★ **Taxi cabs.** "If it pictures an American taxi cab, I'll buy it," says Henry, who seeks a wide variety of taxi related items. If you have something that is in any way related to taxis, drop him a line.
> Henry Winningham
> 3205 South Morgan Street
> Chicago, IL 60608
> (312) 847-1672

AUTOMOBILES

★ **Classic American and foreign automobiles.** One of the nation's largest auctioneers of high quality foreign and old domestic automobiles. If you have anything fast, sleek, limited production, or unusual, give Cole a call and discuss putting it up for sale in California's lucrative automobile market. Also *Corvettes, T-Birds*, older convertibles, and fine condition high quality American cars of the 1950's and 1960's. Don't sell your old car for too little.

> Rick Cole Auctions
> 10701 Riverside Drive
> North Hollywood, CA 91602
> (818) 506-6533

★ **Race car "speed equipment"** to hop up automobiles from the 1930's, 40's, 50's, and 60's. Whether factory equipment or aftermarket, if it's designed to make a car go faster, and you want to sell it, give Dale a call. He'd especially like to find early *Ford* flathead engine cylinder heads, intake manifolds, and camshafts. 1955 to '58 *Chrysler* aftermarket intake manifolds or valve covers will bring top prices. He personally does not want complete cars, complete engines, or "any items that can't be shipped U.P.S." But, if you have these things for sale, you might inquire as he adds, "I do have quality buyers for this type item." Describe what you have, including manufacturer and date, when possible. Dale publishes *RPM*, a monthly catalog which includes 30 pages of classified ads for folks buying and selling speed parts. You can subscribe for $20 a year.

> Dale Wilch
> 2217 North 99th
> Kansas City, KS 66109
> (913) 788-3219   Fax: (913) 788-9682

★ **Automobiles made between 1940 and 1969** that are well maintained low mileage, especially a *Cadillac* convertible from the 1950's or 60's. "I'd keep it as long as I live!" Also buys **automotive related signs**: auto sales and service, gasoline, motor oil, etc. Also **auto toys**.

> Gus Garton, Garton's Auto
> 5th & Vine
> Millville, NJ 08332

★ *Dan Patch* **automobile** or parts and other ephemera from that brand. Call collect if you know of one of these cars for sale.

> Donald Sawyer
> 40 Bachelor Street
> West Newbury, MA 01985
> (508) 363-2983

AUTOMOBILE EPHEMERA

★ **Paper ephemera, advertising, and promotional items associated with automobiles,** trucks, buses, campers, taxis, auto racing, police cars, ambulances, and hearses. Jay operates a large mail order business selling **transportation memorabilia of all sorts** and always needs clean old items such as catalogs, promotional items, emblems, promotional models given away by car dealers, auto company service pins, owner's manuals, and other small items associated with any form of vehicle. Will buy U.S. and foreign items, and multiples of some things. Will accept boxes sent on approval and "will make immediate offers to buy." Requests you include your phone number. Does not want shop manuals, parts lists, and magazine ads.

> Jay Ketelle
> 3721 Farwell
> Amarillo, TX 79109
> (806) 355-3456

★ **Automobile related memorabilia** including promotional giveaways, **owner's manuals**, repair manuals, radiator emblems and caps, dial type tire gauges, fancy gear shift knobs, car clocks, **spark plugs**, horns, dash panels, brass speedometers, **DAV keychains**, automobile **magazines**, plant employee badges, canceled checks from auto companies, **stocks and bonds**, porcelain or leather license plates, driving awards and anything you can imagine having to do with automobiles except magazine ads.

> Joseph Russell
> 455 Ollie Street
> Cottage Grove, WI 53527
> (608) 839-4736 eves

★ **Automobile and truck dealers' showroom brochures,** 1900-1970, for any makes, American or foreign. Also buying selected automobile owner's manuals, shop manuals, and parts manuals issued by the companies themselves. Also **auto dealer promotional items**, including signs, banners, date books, etc., that were originally in a car dealer's showroom. Not interested in reproductions, reprints, magazines, clipped ads, *Motor's* or *Chilton's* manuals, and items not issued by the auto company. This 25 year veteran collector and dealer says a good description includes measurements, color, number of pages, and condition, listing any visible flaws. Photocopies are appreciated but not essential. Please include your phone number.

> S.E. Penning
> PO Box 16171
> Fresno, CA 93755

★ **Automobile sales catalogs, brochures, owner's manuals** and **repair guides** printed by the auto company. Wants material for all cars and trucks, American or foreign, especially pre-1970. No magazines, clipped ads, *Motor's Manuals, Chilton's Manuals*, or books not printed by the auto company. Also buys **auto dealer promotional items** including signs, salesman's awards, and the like. "Please send me a list of each item by year and make. If a list is not practical, give me a count by decade, such as 'so many brochures from 1950 to 1959,' etc."

> Walter Miller
> 6710 Brooklawn Parkway
> Syracuse, NY 13211
> (315) 432-8282

★ **Books, magazines, and factory literature about cars, trucks, motorcycles, and bicycles.** Also buys newsletters and magazines produced by automobile clubs devoted to one particular make of vehicle or another. Documents related to vehicle history 1895-1990 also purchased.

> Ralph Dunwoodie
> 5935 Calico Drive
> Sun Valley, NV 89433
> (702) 673-3811

★ **Books, catalogs, and owner's manuals.** Books may be on automobiles, auto history, racing, biography, auto travel, etc. Not interested in technical and repair manuals. Give standard bibliographic information, and note condition of cover, pages, spine, binding, and dust jacket. Also buys some photos of cars.

> David King's Automotive Books
> 5 Brouwer Lane
> Rockville Center, NY 11570
> (516) 766-1561

★ *Ford* **Motor Company memorabilia** from before 1955, including books, coins, badges, pins, postcards, and literature.

> Tim O'Callaghan
> 46878 Betty Hill
> Plymouth, MI 48170
> (313) 459-4636

★ *Ford* **Motor Company** memorabilia and other items related to Ford automobiles: postcards, books, photos, Christmas cards, sheet music, records, pens, pins, china, silverware, menus, sales literature, joke books, and what have you. Also wants items related to **Henry Ford**. Has a special interest in sales literature from 1928 to 1936.

> Cliff Moebius
> 484 Winthrop Street
> Westbury, NY 11590
> (516) 333-3797

★ **Advertising literature for the** *Chevrolet Corvette,* 1953 on, including newspaper and magazine ads, sales brochures, direct mailings, race programs, sports programs, and auto show literature. Also "related *Corvette* memorabilia," including promotional giveaways. No reprints.
David Facey, Auto-Ads
7015 Klein Road
Lakeland, FL 33813
(813) 644-8369

★ **1932** *Chevrolet* parts, accessories, go-withs, and paper ephemera including ads, showroom literature, catalogs, repair manuals, and what have you. Will buy nearly any original parts, but especially needs dash clock, heater, various switches, tools, defroster, and many other items. If you regularly come across parts, send for his wants list.
Reed Fitzpatrick
9925 SW 178th Street
Vashon, WA 98070
(206) 463-3900 days

★ *Buick* **promotional items.**
Alvin Heckard
Route #1 Box 88
Lewistown, PA 17044
(717) 248-7071

★ *Mercedes* **and** *Rolls-Royce* radiator mascots and other parts, accessories, manuals, and literature made before 1960.
Joseph Weber
604 Centre Street
Ashland, PA 17921
(717) 875-4401 from 3 to 5 p.m.

★ *Rolls Royce* **advertising,** pamphlets, cards, toys, and other information. Has particular interest in all models from the years 1957 through 1962, *Princess* through *Silver Cloud.*
Richard Melcher
1206 Okanogan Street
Wenatchee, WA 98807
(509) 662-0386

★ *Cunningham Auto Company* **ephemera.** "I want anything regarding this 1920's Rochester, NY, auto maker. Priced approvals are requested. Your postage will be reimbursed."
David Lamb
48 Woodside Drive
Rochester, NY 14624

★ **Parts and ephemera for** *Gardner* **and other autos made in St. Louis** such as *Moon, Diana, Ruxton*, and *Windsor*. Buys parts, hubcaps, mascots, owner's manuals, and the like. Will pay $75 for a single brochure on the front drive of a 1930 *Gardner*.
  Robert Owen
  PO Box 204
  Fairborn, OH 45324

★ **Odd looking spark plugs.** "I'll buy as many as you have, the odder looking the better." He especially wants those with priming cups. No *AC* or *Champion* plugs.
  Joseph Weber
  604 Centre Street
  Ashland, PA 17921
    (717) 875-4401 from 3 to 5 p.m.

★ **Factory original automobile AM radios 1926-1962.** Only AM-FM from 1963-77. Wants brand and model number. Also auto wheel-covers (*not hubcaps*), 1950 to the present. Tell him the make, model, condition, and quantity. Include your price, phone number and hours to reach you.
  John Sheldon
  2718 Koper Drive
  Sterling Heights, MI 48310
    (313) 977-7979 days   Fax: (313) 977-0895

★ *Firestone Tire Company* **promotional items** especially those shaped like tires including tire ashtrays, clocks, pen holders, cigarette cases. Also radios shaped like batteries, and other figural selling aids. List everything printed on the tire and on the insert. Does not want domestic ashtrays made after 1950. Pays $20-$35 for most items.
  Wayne Ray
  10325 Willeo Creek Trace
  Roswell, GA 30075
    (404) 998-5325

★ **Tire company promotional items** especially tire ashtrays, tire clocks, pen holders, radios, globes, *Tires* magazines, tire catalogs, and other literature and promotional items. "Will pay $50 for any original *Michelin* or *Overman* rubber tire ashtray." Also want foreign tires, tires with commemorative inserts, and other unusual promotional tires. Long priced wants list available.
  Jeff Mc Vey
  PO Box 50091
  Billings, MT 59105

LICENSE PLATES

★ **License plates before 1920,** especially undated plates made of leather, brass, or porcelain. Will buy old collections or accumulations. Describe condition carefully, including damage, chips, and crazing. He offers to answer questions about license plates and says "If I don't want your plates, perhaps I can find someone who does." Gary is secretary of the Automobile License Plate Collector's Association and a valuable source of information.

> Gary Brent Kincade
> PO Box 712
> Weston, WV 26452
> (304) 842-3773 eves

★ **Extraordinary license plates, especially undated** or those made of porcelain, leather, or wood. Also all license plates issued on or for Indian reservations. Also U.S. pre-1915; all motorcycle pre-1950; all foreign pre-1950; all Southern and Southwestern plates pre-1935; New Mexico, Alaska, and Hawaii pre-1950 in good condition and pre-1920 in any condition; and personalized plates "with cute names or phrases." Also any pictorial plates. Will buy any good condition pre-1935 plate plus collections or accumulations of plates. George also buys **miniature plates from DAV,** *Goodrich, Wheaties,* or *Post* cereals. Also **car club emblems** such as AAA, especially foreign ones or those before 1925. Also all pre-1940 **chauffeur's badges** in good original condition. List the type of item, place of origin, date, number, condition, quantity, and price (if possible). Will make offer on any item if two loose stamps are sent. "If you don't like what I offer for your license plate, I'll let you run a free ad in my *License Plate Corner* magazine so you can try to sell it for more."

"Plates from populated states like NY, OH, and PA are worth little even if they date back to 1915 whereas plates from Alaska, Hawaii, and Puerto Rico are wanted from any year even in poor shape."

> George Chartrand
> PO Box 334
> Winnipeg, MB
> R3C 2H6 CANADA
> (204) 774-1186

★ **Ordinary license plates** such as found in wrecking yards and garage sales, but only in nearly new condition. Will pay 25¢ each, up to $5 each for harder to find ones. Will accept shipments of up to 200 plates; write if you have more than that.

> George Chartrand
> PO Box 334
> Winnipeg, MB
> R3C 2H6 CANADA

★ **Porcelain license plates** from U.S. and Canadian cars, trucks, and motorcycles before 1923. Also wants early **photos and photo postcards of vehicles clearly showing readable plates.** Pays especially well for plates from Southern and unpopulated Western states. Does not buy painted metal plates. Photocopies suggested.

> Rodney Brunsell
> 55 Spring Street
> Hanson, MA 02341

★ **All types of old license plates.** "I buy license plates from anywhere issued to any type of motor vehicle at any time. My number one find would be a 1905 VT porcelain plate, for which I'd pay $1,500 if in good condition." Describe all chips, bends, repainting, rust, etc.

> Andy Bernstein
> 154 Murray Drive
> Oceanside, NY 11572
>   (516) 764-0273 or   (516) 536-3635

★ **License plates from vehicles other than trucks and automobiles** such as motorcycles, bicycles, snowmobiles, etc. George will also buy **license plates issued by cities** from before 1920, and pay $40 to $1,000 for them, depending on rarity. List the type of item, place of origin, date, number, condition, and price (if possible).

> George Chartrand
> PO Box 334
> Winnipeg, MB
> R3C 2H6 CANADA

★ **License plates from Southern states pre-1958,** and other states pre-1935. Wants *only* automobile plates except from Mississippi, a state from which he will buy all types and classes of plates. 1912 and 1913 Mississippi plates are worth up to $1,000 each. Wants first year of issue plates from all 50 states, as well as any undated or handmade plates.

> Eugene Gardner
> 10510 Rico Tatum Road
> Palmetto, GA 30268
>   (404) 463-4264

★ **License plates from Missouri, Kansas, and Colorado.** Also wants other states from the years 1936, 1976, and 1989. Also miniature key chain license plates produced by *B.F. Goodrich* or the DAV. Provide a list of the items you have and the price you'd like.

> George Van Trump, Jr.
> PO Box 260170
> Lakewood, CO 80226
>   (303) 985-3508

★ **License plates from Washington and Alaska**. Very early leather and porcelain plates are wanted, but "I'll buy any Washington State plates 1915-1959 in most any condition. All Alaska plates are of interest. Unusual plates such as mobile home, taxi, trailer, state representative, etc., are particularly welcome." Also buys old **printed matter about vehicle licensing**, including titles, certificates, tonnage slips, etc. Also buys **license plate frames** with Washington and Alaskan car dealership names, and piggyback **plates that carry an advertising message** and fasten just above or below a license plate. Brass plaques, **auto club insignias**, and the like are of interest too. "When you contact me, I want to know the state, year, type of plate, whether you have a single plate or matched pair, condition (including rust, extra holes), and the material. I'll also consider **plates from other states** that are suitable for trading."

    Reed Fitzpatrick
    PO Box 369
    Vashon, WA 98070
       (206) 463-3900

★ **British Columbia license plates** before 1922 in any condition. Later BC plates will be considered if unusual, as will pre-1960 Yukon plates, Canadian motorcycle plates, and BC chauffeur's badges and key tags.

    Don Schneider
    PO Box 1570
    Merritt, BC
    V0K 2B0   CANADA

★ **License plates and license plate related items**, chauffeur's badges, hack (taxi) badges, Disabled Veterans key chain tags, *B.F. Goodrich* key chain tags, dashboard discs, registration windshield stickers, inspection windshield stickers, early driver's licenses and auto registrations.

    Dr. Edward Miles
    888 8th Ave.
    New York, NY 10019
       (212) 765-2660

★ **B.F.Goodrich and DAV keychain license plate tags.** Pays 50¢ to $1 each, depending on age and state. The older the better.

    Dennis Schulte
    8th Avenue NW
    Waukon, IA 52172

★ **Aluminum license plate attachments.** "I'll buy unusual and attractive licence plate attachments which promote cities, states, turnpikes or special events. I don't need more Florida cities, but want other decorative aluminum brackets designed to fit above a license plate."

    Peter Capell
    1838 West Grace Street
    Chicago, IL 60613
       (312) 871-8735 eves

OFFICE MACHINES

★ **Unusual antique typewriters.** Wants items dating between 1870-1920. Look for typewriters with odd designs, curved keyboards, no keyboards, pointers, or more or less than the standard four rows of keys. The most desired machine is a *Sholes & Glidden*, worth as much as $5,000 in outstanding condition. Give the make and model number if it can be found on the machine, the serial number, and "an in-focus photo."

"If you recognize the brand name on your typewriter, collectors probably don't want it. Remington, Smith-Corona, Underwood, and Oliver are common, not of interest to collectors."

Rehr will provide you with a free checklist to help you describe your machine to him. Also buys ribbon tins and early literature and catalogs of typewriters as well as early **small calculators**. Include an SASE with inquiries or to receive a free packet about the Typewriter Association.

Darryl Rehr
Early Typewriter Collectors Association
2591 Military Ave.
Los Angeles, CA 90064
(310) 477-5229 phone or fax

★ **American typewriters and ephemera** before 1925 including ribbon tins, ribbon, tools, accessories, oilers, advertising, catalogs, instruction manuals, shipping cases if they are imprinted with the name of a typewriter, catalogs for business schools if they picture early typewriters, cardboard or metal signs, paperweights, blotters, clocks, rulers or any other item imprinted with the name or illustration of a typewriter. Also early **typewriter tables** with fancy cast iron frames or legs (they usually have two drop leaves and a center drawer). Also typewriting instruction books pre-1910. **Some small very early hand held adders and calculators** are of interest. Provide the name, model, type of lid and base, and condition. Photocopy accessories. "Never ship a typewriter until a deal is made. I will give shipping and packing instructions first. I am not a dealer and do not buy typewriters for stock. If the machine is not one that I want, but may be wanted by another collector of early typewriters, I will help you find a buyer." His *American Typewriters: A Collector's Encyclopedia,* is available from the author for $55.

"If in doubt, write or call. I'll happily answer any inquiry rather than risk missing an item I would like to hear about."

Paul Lippman
1216 Garden Street
Hoboken, NJ 07030
(201) 656-5278 eves   Fax: (201) 714-9350

★ **Typewriters** made before 1910, especially those with fancy or strange mechanisms, such as the *Sholes & Glidden* from the 1870's which strikes from below so the typist can't see her work. "I'm always willing to give you *"I will never try to buy your machine for less than it's worth."* an opinion about a machine if you send a picture or good description."
>
> Joseph Weber
> 604 Centre Street
> Ashland, PA 17921
>   (717) 875-4401 from 3 to 5 p.m.

★ **Check writers and check protectors,** pre-1910, in working condition. May be home, office, or hand held models. No machines by *Todd, F & E Lightning, Hedman, Paymaster,* or *Safeguard.*
>
> William Feigin
> 45 West 34th Street   #405
> New York, NY 10001
>   (212) 736-3360

★ **Telegraphones and other unusual magnetic recorders, especially wire.** Not interested in *Webster* machines.
>
> Harold Layer, SFSU-AV
> 1600 Holloway Ave.
> San Francisco, CA 94132

★ **Calculating devices before 1915** and associated ephemera including catalogs and advertising. Wants mechanical calculators such as arithmometers, generally in wooden cases. Brand names to look for include *Autarith, Baldwin, Calculmeter, Grant, Madas, Spalding, Thomas,* but interested in anything odd. Also rotary machine, heavy devices operated by a crank, and other types of calculators including **slide rules** (if they don't have patent numbers). He buys comptometers with wooden cases as well as **planimeters**, devices for measuring area on maps. Give a photo or sketch of what you have plus describe markings, serial numbers, etc. Weight and dimensions helpful. Photocopy your paper goods.
>
> Robert Otnes
> 2160 Middlefield Road
> Palo Alto, CA 94301
>   (415) 324-1821 eves

★ **Unusual calculators and adding machines.** "I buy unusual and scarce calculators and adding machines, and pay for information leading to them. Will travel worldwide and pay immediate cash, no fuss, for the right items. I am happy to buy single items or entire collections."
>
> Peter Frei
> PO Box 500
> Brimfield, MA 01010
>   (800) 942-8968 or in Mass: (413) 245-4660

★ **Decorative resellable things found in the offices** of doctors, dentists, undertakers, blacksmiths, watchmakers, gunsmiths, locksmiths, opticians, jewelers, mines, hotels, brothels, police stations, prisons, firehouses, asylums, saloons, roadhouses, arcades, breweries, boat wrights, etc., including furniture, cash registers, glass counters, tools, and the like. "I will respond to any honest inquiry for help to identify an item for sale." He requests a complete description indicating all wear or broken parts. If you know the item's history, it is helpful. Photos of larger items and photocopies of smaller ones are recommended. "I'd rather buy an entire store or business than a single item. No lot is too large!"

"Readers should not expect to get rich from decorator items. It is expensive for dealers to buy, transport, restore, and then try to find buyers for items. If I can resell their item quickly, the offer will be more than if I must warehouse the item."

Larry Franklin
3238 Hutchison Ave.
Los Angeles, CA 90034
(310) 559-4461

★ **Cash registers made of brass or wood,** especially early wooden registers with inlaid cabinets, dial registers, or multiple drawers. Also registers that ring only to $1. He also buys AMOUNT PURCHASED signs that were on top of registers, and literature about registers. Machines can be in any condition since he uses damaged machines for parts. Give both the brand name and model number of your machine and include the serial number. Provide your phone number so Ken can make arrangements to pick up your machine. Nothing after 1917.

Ken Konet
849 Oak Hill Road
Barrington, IL 60010
(708) 382-7799   Fax: (708) 382-7803

★ **Stock market tickers, books, and other memorabilia** having to do with speculation, panics, commodities, cycles, and other activities pre-1940. Also turn of the century prints depicting the stock market, and **stock market magazines** pre-1935.

R.G. Klein
PO Box 24A06
Los Angeles, CA 90024

★ **Stock market tickers.** "I'll pay $2,000 for *Edison* glass domed tickers and $1,500 for those made for *Western Union*."

Frank Guarino
PO Box 89
DeBary, FL 32713

★ **Banking relics** such as old bank safes, money bags, bullion and stage coach boxes, *Wells Fargo and Co* or *Railway Express* locks, assay office items, scales, and **three fingered lock boxes** (which cut off your fingers if you put them in the wrong holes to open the box). Wants things before 1900. Not interested in paper.
>Larry Franklin
>3238 Hutchison Ave.
>Los Angeles, CA 90034
>>(310) 559-4461

★ **Mimeograph memorabilia.** Advertising, instructions, service manuals, etc. If it's very *old* and about mimeos, he may be interested.
>Walley Francis
>PO Box 6941
>Syracuse, NY 13217
>>(315) 478-5671

★ **Microcomputer literature and computers** including just about anything, machines, literature, catalogs, you name it, if it's from the pre-*Apple* pre-*Radio Shack* days (before 1977). Look for *Mark-8, Sphere, Scelbi, Intel* and other machines created for "do it your selfers."
>Harold Layer
>SF State University-AV
>1600 Holloway Ave.
>San Francisco, CA 94132

★ **Time clocks.** Give the brand name, model number and condition.
>Steve Chyrchel
>Route #2 Box 362
>Eureka Springs, AR 72632
>>(501) 253-9244

★ **Telephones made before 1930,** especially unusual or early pay phones. His wants list and parts catalog's handy numbered illustrations will help you describe what you want to sell. Also buys **telephone books** pre-1950, "the earlier the better."
>Gerry Billard, Old Telephones
>21710 Regnart Road
>Cupertino, CA 95014
>>(408) 252-2104

★ **Telephones, parts of phones, and phone company memorabilia** especially signs and pre-1900 magazines with telephone ads. No modern or electronic phones. They offer the *History and Identification of Old Telephones* with 6,000 pictures of old phones for $58.
>Ron and Mary Knappen, Phoneco
>Route #2 Box 590
>Galesville, WI 54630
>>(608) 582-4124

★ **Telephones made before 1905,** porcelain signs featuring phones, telephone watch fobs, telephone pocket mirrors, and similar quality phone related items. **Also spring driven telegraph registers and fire station bells.** No interest in paper. "A photo is worth 1,000 words."
Paul Engelke, Key Telephone Company
23399 Rio Del Mar Drive
Boca Raton, FL 33486
(407) 338-3332

★ **Rare glass insulators.** Describe the color, dimensions, embossing, whether it has threads, and its condition. Requests you describe insulators using numbers found in Milholland's *Most About Glass Insulators,* available from Linscott with price guide for $39. No damaged insulators are wanted. Color of your insulators is particularly important.
Len Linscott
3557 Nicklaus Drive
Titusville, FL 32780
(407) 267-9170

★ **Telegraph instruments** if old, complete, and professional quality, especially from railroads.
Scott Arden
20457 Highway 126
Noti, OR 97461

★ **Telegraph instruments and ephemera** from before 1900 including keys (worth $50-$100), sounders, relays, signs, catalogs, and stationery, especially railroad instruments. Wants registers (clockwork driven devices that inscribe dots and dashes on paper tape) and will pay to $800-$1,000 for them. Also seeking linemen's sets of very small portable keys in a hard rubber case. Items do not need to be in perfect condition. No *Boy Scout, Menominee, Western Electric,* or *Signal* equipment or post 1900 paper or telegrams, but he loves to find signs advertising telegraph companies before 1890. A photo or crude sketch is appreciated.

"Names to look for include L.G. Tillotson, Patrick and Carter, Greeley, Chester, Clark, Davis, Redding, Jones, Williams, Pope, and 100 others."

Roger Reinke, Brasspounder
5301 Neville Court
Alexandria, VA 22310
(703) 971-4095

★ *Western Union* and *Postal Telegraph* instruments and ephemera. List all marks on items you wish to sell. No cracked or damaged pieces.
Charles Goodman
636 West Grant Ave.
Charleston, IL 61920

BUSINESS RELATED PAPER

★ **Business cards of all types.** "We buy business cards of all types with particular interest in cards 1700-1960. We even buy cards that are damaged or written upon if they are rare ones. We also buy other paper items such as **photos, letters, and bill heads related to business cards.** We will pay postage both ways on items sent to us on approval." Few business cards have much value, but Jack will pay well for Mathew Brady and Benjamin Franklin. Jack emphasizes that chromolith (color printed) cards were stock items issued in large quantities. Photocopies are the best description. Jack edits *The Business Card Journal.*

> Jack Gurner
> 116 Dupuy Street
> Water Valley, MS 38965
> (601) 473-1154

★ **Business cards.** "I'll consider buying business cards that are unique, unusual, or have an interesting story. Cards from exotic or unlikely materials such as stainless steel, plastic, papyrus, tin, etc., and cards from celebrities. Looks for creativity, which is "timeless," so will consider anything imaginative in shape, color, message, or material. "I love cards that make you laugh." Photocopy what you have if possible, otherwise describe it [them] as best you can. Some **trade card collections** will be considered if they are suitable for resale or auction. Avery is President of The American Business Card Club.

> Avery N. Pitzak
> PO Box 460297
> Aurora, CO 80046
> (303) 690-6496

★ **Envelopes with color advertising for products** on the front or back, but only if they are from before 1940.

> Gordon McHenry
> PO Box 1117
> Osprey, FL 34229
>   Fax: (813) 966-4568

★ **Trade catalogs and piles of business letters,** pre-1920, from manufacturers, wholesalers, and retailers. "The earlier the better," says Jim. Most common catalogs bring from $5-$10, but "we have paid as high as $400 for some." Please check that all pages are present as you list the company name, the type of products, size and number of pages, and the type and number of illustrations. Photocopies are helpful. Mention *Where To Sell It!* for a free copy of Jim's catalog of catalogs.

> Jim Presgraves
> Bookworm & Silverfish
> PO Box 639
> Wytheville, VA 24382

★ **Trade catalogs** for consumer products. "These are exciting peeks into their time, giving the unvarnished truth about their era. Prices vary from two figures (most catalogs are $10-$90) to over $10,000 for rare and desirable ones."
> Ivan Gilbert, Miran Arts & Books
> 2824 Elm Ave.
> Columbus, OH 43209

★ **Christmas catalogs** from *Sears, Montgomery Wards, JC Penny, Alden* and *Spiegel*, dating between 1958 and 1969 only. "Please contact me with prices and what you have."
> David Snow
> East 4217 22nd Ave.
> Spokane, WA 99223

★ **Trade cards,** especially better quality and specialized collections. Especially interested in clipper ships, mechanical banks, *Currier & Ives*, metamorphic and mechanical, and other better items. Will pay $300 up for fine cards depicting mechanical banks, and $150+ for clipper ships. No interest in damaged common cards or stock cards with no company name. Must actually see an item in person before making offers. Will not do phone appraisals or evaluations of items not for sale.
> Russell Mascieri
> 6 Florence Ave.
> Marlton, NJ 08053
> (609) 985-7711   Fax: (609) 985-8513

★ **Advertising trade cards** for chewing gum and **insert cards** issued by candy, gum, bakery, beverage, cereal or tobacco companies. Photocopy your cards and tell me what you want for them, or "I welcome approvals, pay all postage, and respond within 48 hours of receipt. Condition is important as I do not collect trimmed cards, badly creased or otherwise battered items."
> William Nielsen
> PO Box 1379
> Brewster, MA 02631
> (508) 896-7389

★ **Vegetable and oyster people trade cards** are wanted. Photocopy.
> Linda Mellis
> 1115 West Montana
> Chicago, IL 60614

★ **Employee photo ID passes.** All photo ID badges are wanted, especially the celluloid buttons with pin backs. Rich pays $2 each except for older ones. Don't bother to inquire, just drop your badge in the mail.
> Rich Hartzog
> PO Box 4143 BFT
> Rockford, IL 61110

PACKAGING & ADVERTISING

★ **Salesmen's samples** and other well-made miniatures of real objects. "If your item is in miniature, all parts to scale, and complete, it can be well worth your while to contact me about it. A sample barber's chair, for example, is worth $10,000 to me. So is a *Wooten* desk sample. Other samples are worth from $300 to $5,000. I'm not interested in doll house miniatures, but want to hear about just about any other small well-crafted items. Since I am writing a book on salesmen's samples, I would like to hear from you even if your piece is not for sale." A photo is almost essential. Include dimensions. Note all repairs. Describe any marks or labels. Describe the case and its condition.

> John Everett
> PO Box 126
> Bodega, CA 94922
>   (707) 876-3513

★ **Three-dimensional advertising trademarked character displays from stores.** "I buy plaster, composition, plastic and wooden store figures depicting cartoonish advertising characters. Items wanted are store displays and statuettes, and promotional banks, figural ash trays, and bobbing head dolls. I'm particularly interested in items of the 1940's through 1970's. Some character examples include *Speedy Alka Seltzer*, *Reddy Kilowatt, Elsie the Cow, Philip Morris*'s Johnny, the *Esquire* man, *Pep Boys* figures and other characters. Please provide a good description, paying close attention to damage. I prefer dealers to price goods, but will make offers to amateur sellers."

> Warren Dotz
> 2999 Regent Street
> Berkeley, CA 94705
>   (510) 652-1159

★ **Canning machinery, catalogs and tools** of the *Ferracute Machine Company* of Bridgeton, NJ, are sought by this researcher who also wants anything related to company founder, **Oberlin Smith**. The Oberlin Smith Society is particularly interested in advertising, catalogs, small presses, medals and tokens, but will consider anything related to FMCo or Smith himself. The OSS is a 501(c)(3) organization and seeks donations, too.

> James Gandy, Oberlin Smith Society
> Route #2 Box 109, River Road
> Bridgeton, NJ 08302
>   (609) 451-5586

★ **Tin can and box making ephemera and artifacts** including items related to **commercial stone lithography** (label printing) before 1925, especially the printing of packages, labels, tin cans, and advertising.

> Tony Hyman
> PO Box 3028
> Pismo Beach, CA 93448

★ **Motion display advertising,** especially by *Baranger*. These are small pieces, under 3' high, usually with animated people advertising watches from the 1930's and 40's, but other products are also found.

> Frank Novak
> 7386 Beverly Blvd.
> Los Angeles, CA 90036
> (213) 683-1963   Fax: (213) 683-1312

★ **Neon advertising clocks and signs,** 1920-50. Buys those entirely of neon as well as those with "reverse painting on glass" that are lit by neon. Prefers smaller sizes that can be safely shipped via UPS. His favorite clocks and signs are "point of purchase" which sit on counter tops, although he buys wall models, too. He is particularly interested in signs with neon glow tubes made by AMGLO. Also buys **signs that bubble, create optical illusions, or are animated**. Value is based on visual appeal so a photo is essential. Does not want new neon beer signs, plastic signs of any sort, or signs lit by fluorescent tubes.

> Roark Vane
> 6839 Havenside Drive
> Sacramento, CA 95831
> (916) 392-3864

★ **Porcelain signs, clocks, thermometers, and door pushes** for any product, but has special interest in colas. Wants fine condition items with good graphics only. Photograph suggested. Give dimensions. Dealers price your goods, but he will make offers for amateur sellers.

> Van Stueart
> Route 3   Box 216
> Nashville, AR 71852
> (501) 845-4264

★ **Tin, porcelain, and cardboard advertising** from before 1920 including signs, posters, cans, trays, calendars, syrup dispensers, etc., for candy, gum, groceries, soft drinks, ammunition, tobacco, beer, and the like. No magazine or newspaper ads. "We pay the highest prices but do not make offers. Let us know what you have and what you want for it."

> Don Stuart
> 4751 NE Ocean Blvd.
> Jensen Beach, FL 34957
> (407) 225-0900

★ **Typewriter ribbon tins.** "I'm interested in any typewriter tin in good condition. I especially want tins made to hold ribbon wider than 1/2" and boxed sets of tins. Large quantities eagerly accepted, but no cardboard boxes of any type." Please send a photocopy.

> Darryl Rehr
> 2591 Military Ave.
> Los Angeles, CA 90064
> (310) 477-5229   phone or fax

★ **Advertising china made by** *Royal Doulton.* All types including ashtrays, jugs, mugs, bottles, ginger beers, display signs. Old and rare pieces do not have to be in perfect condition to be considered for purchase, but you must indicate any flaws in your description. Make sure to mention the item, the product being advertised, size, color, condition, and any markings.
> Diane Alexander
> 20834 San Simeon Way #70-C
> North Miami Beach, FL 33179
> (305) 770-4422

★ **Colorful tin cans, signs and trays** advertising beer, whiskey, soda pop, medicines, tobacco, and food such as peanuts, peanut butter, tea, coffee, and the like. Especially likes rare peanut butter pails and one-pound coffee cans from New York companies. Nothing rusty or damaged. Describe colors. Photocopy please.
> Burton Spiller
> 49 Palmerston Road
> Rochester, NY 14618
> (716) 244-2229

★ **Porcelain enamel signs,** 1880-1950, advertising any U.S. bicycles, automobiles, motorcycles, gasoline, oil, soda pop, food, soap, clothing, telephones, telegraph, money orders, etc. Likes all types of porcelain signs, including those with **neon trim, thermometers**, and the like, especially interesting figurals. Prices are always best for those in multiple colors which depict animals, people, products, or fancy logos. Condition is very important. He is not interested in repros (look for brass grommets in the hanging holes). No signs bigger than 8 feet long or high. "I want a close up photo, dimensions, and any information the seller has on the item's background. Make certain to include your home phone."
> Robert Newman
> 10809 Charnock Road
> Los Angeles, CA 90034
> (310) 559-0539

★ **Tin plates** from the turn of the century depicting women and/or advertising. Plates were usually printed by *Meek, Beech* or *Shonk.* Plates must be in fine condition. Photos of what you have are almost essential.
> Lisa Van Hook
> PO Box 13256
> El Cajon, CA 92022

★ **Damaged, bent, or rusty tin cans or signs** which are difficult to sell. They aren't worth much, but few people will buy them at all.
> Ron Knappen
> Route #2 Box 590
> Galesville, WI 54630

★ **Celluloid advertising mirrors** and other small advertising items such as bookmarks, pin back buttons, blotters, stamp cases, etc. "I run auctions of these items, so buy anything, but you may also consign your items to my auction after discussing them with me first by phone." Especially likes pocket mirrors with colorful pictures of women, children, nudes, or pictures of the product. Send a photocopy of your mirror, along with notations as to color and any imperfections.

> John Andreae
> 51122 Mill Run
> Granger, IN 46530
> (219) 272-2337   Fax: (219) 271-1146

★ **Advertising mirrors of all types,** both pocket and paperweight style. Higher prices paid for anything from Illinois, Florida, or Michigan. Better prices paid for those with a product or female or both. Spots, rips, brown areas, foxing, etc., in the celluloid will lower the value substantially. Please ship or send a photocopy for offer. Particularly wanted *"Condition of the picture side is important; mirrors, unless missing or broken, don't matter."* are any mirrors with GOOD FOR 10¢ IN TRADE or similar variation for which he pays from $35 to $2,000. "I consider paperweight mirrors to be less desirable than pocket mirrors, and seldom pay over $20 for them, even ones you think might be unusual."

> Rich Hartzog
> PO Box 4143 BFT
> Rockford, IL 61110
> (815) 226-0771

★ **Advertising pocket mirrors** of all types, especially marked as being GOOD FOR TRADE. Making a photocopy is suggested by this author and expert in the field of mirrors.

> Stephen P. Alpert
> PO Box 66331
> Los Angeles, CA 90066
> (310) 478-7405

★ **Advertising buttons** from North Carolina and South Carolina products, companies, or any topic at all, including politics, meetings, etc. Make a photocopy of what you have.

> Lew Powell
> 700 East Park Ave.
> Charlotte, NC 28203

ADVERTISING FOR VARIOUS INDUSTRIES

★ **Coffee cans with pictures printed onto the tin** are wanted, especially the tall one pound cans with slip tops. No vacuum (key open) cans are wanted. $500 to $1,000 each will be paid for *Army & Navy, Blue Parrot, College Town, Convention Hall* (green or yellow only), *Festall Hall, Mayflower* or *Town Crier.* Most paper label cans are not as desirable, but some are collectible, but bring a substantially smaller selling price. Send the name of the tin, height and diameter, and state whether the condition is like new or scratched and worn. The *Luzianne* can is common, worth about $15.

> Tim Schweighart
> 1123 Santa Luisa Drive
> Solana Beach, CA 92075
> (619) 481-8315

★ **Cigar advertising boxes, labels and tins,** especially boxes featuring nudes, sports, gambling, comic characters, and other colorful scenes. Also **gambling devices, trade figures, or signs related to cigars.** Also tin **tobacco cans** and boxes. Photocopy the inside lid of boxes you'd like to sell. Long SASE will bring you a priced illustrated wants list. Don't want items covered with cigar bands except as a gift. Nothing in poor condition. Will pay $400+ for *Asthma Cure, Cheez It* or any xxx rated box. *Handbook of American Cigar Boxes,* an illustrated limited edition is available for $14.95 postpaid with price guide.

> Tony Hyman
> PO Box 3028
> Pismo Beach, CA 93448
> (805) 773-6777   Fax: (805) 773-0117

★ **Gun and ammunition related advertising.** "I buy posters, calendars, envelopes with ads, cardboard shotshell boxes, gunpowder cans, pin back buttons, glass target balls, catalogs, etc. but I am only interested in items produced by a gun or ammunition maker (not secondary vendors) before 1940."

> Ron Willoughby
> 1072 Route 171
> Woodstock, CT 06281
> (203) 974-1226

★ **Gun company advertising depicting cowboys, cowgirls or cattle.** Advertising from other products considered, but particular interest in items with Western orientation. Also wants all **original art for gun and ammunition company ads.** Please send color photo.

> Johnny Spellman
> 10806 North Lamar
> Austin, TX 78753
> (512) 836-2889 days   (512) 258-6910 eves

★ **Fire service and fire insurance items** such as badges, histories of insurance companies, pre-1900 fire insurance policies, firemarks, signs, advertising, and postcards. Doesn't want anything except fire related items, and nothing modern. Please quote books that are fire related.

Glenn Hartley
2859 Marlin Drive
Chamblee, GA 30341
(404) 451-2651

★ **Anything relating to fire insurance companies** before 1940. Wants fire marks, illustrated policies, advertising, signs, and giveaways. Does not make offers, so price what you have.

Ralph Jennings
301 Fort Washington Ave.
Fort Washington, PA 19034

★ **Stove company samples and toy stoves.** Wants salesmen's sample stoves, particularly made by *Majestic, Quick Meal, Engman-Matthews* and *Home Comfort*. Desirable toy stoves include *Dolly's Favorite* and all models of *Buck's Jr*. Also wants toy cooking utensils that accompany these stoves (skillets, Dutch ovens, and especially tea kettles up to 4" high) by such makers as *Wagner Ware* and *Griswold*. Dimensions and condition are helpful but a "picture is usually all I need."

Ed Hullet
5200 North Lorraine
Hutchinson, KS 67502
(316) 662-9381

★ **Stove company samples.** "I'll buy salesmen's sample stoves finished in porcelain enamel such as those made by *Beauty Banquet, Monarch, Qualified,* and *Home Comfort*. I especially want a miniature *Monarch* range which is 32" tall to the top of the warming ovens and comes in green, yellow, and white." She would like to correspond with other collectors or owners of miniature stoves.

Marilyn Wren
9073 Weidkamp
Lynden, WA 98264

★ **Old salmon can labels.** Singles, samples, or collections from any state. Also buys postcards, letterheads, and views of canneries, fish traps, etc. Only items dating from before 1960 are wanted. You may send fine condition early items on approval.

W.E. Nickell
102 People's Wharf
Juneau, AK 99801
(907) 586-1733

★ **Fruit crate labels and other advertising** from the packing, **canning and bottling trades** such as posters, tin signs, sales displays, letterheads, magazine ads, and other promotional items. He says he'll buy fruit and vegetable labels, American or foreign, but especially West Coast. Will consider singles, bulk quantities, and labels on crates. Especially interested in *Sunkist, Del Monte, Libby's*, etc.
>T. Pat Jacobsen
>437 Minton Court
>Pleasant Hill, CA 94523
>>(510) 930-8531

★ **Florida citrus labels.** Also advertisements and other paper related to the Florida citrus industry.
>Jerry Chicone
>PO Box 547636
>Orlando, FL 32854
>>(407) 298-555

★ **Southern advertising for products.** Wants decorative advertising and packaging in any form, including signs, posters, labels, paper bags, **feed and flour sacks,** bottles, boxes, etc., for any product or company located in the South. Items may be old or new, but "we prefer unused stock." Buys only in quantity for resale. Does not buy or do appraisals on single pieces. Photocopies helpful. Publishes *The Southern Label Collector's Newsletter.*
>D.W. King & Associates
>PO Box 24811
>Tampa, FL 33623
>>(813) 888-8057

★ **Popcorn memorabilia** including boxes, cans, crates, brochures, catalogs, old machines, parts of machines, *Creator's* steam engines, and everything else related to popcorn.
>Jack Cory
>3395 West Pinks Place
>Las Vegas, NV 89102
>>(702) 367-2676

★ **Advertising for medicine and whiskey companies.**
>Robert Daly
>10341 Jewell Lake Court
>Fenton, MI 48430
>>(313) 629-4934

ADVERTISING FOR SPECIFIC COMPANIES

★ *Cracker Jack* **prizes, advertising** and related items, including tins, jars, store advertising, point of sale, and dealer items from any of the following companies: *Checkers Confections, Angel Marshmallows, Shotwell Mfg. Co., Rueckheim Bros.* and *Eckstein Co.* He does not want plastic *Cracker Jack* toys and prizes. Note any obvious signs of wear. Price if you can.

> Edwin Snyder
> PO Box 156
> Lancaster, KY 40444
> (606) 792-4816

★ *Planters Peanut* **memorabilia.** "I'll buy all rare and unusual items" with particular interest in any and all figural, 3-D, *Mr. Peanuts* such as:
> Wooden jointed doll;
> "Blinker" with lighted eyes;
> "Tapper" which taps on a window;
> Scale made of cast iron and aluminum, 4' high;
> Rubber squeeze toy about 8" tall;
> *Mr. Peanut* hand puppet;
> Fence sitter, cast iron, 42" high;
> Parade costume and anything papier maché;
> Any tin displays and 5# and 10# peanut tins;
> Unopened key wind tins of peanuts;
> Cardboard display boxes peanuts came in;
> Wooden shipping boxes;
> Old jars with peanut finials.

Does not want reproductions or anything from the 1970's or 80's. Does not want plastic items, or tin nut dish sets except World's Fair set (worth about $20). No broken or incomplete items. Send a photo and complete description, including condition of the surface and paint. Enclose an SASE for picture return. Richard is author of *Planter's Peanut Advertising and Collectibles*.

> Richard and Barbara Reddock
> 914 Ilse Court
> North Bellmore, NY 11710
> (516) 826-2032 eves

★ *Elsie the Cow* **and other** *Borden's* **ephemera** including games, toys, cookbooks, comic books, cups, glasses, Xmas cards, employee magazines, neon signs, milk bottles, and trade cards. Would especially like an *Elsie* string puppet and a *Borden's Good Food Line* train. No *Elsie* postcards or charms. Also buys milk bottles and advertising from Du Page County, Illinois. Describe and price your items.

> Ronald Selcke
> PO Box 237
> Bloomingdale, IL 60108
> (708) 543-4848 eves

★ *Sunshine Biscuits* **ephemera** including tins, boxes, signs, display racks, novelties, games, calendars, pin back buttons,trade cards, invoices, stationery and "things we have yet to imagine." Buys items from all brands produced by *Sunshine* or its predecessor, *Loose-Wiles Company*. These companies made potato chips, cookies, crackers, marshmallows, pretzels, candy, and several cereals. "We especially want uncut sheets of stuffed animal toys (worth $150 each), *Ann Hathaway* cookie tin ($250) and neckties advertising their products ($25 up)." Complete descriptions include size, shape, condition, what is pictured, and a photograph or photocopy of the best and worst side. "I will discuss an item with a seller on the phone but prefer a letter with pictures and SASE. I will not agree to purchase nor can I make an offer to buy or appraise an item without seeing it in person. I pay or reimburse for postage on anything I request be sent for inspection.

Liz and Dick Wilmes
38W 567 Brindlewood
Elgin, IL 60123
(708) 697-9679

★ *Larkin Soap Company* **items.** "We're primarily interested in catalogs and other historically interesting paper ephemera pre-1920." *Larkin* is also known as *Larkin Mfg., Larkin, Inc., Larkin Co.,* and *People's Mfg. Co.* Ayars and his wife wrote and published *Larkin Oak* ($16) and are working on *Larkin China and Pottery*. "Readers who have questions about *Larkin* are welcome; there is no charge for our research." Include title, year, issue number, or a photocopy of the cover.

Walter Ayars III
PO Box 279
Summerdale, PA 17093
(717) 732-9886

★ *Larkin Soap Company* **items.** "I'll buy items made by or relating to the *Larkin Company,* including products, trade cards, catalogs, advertising, calendars and other paper items. If the item says LARKIN, I'm interested. I want info about the *Larkin* administration building designed by Frank Lloyd Wright and would love to find dedication programs, etc." Please make sure you describe condition.

Jerome Puma
78 Brinton Street
Buffalo, NY 14214
(716) 838-5674

★ *Larkin Soap Company.* "I'm interested in everything!"
Thomas Knopke
1430 East Brookdale Place
Fullerton, CA 92631
(714) 526-1749

★ *Speedy Alka Seltzer* **dolls, toys and ephemera** wanted.
Jim Frugoli
960 North Northwest Highway
Park Ridge, IL 60068

★ *Walgreens Drug Store* **products and ephemera.** "I'll buy a wide
range of products marketed by this national chain between 1901 and
1960, including non prescription drug and health aids, candy, tobacco,
coffee, toys and what have you.
Items were sold under many different
brand names among which are: *Walgreens, Myers, Union Drug, Keller,
Valentine, Carrel, Glide, Amoray,
Ladonna, Olafsen, Orlis, Triomphe,
Hill Rose, CRW,* and others. I'm
especially interested in finding
Walgreens tin cans for coffee and
other products. I do not want any
product marked with the words AGENCY or WALGREEN AGENCY, nor do
I want heating pads, water bottles, or ice caps." To sell to this 10 year
veteran collector, you need to tell him what you have, and its size, color,
and condition. Indicate whether you have the original box or not, and
give the original selling price, if it's marked on the container.

> *"There are only a few
> collectors of Walgreens
> so there isn't a lot of
> competition. But some
> items are quite rare and
> I'd love to hear from you
> if you have one."*

Gordon Addington
260 East Chestnut #2801
Chicago, IL 60611
    (312) 943-4085

★ *State Farm Insurance Company* **memorabilia,** 1922-52. He wants
all items marked with their 3 oval emblem depicting a car, fire helmet,
and cornucopia. Also selected items marked with the home office or an
old *Buick*. He buys ashtrays, pocket knives, pencils, tape measures,
signs, stationery, and everything else. He does not want anything marked
with the three ovals and the words AUTO, LIFE and FIRE.
Ken Jones
100 Manor Drive
Columbia, MO 65203

★ *Flaccus, Hunter and Exwaco* **bottles and jars** with colorful labels.
"All West Virginia food companies from before 1910 are wanted. Has
special interest in food jars, bottles, and crocks from the above, but buys
any jars marked as made or used in Wheeling or Wellsburg, WV.
Give the color of the glass and its size. Report *exactly* what is written on
the jar or crock, and note any cracks, chips, dings, or unwashable stains.
They will pay $200 if you sell them a *Flaccus* stoneware water cooler.
Tom and Deena Caniff
1223 Oak Grove Ave.
Steubenville, OH 43952
    (614) 282-8918

SOFT DRINKS

★ *Coca-Cola* **memorabilia** from before 1945, including fancier *Coke* items with pretty girls and lots of color especially cardboard cut out signs and back bar decorations. He will pay up to $5,000 for pre-1900 calendars. Pays well for metal tins, trays, and signs. Magazine ads are wanted only if before 1932. No commemorative bottles, please.

> Randy Schaeffer, C-C Trayders
> 611 North 5th Street
> Reading, PA 19601
> (215) 373-3333

★ *Coca-Cola* **advertising** of all type before 1940. Buys cardboard cutouts, festoons, and calendars, but has most interest in small items such as watch fobs, openers, pocket knives, and the like. "I will pay premium prices for all advertising for *Coca-Cola* chewing gum." Thom says he "will be glad to help you evaluate the worth of your *Coca-Cola* items."

> Thom Thompson
> 123 Shaw Ave.
> Versailles, KY 40383
> (606) 255-2727 days   (606) 873-8787 eves

★ *Coca-Cola* **advertising.** "I'll buy pre-1960 calendars, trays, small signs, syrup bottles, clocks, thermometers, menu boards, ashtrays, playing cards, lighters, and just about anything else free of rust or wrinkles that says *Coca-Cola*." Loves to find salesman's sample coolers and dispensers. Does not want reproduction trays, bottles of any sort including commemorative, or magazine ads. Describe condition carefully.

> Terry Buchheit
> Route 7   Box 62
> Perryville, MO 63775

★ *Coca-Cola* **ephemera.** Wants pre-1960 signs, clocks, calendars, bottles and carriers, dispensers, machines, uniforms, etc. Will consider any item that reads "Drink *Coca-Cola*." Those that read "Enjoy *Coca-Cola*" are new. Please include your phone number.

"If your item says Enjoy Coca-Cola it's too new."

> Marion Lathan
> Route 1   Box 430
> Chester, SC 29706
> (803) 377-8225

★ *Coca-Cola, Pepsi-Cola* and *Chero-Cola* **advertising.** Wants small pieces such as trays, tip trays, smaller signs, door pushes, match strikers, etc., especially porcelain on tin. No paper.

> Dick Shay
> 514 Stevenson Ave.
> Worthington, OH 43085

★ *7-Up* **memorabilia.** "I'll buy almost any item that advertises *7-Up*, especially American made items from the 1930's through the 1950's. I want historical items, company memos, photos of store displays and the like. The older the better. Watch for ads or items from Howdy Company's *Bib-Lable Lithiated Lemon-Lime Soda* which later became *7-Up*. Your description should include the shape of the *7-Up* logo (round, oval, square, or rectangular). Not interested in foreign items or most stuff after 1960."

"I am a collector and will try to help find a buyer if your stuff's any good."

> Don Fiebiger
> 1970 Las Lomitas Drive
> Hacienda Heights, CA 91745
>   (310) 693-6484

★ *Dr. Pepper* **memorabilia** and advertising such as trays, posters, signs, clocks, and other items from before World War II. Describe what you have thoroughly, emphasizing condition.
> Ed Royse
> PO Box 33489
> Fort Sill, OK 73503
>   (405) 357-8000

★ *Hires Root Beer* **memorabilia** pre-1930 in fine to mint condition. Wants trays, dispensers, and signs. No syrup extract bottles or reproductions of any *Hires* items.
> Steve Sourapas
> 1413 NW 198th Street
> Seattle, WA 98177
>   (206) 542-1791

★ **Root Beer advertising** such as bottles, mugs, signs, caps, cans, syrup dispensers, and paper items. It *must* have the words "root beer" on the item. "If you don't recognize the brand name, or if it was sold only in a limited area, I'll probably be interested. I'd love to find *Dr. Swett's* root beer mug in majolica with a false bottom half way up the mug and will pay $200 for a perfect one. For many of the 400 makers of root beer, only bottle caps survive. I pay $3 each for bottle caps I don't have." Doesn't want anything from brands sold on the market today or any *A&W* mugs except those that say 5¢. No photograph is needed if you give a good complete written description.
> Tom Morrison
> 2930 Squaw Valley Drive
> Colorado Springs, CO 80918
>   (719) 598-175

★ *Moxie* **memorabilia.** Wants signs, fans, toys, advertising posters, metal trays, and other pre-1940 items associated with this old time soft drink. Will buy *Moxie* bottles only if the name of a town is part of the inscription. Bowers is the author of *The Moxie Encyclopedia*, a 760 page illustrated history available for $19.95.

Q. David Bowers
PO Box 1224
Wolfeboro, NH 03894
(603) 569-5095

★ **Soda pop cans** pre-1965, especially small local brands. Will buy quantities of rare cans, but no rusty cans are wanted by this 10 year veteran collector-dealer. "Some light spotting and aging is natural. I do require cans be sent before a final purchase offer is made because condition so greatly affects the value and I need to examine cans closely."

Tony Steffens
615 Chester
Elgin, IL 60120
(800) 443-8712

★ **Soda pop bottles with painted labels from New England.** If you are offering one of these for sale, pay particular attention to describing all the colors that appear on the label, and accurately writing down what is printed on the bottle.

Steve Daniels
PO Box 218
Medfield, MA 02052

★ **Soda pop bottles with painted labels** (called ACL's or applied color labels) are wanted, particularly minor bottling companies anywhere in North America. "I think I have West Virginia well covered, but I'm buying bottles from anywhere, including foreign soda pop bottles." **Ephemera related to local and regional bottlers** is also wanted, including factory or publicity photographs and soda pop advertising. Would love to find a three colored *Uncle Tom's Root Beer* from California. Please describe the color of the glass, all colors that are on the label and the exact wording "so I can make the best offer."

Gary Brent Kincade
PO Box 712
Weston, WV 26452
(304) 842-3773 eves

SODA FOUNTAIN MEMORABILIA

★ **Ice cream and soda fountain memorabilia:**
  Postcards depicting ice cream or soda fountains, ice cream
    trucks, factories or any other ice cream topic (any year);
  Photographs of soda fountain interiors;
  Letterheads, envelopes and other **paper** with ice cream images;
  Magazines from soda fountain and ice cream trade, pre-1930;
  Trade cards with ice cream parlors, freezers, or soda fountains;
  Catalogs pre-1920 (except *Mills* #31);
  Advertising giveaways, fobs, buttons, tape measures, etc.
Allan buys a wide range of ice cream related items, but says his focus for
the last few years has been on postcards with historical photos. He buys
nothing damaged or made after 1945. He does not make offers, and re-
quests you price what you have.
  Allan "Mr. Ice Cream" Mellis
  1115 West Montana
  Chicago, IL 60614
  (312) 327-9123

★ **Soda Fountain memorabilia** and historical ephemera related to
soda fountain operations such as **photographs, trade catalogs**, bill and
letterheads, recipe and formula books, **trade magazines** (like *Soda
Dispenser* and *Soda Fountain*), and the like. Also wants **19th century
soda fountain items** such as **hand crank milk shakers**, tumbler
holders, **root beer mugs**, etc. Wanted items from the 20th century include unusual straw dispensers, glasses marked with a product name,
True Fruit advertising from the *J. Hungerford Smith Co.* of Rochester,
hand held **advertising fans** showing ice cream or with a soda fountain
theme, **pink ice cream soda glasses**, and **banana split dishes**. The
favorite find of this 20 year veteran collector would be an equipment and
supplies catalog from before 1870. He does not want syrup well inserts
for later fountains, nor does he want match book covers, or trinkets
related to the ice cream industry. "Please give as much reasonable detail
as possible. A photo or photocopy is helpful." Dealers should price your
goods. Amateurs may request an offer.
  Harold Screen
  2804 Munster Road
  Baltimore, MD 21234
  (410) 661-6765

★ *Dixie* **ice cream cup picture lids** and other memorabilia 1930-54
including premium pictures and offers, albums, scrapbook covers, ads,
and company literature. Also buys some non-*Dixie* pictorial ice cream
cup lids such as *Tarzan* or American Historical Shrines series.
  Stephen Leone
  94 Pond Street
  Salem, NH 03079
  (603) 898-4900

BARBERSHOP ITEMS

★ **Decorated shaving mugs** depicting the owner's occupation, trade, or hobby above or below his name. Also hand painted personal occupational barber bottles. Since each was custom made, they must be evaluated individually. Also **salesman's sample barber chairs** made in porcelain or wood. No Japanese reproductions or "Sportsman's Series" mugs from the 1950's.

Burton Handelsman
18 Hotel Drive
White Plains, NY 10605
(914) 761-8880

★ **Shaving mugs depicting occupations.** Must have both a picture and a man's name. "I'll buy those with photo portraits for $500 and up and will pay $500-$1,500 for athletes (especially a high jumper), $400-$1,200 for automobile related professions, $500-$750 for an undertaker, and $500-$1,000 for a tugboat worker. Will also buy some mugs with emblems of fraternal organizations. Please give any maker's name on the bottom of the mug and indicate any damage, hairline cracks, or chips no matter how small."

Robert Fortin, Barber Shop
459 South Main Street
North Syracuse, NY 13212
(315) 458-7465

★ **Barbershop memorabilia of all types** including any good quality item associated with barber shops such as decorated shaving mugs, barber bowls, bottles, waste jars, catalogs, straight razors with scenes or names engraved on the blades, barber's emblem pins, barbershop trade or business cards, salesmen's samples of barber chairs, and much more. Powell both collects and deals so buys a wide range of fine items or accepts them on consignment. Names to look for include *Koken, Kochs, Kern, Archer, Buerger,* and others. Include a tracing or close up photo. New shaving mugs are not wanted. This well known historian is the only member of the Barber's Hall of Fame who isn't a barber.

Robert Powell
PO Box 833
Hurst, TX 76053
(817) 284-8145

FOOD & LODGING MEMORABILIA

★ *McDonalds* memorabilia including:
   Uniforms, employees, with the M logo;
   Paper goods including boxes, place mats, napkins, flyers;
   Displays and promotions such as signs, decals, posters;
   Anything in foreign languages;
   Not for public items such as ID cards, newsletters, bulletins,
      sales and procedures manuals, and worksheets;
   Fixtures, signs, and lights.
Does not want items that are currently available in all restaurants.
   Matt Welch
   PO Box 30444
   Tucson, AZ 85751
      (602) 886-0505

★ *McDonalds* happy meal counter displays.
   Mike Dyer
   230 Eldon Drive NW
   Warren, OH 44483

★ *Bob's Big Boy*, *Kentucky Fried Chicken*, and *Coon Chicken Inn*
restaurant memorabilia such as ceramic ashtrays and salt & peppers,
cups or dishes with logos, lunch boxes, game boards, toys, comics,
figurines, and other unusual pieces. Please write or fax with a
description, noting all repairs. Dealers must set the price they want;
amateurs may request offers. Vinyl plastic doll banks are not wanted.
   Glen Grush
   8400 Sunset Blvd. #3A
   Los Angeles, CA 90069
      (213) 656-4758   Fax: (213) 656-4158

★ *Bob's Big Boy* and *Kentucky Fried Chicken* premiums.
   William Hamburg
   PO Box 1305
   Woodland Hills, CA 91365
      (818) 346-9884

★ *Bob's Big Boy* items, especially menus, lamps, matches, ashtrays,
salt & pepper shakers, and nodders. No plastic banks.
   Steve Soelberg
   29126 Laro Drive
   Agoura Hills, CA 91301
      (818) 889-9909

★ *Coon Chicken Inn* memorabilia of all kinds that features Blacks.
   Diane Cauwels
   3947 Old South Road
   Murfreesboro, TN 37129

★ **Fast food chain ephemera including kid's meal toys and boxes** from before 1988. Also crew pins, displays, and other fast-food related items that are odd or unusual. Wants *Wendy's, Sonic Drive-In, Arby's, Burger King, Roy Rogers, Hardees, Carls Jr., What-a-Burger*, and other similar chains.
Ken Clee
PO Box 11412
Philadelphia, PA 19111
(215) 722-1979

★ *Isaly's* **ephemera.** Wants advertising, paper ephemera and souvenirs from this dairy/deli chain from Western Pennsylvania and Ohio. Buys postcards, photos, guidebooks, roadside signs, etc.
Brian Butko
2640 Sunset Drive
West Mifflin, PA 15122

★ **Items associated with famous Chicago hotels** and their shops. Wants furniture, menus, stationery, fixtures, signs, etc., from places like the *Lexington, Metropole, Hawthorne Inn, Hawthorne Smoke Shop*, and *Scholfields Flower Shop*.
Michael Graham
345 Cleveland Ave.
Libertyville, IL 60048
(708) 362-8531 eves

★ **Swiss hotels paper ephemera,** pre-1930. Will buy illustrated bills, letterheads, wine lists, rate cards, envelopes, postcards and anything else pictorial showing Swiss hotels before 1930.
Ronald Lowden, Jr.
314 Chestnut Ave.
Narberth, PA 19072
(215) 667-0257 anytime

★ **Tourist courts, tourist camps, and motel ephemera.** Wants *Tourist Court Journal* magazine and other pre-1950 ephemera related to motor travel lodging.
Kevin Regn
2127 15th Street NW
Washington, DC 20009

★ **Youth hostel ephemera** such as handbooks, pins, magazines, etc.
Walley Francis
PO Box 6941
Syracuse, NY 13217
(315) 478-5671

OIL COMPANY MEMORABILIA

★ **Oil company memorabilia** from the 1920's including advertising of all sorts, from giveaways to stationary, point of purchase advertising, signs, pump globes, etc. Also seeks informative material such as early gas station photos, **trade publications**, and the like, from any company, as long as its generally from the 1920's era. This 20+ year veteran collector does not want reproductions of any sort. Give him the name of the company, and a description of the item you have.

    Bill Allard
    1801 Fernside
    Tacoma, WA 98465
    (206) 565-2545

★ **Oil company memorabilia 1859-1939.** Wants "virtually anything" connected to specific companies, wells, or famous oil pioneers including pre-1900 books about oil and oil exploration, oil stocks (especially early with engraved views of oil fields), sheet music (from the 1860's), newspapers from early Pennsylvania oil towns, clippings, photos, deeds, and engravings.

    Jeffrey Viola
    475-B Eltone Road
    Jackson, NJ 08527
    (201) 928-0666 eves

★ **Gasoline and service station advertising and promotional items** from local, regional and independent dealers including banks and salt & pepper shakers shaped like gas pumps, 4 ounce oil can banks, thermometers, radios shaped like oil cans or gas pumps, and full size original gasoline pump globes. He does not want salt and pepper shakers from national brands, or reproductions of gas pump globes. Give him a description, the brand name, and its condition. Price if you can.

    Peter Capell
    1838 West Grace Street
    Chicago, IL 60613
    (312) 871-8735 eves

★ *Gulf Oil* **memorabilia** including signs, cans, maps, advertising junk mail, magazine ads, blotters, postcards, ashtrays, key chains, and anything else marked *Gulf*, especially older correspondence, paper items, and signs. This retired petroleum geologist also wants postcards which depict oil fields and wells. Prefers you to contact him first, then send your items on approval.

    Charles Roach
    3212 Tudor
    Oklahoma City, OK 73122
    (405) 942-4520

★ *Mobil Oil* **memorabilia** including "anything picturing the red horse." Also collecting service pins given to *Mobil* employees. Also buys porcelain signs from *Gargoyle, White Eagle*, and *Magnolia* gas and oil. No repros...and Billie says she has enough globes. She insists that the seller set the price wanted as she and Bob do not make offers for additions to their herd.

Bob and Billie Butler
1236 Helen Street
Augusta, KS 67010
(316) 775-6193

★ **Oil cans in all sizes, all types, and all materials,** including brass, aluminum, glass, tin, granite-wear, or plastic. Wants everything from small sewing machine size up to and including railroad oil cans, advertising cans, and novelty cans. Pays $10-$25 for a graniteware can especially with the name WHITE on it, $10-$15 for most others, more for railroad cans. Not all desirable cans have names on them. Make a sketch. If it is a pump can, tell Robert whether the pump works.

Robert Larson
3517 Vernal Court
Merced, CA 95340
(209) 723-7828

★ **Oil cans from Canada,** especially British Columbia oil in tin cans, and any quart oil cans related to motorcycles.

Don Schneider
PO Box 1570
Merritt, BC V0K 2B0 CANADA

★ **Oil company road maps,** particularly from the 1920's and 30's. "I like city maps, state maps, and regional maps, foreign or domestic." Must be in good condition. Mass quantities are wanted. Also will buy old Official State Highway Department maps, the earlier the better. **Other oil company items** such as credit cards, and pocket **calendars** are also purchased. He says you may send your items for his immediate offer and a return check.

Noel Levy
PO Box 595699
Dallas, TX 75359
(214) 987-3513

FARMS, HORSES & TRACTORS

★ **Antique farm equipment,** horse drawn vehicles, and "tools of all type" that are unusual, suitable for display in a museum of the odd and unusual. Send a photo and description of condition. "Farm equipment must be something out of the ordinary to find a buyer," he cautions.
> Harvey Lee Boswell's Palace of Wonders
> PO Box 446
> Elm City, NC 27822

★ **Wagons, carriages, and commercial horse drawn vehicles,** in whole or in part. Buys carriage lamps, dashboard clocks, wagon tools, nameplates, wheel making machines, coachman's and groom's clothing, jacks, tack room fixtures, whip racks, wagon odometers, hitching post statuary, rein clips, wagon seats, wagon poles, veterinary tools, lap robes, life size harness makers horses, **zinc animal heads**, and anything else related to carriages and wagons. Offers from $500 to $2,500 for lamps marked *Studebaker, Brewster,* or *Healey.* Also buys **goat and dog carts**. If your item is old, genuine, and in good condition you may ship it on approval. No harnesses, please. Don will send you a large illustrated wants list if you send an SASE with four stamps on the envelope.
> Don Sawyer, West Newbury Wagon Works
> 40 Bachelor Street
> West Newbury, MA 01985
> (508) 346-4724 days   (508) 363-2983 eves

★ **Everything related to work or play with horses** including polo, horseback riding, carriage driving, sidesaddle, draft horses, **horseshoeing, veterinary**, etc. Wants horse farm catalogs, brochures, posters, prints of riding and recognized horse breeds, books (1st editions in dust jackets only), magazines, postcards (if horse is named), stud books, and breed registers. "I don't buy common books still in print, book club editions, *Diseases of the Horse,* books on racing or horse race betting, or books with highlighting or underlining in the text. Everything must be in fine condition for resale."
> Barbara Cole's October Farm
> Route 2   Box 183-C
> Raleigh, NC 27610
> (919) 772-0482

★ **Horse bits.** "I'll buy old iron, fancy, or strange horse bits as well as foreign, military, and medical bits. I also buy reference material about horse bits, including catalogs. I'd like to find Civil War bits and cowboy bits decorated with buffaloes. Draw me a picture of what you have."
> Jean Gay, Three Horses
> 7403 Blaine Road
> Aberdeen, WA 98520
> (206) 533-3490

★ **Tractor memorabilia** including all sorts of paper ephemera and small trinkets given away as advertising promotion by tractor makers and dealers, such as watch fobs, pens, cigarette lighters, etc. You may ship on approval if it's old, original, and clean.

> Jay Ketelle
> 3721 Farwell
> Amarillo, TX 79109
> (806) 355-3456

★ **Tractor, farm machinery, and gasoline engine paper ephemera** including pre-1970 manuals, catalogs, parts books, in-house publications, and sales literature. Also buys farm magazines such as *Implement Record, Farm Machinery & Hardware,* and *Farm Mechanics.* Also buys "giveaways" such as signs, ashtrays, buttons, etc. associated with any farm machinery. No textbooks or reprints are wanted. Please indicate the color of the item and the price you'd like.

> Alan C. King
> PO Box 86
> Radnor, OH 43066

★ *J.I. Case Tractor Company* **memorabilia** including tractors and implements, toy tractors, advertising signs, catalogs, books, and anything else marked *J.I. Case.* If you're trying to sell an old *Case* tractor, make certain to tell them where it is presently located.

> Ed and Carla Schuth
> Route 2 Box 6
> Wabasha, MN 55981
> (612) 565-4251

★ **Windmill ephemera,** especially cast iron windmill weights, display model windmills and salesman's sample windmills. He does not want reproductions, damaged or repaired items, items with new paint, or "short tail horse" windmill weights. Please send a color photo, your phone number, and the price range you'd like to get.

> Richard Tucker, Argyle Antiques
> PO Box 262
> Angyle, TX 76226
> (817) 464-3752

★ **Poultry raising.** Wants books, magazines, and paper ephemera about raising any kind of poultry (ducks, chickens, geese, etc.) from before 1930. Make a photocopy of what you have.

> W.L. Bill Zeigler
> 10 Lincolnway West
> New Oxford, PA 17350
> (717) 624-2347

MILK & DAIRY EPHEMERA

★ **Milk or dairy industry items marked with the name and address of a dairy** including old and unusual bottles, advertising, toys, and signs, especially from institutional bottlers such as prisons, colleges, railroads, hotels, and the like. Any bottles with character endorsements (sports, *Hopalong Cassidy*, etc.) are wanted with cartoon characters particularly desirable (Disney bottles bring $100+ each). Bottles and posters with WWII slogans are also sought. Unusually shaped bottles with faces or heads or those made of colored glass are always wanted, as are creamer size bottles marked with the name of a dairy, hotel, or restaurant. Bottles with glass lids, tin handles or lids and pour spouts can go as high as $300. Just about anything related to *Borden's* or their *Elsie the Cow* **trademark** is wanted, especially their ruby red bottles which bring from $700-$1,000 each. "I'll buy **catalogs of bottle makers** which show design variations offered." Large items like cream separators, churns, milk cans, and the like are not wanted. "If in doubt about the authenticity of what you own, feel free to call or send me a good photo. I will verify what you have and answer your questions about it, if you include a Self-Addressed Stamped Envelope."

"You can never give too much information in a description when you are detailing condition. List all flaws, scratches, chips, tears or cracks. I can give you a good appraisal only if you give me a good description."

Ralph Riovo
686 Franklin Street
Alburtis, PA 18011
(215) 966-2536

★ **Round milk bottles with dairy names** embossed or printed on them. Square bottles are OK if amber colored or from any Western states. Nothing worn, cracked, or chipped is wanted.

Leigh Giarde
PO Box 366
Bryn Mawr, CA 92318
(909) 792-8681

★ **Dairy creamers** made of glass with the names of dairies embossed or printed on are sought. He does not want ceramic creamers or those without names. Also **milk bottles** with cop tops, baby tops, or war slogans, but only in excellent condition.

Ken Clee
PO Box 11412
Philadelphia, PA 19111
(215) 722-1979

PLANTS, TREES & LUMBER

★ **Everything about fruit and vegetable growing, packing and canning** is wanted, such as labels, photographs, postcards, magazines, buttons, ribbons and giveaway trinkets of all types. Wants all sorts of paper ephemera from various organizations and events promoting fruit and vegetable growing and packing. Buys **orange juicers, reamers and extractors** from major packers, if company name is impressed.

    T. Pat Jacobsen
    437 Minton Court
    Pleasant Hill, CA   94523
       (510) 930-8531

★ **Everything about fruit raising and varieties before 1900,** including illustrated books, magazine articles, ceramic tiles depicting fruit, postcards, prints, folders, and greeting cards depicting apples. Especially wants books and paper with color plates or descriptions of fruit varieties. May be in any language. No tropical fruit, or anything later than 1940. This veteran horticulture experimenter wants **cuttings from uncommon tree fruit varieties** you have on your farm. He wants temperate climate fruits, especially apples, but also pears, plums, quinces and medlars. Also buys **books on fruit propagation** printed before 1920.

    Fred Janson
    Pomona Book Exchange
    Rockton PO, Ontario
    L0R 1X0   CANADA

★ **Canning machinery, catalogs and tools** of the *Ferracute Machine Company* of Bridgeton, NJ, are sought by this researcher who also wants anything related to company founder, **Oberlin Smith**. The Oberlin Smith Society is particularly interested in advertising, catalogs, small presses, medals and tokens, but will consider anything related to FMCc or Smith himself. The OSS is a 501(c)(3) organization and seeks donations too.

    James Gandy, Oberlin Smith Society
    Route 2   Box 109,   River Road
    Bridgeton, NJ   08302
       (609) 451-5586

★ **Lumber company and store tokens, scrip, stocks and bonds.** Please make a photocopy of your items.

    "Tip" Tippy
    22 Cottonwood Lane
    Carterville, IL 62916

MINING MEMORABILIA

★ **Mining items** including safety lamps, oil wick cap lamps, carbide lamps, blasting cap tins and blasting machines, candle holders, and hundreds of other small tools, photos, souvenirs, and advertising items related to mining. Will even buy ore carts and buckets. Also wants ribbons, banners, and badges from the **United Mine Workers** (UMWA) and the Western Federation of Miners (WFM). Dave says he's willing to pay you in cash in you prefer.
>David Crawford
>1308 Halsted Road
>Rockford, IL 61103
>(815) 637-6720

★ **Coal company scrip, stocks and bonds,** and **cap lamps** worn by miners when underground.
>"Tip" Tippy
>22 Cottonwood Lane
>Carterville, IL 62916

★ **Mining company memorabilia,** primarily Pennsylvania and the Western U.S. Buys books, stocks and bonds, sheet music, photographs, and selected artifacts.
>Jeffrey Viola
>475-B Eltone Road
>Jackson, NJ 08527
>(201) 928-0666

★ **Colorado mining memorabilia 1859-1915** including photos, paper ephemera, stocks, maps, stereoviews, advertising, and small souvenirs, especially from towns of Cripple Creek, Victor, Central City, Leadville, Breckenridge, Idaho Springs, Telluride, etc. Also books about Colorado mining and any city directories pre-1915. No interest in "flatland cities" like Denver or Colorado Springs, nor in Colorado tourist attractions and parks. No photos of mountains unless a mine or mining town is featured.
>George Foott
>6683 South Yukon Way
>Littleton, CO 80123
>(303) 979-8688

★ **Mining ephemera, especially paper goods from Arizona and Colorado mines.** Interested in buying stock certificates and other paper pertaining to mining other than coal. Buys books on mining and gems, catalogs of mining equipment, photographs, etc.
>Russell Filer Mining
>PO Box 487
>Yucaipa, CA 92399
>(909) 797-1650

ARCHITECTURE & BUILDING ITEMS

★ **Architectural antiques,** including large chandeliers, wall sconces, statuary, gargoyles, gates, large quantities of iron fencing, stained glass windows and doors, and the like. Please send complete details and measurements. Collect calls OK, but only if you're a serious seller.
Architectural Antiques
801 Washington Avenue North
Minneapolis, MN 55401
(612) 332-8344

★ **Architectural antiques.** If you have mantles, stained glass windows, chandeliers, iron fencing or gates, garden statuary, and other architectural relics, it may be profitable to give this giant dealer a call.
United House Wrecking
535 Hope Street
Stamford, CT 06906
(203) 348-5371

★ **Parts from buildings** such as cornices, gargoyles, arches, fireplaces, mantels, and anything unusual, as long as it dates before 1930.   No material not related to building.
Robert Des Marais
618 West Foster Ave.
State College, PA 16801
(814) 237-7141

★ **Pieces of famous buildings, structures, monuments, aircraft, etc.,** such as the Statue of Liberty, Independence Hall, The Eiffel Tower, etc. "These must be legally acquired pieces and not vandalized items. They must be well documented for me to purchase them."
Paul Hartunian
127B East Bradford Ave.
Cedar Grove, NJ 07009
(201) 857-7275

★ **Stained or beveled glass windows.** Send photos of the window, note all cracks or missing pieces, and include your phone number.
Carl Heck
PO Box 8416
Aspen, CO 81612
(303) 925-8011

★ **Sidewalk or paving bricks** marked with the name and or address of a maker. "They're hard to mail, but fun to collect." No fire bricks.
Ken Jones
100 Manor Drive
Columbia, MO 65203

★ **Display cases and lighting fixtures,** especially from old drugstores. Wants early counter-top display cases with original glass, especially revolving cases, bow-front cases, and double tower cases. Also wrought iron or tin **lighting fixtures,** especially from commercial buildings. List all damage and give all data on maker's plate. Nothing after 1900.

> Jerry Phelps
> 6013 Innes Trace Road
> Louisville, KY 40222
> (502) 425-4765

★ **Ornate doorknobs and other builder's hardware** including knockers, hinges, escutcheon plates, doorbells, push plates, bin pulls and any other fancy Victorian hardware. "I'll pay up to $200 for some knobs. No plain porcelain or common octagonal glass knobs are wanted. Sets of knobs routinely bring $20-$30, but get my offer before you sell. Send SASE for my illustrated wants list. Photocopies speed offers."

> Charles Wardell
> PO Box 195
> Trinity, NC 27370
> (919) 434-1145

★ **Antique doorknobs.** Loretta is editor of the club's newsletter and can put you in touch with collectors all over America who are interested in antique doorknobs and other door hardware. Send a good close up photo or a photocopy.

> Loretta Nemec, Antique Doorknob Collectors of America
> PO Box 126
> Eola, IL 60519
> (312) 357-2381

★ **Catalogs related to architecture and building materials,** 1850-1960. Will consider anything informative, including architects' publicity books, house designs, catalogs of plaster ornaments, roofing materials, signs, store fronts, paint, etc. Send a photocopy of what you have.

> Herbert Mitchell
> Avery Library
> Columbia University
> New York, NY 10027

★ **Items related to building and architecture** pre-1930 including books about architecture, building, carpentry, and surveying. Also manuals and catalogs of cast iron, steel, plumbing, hardware, paint, and other building materials. Also **blueprints, architects renderings,** drafting instruments made of brass, early drafting or drawing machines, slide rules, and watercolor boxes.

> Robert Des Marais
> 618 West Foster Ave.
> State College, PA 16801
> (814) 237-7141

★ **Blueprints for buildings or machines.**
Jim Presgraves, Bookworm & Silverfish
PO Box 639
Wytheville, VA 24382

★ **Architect's renderings** and other paintings of skyscrapers, houses, and other buildings.
Charles Martignette
PO Box 293
Hallandale, FL 33009
(305) 454-3474

★ **Antique surveying instruments,** including compasses, transits, levels, wire link measuring chains, circumferentors, semi-circumferentors, railroad compasses, and solar compasses. Tools may be wood, brass, or wood and brass. "Also have interest in **mathematical and philosophical instruments** of the past." Give all names and numbers found on the body or lens.
Michael Manier
PO Box 100
Houston, MO 65483
(417) 967-2777 anytime

★ **Old tools of the trades and crafts** especially those used by wood-workers: wooden and metallic planes, folding rulers, chisels, levels, saws, plumb bobs, scribes, spokeshaves, hammers, squares, axes, trammel points, measuring devices, drills, bit braces, marking gauges, wrenches, fancy tool boxes, and hand or foot powered machinery. Also wants advertising items and hardware store displays, catalogs, and documents. "I'll pay $200+ for *Stanley* tool catalogs from before 1900. I especially want tools made in Ohio, although they're not worth as much as tools from New England." Does not want mechanics' tools, electric tools, agricultural and farm tools, or any that have been "reconditioned." Give all markings. Keep your eyes open for an ivory plow plane made in Ohio, because "I'll pay $10,000 for one." John will accept select consignments at 10% commission for inclusion in his good looking quarterly newsletter on tools. John produced *Antique & Collectible Stanley Tools: A Guide to Identity and Value*, a detailed 455 page illustrated guide which you can obtain from him for $25.
John Walter
The Tool Merchant
208 Front Street
Marietta, OH 45750
(614) 373-9973

★ **Joiner's planes and other tools.** "I'll buy planes or any pre-1900 paper ephemera about them. I'll also buy, and pay retail prices for, fancy old woodworking hand tools."
Richard Wood, Alaska Heritage Books
PO Box 22165
Juneau, AK 99802
(907) 586-6748

ELECTRICAL DEVICES

★ **Electrical devices pre-1900** manufactured by *Stanley Electric, Edison General Electric, Thomson-Houston, Weston, Westinghouse, Crocker Wheeler* and *Sprague.* "I want small open frame bipolar motors and generators, switchboard voltmeters and ammeters, carbon arc lamps, **electric fans with brass blades**, and watt-hour meters. I also want catalogs, photographs and paper related to these companies printed before 1905." Provide all nameplate data including patent dates and numbers. Prefers the seller to set the price, but will make offers.
William F. Edwards
State Road
Richmond, MA 01254
(413) 698-3458

★ **Electrical apparatus, tubes, test equipment, open frame motors, generators,** switch board meters, knife switches, **neon signs, fans,** Tesla coils, **quack medical devices** (Violet Ray, etc.), **unusual clocks,** etc., as well as books on radio and electrical theory and practice. Give info from the item's ID plate, and include a sketch or photo.
Hank Andreoni
504 West 6th
Beaumont, CA 92223
(909) 849-7539

★ **Early electrical meters, gauges, and other apparatus** made by *Thompson-Houston,* or of the 133 cycle type. Also early direct current watthour meters, type CS, manufactured by *G.E.* Any very old unusual electrical items will be considered by the veteran collector and electrical museum owner. Give him the information found on the item's ID plate, measurements and weight. "I prefer the seller to set the price. I may need to see the item before buying."
Tommy Bolack
3901 Bloomfield Highway
Farminton, NM 87401
(505) 325-7873

MEDICAL EPHEMERA

★ **Unusual medicines and healing devices.** "I'll buy pills, liquids, mixtures, devices and things promoted to cure ills or bring on better health. I'll consider items whether they work or not, whether scientific or crackpot, drab or colorful, sincere, absurd, or ridiculous. I'll even buy brand new items if they are odd or come with an interesting story."

> **Bottles and containers,** empty of full of pills and powders;
> **Bottling and filling materials;**
> **Advertising flyers** and trade cards of all sort for medicines;
> **Medical catalogs;**
> **Health devices, real or quack,** such as vaporizers, electric
> gadgets, etc., the more unusual the better;
> **Any product that makes a health claim** such as tobacco,
> mineral water, etc.;
> **Books and booklets,** serious or humorous, on medicines;
> **Medical teaching devices.**

"I'd like as complete a description as possible, including the item's age, condition, price, and what you feel to be its unique characteristics."

> August Maymudes
> 10564 Cheviot Drive
> Los Angeles, CA 90064
> (310) 839-4426 eves   Fax: (310) 481-8169

★ **Medical and apothecary (drug store) equipment** from before 1900 including **doctor's instruments,** bleeding bowls, leech jars, apothecary tools, colored and pontiled **patent medicine** bottles, patent medicine tax stamps 1860-80, and all patent medicine advertising in *any* form especially signs, clocks, tins, and 3-dimensional papier maché figures. A 26 year veteran collector dealer, he'll pay from $150 to $3,000 for leech jars and up to $1,500 for figures.

> Jerry Phelps
> 6013 Innes Trace Road
> Louisville, KY 40222
> (502) 425-4765

★ **Medical and drug store items** including trade cards, catalogs, advertising, journals, ledgers, photos, and other similar ephemera pre-1910. Also patent medicines, instruments and quack devices.

> Doug Johnston
> 529 West Encanto
> Phoenix, AZ 85003

★ **Stethoscopes.** "I'll buy antique and unusual physician's stethoscopes, both monaural and binaural." Give all markings, patents, etc.

> Chris Papadopoulos
> 1107 Chatterleigh Circle
> Towson, MD 21204
> (410) 825-9157 eves

★ **Medical instruments such as monaural stethoscopes, ear trumpets and conversation tubes,** brass anesthesia masks from the drop ether days, all bleeders especially mechanical, and old dental instruments if made from wood or ivory.
Lucille Malitz, Lucid Antiques
PO Box KH
Scarsdale, NY 10583
(914) 636-3367

★ **Microscopes and other medical or scientific instruments.** "I'll buy pre-1900 microscopes by the following makers: *Zentmayer, Grunow, Bullock, McAllister, Gundlock, Tolles, Queen, Pike* and *Charles Spencer.*" Give the maker's name and serial number. Describe overall condition of the instrument, case, and accessories. "Don't clean or polish anything," he warns.
Dr. Allan Wissner
PO Box 102
Ardsley, NY 10502
(914) 693-4628

★ **Enema and douche equipment.** Wants a variety of rubber fountain syringes, sinus fountain syringes, bulb syringes, etc., especially in different colors. Especially interested in the *Buckingham* and *Boots* enema syringes, both of which come in a metal box. Also buys books and catalogs related to the subject, from any maker. "No new type fountain syringes with white plastic hoses." Items must be made of rubber, not plastic, and have black, not white, fittings. Do you have the original box?
Helen Roman
115 Baldwin Street
Bloomfield, NJ 07003

★ **Electric and pre-electric vibrators and hand held massagers.** "I especially like those with metal casings rather than plastic, those with hand-cranks, and vibrators with wooden handles or parts. Not interested in battery operated devices. You won't make a fortune selling to me, but your item could reside in the world's only vibrator museum and will be happier than in your attic." No *Oster* vibrators which are worn on the back of the hand. Describe, give numbers, and indicate whether the box and any attachments or instructional inserts are present. Will buy items which do not work but are not physically broken.
Joani Blank, Good Vibrations
PO Box 2086
Burlingame, CA 94011

★ **Homeopathic medicine.**
Julian Winston
2067 East Clearfield Street
Philadelphia, PA 19134

★ **Embalming tools and bottles.** Embalming kits and tools are often in black bags and can be recognized by long aspiration needles. Many tools and bottles are marked with skulls and crossbones. Look for *Dioxin* brand, and others. "I have enough embalming tables unless they're priced at $20 or less."
> Steve DeGenaro
> PO Box 5662
> Youngstown, OH 44504

★ **Medically related advertising and memorabilia** especially tin containers, trays, signs, match holders, trade cards, advertising envelopes, calendars, old corked and labeled medicine bottles, pin back buttons, mirrors, **instruments**, and the like. Among tins, he wants medical, dental, veterinary, talcums, prophylactics, etc. Fine condition items only.
> Eugene Cunningham, MD
> 152 Wood Acres Drive
> East Amherst, NY 14051
> (716) 688-9537

★ **Old quack medical devices** which shock, spark, buzz, vibrate, or do nothing at all. Most devices were built into fancy boxes with dials, wires, hand electrodes, plated terminals, coils, and levers. Other devices consisted of therapeutic gloves, brushes, charms, and the like. There is an extensive list of brand names he seeks but he does not want common massage vibrators, violet rays, and *Electreat* devices. He also buys books, catalogs, pamphlets, and other paper ephemera promoting quack electrical items or other therapeutic gimmicks. Keller prefers you price your item but will make offers.
> Leland Keller
> 1205 Imperial Drive
> Pittsburg, KS 66762

★ **Medical books and ephemera.** Wants quality items including books from before 1840, medical broadsides, pamphlets, hand colored illustrations, stereo views, letters, documents, and catalogs. "I'll pay well for quality material," he states.
> Ivan Gilbert, Miran Arts & Books
> 2824 Elm Ave.
> Columbus, OH 43209
> (614) 236-0002

★ **Chiropractic equipment and books** especially electronic diagnostic gear or items from the Palmer College/School. Pre-1960 only, please.
> Mel Rosenthal
> 507 South Maryland Ave.
> Wilmington, DE 19804
> (302) 322-8944

★ **Twins, multiple births, and freak parasitic twin births.** This dedicated nurse archivist wants photos, newspaper clips, souvenirs, personal information, and *anything* statistical, scholarly, or informative. If you are one of a multiple birth, this is the lady who will preserve the experience. She always wants first hand information from multiples about their lives. *She does not want* undated clippings or items that have been damaged by pinning, pasting, or taping. When describing scrapbooks, make certain to note whether the clippings are dated. "My collection is not a hobby but a full time job in research, internationally recognized for its accuracy and extent, a source of factual information for physicians, researchers, and news media of all types." She has been at it since 1939, but Miss Helen always appreciates help, especially people sending clippings from local papers and obscure magazines about twins (as long as you tell where it came from and the date). Especially wants **photos and other Dionne quints** memorabilia.

    Miss Helen Kirk's Multiple Birth Museum
    PO Box 254
    Galveston, TX 77553
       (409) 762-4792

★ **All human glass eyes** in any size or color, rights or lefts.
    Donald Gorlick
    PO Box 24541
    Seattle, WA 98124
       (206) 824-0508

★ **Unusual eye cups.**
    W.T. Atkinson
    1217 Bayside Circle West
    Wilmington, NC 28405

★ **Dental cabinets, instruments, and catalogs,** but only before 1920.
    Peter Chu, DDS
    5470 Folkestone Drive
    Dayton, OH 45459
       (513) 435-6849

★ **Dental trade cards.** "I'll buy trade cards from dentists, dentifrices, pain medications, dental parlors, breath fresheners, and the like." Will consider any paper ephemera related to dentistry.
    Ted Croll, DDS
    East Street and North Main Street
    Doylestown, PA 18901

★ **Veterinary medicine ephemera** from before 1900.
    Barbara Cole, October Farm
    Route 2 Box 183-C
    Raleigh, NC 27610

★ **Drug store memorabilia** including apothecary bottles with glass labels and stoppers, show globes, all **related advertising, and catalogs**. No scales or mortar and pestle sets are wanted.
>   Mart James
>   8269 Scarlet Oaks Cove
>   Cordova, TN 38018
>   (901) 757-0214

★ **Patent medicine advertising.** "I'll buy 19th century advertising, trade cards, almanacs, booklets, postcards, posters, sheet music, tokens, and giveaway items related to any patent medicine. I have a particular interest in *Hadacol* items, and will purchase them as late as 1950. In trade cards, I am looking for 'private' cards, made for one manufacturer, not stock cards with overprints. Please send a photocopy or send the item itself on approval." Walker has a new book forthcoming on the history of patent medicine advertising.
>   A. Walker Bingham
>   19 East 72nd Street
>   New York, NY 10021
>   (212) 628-5358

★ **Almanacs published by patent medicine companies, between 1840-1920.** Many of these pay $20-$30. If you have many of them to sell it is advisable to have his detailed wants list. There were dozens of almanac companies that are wanted. He does not want any of the three most common almanacs: *Swamp Root, Nostetters*, or *Ayers*. No foreign language editions, either. The only almanacs he wants are printed before 1920. Please don't offer medical booklets, pamphlets, cookbooks, etc.
>   Rodney Brunsell
>   55 Spring Street
>   Hanson, MA 02341

BOTTLES

★ **Early American bottles and historical flasks.** Wants hand blown figural bottles or those with embossed figures and portraits. Will pay $3,000 for *"The American System"* flask depicting a paddle wheeler. Also wants **figural bitters bottles** and hand-blown, pontil marked, **colored ink** and **medicine bottles.** Burt also buys **rare fruit (canning) jars** complete with lids, round and **colored milk bottles** and mineral water bottles. No cracks, chips, or bad stains are acceptable. Burt advises reading McKearin's *American Glass* to see bottles which attract top dollar. No machine made bottles or reproductions.

> Burton Spiller
> 49 Palmerston Road
> Rochester, NY 14618
> (716) 244-2229

★ **Antique American medicine and beer bottles,** both glass and pottery, especially from the Buffalo area. Has a particular interest in the patent medicine bottles of *G. W. Merchant* of Lockport, NY. Also wants mineral waters, poisons, and **barber shop bottles.** Buys trade cards, advertising, billheads, and other **items associated with makers or users of bottles in Western New York state.** Sven publishes the newsletter of the Western New York Bottle Collectors Association.

> Sven Stau
> PO Box 437
> Buffalo, NY 14212
> (716) 825-5448 or (716) 822-3120

★ **Early American bottles.** Buys a wide range of glass bottles, including bitters, campaign bottles, figurals, whiskey flasks and **glass jugs with handles.** Wants glass bottles with agricultural symbols, flags, sunbursts, portraits of national heroes, and the like, or bottles in the shape of log cabins, cannons, lighthouses, pigs, etc. Many of these items are worth in excess of $1,000. **Pottery pig bottles** are also wanted, but no *Jim Beam* type whiskey bottles.

> Robert Daly
> 10341 Jewell Lake Court
> Fenton, MI 48430
> (313) 629-4934

★ **Patent medicine bottles.** "I'll buy pontilled, embossed bottles, especially colored and labeled ones, and will pay from $500 to $6,000 for fine ones. Also buys patent medicine advertising.

> Jerry Phelps
> 6013 Innes Trace Road
> Louisville, KY 40222
> (502) 425-4765

★ **Bottles and bottle company ephemera** of all types such as calendars, brochures, and signs. *Gayner Glass Co.* is of special interest, as are Salem squats, a New Jersey soda bottle.

"I 'm glad to help everyone I can."

  Charles McDonald's Bottle Museum
  4 Friendship Drive
  Salem, NJ 08079
  (609) 935-5631

★ **Dark blue medicine and poison bottles.** Bottles must be cork tops, not screw tops. Particularly looking for bottles which held various types of salts by *John Wyeth and Bro.* that have dose caps, contents, and paper labels. Also want *Warner's, Mulford's*, and other cobalt blue and green bottles complete with contents and labels.Pays $60+ for *Kickapoo* bottle with original stopper. No bottles marked TAIWAN or WHEATON or modern milk of magnesia. Give the color, size, and embossed letters or designs, and note existence of chips, cracks, labels, screw threads, etc.

  Adrienne & David Escoe
  PO Box 342
  Los Alamitos, CA 90720

★ **Bottles from California and the old West.** "I'll buy whiskey, medicine, food and other bottles from the days of miners, loggers, and cowboys in the West. I especially like bottles with the names of California towns and companies on them." He wants **whiskey bottles with pictures** embedded in the glass, which bring from $100 to as much as $2,500 for a *California Club* bottle. "Bottles without names or designs embossed in the glass are generally

"If your bottle says FEDERAL LAW FORBIDS THE RESALE... it isn't old enough to be of interest to collectors."

valueless to collectors as are most cracked or chipped ones." Tell him what it says on all sides of your bottle, what color it is, and what condition it is in, with particular attention to neck chips.

  John Goetz
  PO Box 1570
  Cedar Ridge, CA 95924
  (916) 272-4644

LAW ENFORCEMENT MEMORABILIA

★ **Law enforcement memorabilia** such as badges, patches, nightsticks, handcuffs, and restraints from all types of law enforcement officers including fish and game, railroad security, sheriffs, marshals, constables, Indian police, city police, and other. Also likes studio **portraits of law enforcement officers**. Make a photocopy of the front and rear of your badge or photo and give its history if you can. No security company, college police, or "gun show" brass badges. Include any wording or numbers you find on handcuffs or leg irons.

> Gene Matzke
> Gene's Badges
> 2345 South 28th Street
> Milwaukee, WI 53215
> (414) 383-8995

★ **Western peace officer's badges,** especially from Oklahoma and the Southwest. "I am especially interested in suspension badges (which hang from a bar by chains), stars, circles with cut out stars, shields, and some others, depending on age and appearance. I will also buy some contemporary badges, depending on their hallmark and where they are from. Indian police badges from anywhere are also wanted, as is a genuine Arizona Ranger badge. Note there are a lot of fake badge #11 on the market; a genuine one is made of sheet silver and hand engraved. I am not interested in reproductions, phonies, fakes and cheap brass badges." This 30 year veteran collector and author warns that lots of fake badges exist and that it is important to have any badge authenticated by someone who really knows what he's doing. If you write him, he wants to know the style of badge, the wording, who wore it and where, any hallmarks, and what you think the age of the badge is. "If in doubt, send the badge insured and I will inspect it, make an offer, or return it."

> Ron Donoho
> PO Box 13170
> Las Vegas, NV 89112
> (702) 458-7731

★ **Handcuffs, leg irons, torture and execution devices, and electric chairs,** both authentic or reproduction. Also wants photographs of these devices in use. Please photocopy any photographs you want to sell.

> Harvey Lee Boswell's Palace of Wonders
> PO Box 446
> Elm City, NC 27822

★ **All items related to imprisonment, locking and restraint** including handcuffs, shackles, ball & chains, leather restraints, straight jackets, prison uniforms and antique or unusual **padlocks**. Also wants magician's escape locks, lock picks, and books about lock picking. These well known dealers in magic and escape devices offer a catalog for $2.

> Joe and Pam Tanner
> Tanner Escapes
> PO Box 349
> Great Falls, MT 59403
> (406) 453-4961

★ **Old handcuffs, leg irons, and other police or prison restraint devices.** Also police department badges, photos, and histories of police departments especially from Ohio. Mention whether your item works and has a key.

> Stan Willis
> 6211 Stewart Road
> Cincinnati, OH 45227
> (513) 271-0454 days

★ **Northwest Mounted Police items** from before 1950. Also the Royal Northwest Mounted Police, the Royal Canadian Mounted Police, the BC Provincial Police, or the Alberta Provincial Police. Especially awards and medals, cap badges, collar badges, uniforms, and law enforcement items marked with the initials of one of these agencies.

> Michael Rice
> PO Box 286
> Saanichton, BC
> V0S 1M0 CANADA
> (604) 652-9047 eves

★ **Law enforcement memorabilia from prohibition era Chicago** including photos, police bulletins, warrants for arrests, court transcripts, police uniforms (1920's only), badges, and personal items from police chiefs Garrity, Fitzmorris, Collins, Hughs, and Russell. Only well documented personal effects, please, with value in part dependent upon the authenticity and story accompanying the item. If offering personal effects, tell how you obtained them and provide your phone number.

> Michael Graham's Roaring 20's
> 345 Cleveland Ave.
> Libertyville, IL 60048
> (708) 362-4808 days or 362-8531 eves

★ **Prison, jail, or penal colony related memorabilia** including items from juvenile detention centers and reform schools. Items include coins, tokens, uniforms, weapons, badges, letters about prison life, restraint devices, photos of prisons, items made by prisoners, postcards, and "just about anything at all." His prime interest is in **scrip**, the paper money used in institutions as a medium of exchange. If you have genuine prison material you may send it for his offer.

> "Jailhouse Jerry" Zara
> 2414 Mark Place
> Point Pleasant, NJ 08742
> (908) 899-1016

★ **Jail, prison, and law enforcement memorabilia,** with emphasis on all types of restraints, including U.S. or foreign military, third world, and Eastern European. Wants handcuffs, ball and chains, manacles, leg irons, thumb screws, nippers, iron claws, and comealongs. Also wants literature from manufacturers, copies of *Detective*, a peace officer trade magazine, and patent information on locks and restraints. Wants to find magician's key rings as well as restraint keys marked with the maker's name. He says now is a particularly good time to sell.

> Larry Franklin
> 3238 Hutchison Ave.
> Los Angeles, CA 90034
> (310) 559-4461

★ **San Quentin and Folsom prison and prisoner memorabilia,** 1890-1915 with special interest in prisoners Ed Morrell, Donald Lowrie, Jake Oppenheimer, Sir Harry Westwood Cooper, Jack Black, Christopher Evands, and George Sontag. Do you know or have anything about these people? If so, Jack wants to hear from you.

> Jack Fleming
> 1825 Vine #2
> Berkeley, CA 94703

★ **Fingerprinting equipment.** "I'll buy old police fingerprinting equipment including *Bertillon* equipment, fingerprint cameras, microscopes and especially books and magazines concerning fingerprinting." Also buys WANTED posters and police mug shots.

> Michael Carrick
> 1230 Hoyt Street SE
> Salem, OR 97302
> (800) 852-0300

GOVERNMENT SERVICES ITEMS

★ **School, teacher, and student memorabilia** from before 1920, especially diaries, postcards, photographs, teaching certificates, teacher souvenirs, rewards of merit, report cards, letters, student assignments, and books having to do with teaching or operating schools. No student textbooks except those from before 1860. Has particular interest in ephemera associated with New England educator **Samuel Read Hall** (1795-1877), a prominent early textbook author.
> Tedd Levy
> PO Box 2217
> Norwalk, CT 06850

★ **Civilian Conservation Corps (CCC)** memorabilia from the 1930's such as belt buckles, scarves, uniforms, sweetheart pillows, china, etc., which run $15 and up. Items marked with the unit camp number are the most desirable, especially the sleeve unit patches designed by the individual camps, worth $25 up. Honor awards will bring $150 each, more if found complete with original ribbon in good condition. Send photo, sketch or photocopy of what you have.
> Tom Pooler
> PO Box 1861
> Grass Valley, CA 95945
> (916) 268-1338

★ **Civilian Conservation Corps (CCC)** memorabilia from the 1930's.
> Ken Kipp
> PO Box 116
> Allenwood, PA 17810
> (717) 538-1440

★ **U.S. Post Office memorabilia** including steel postmarking devices, locks and keys, uniform badges and buttons, scales, marked handguns, and postcards depicting post offices. Many other items are also wanted, but not postage stamps. His large illustrated wants list can be had if you send first class postage on a large self addressed envelope. If you have a postmarking device to sell, make an imprint. Only obsolete items no longer in use, please.
> Frank Scheer
> 12 East Rosemont Ave.
> Alexandria, VA 22301
> (703) 549-4095 eves

FIRE FIGHTING EPHEMERA

★ **Fire fighting and fire insurance ephemera** including, but not limited to, fire grenades, awards, helmets, buckets, axes, badges, **toys**, fire marks, fire insurance signs, advertising items, nozzles, apparatus parts, alarm equipment, photos, lanterns, **extinguishers**, postcards, books, salesmen's samples, models, etc., especially from pre-1900. Nothing made after 1940 is of interest.

Ralph Jennings, Jr.
301 Fort Washington Ave.
Fort Washington, PA 19034
(215) 646-7178 eves

★ **Wood cased fire station gongs.** "I'll buy any wood cased fire station gong, working condition or not, made by *Gamewell Fire Alarm Telegraph Co., Star Co., Moses Crane Co.*, or other manufacturer. Gongs have wooden cases, glass doors, and key wind movements." Also wants literature describing gongs or photos of fire station watch desks showing a wall gong.

Gary Carino
805 West 3rd Street
Duluth, MN 55806
(218) 722-0964

★ **Fire and casualty insurance company memorabilia,** especially reverse on glass signs, and automobile bumper and grill tags that have an insurance company's name. Your description should include the name of the insurance company, size, material, and condition. "Best to send a photo, along with the dimensions." If he doesn't want your item, he will give you the name of another collector who might be interested in what you have, whenever possible. No life insurance items.

Byron Gregerson
PO Box 951
Modesto, CA 95353
(209) 523-3300

★ **Glass fire grenade bottles** in any color if embossed with a brand name and "fire grenade." He is particularly interested in finding those with the name of a railroad. He does not want glass bulb grenades from the 1940's that are filled with carbon tetrachloride. List the color, size, and all defects, especially chips, cracks, or damage to any labels.

Larry Meyer
4001 Elmwood Ave.
Stickney, IL 60402
(708) 749-1564

★ **Fire fighting antiques and alarm equipment,** especially fire alarm boxes and wood cased gongs in any condition and quantity (would like to buy entire systems or collections). Will also buy extinguishers, nozzles, bells, lanterns, helmets, badges, **fire grenades, fire related toys,** and catalogs. Your description should give all markings, dimensions, and any history of the piece you know. Make sure you include your phone number and best time for him to call.

Stan Zukowski
1867 Ellard Place
Concord, CA 94521
    (510) 687-6426

★ **Fire fighting antiques** such as early leather fire helmets, leather fire buckets with paintings on them, speaking trumpets with fancy engraving, early fire nozzles from hand operated pumpers, fire department lanterns that burn kerosene or whale oil and have two color glass globes, gold or silver presentation badges, etc. **Anything from the Chicago Fire Department** from before 1940. Very old fire alarm boxes, wood cased fire gongs, fire alarm registers, and other old equipment marked *Gamewell, Star, Moses Crane, American,* or *U.S. Police & Fire* is wanted by this veteran fire fighter.

Larry Meyer
4001 Elmwood Ave.
Stickney, IL 60402
    (708) 749-1564

Weapons and military items

Anyone who listens to the news these days knows guns are an international medium of exchange. Buyers for guns, like coins and gold, seem to be everywhere. But the market for antique and collectible guns is less active, and it can be tough to find the right buyer. I am always on the look-out for people who are both fair and knowledgeable.

Edged weapons, knives and swords, should be treated as fragile objects. Careless mishandling or storage can damage valuable blades.

When you are describing a sword, dagger, or bayonet you should give the measurements from end to end and from the tip of the blade to the handle guard. Measure the width of the blade at the point it attaches to the handle guard. Mention every word or number found on the blade, hilt, or handle. Trace or photocopy any decoration on the blade or sheath. The condition of the scabbard or sheath is important to describe.

If you wish to sell a gun, the first step, before you do anything else, is to make certain it is not loaded, so you can inspect it carefully.

What do you tell a gun buyer about your gun? Pistol buyer Jim Supica answers that question:

> "Any gun buyer wants to know make, model, serial number, caliber or gauge, barrel length, type and percent of finish, type of stock or grips, mechanical condition and the condition of the bore. If the serial numbers do not match from one part to another, note that fact. Describe all markings inside and out, list alterations, mention all dings and defects."

Regulations for shipping guns are strict but not difficult to follow. Anyone who buys your gun will tell you how to ship your gun. Follow regulations exactly and you won't run afoul of the law. When rare or valuable weapons are involved, the buyer may pick them up personally or arrange for the weapon to be picked up by messenger.

If you are in the unusual position of selling a tank (don't laugh, a VFW lodge in process of disbanding sold the anti-aircraft gun in front of their hall) or other large weapon, you must take two steps. First you will need a good set of color photographs taken from all sides. You will also need to locate the item's ID plate and copy down all information. Note if it has an engine, even if it doesn't run. Also copy everything on the engine's ID plate as well.

To describe most war souvenirs, relics, and ephemera, list the material(s) from which it is made, color(s), dimensions, serial numbers and other marks, what you know of its history, and the item's condition.   If it's supposed to do something, does it do it? Are all parts and pieces there? Is it for sale or do you "just want a price"?

When you offer a uniform for sale, you should note the insignia, badges, and ribbons since they will be a major determiner of the uniform's value. Condition of your uniform is critical, of course. Collectors are more forgiving about moth holes in a Revolutionary War outfit than they will be about a WWII dress or combat uniform.

This whole procedure can be simplified greatly by photocopying small items whenever possible. A good honest description following these guidelines is usually enough to sell what you have if it is collectible.

In general, most buyers like to obtain military items directly from the soldier, sailor, or marine who received them. When that is not possible, they prefer to buy from the soldier's family or descendants. Tell whatever you can of an item's history.

SWORDS & KNIVES

★ **American swords from 1789-1902.** Especially wants swords with presentations or inscriptions to military persons with dates and rank, either etched or engraved on the blade or on the metal part of the scabbard. Inscribed Civil War swords are particularly desirable. The best makers marks are *Ames, Starr, Roby, Rose, Widman, Horstmann,* or *Glaze.* It is most important for sellers to send a very good drawing or photo of the hilt handle (guard and grip) of the sword. List all markings on the blade. Indicate the type of metal the guard is made from (brass, iron, aluminum), the type of grip or handle (ivory, bone, metal, wood, leather covered wood, or plastic). Note if the scabbard or sheath is included, and the condition of the sword and scabbard (rust? pitting?), and whether the scabbard is dented. Indicate the width of the blade at the handle, the length of the blade, and any engraving or etching. This 30+ year collector and dealer is interested in most swords, including early fakes and reproductions as long as the seller knows that the price will be considerably less than for an original. Common original swords are also purchased for resale. Ron is author of two books on swords and is active in gun and sword societies.

"We do not buy or appraise nonmilitary swords such as Masonic lodges, Knights of Columbus, Knights Templar, and the like."

Ron Hickox
Antique Arms & Militaria
PO Box 360006, Dept. T
Tampa, FL 33673
   (813) 968-1571   Fax: (813) 935-0190

★ **American swords and large knives** from before 1900. Please describe thoroughly, including any numbers or writing found on the weapon. Make a photocopy of the knife and of the sword handle if you can. Otherwise photograph it or make a good sketch. No fraternal, lodge or ceremonial swords, please. SASE requested.

Charles Worman
PO Box 33584 (AMC)
Dayton, OH 45433
   (513) 429-1808 eves

★ **U.S. and German bayonets and daggers,** either standard fighting issue or dress type. Other countries also purchased. He prefers to buy directly from the veteran or family, and would like information about your weapon's history. Free appraisals of all military swords and edged weapons available to private parties from this 25 year expert appraiser.

Hank McGonagle
26 Broad Street
Newburyport, MA 01950
   (508) 462-2354

★ **British and American military knives** of WWI and WWII especially British Commando daggers, *Wilkinson Sword* fighting knives (marked FS FIGHTING KNIFE), and American special unit fighting knives. Value ranges from $50 to $1,500 depending on rarity, condition, and its scabbard. It is very important for you to copy every word and symbol on the blade, handle, guard, and scabbard. John does not want bayonets that attach to the end of a rifle.

John Fischer
7831 Peachtree Ave.
Panorama City, CA 91402

★ **German swords and daggers** from the Nazi era (1933-1945). Will buy both common and rare variations, with etched or with plain blades. Especially wanted are swords and daggers with presentation inscriptions giving name, date, and military unit etched on the scabbard or blade. Make a drawing or photocopy of the item, noting all rust, pitting, scabbard dents, etc.

Ron Hickox
Antique Arms & Militaria
PO Box 360006, Dept. T
Tampa, FL 33673
(813) 968-1571   Fax: (813) 935-0190

★ **Japanese swords,** daggers, armor and Samurai items, especially fine swords and daggers, and sword and dagger parts. No other guns, bayonets, or non-Japanese items. Ron will send you a checklist to help you describe a sword for sale. Ron has been treasurer of the Japanese Sword Society and editor of its newsletter for ten years. Ron appeals, "Many of these items were brought back to America after WWII and now rust away in basements and attics. It is important that these items be preserved by placement into a collection."

Ron Hartmann
5907 Deerwood Drive
St. Louis, MO 63123

★ **Italian daggers** from WWI through the Fascist era up to and including WWII. "Premium prices paid for those with white handles or engraved blades. When writing, please include your phone number and best time to call. I guarantee postage both ways if you send a dagger for my inspection. I will help you identify any Italian dagger free of charge if you send an SASE with your inquiry, or call me after 7pm East coast time." Be prepared to describe the handle style, crossguard, color of grips, style of the blade, all markings, the length, and what the scabbard looks like. Not interested in swords, bayonets, or daggers that have been shortened, filed, or otherwise damaged.

Joseph Venanzi
46 Wolfpack Road
Trenton, NJ 08619
(609) 586-3414

GUNS

★ **Antique and modern firearms.** "I'll buy a wide range of items, from Civil War carbines, Indian wars guns, trap doors, rolling blocks, cap and ball, etc., to early *Winchester, Marlin, Savage*, and *Remington*. This 25 year dealer also buys some *Colt* **handguns**. If your gun or rifle is pre-1964 and all wood and metal surfaces are original and unrestored, it might be worth a call. Although he buys *Krag, Springfield* and others for parts, he does not want reworked guns or reproductions. Rudy offers a catalog of guns for sale.

> Rudy Dotzenrod
> Route 2   Box 26
> Wyndmere, ND 58081
> (701) 439-2646

★ **Guns and gun collections** of all types. "I'm always searching for **Gattling guns.**"

> Ed Kukowski
> Ed's Gun House
> Route 1
> Minnesota City, MN 55959
> (507) 689-2925

★ **Black powder antique guns** made in Western New York State. Makers of interest include *Artis, Cutler, Ellis, Gardner, Lefever, Marsley, Miller, Plimpton, Southerland, Walker, Wood* and several others. Antique guns only.

> Alan Stone
> PO Box 500
> Honeoye, NY 14471
> (716) 229-2700

★ **American percussion and early cartridge firearms,** both long guns and revolvers, 1840-1920. "I'll buy guns by any maker, but especially *Colt, Winchester, Remington, Marlin, Smith & Wesson, Manhattan, Sharps, Stevens,* and *Bacon*. I like to buy derringers of all types, especially those that are particularly small or short barreled, those that are very large caliber (.41 cal. up), or those which take metallic cartridges. I also like finding any pocket size pistols made by *Colt, Remington, Bacon, Marston, Moore, National, Reid, Terry, Warner,* and *Williamson*, among others." Pays $300 to $3,000 for these guns. Wants photos or photocopies of both sides of the weapon and all markings and numbers found anywhere on the gun.

> Steve Howard
> Past Tyme Pleasures
> 101 First Street #404
> Los Altos, CA 94022
> (415) 484-4488 eves

★ **Revolvers (pistols).** "I'll consider any antique or collectible firearms to build my dealer's inventory or to enhance my personal collection, but my special interests are:

Serial number one guns, antique or modern;
Antique *Smith & Wesson* large frame top-break revolvers;
Antique engraved revolvers;
Unusual hammerless revolvers;
Guns owned by famous individuals.

"I can travel if needed. Confidentiality assured. I try to be considerate and helpful in cases of divorce, bankruptcy, and estate liquidation. I can pay immediately or arrange auction or consignment sales. I'm more interested in unusual or oddball older guns that many other collectors avoid. I will consider heavily worn, broken, or refinished items only if they are rare or have documented historical connection. Honest wear and alterations from the period of use are OK, but do affect the value of the piece. I am not interested in fakes, reproductions or modern guns. If offering an historic gun, quality of documentation is important. Send a photocopy of documentation and what you will swear to in a notarized affidavit. A personal inspection is required before final offer can be made, especially on finely engraved guns. Please don't offer anything stolen or illegal. I won't buy it." Specific regulations govern shipment of firearms. Jim has the necessary licenses, but check with him for shipping instructions. If you don't want to sell your gun but would like an informal appraisal, Jim charges only $1 each to appraise most handguns.

"Any gun buyer wants to know make, model, serial number, caliber or gauge, barrel length, type and percent of finish, type of stock or grips, mechanical condition and the condition of the bore. Describe all markings inside and out, list alterations, note dings and defects."

Jim Supica, Jr.
Old Town Station
PO Box 15351
Lenexa, KS 66285
(913) 492-3000   Fax: (913) 492-3064

★ **American guns** from before 1900, especially those with historic association. No interest in reproductions. If possible, send a clear photo of the item and write down all markings found anywhere on it. If it is a pistol, please make a photocopy, or draw a pencil outline. Mention any broken or missing wood, metal that is pitted, parts missing, etc. Does it work? Worman wrote a book on firearms of the American West and was firearms editor of *Hobbies* magazine for sixteen years. SASE please.

Charles Worman
PO Box 33584 (AMC)
Dayton, OH 45433
(513) 429-1808 eves

★ *Colt* **pistols with factory engraving.** "I'll buy single action *Colts* in 95% or better original condition, if they predate WWII and have factory engraving." Give the serial number when you write, and, if possible, a good close up photo of the artwork. Some newer single actions are also wanted. Also wants **guns from outlaws and lawmen** if they have proper documentation. All early **memorabilia from the *Colt* company,** including all advertising and literature are wanted, including *Coltrock* brand products and the boxes they came in.

> Johnny Spellman
> 10806 North Lamar
> Austin, TX 78753
>   (512) 836-2889 days   (512) 258-6910 eves

★ *Colt Firearms Manufacturing Company* **ephemera** including all correspondence on factory letterhead, pamphlets and brochures by *Colt*, empty black and maroon boxes that *Colt* guns were packed in, instruction sheets and manuals, and "anything else pertaining to *Colt* products." John wants *Colt* factory catalogs, 1888-1910, for which he pays from $40-$500. 1910-1940 catalogs bring $20-$75. John also buys plastic and electrical items marked *Coltrock* as well as *The Book of Colt Firearms* by Sutherland and Wilson, 1971, for which he'll pay over $100.

> John Fischer
> 7831 Peachtree Ave.
> Panorama City, CA 91402

★ *Iver Johnson* **products and memorabilia** including **guns, bicycles, catalogs,** etc. Special wants include engraved presentation guns and awards and any other unusual *Iver Johnson* item. This 30 year veteran collector does not want "common handguns in less than mint condition." Send a complete description, including a sketch or photo. Prefers seller to price, but will make offers.

> Charles Best
> 6288 South Pontiac
> Englewood, CO 80111

★ *Newton Arms Co.* **guns and other memorabilia** from this progressive 1916-18 gunsmith. "I'll buy rifles, catalogs, **loading tools,** letters, stock, cartridges, and any other paper or memorabilia from the *Newton Arms Co.* or the *Chas. Newton Rifle Corp.* I will pay $5,000 for a .276 *Newton* rifle or a rifle in .280, .33 or .40 (.400) calibers if in mint condition, and will consider all other *Newton* guns at lesser prices. Also want these and other unusual *Newton* cartridges. I will gladly pay a finder's fee for *Newton* guns I buy. I'll take anything signed by Chas. Newton but nothing marked *Buffalo Newton Rifle Co.* Any items other than guns must be original condition."

> Bruce Jennings
> 70 Metz Road
> Sheridan, WY 82801
>   (307) 674-6921

★ **German pistols, parts and accessories** such as holsters, stocks, magazines, etc. This 30 year veteran dealer buys and stocks parts for *Luger, Mauser, Walthers*, and many others. He wants to buy mismatched *Lugers* for parts (at $200 up) and will sell perfect matched pistols on consignment in the $500 to $2,000 range. He is willing to buy in quantity from other dealers, police departments, veterans groups, etc., including nonworking guns in volume. If you have a captured WWII pistol with an interesting story, he'd love to hear from you. He does not want reproduction parts or accessories. If you wish to sell a gun, he wants you to tell him the name of the manufacturer, the model number (usually on the slide), the caliber, the serial number, and anything else printed or stamped anywhere on the pistol. He will give free verbal appraisals over the phone, but charges for formal written assessments. He also sells accessories for most European pistols from 1900 to the present and a selection of books on guns.

Tom Heller, Heller Arms, Ltd.
PO Box 578
San Bruno, CA 94066
(415) 359-2290

★ **High grade shotguns,** fine sporting rifles, and English double rifles. "I'll pay up to $5,000 for pre-1964 *Winchester* Model 70 rifles, and up to $250,000 for *Parker* shotguns, and $100,000 for English double rifles and shotguns. I don't want old worn guns with little or no original finish. Give the make, serial number, gauge and condition if you want an offer."

Alan Phillips
PO Box 276
Thousand Palms, CA 92276

★ **Old double barrel shotguns** are wanted in any condition. "I will buy any kind of double barrel made before 1940 that is worth $300 or less. I especially want old side plate *Lefevers, L.C. Smith*, and most English or Belgian guns. Describe the condition, amount of bluing, rust, missing parts, engraving, butt plates, etc."

Charles Black, The Gun Doctor
Route 6 Box 237-D
Athens, AL 35611
(205) 729-1640

★ **Junk guns and gun parts** in any condition. "I'm in the parts business and will travel to pick up large lots." Wants nothing having to do with current guns. Describe, including all markings and numbers. Bob is available for insurance appraisals of fire damaged gun collections.

Robert Fay
Star Route Box AF
Whitmore, CA 96096
(916) 472-3132

TANKS & HEAVY WEAPONS

★ **Tanks, artillery, armored vehicles and machine guns and their parts and accessories.** "We are a Federally licensed machine gun manufacturer and dealer, and seek to buy registered operational machine guns and other military equipment, including **muzzle loading cannon** and **Gattling guns.** We buy machine gun parts and accessories including, but not limited to, barrels, buttstocks, magazines, clips, drums, bipods, tripods, mounts, loading machines, linkers, armorer's kits, etc. We are particularly interested in mounts for *Maxim* machine guns and will pay $150+ for them. We will buy most anything made in the 19th or 20th centuries. Parts and guns do not have to be in perfect condition. We will look at all items, but clear photos are a must. A VHS video is even better. Include dimensions and condition of accessories. Copies of any accompanying paperwork or manuals are helpful. If, after inspection, our offer in unacceptable, I will pay shipping both ways." Not interested in toys, miniatures, stolen firearms or U.S. Army manuals.

> Greg Souchik
> T.M.P. Company
> PO Box 133
> Custer City, PA 16725
> (814) 362-2642 Fax: (814) 362-7356

★ **Half tracks, armored cars, tanks,** **Gattling guns,** howitzers, and cannons, especially a *FT-17 Renault* (M1917) tank in any condition. Larry will arrange for transporting what you have. Also wants:

> **U.S. women's uniforms** and accessories, WWI or WWII but only in fine condition;
> **Military diving** equipment and related items including sales catalogs;
> *Mercedes Benz 500K* or *540K* autos from between 1930-40;
> **German military staff cars;**
> **Military aircraft** from any country pre-1940.

Provide all the information printed on the machine's data plates. In most cases when you are trying to sell large equipment, a few photographs from different angles would be recommended.

> Larry Pitman
> Zanzibar War Museum
> 5424 Bryan Station Road
> Paris, KY 40361
> (606) 299-5022

★ **WWII era halftrack parts,** uniforms, insignia, accessories, manuals, and anything else. "The boys and I are trying to rebuild one, and can use a lot of different things. Call with what you have."

> Charles Eberhart
> 33616 Seward
> Topeka, KS 66616
> (913) 235-1016

★ **Ammunition and exploding devices** such as grenades, mines, bombs, and fuses of all type, from the beginning of time to the present. "We buy everything from stone cannon balls to the smart weapons used in Operation Desert Storm. Also want books, films, reports, and videos about ordnance in any format or language." Schmitt's family has been making ammunition since 1849, so he particularly wants things marked with the *Crittenden* name. He is willing to pay $2,000 for a .69 caliber *Crittenden and Tibbals* Rimfire cartridge. He wants the measurements, condition, and all markings on what you have, preferring you also include a photo. He has no interest in store stock items. Schmitt is a contributing editor of two gun magazines and involved with cleaning up explosive ordnance from the Iraq/UN war.

 J. Randall Crittenden Schmitt
 Court House Station
 PO Box 4253
 Rockville, MD 20849

★ **Brass military shell casings.** "I want to buy the casings for shells and projectiles in 37mm and larger sizes. Particularly wants an 8" Navy shell. I'll buy shell casings of all weapons, all nations."

 Charles Eberhart
 33616 Seward
 Topeka, KS 66616
  (913) 235-1016

EARLY & PRIMITIVE WEAPONS

★ **Napoleonic arms and armor.** This 30 year veteran collector/dealer in Western ephemera does not make offers. Requires you to send a photo and complete description including information about where you got it, and your asking price. No fakes or reproductions are wanted.

 Pierre Bovis
 The Az-Tex Cowboy Trading Co.
 PO Box 460
 Tombstone, AZ 85638
  (602) 457-3359

★ **Primitive weapons from around the world.** Also trade beads from various cultures.

 David Boone Trading Company
 562 Coyote Road
 Brinnon, WA 98320
  (206) 796-4330

WAR & MILITARY SOUVENIRS

★ **French and Indian War,** the **Revolutionary War** or the **War of 1812** in northern New York especially the Lake Champlain, Lake George, or Fort Ticonderoga area. All ephemera about the campaigns and the men involved especially Benedict Arnold and Rogers' Rangers.
Breck Turner
With Pipe and Book
91 Main Street
Lake Placid, NY 12946

★ **Mexican War** (1846-48) photos and documents are sought.
Johnny Spellman
10806 North Lamar
Austin, TX 78753
(512) 836-2889 days   (512) 258-6910 eves

★ **Civil War artifacts of all types** including guns, knives, canteens, uniforms, documents, swords, and prisoner of war items. Reproductions not wanted. It is important to indicate any markings. SASE requested.
Charles Worman
PO Box 33584 (AMC)
Dayton, OH 45433
(513) 429-1808 eves

★ **Confederate Civil War letters,** envelopes, **paper money**, posters, pardons, passes, and other ephemera. Also, some other Civil War items, and **Lincoln photos** and manuscripts.
Gordon McHenry
PO Box 1117
Osprey, FL 34229

★ **Civil War, especially Southern Unit histories,** battle accounts, biographies, and personal memoirs. Has detailed wants list for those who deal in Civil War material. No books published by Grosset & Dunlap.
James Baumhofer
PO Box 65493
St. Paul, MN 55165
(612) 6987151

★ **G.A.R. china, mugs, and spoons.** Any pieces marked G.A.R. (Grand Army of the Republic).
Don McMahon
385 Thorpe Ave.
Meriden, CT 06450

★ **Civil War regimental histories** and first person narratives.
Jim Presgraves, Bookworm & Silverfish
PO Box 639
Wytheville, VA 24382

★ **Military unit histories** from any branch of the service, American or British. Collects all eras, but especially needs Korean and Vietnam wars. Guarantees "highest prices" for WWII fighter or bomber groups, paratroopers, tank units or units of Black soldiers. "I am not interested in reprints or later editions. I also collect **unit photos**, military postcards, holiday menus, distinctive unit insignia, shoulder patches, **medals**, guidons, scrapbooks and berets. If you have an item for sale and want an offer, send it for my examination. I will pay all postage, both ways."
Lt. Col. Wilfred Baumann
PO Box 319
Esperance, NY 12066
(518) 875-6753

★ **U.S. Navy memorabilia** including postcards, ship or station postmarks and documents. Describe. Pricing appreciated.
Frank Hoak III
PO Box 668
New Canaan, CT 06840

★ **Merchant Marine** photos, uniforms, and medals.
Harvey Lee Boswell
PO Box 446
Elm City, NC 27822

★ **U.S. Marine Corps memorabilia** of all kinds including recruiting posters and materials, books, photos, belt buckles, cigarette lighters, steins, mugs, documents, autographs, postcards, **trench art**, bronzes, and **John Philip Sousa** ephemera. Also buys **toy soldiers, trucks, and planes** with Marine markings. Describe or make a photocopy.
Dick Weisler
5307 213th Street
Bayside, NY 11364
(718) 626-7110 days   (718) 428-9829 eves

★ **U.S. Marine Corps everything.** Anything used and/or worn by Marines from 1776 to 1946, such as **uniforms**, **medals**, helmets and weapons. Also buys unit histories, documents and **recruiting posters**. Wants photos of Marines at war, work, or play, especially amateur photos. Also wants trench art created by Marines and souvenirs of war brought home by Marines. Tell what you can of the item's history.
Bruce Updegrove
Route 5 Box 546
Boyertown, PA 19512
(215) 369-1798 eves

★ **Army Air Force A2 flight jackets,** AAF pocket insignia, sterling military aviation wings and WWI enlisted man's round collar discs. Nothing later than the Korean War.

> Jerry Keohane
> 16 Saint Margaret's Court
> Buffalo, NY 14216

★ **WWII leather or cloth aviation jackets** with squadron patch and or painted artwork on the back, from any branch of the service, any branch of aviation. Needs information on jacket label, condition of the jacket and its patches or art, plus details about the art. Photo helpful. I don't want currently made flight jackets with antiqued paintings or patches.

"If the seller did not acquire the jacket from the veteran or his family, it is probably not old."

Buys documented **Flying Tiger memorabilia, squadron patches and histories** and photos of **airplane nose art.**

> Gary Hullfish
> 16 Gordon Ave.
> Lawranceville, NJ 08648
> (609) 896-0224

★ **WWI aviation relics from all nations,** especially log books, diaries, awards and **medals,** aircraft insignia and maker's plates, **trench art** made from aircraft parts, and anything belonging to **WWI aces.** Send detailed description, sketch or photo and "your lowest price." Also buys **pulp magazines with air war themes.** No photos, books or other mags.

> Kenneth Smith
> 345 Park Avenue 42nd Floor
> New York, NY 10154

★ **Photos and bits and pieces of WWII aircraft.** It doesn't matter whether allied and axis, crashed or operational, Ken wants single snaps, albums, or negatives of photos of any aircraft used in WWII. Also wants **instruments, gauges,** fabric, fittings, data plates, unit or group insignia, and miscellaneous bits and pieces of the combat aircraft of any nation.

> Ken Francella
> PO Box 234
> Granite Springs, NY 10527
> (914) 248-8138

★ **Airplane identification models,** 1940-1970. Also promotional models, travel agency models, and **squadron and bomb group unit histories.** When writing, copy all info printed on the plane.

> John Pochobradsky
> 1991 East Schodack Road
> Castleton, NY 12033
> (518) 477-9488

★ **Canadian military medals and cap badges.** "I'll buy all cap badges with the initials CEF on them, or badges with a number and the words "overseas battalion" and CANADA or CANADIAN on them. I'll buy any war or period. Look for the name rank and military unit on the rim of medals as some can be worth $1,000 or more." Will answer all inquiries.
Michael Rice
PO Box 286
Saanichton, BC V0S 1M0 CANADA

★ **Military items of Great Britain or Commonwealth nations.** "I'll buy hat, collar or shoulder badges, headdresses, uniforms, field equipment (belts, packs, pouches), **edged weapons,** particularly Scottish bagpipers' headdress and badges, kilts and sporrans (leather kilt purses), dirks, and knives." This 45 year collector will consider 1910-1945 items from other countries, especially cloth patches. No fakes or repros. Describe the material the item is made from, colors, etc. Note if anything seems to be missing and chips, dents, nicks, cracks, moth holes, stitch marks, corrosion, fading, stains and polish wear. Please photocopy.
Charles Edwards, Pass in Review
PO Box 622
Grayslake, IL 60030
(708) 223-2332

★ **Military items from the Coldstream Guards.** The museum wants to buy uniforms, equipment, badges, and miscellaneous items used by the British Coldstream Guards before 1900. Other British Army ephemera from before 1900 may also be of interest. A full description includes dimensions, materials, and age. Indicate anything you believe to be unique. Donations acknowledged. No U.S. items.
Ernest Klapmeier
Coldstream Guards Living History Museum
PO Box 334
Wayne, IL 60184
(708) 584-1017 days (604) 652-9047 eves

★ **French or British military forces** overseas, British Indian Native States forces, Spanish or **French Foreign Legion,** Abraham Lincoln Brigade, Camel Corps, Free French & Vichy forces, French forces in China, Devil's Island, White Russian forces, Chinese Customs Service, Chinese bandits or pirates, China Navigation Company, international settlements in China, Chinese airlines, and similar topics. Wants badges, banners, **medals,** photos, certificates, souvenirs, etc. Material about American volunteers or **famous soldiers of fortune** of any nationality is particularly welcome. No repros of Devil's Island folk art or souvenirs produced by the Foreign Legion Veteran's Home.
Gene Christian
3849 Bailey Ave.
Bronx, NY 10463
(212) 548-0243

★ **Nazi notables** especially Heinrich Himmler, commander of the SS and Gestapo. Wants items given by or to Hitler, Goering, Goebbles, Hess, etc., including promotion and award documents, letters, trophies, **uniforms** or **medals**. "I am generally not interested in any item you or a member of your family did not personally bring back from overseas." He prefers you to call him with the item in hand. Otherwise write, describe what you have, make a photocopy, and include your phone number. Tom will pay $10,000 cash for some Nazi documents.

    Thomas Pooler
    PO Box 1861
    Grass Valley, CA 95945
        (916) 268-1338

★ **German and Japanese military** wanted, especially daggers and dagger parts, medals, badges, spike helmets, **swords** and flagpole tops. Pays $50 each for **German WWII helmets** complete with liner. "I will also buy flags, but the bigger the flag, the less they're worth. You may write, giving me your phone number. Take a photo or send insured for cash offer." This is a hobby for Dick, so he says that he's happy to help people if they send him a SASE. Makes offers only on items for sale.

    Dick Pankowski
    PO Box 04421
    Milwaukee, WI 53204
        (414) 421-7056 days   (414) 421-5212 eves

★ **Cloth shoulder insignia** of divisions, regiments, brigades, and other units from the Civil War to Vietnam. WWI U.S. and German insignia are of special interest. Complete uniforms welcome. He prefers to buy directly from the veteran or family. Condition is important. This 25 year veteran does not want fakes or reproductions.

    Hank McGonagle
    26 Broad Street
    Newburyport, MA 01950
        (508) 462-2354

★ **Regimental and Battalion unit flags** from all nations and periods of history. "I'll also buy flag related items such as U.S. Army spear pole tops, color woven flag cords and tassels, engraved battle honor rings and battle streamers, canvas issue flag cover bags, and close up or parade photos showing unit flags." No national flags or reenactment group flags. Please make a sketch of the flag, noting size and material. Ben can provide info about unit flags if you send an SASE with your inquiry.

    Ben Weed
    PO Box 4643
    Stockton, CA 95204

★ **Military medals and decorations** from all countries and periods. Also any documents or certificates related to military awards, medals and decorations. He prefers to buy directly from the vet or his family, and would like all associated paperwork and any information about the medal's history. Condition is important, and a photocopy is requested.

> Hank McGonagle
> 26 Broad Street
> Newburyport, MA 01950
> (508) 462-2354

★ **Medals, Decorations, and Orders** for military gallantry and other campaign medals of the U.S. and British Empire, 1780 to the present. Especially wants U.S. Medals of Honor and British Victoria Crosses and U.S. Purple Hearts for WWII officially named to the Navy and Marines. Does not want reproductions. Photocopy both sides of the medal.

> Alan Harrow
> 2292 Chelan Drive
> Los Angeles, CA 90068

★ **Small U.S. military relics and photographs** including ribbons, awards, paperwork, letters, buttons, canteens, **knives**, insignia, flags, etc. Rex operates a large mail auction of Americana and always needs new stock, especially 19th century. Do not contact him if you are only "fishing for free information," if your goods are damaged, or if your items are not for immediate sale.

> Rex Stark
> 49 Wethersfield Road
> Bellingham, MA 02019
> (508) 966-0994

★ **Military newsreel and training films** from WWII on any military, naval, or aviation subject. British, American, Canadian, German, or Russian, but must be 16mm sound films shot 1939-45. Films may be training, propaganda or documentary. Buys military aviation films 1903-1985, especially WWI, Korean Conflict, and Vietnam. Give complete title, producer, length and defects. If possible, give brief summary of contents. Nothing damaged. Also buys **military magazines.**

> Edward Topor
> 14313 South Marshfield Ave.
> Chicago, IL 60609
> (312) 847-6392

★ **Photos or photo albums taken or collected by soldiers** during WWI or WWII. Please set the price you'd like.

> Ted Fonseca
> 785 South Bryant
> Denver, CO 80219

★ **General Douglas MacArthur memorabilia** of all types is wanted. "I'll buy books, scrapbooks, autographed items, pictures, documents, toys, dolls, medals, coins, any item with 'I shall return' or 'I have returned' on it, buttons, statues, and any item documented as having belonged to MacArthur." Please send a photocopy if you'd like an offer.
> Gaal Long
> Route 1   Box 40
> Sardis, MS   38666
> (601) 487-2457

★ **Trench art brass vases and lamps** made from shell casings. "I am only interested if they are engraved or embossed." No plain casings are wanted. Make a sketch or take a photo and include dimensions.
> Al Lanzetta
> PO Box 2082
> New York, NY   10185

★ **Home Front and anti-fascist collectibles** from World War II especially related to important events or phenomena including the **Holocaust,** resistance, women during war, chaplaincy, soldier benevolent funds, etc. Anything related to **anti-Semitism** or the Allied war effort, from paper to pottery, considered if made 1939-1946.   Items directly related to military occupation of Germany or Japan 1945-1955 considered. Interested in the rare or unusual.   Does not want military uniforms, weapons, medals, or insignia, nor does he want souvenirs from Germany or Japan other than related to anti-Semitism.   No magazines, news-papers, or damaged items.   Requires some items be sent on approval.   Reimburses postal costs.
> Richard Harrow
> 8523 210th Street
> Hollis Hills, NY   11427
> (718) 740-1088

★ **Rationing material** worldwide. CSU owns most American items, buys only paper and "wants many foreign items." No U.S. ration books.
> Ronald Mahoney, Head Special Collections
> Madden Library
> California State University
> Fresno, CA   93740
> (209) 294-2595

★ **Ration tokens.** Pays 2¢ each for red tokens, 3¢ each for blue. After 250, he pays 1¢ each, but much more for error tokens. Ship for his check.
> Rich Hartzog
> PO Box 4143 BFT
> Rockford, IL   61110

Coins and currency

Looking up the value of U.S. coins is easy. The most used price guide to coins is *A Guide Book of United States Coins* by R.S. Yoeman. Popularly called "The Red Book of Coins," it gives you the average retail values of coins around the U.S. Another useful Yoeman book, *The Handbook of United States Coins* ("The Blue Book of Coins") gives typical prices dealers pay for coins. Both of Yoeman's guides can be purchased at book, coin, or stamp stores or borrowed from most libraries.

Dealers tend to pay from 30%-50% of prices listed in the Red Book, and fairly close to blue book prices. If you own anything that appears to catalog over $100, you have a good item and should be extra careful about its dispersal. Coins with values listed at under five dollars will find few takers unless heavily discounted.

How much cash you get for a coin will depend on how the buyer grades it. Both of these handy books contain information you should read about coin grading, because amateurs over-estimate condition of coins and currency. Collectors and dealers grade severely, especially when they're buying. If you are not happy with how your coins are graded, go to someone else. Before you challenge someone's grading, however, read the grading criterion in the red or blue book. A tiny spot of wear at the tip of an eagle's wing, can cost a coin 5 grade points and hundreds of dollars.

For those interested in modern paper money of the U.S., *A Guide Book of Modern United States Currency* by Neil Shafer will be informative. Other standard works include William Donlon's *Price Catalog of United States Small Size*

Paper Money, which is issued periodically and available in libraries. More difficult to find is the detailed *Standard Handbook of Modern U.S. Paper Money* by Goodman, Schwartz and O'Donnell.

Money issued by small banks is always sought, as are the hundreds of variations of modern circulating currency. Bills with printing errors have premium value. An error bill with a star at the beginning of a serial number is desirable since bills with stars were printed to replace bills damaged in printing. Large denomination error bills such as $50's and $100's are less desirable than small denominations.

I frequently get questions when on the air about large denomination German currency from the 1920's. This was a time of great inflation, and enormous denomination bills called *notgeld,* were printed, often in the millions of marks. Interesting though they may be, these bills were worthless then, and for the most part carry little value other than curiosity today.

The ease of photocopying makes it possible to check the value of your money easily and quickly. If inquiring about the value of modern currency, it is important to note the color of the Treasury seal to the right of the portrait on the face of each bill. Colors can be blue, green red, brown, gold, or yellow, with different values for different colors.

The coin world has attracted more than its share of shady characters over the years. Never sell coins, watches or jewelry to someone buying out of a motel room. You get much less than you would from well-established dealers.

COINS & PAPER MONEY

★ **Ancient Greek and Roman coins** of high quality. He also buys books related to ancient Greek and Roman coins. In business 20 years, he issues sales catalogs and holds auctions of coins and related books.
Thomas McKenna
PO Box 1356
Fort Collins, CO 80522

★ **Ancient coins, especially Biblical, Greek, and Roman.** Also other ancient artifacts including Egyptian, Greek, Roman, and Biblical pottery, glass and relics. Wrote *Guide to Ancient Jewish Coins* and other books. A 20 year veteran collector/dealer, he issues periodic catalogs.
David Hendin, Amphora
PO Box 805
Nyack, NY 10960

★ **Spanish pieces of eight.** Wants *reales* minted in Spanish or South American mints. Seeks coins with globe and pillars known as "pillar dollars," "pieces of eight," or "pirate dollars."
Sven Stau
PO Box 437
Buffalo, NY 14212
    (716) 825-5448 or (716) 822-3120

★ **Coin collections of all types,** "from pennies to gold." Also individual gold coins, medals, and artifacts. Also pre-1930 U.S. banknotes and commemorative coins. No pennies after 1955, nickels after 1939, dimes, quarters, and halves after 1964, or silver dollars after 1936.
Ron Aldridge
14908 Knollview
Dallas, TX 75248
    (214) 239-3574 eves

★ **Silver and gold coins from any country** but especially wants perfect proof U.S. silver dollars. "No junk coins."
Robert Hiett, Maple City Coin
PO Box 47
Monmouth, IL 61462
    (309) 734-3212 Fax: (309) 734-8083

★ **Paper money.** "I buy all U.S. paper money issued before 1929, all **Confederate money** and all broken bank notes from any state. I especially want **items made of ground up paper money**, and will pay 60% of retail. I recommend making photocopies of bills you'd like to sell."
William Skelton, Highland Coin
PO Box 55448
Birmingham, AL 35255
    (205) 939-3166 ext #3

★ **Paper money.** "We'll buy any foreign and obsolete U.S. and **Confederate banknotes**. We will buy currency in any condition and quantity in order to supply fellow collectors in all parts of the world. We deal by mail only but telephone calls are welcomed. We will buy collections as well as single notes, but we do not want U.S. currency after 1928." A description should include the date, denomination, and the country of issue. A photocopy is the best way to describe currency. With his available research library, he is "able to identify and appraise any banknote ever issued."

"Modern small size bills were made after 1928."

    Josef Klaus, World Wide Notaphilic Service
    PO Box 5427
    Vallejo, CA 94591
        (707) 644-3146 or (707) 643-8616

★ **Paper money.** "I'll buy collections, accumulations, and individual items of U.S. and foreign paper money. Send clear photocopies of both sides. Please understand that much of what I look at will not be of interest because of poor condition or lack of collector demand." Over thirty years' experience.
    Douglas Swisher
    PO Box 52701
    Jacksonville, FL 32201
        (904) 448-6214

★ **All foreign paper money.** "I'll buy collections, accumulations, dealer's stock, hoards, rarities, German inflation currency, specimens, printer's proofs, banknote presentations, sample books, and entire **numismatic libraries**." Will travel. Has been buying since 1964.
    AMCASE
    PO Box 5376
    Akron, OH 44334
        (216) 867-6724

★ **U.S. Coins and paper money.** Wants estates, collections and accumulations of early **U.S. silver and gold coins**, paper money, and all other U.S. coins from 1793-1900. This nationally known dealer has been around for 40 years, and will travel to see large lots and better collections. Send a list and description. Photocopy suggested.
    Littleton Coin Co., THCC
    253 Union Street
    Littleton, NH 03561

★ **German coins.** Please list or photocopy.
    Ronald Selcke
    PO Box 237
    Bloomingdale, IL 60108

★ **Printed or manuscript items relating to coins, currency, medals, tokens, or counterfeiting.** Especially scholarly books on coins from any period or language. Also scholarly **numismatic periodicals** and catalogs of coin auctions pre-1940 in any language. Also **counterfeit detectors and bank note reporters** issued in the U.S., 1820 and 1900. No modern works or general surveys of numismatics. Makes offers on better items.

> George Frederick Kolbe
> PO Drawer 3100
> Crestline, CA 92325
> (909) 338-6527

★ **Items made from macerated (ground up) currency** by the mint, including statues, plaques, postcards, shoes, hats, etc., have a small tag reading, "This item made of U.S. greenbacks redeemed and macerated by the U.S. Government." Describe carefully, noting damage.

> Donald Gorlick
> PO Box 24541
> Seattle, WA 98124
> (206) 824-0508

ERROR COINS & ELONGATES

★ **Mis-strike and error coins created by the U.S. Mint.** Under most circumstances, it is best to send a good clear pencil rubbing or photocopy for evaluation if you wish an offer. Also **paper money of 1929 issued by banks.** Include photocopy and SASE for free appraisal.

> Neil Osina
> Best Variety Coin Center
> 358 West Foothill Blvd.
> Glendora, CA 91740

★ **Error coins** created by the mint. Send a photo or a rubbing.

> George VanTrump, Jr.
> PO Box 260170
> Lakewood, CO 80226

★ **Elongated coins pre-1960.** Also **machines to make them.**

> C. Meccarello, Elongated Coin Museum
> 228 Vassar Road
> Poughkeepsie, NY 12603

★ **Elongated coins.** If what you have is pre-1930, ship it for an offer, but *do not* ship COD. Hartzog pays $1-$5 and up for elongates before 1940. Large collections especially wanted.

> Rich Hartzog
> PO Box 4143 BFT
> Rockford, IL 61110

COUNTERFEITING DEVICES

★ **Any machine or device used to detect counterfeit coins or currency** including coin scales, coin detectors, scanners, grids, magnifiers, Detectographs and other devices to check weight, thickness or diameter of coins. Also any scale with markings in amounts, such as "20 dol."
> Donald Gorlick
> PO Box 24541
> Seattle, WA 98124
> (206) 824-0508

★ **Coin scales, coin detectors, and counterfeit detectors.** Will buy the devices and/or books about them and the processes. Buys outright or accept on consignment for auction.
> Rich Hartzog
> PO Box 4143 BFT
> Rockford, IL 61110
> (815) 226-0771   Fax: (815) 397-7662

CREDIT CARDS

★ **Credit cards.** "I'll pay a flat $2 each for credit cards, charga-plates, and charge coins made of celluloid, metal, paper or plastic, U.S. or foreign, as long as they are not abused. Ship what you have, for prompt payment." ATM and sample credit cards are only worth 25¢ each.
> Lin Overholt
> PO Box 8481
> Madeira Beach, FL 33738

★ **Credit cards.** "I've collected credit cards for over ten years an am seriously interested in buying both the older metal charge cards and modern plastic cards. Please ship any quantity of used or new cards. I pay $4 up for older metal charge cards and will pay *at least* $15 for any metal one I need for my own collection. Pre-1980 plastic cards bring $1 up, and those before 1970 average $2. More paid for local businesses, unusual types, etc. Post-1980 cards are worth 50¢ each, a few bring more. I will also reimburse your postage. Please ship for my check."
> Rich Hartzog
> PO Box 4143 BFT
> Rockford, IL 61110

★ **Credit cards** from any source, paper or plastic, are desired. "Send items for immediate offer and check. I pay postage both ways."
> Noel Levy
> PO Box 595699
> Dallas, TX 75359

STOCKS, BONDS & FISCAL PAPER

★ **Fiscal paper** including **rare currency (U.S. and foreign)**, checks, stocks and bonds, certificates of deposits, books on money, other items. He is particularly expert in **California currency, national currency and Mexican currency.** Doesn't want items after 1935 or any kind of reproduction. A photocopy will often do, but "I'll usually request to see the item in person before making an offer."

> Lowell Horwedel
> PO Box 2395
> West Lafayette, IN 47906
>   (317) 583-2784

★ **Elaborately illustrated stocks and bonds.** All are wanted but have particular need for pre-1920 railroads, mining, telegraph, aviation, oil, and automobiles. Also stocks from unusual companies like a maker of life rafts. Items pre-1870 given special consideration. Especially want Western paper with autographs of important people like Rockefeller, Carnegie, Gould, James Hill, U.S. Presidents, and other recognizable people. "Send a photocopy and an SASE for fast payment."

> David Beach's Paper Americana
> PO Box 2026
> Goldenrod, FL 32733
>   (407) 657-7403   Fax: (407) 657-6382

★ **Stocks and bonds from any industry** but especially mining, railroads, automobile companies, expositions, and aviation. Also other stocks if they are well illustrated and pre-1900. Stocks signed by famous people can be worth up to $1,000. Please include your phone number.

> Ken Prag's Paper Americana
> PO Box 531
> Burlingame, CA 94011
>   (415) 566-6400

Fiscal paper is documents having to do with money, including stocks, bonds, checks, mortgages, scrip, IOU's, revenue stamps, and the like. Collectors buy financial "fiscal" paper for the elaborate pictorial engravings called vignettes. Fiscal paper is also sought if signed by famous people or if it is pre-1830. The value range is from $1 to $500, with most selling for less than $30.

★ **Stocks and bonds** issued in the United States before 1910, especially mining, railroads, or unusual companies. "I am not interested in stocks that were never issued and are unsigned. Stocks and bonds must have an original company seal."

> Phyllis Barrella
> Buttonwood Galleries
> PO Box 1006, Throggs Neck Station
> New York, NY 10465

★ **U.S. and Canadian stocks and bonds,** especially railroads, mining, oil, shipping, automotive, aviation, expositions, and others. Also stocks or bonds signed or owned by someone famous. Also seeks documents with a **printed revenue stamp**. This past president of the Bond & Share Society also wants all pre-1800 certificates from any company.

> Bob Kluge
> American Vignettes
> PO Box 155
> Roselle Park, NJ 07204

★ **Stocks, bonds, checks,** drafts, and warrants from Western states before 1930. Signed, illustrated, used documents are desired, with premium paid for Western items before the Civil War.

> Warren Anderson
> American West Archives
> PO Box 100
> Cedar City, UT 84720
> (801) 586-9497

★ **All paper items printed with fancy engraved illustrations by security printers,** including railroad passes, semi-postals (advertising stamps), souvenir cards, and annual reports. Security printers include the Bureau of Printing & Engraving, U.S.P.S, American Bank Note Co., Canadian Bank Note Co., and Homer Lee Bank Note Co. Wants to find *Annual Reports* of American Bank Note Co. and other security printers and engravers.

> Robin M. Ellis
> PO Box 8468
> San Antonio, TX 78208

★ **Fiscal paper from South Carolina** pre-1910, especially from the city of Charleston.

> Bob Karrer
> PO Box 6094
> Alexandria, VA 22306

Tokens and medals

Tokens and medals are issued by governments, civic and athletic organizations, charities, schools, and other groups. Military valor awards bring the most money, especially if they have their original paperwork. Many other medals and exonumia (*see below*) sells for bargain prices (under $20). Buyers of medals and tokens will be found throughout *Where To Sell It!*

Collecting tokens is popular in part because they are inexpensive, with most tokens retailing for 25¢ to $3. Dealer evaluation is called for, however, because a few are worth $500 and up. They are difficult for most people to evaluate on their own, because more than 300 books are in print about tokens.

The following definitions should be helpful when you're faced with describing "a little round thing" to a potential buyer.

Exonumia is a word created to cover the entire field of non-money coin-like objects. It refers primarily to tokens, but has come to include medals, orders, decorations, plaques, awards, ribbons, and the like. Dealers of exonumia often sell advertising mirrors (they were frequently trade tokens) and other small collectibles as well.

Coins are money, generally issued by governments. Most modern coins contain the name of the issuing agency, the denomination, and the date of issue. You will find buyers for coins on pages 341-345 in *Where To Sell It!*

Tokens are money substitutes, often marked with a value, such as "good for 5¢ in trade." Tokens were issued by local businesses for a wide variety of reasons, usually but not exclusively for advertising. Sometimes they were issued because no legal coinage was available.

Medals are "any piece of metal marked with a design or inscription, made to honor a person, place or event," according to one of our buyers. Medals vary in size and shape, although most are round. Medals larger than 3" in diameter are usually called **medallions**. Small rectangular medals are called **plaquettes** and larger ones, meant to hang on the wall are **plaques**.

Orders and **decorations** are an important separate category, generally related to diplomacy and the military. They are often worn around the neck or on sashes across the wearer's breast.

Military medals are emblems of honor normally made with ribbons so they can be worn. **Badges** have a top pin or device, with or without a ribbon, so they too can be worn. Both usually have a medallic device hanging from them (what amateurs think of when someone says "medals").

Ribbons are commemorative items, printed with information about the event commemorated. They are usually associated with lodges, fraternal organizations, conventions, and the like.

Whichever one of these you have, make a pencil rubbing or a photocopy and let the buyers tell you exactly what you own and what they'll pay.

TOKENS & MEDALS

★   **All types and quantities of tokens, medals, ribbons, badges, and related items.**   He buys trade tokens, medals of all sort, hard times tokens, Civil War tokens, transit tokens especially with pictures on them ($10-$750), amusement tokens, telephone tokens, sales tax tokens, **any token or medal made from another item**, medals related to medicine or the arts and humanities, **love tokens, World's Fair medals** and elongated coins, **G.A.R. badges** and tokens, **Indian peace medals** ($1,500 up), **slave tags, Canadian** tokens and medals, **military awards and medals,** counterstamped coins, and just about everything similar to the above including advertising mirrors and **Franklin Mint token sets.** There are literally millions of varieties, and condition plays an important role in value. If what you have is pre-1930, simply ship it to him for an offer, but do not ship COD. Hartzog will send you a check for the lot. "We cannot make individual offers on a long list of material. Our offers are for the entire lot as we want to purchase everything. We are not interested in pricing your material for you to sell to others, sorry!" He claims to pay higher prices than anyone else. If your collection is very early, very large, or very valuable, phone collect and Hartzog will make arrangements to see what you have. Hartzog can auction your materials for you if you prefer. A sample of his auction catalog is available for $3. Hartzog's lengthy wants list shows prices and is recommended.

> Rich Hartzog
> World Exonumia
> PO Box 4143 BFT
> Rockford, IL 61110
>   (815) 226-0771

★   **Tokens and medals of all kinds and countries** including transportation tokens, advertising tokens, **gambling tokens**, merchant GOOD FOR tokens, and the like. All old coin-like items are purchased as well as related items such as **elongated** or encased coins, engraved coins, pre-1900 dog tags, **advertising pocket mirrors**, political buttons, and **stage or movie money**. Also wants **"hobo nickels"** which are buffalo nickels with the Indian head re-engraved into another face. Steve will pay $10 to $35 each for these. Commemorative and award **medals from fairs** are also wanted. Photocopies are usually the best way to describe what you have to sell. No large modern fantasy tokens are wanted. No Franklin Mint medals. No modern arcade tokens. Steve runs mail auctions of tokens and medals and has written books on U.S. tokens, amusement tokens, Scouting tokens and "lucky" souvenir coins, all of which are available from the author at reasonable prices. Steve's useful 300 page illustrated price guide, *Tokens and Medals*, costs $23 postpaid.

> Stephen P. Alpert
> PO Box 66331
> Los Angeles, CA 90066
>   (310) 478-7405

★ **Medals and tokens of all sorts** are wanted by this 22 year veteran dealer. Identify what the token or medal is made from, and provide a photocopy or a good rubbing. "Buys them all," he says.

William Williges
PO Box 1245
Wheatland, CA 95692
(916) 633-2732

★ **Transportation or toll tokens** for bridges, toll roads, ferries, horse-cars, depot hacks, and early streetcars. Tokens *must* be made of metal or plastic. Cardboard tokens are wanted *only* if round, *not* square or rectangular. HOTEL TO DEPOT or TRANSFER LINE tokens are worth $25-$100, more if pictorial. A token reading I GIBBS BELLEVILLE & NEW YORK USM STAGE//GOOD FOR ONE RIDE TO THE BEARER would be worth $1,500 in nice condition.

Rev. John Coffee
PO Box 1204
Boston, MA 02104
(617) 277-8111

★ **Transportation tokens.** Will buy in any quantity from any years. Prices vary. Some old tokens are common, but others can be worth $1,500+ each if they picture a ship, trolley, horse car, ferry, or stage coach. Look for the words DEPOTEL, BAGGAGE, HOTEL, OMNIBUS, DRAYAGE, DEPOT TO HOTEL, and similar wordings. Simply ship your tokens if you want this well known dealer to make an offer.

"We sell bags of 2,500 modern tokens with cut-out letters for $99, so you can see they aren't worth much."

Rich Hartzog
World Exonumia
PO Box 4143 BFT
Rockford, IL 61110
(815) 226-0771   Fax: (815) 397-7662

★ **Medals and medallions from Canada, Britain, and other English speaking countries** issued for coronations, jubilees, town celebrations, victories, fraternal groups, achievement, athletics, and especially military valor medals awarded to Canadians. Also **love tokens** engraved with names, initials, dates, pledges, and the like from around the world especially pre-1900. Also merchant's **GOOD FOR trade tokens** from Canada, Britain, and English speaking countries. Also buys **Canadian paper money**, singles or collections, but only dating before 1937.

Michael Rice
PO Box 286
Saanichton, BC
V0S 1M0 CANADA
(604) 652-9047 eves

★ **U.S., British, and Soviet valor decorations** and war medals. **Foreign awards given to Americans** are of great interest, especially Soviet World War II orders and decorations. All items *must* have supporting documentation of the award to U.S. personnel. Hlinka also buys all letters, certificates, or documents pertaining to valor awards. He seeks a U.S. Medal Of Honor awarded between 1917 and 1970. He encourages you to photocopy both sides of medals and supporting paperwork. Hlinka has been dealing in medals for 40 years and has been an officer in various collectors' societies.

> Peter Hlinka
> PO Box 310
> New York, NY 10028
> (212) 409-6407

★ **Medals, decorations, and orders,** especially military gallantry awards from U.S. and England, but will consider **all governmental awards** from any Western nation. No Asian awards, please.

> Alan Harrow
> 2292 Chelan Drive
> Los Angeles, CA 90068

★ **Indian War medals, badges and awards** issued by the U.S. government, states, or veteran's groups. An Indian scout's Medal of Honor can be worth $20,000. Other items from $100 to $10,000. "No offers based on phone calls or photos. Items must be seen. Ship insured with record of delivery. Your postage will be reimbursed."

> Thomas Pooler
> PO Box 1861
> Grass Valley, CA 95949

★ **Official presidential inaugural medals.** Levine, who has been a dealer for twenty-five years, will pay $4,000 for the Teddy Roosevelt inaugural medal.

> H. Joseph Levine
> 6550-I Little River Turnpike
> Alexandria, VA 22312

★ **Medals commemorating or depicting Black Americans.** "I'll buy medals, medallions, badges, or tokens relating to, or depicting, Afro-Americans or including the words NEGRO, COLORED or BLACK-AMERI-CAN. Items may be positive or negative in tone. "I'll pay $1,200 for the Franklin Mint set of 70 American Negro Commemorative Society medals." Tell him the material (silver, bronze, or aluminum), the size in millimeters, and inscriptions on both sides.

> Elijah Singley
> 2301 Noble Ave.
> Springfield, IL 62704
> (217) 546-5143 eves

★ **Medals, especially foreign,** related to medicine, photography, printing, cycling, railroads, aviation, Judaica, ships, Olympic Games, Africa, Australia, West Indies, Far East, Monaco, or New Zealand. No badly worn items will be purchased.
>Hedley Betts
>PO Box 8122
>San Jose, CA 95155
>(408) 266-9255

★ **Tokens, medals, and exonumia (non money coinage) from Georgia** including "good for" tokens issued by merchants, saloons and lumber companies, encased and **elongated coins**, advertising and commemorative medals and tokens, including those issued for the 1895 Atlanta Cotton States Exposition, and any agriculture awards and medals from Georgia state fairs, the earlier the better. "Top prices paid for collections or single items."
>R.W. Colbert
>4156 Livsey Road
>Tucker, GA 30084

★ **Animal rescue, school attendance, heroism or truant officer's** medals and badges.
>Gene Christian
>3849 Bailey Ave.
>Bronx, NY 10463

★ **Masonic chapter pennies** all varieties and countries, but especially from Maine. Indicate chapter name, number, and location. Will pay from $3-$40 each. No modern coins counterstamped with Masonic emblems.
>Maurice Storck, Sr.
>775 West Roger Road #214
>Tucson, AZ 85705

★ **Franklin Mint and other private mint issues.** "I will purchase all bronze, silver and gold singles, sets and other items such as plates, bronzes, etc., in any quantity. Many silver or gold pieces are worth substantially above issue price. Bronze tokens and medals are worth less than their issue price, most of them under 25¢ apiece. I pay reasonable prices for all modern mint items. Since I do not specialize in *Franklin Mint* items, do not ship them without inquiring first. State the price you want, or request my offer. If my offer is not accepted, I do not pay return postage on modern mint medals that have been shipped." There is little market for *Franklin Mint* items, so it's best to contact Rich first by phone or letter so you fully understand their value or lack of it. Rich is the nation's largest dealers in exonumia (coins that aren't legal money).
>Rich Hartzog
>PO Box 4143 BFT
>Rockford, IL 61110
>(815) 226-0771

Stamps

Few 20th century U.S. stamps have substantial value, but watch for stamped and unstamped envelopes and letters dating before the Civil War, as they can be worth hundreds of dollars! Value is affected by the stamp, the cancellation, the carriers, and where it was mailed from and to. Empty envelopes sell, but an enclosed letter with interesting contents is best. Decorated stamped envelopes sell too. Condition crucial!

When looking at stamped envelopes, look for letters about travel, Indians, mining, colorful people, disasters, famous events, business, military service, personal history, and the like, especially those which give details. Someone looking for stamps paid $20 for a box of envelopes at a yard sale. Letters in those envelopes sold to experts for more than $130,000!

Buyers of early letters are often interested in postmarks. Examine them with an eye toward historic places, vanished cities, and unusual cancellations as on board a riverboat, airplane, or military ship.

Don't be surprised if most foreign stamps turn out to have little value. Enough valuable ones do exist, however, to make it worthwhile checking them, especially when they are on interesting envelopes. If you own a few foreign stamps you can look them up in *Scott's Standard Postage Stamp Catalogue*. U.S. stamps are found in *Scott's Specialized Catalogue of United States Stamps*. Both are available at most public libraries. If you own many stamps, you are facing a tedious chore. Let experts do it for you. They are both faster and more efficient.

STAMPS

★ **U.S. and foreign stamp collections and accumulations** are wanted by this 35 year veteran dealer who buys:

> **Albums** from any country or from mixed countries;
> **Stockbooks** and **unsorted boxfuls** of duplicate stamps;
> **Old envelopes** with stamps from any country;
> Mint sheets and blocks;
> Old **revenue (tax) stamps** on documents of all kinds;
> **Duck hunting** and fishing permit stamps, mint or used,
>   especially on licenses;
> Stamp-like labels and seals of all kinds;
> **Postal related souvenirs** including booklets, cards, and
>   stamp announcements;
> **Philatelic reference books** from any period or country in any
>   language;
> **Stamp magazines** pre-1945;
> **Worldwide stamp catalogs** pre-1925;
> **Philatelic auction catalogs** pre-1945;
> **Photos or real photo postcards** of mail carriers, mail trucks,
>   post offices, and mail delivery.

"If in doubt, include it! I must be one of the last people who collect EVERYTHING in stamps and stamp-related items." Doug says stamp collecting is a highly specialized hobby, and that even the most common looking items (especially envelopes with unusual markings) may have value. "Because of their nature and sheer numbers, stamps have to be sent for my personal inspection. Call first, because I can give you clear shipping instructions and help you eliminate heavy items that have no value, such as newer stamp catalogs, 3-ring notebooks, and empty albums. I can give guidance on how to ship stamps to prevent damage and preserve value. Return postage normally required, but negotiable."

"Three costly errors made by amateurs are
*   (1) Cutting stamps off envelopes and documents;*
*   (2) Improperly storing and handling mint stamps; and*
*   (3) Forgetting that labor costs of preparing stamps for resale will affect how much you are paid."*

Douglas Swisher
PO Box 52701
Jacksonville, FL 32201
    (904) 448-6214 eves

★ **Stamps from any country in any quantity.** "We'll buy everything you have," says Harvey, who has been dealing by the mail since 1934! He wants collections of singles, plate blocks, sheets, covers, and rarities. If you have a large or valuable collection, Harvey Dolin & Company will come to your home. Smaller collections may be shipped to them for their cash offer. "Your satisfaction is always guaranteed," say their ads. Dolin buys **stampless letters** (dating before the first U.S. stamps in 1843, or after), **Confederate stamps and envelopes, Wells Fargo envelopes**, and **Duck Hunting stamps.**

Harvey Dolin & Company
5 Beekman Street #406
New York, NY 10038
(212) 267-0216

★ **Various stamps and envelopes.** McHenry has been in business for 30 years and provides a long list of covers (envelopes) he wants, including Presidential free franks, letters mailed without stamps, color advertising on envelopes, expositions, pioneer flights, and more. You should request his list if you have early or unusual envelopes for sale. In addition to covers, he buys **revenue stamps, Confederate stamps** and **letters, precancels**, and stamps from **U.S. possessions.**

Gordon McHenry
PO Box 1117
Osprey, FL 34229
(813) 966-5563   Fax: (813) 966-4568

★ **U.S. and foreign stamps and covers** (envelopes) have been purchased for resale for over 30 years by this veteran dealer.

Bill Colby, Kenrich Co.
PO Box 248-T
Temple City, CA 91780
(818) 286-3888

★ **U.S. or foreign stamp collections** from before 1960.

Ron Aldridge
14908 Knollview
Dallas, TX 75248
(214) 239-3574

★ **U.S. Internal Revenue special tax stamps,** licenses and permits for making and selling beer, liquor, wine, tobacco, cigars, margarine, firearms, opium and marijuana. Also for businesses such as brokers, pawnbrokers, dentists, lawyers, etc. No stamps from between 1873 and 1885 with punched holes are wanted. Also wants state stamps and licenses for any business, activity, or product including hunting and fishing. **USDA export stamps** and certificates for meat products are also sought. **Ration coupons** for gas, fuel oil and sugar are wanted, but no war books (1,2,3, or 4) or any red or blue tokens. "Photocopies are very helpful."
> Bill Smiley
> PO Box 361
> Portage, WI 53901
>   (608) 742-3714 eves

★ **Federal and state revenue and special tax stamps** including document stamps and all stamps used to show that taxes had been paid on a product. Special tax stamps are large and look like licenses to engage in various occupations, such as liquor dealer, cigar salesman, wine maker, etc. Some of these issues, notably 1875, 1877, 1879, 1883, and 1885, are available in large quantities and sell for very little. Photocopies are strongly urged by this 30 year veteran buyer.
> Hermann Ivester
> 5 Leslie Circle
> Little Rock, AR 72205
>   (501) 225-8565 eves

★ **Stamps, covers, and postal stationery from Hong Kong and Macao.** Covers are decorated or embellished envelopes, and among philatelic items sought by this Hong Kong postcard/stamp dealer, who requests you photocopy and price what you have.
> Kin Leung Liu
> 1517 South Angeline Street
> Seattle, WA 98108
>   (206) 767-3025

★ **Envelopes with stamps mailed in the Orient.** Buys nearly all envelopes with stamps mailed in China, Tibet, Korea, Hong Kong, Nepal, Mongolia and Japan. Advisable to first phone or send a photocopy by mail or fax. Pledges to pay post on items sent on approval.
> Bridgewater Onvelopes Collectibles
> 680 Route 206 North
> Bridgewater, NJ 08807
>   (201) 725-0022   Fax: (201) 707-4647

TIPS ON SELLING

Art

If you are not an art critic, trained to recognize valuable art, get expert advice. Paintings and prints that look sloppy, amateurish or depressing to you may be snapped up by buyers for big dollars. Many paintings and prints have little value but each year, a few turn up worth $10,000 or more.

If a painting has been passed down in your family for more than 50 years, check the current value of that artist's work. Some painters whose work cost $100 at the turn of the century are worth 100 times that today.

A bewildering number of books are available on art, so research is difficult for the amateur. *300 Years of American Art* is frequently helpful because it gives artist biographies, a sample painting and a history of their sale at auction.

Valuing art is subjective, and dependent on auction prices more than any other collectible. In the early 1990's, art is generally in a depressed mode after the record highs of the late 1980's. Many items purchased during the 80's art fever are now selling for 60% of prices they brought then.

Prints signed and numbered in pencil are more likely to have value. Prints from the 1930's are "hot" right now, selling for $300 to $3,000. Some inexpensive prints like Currier & Ives have developed cult status and sell for $30 to $2,000 up! Selling prints requires dimensions of the image and of the border. List signatures and dates. Photocopy if possible.

To sell **paintings**, a good 35mm photo is essential, along with dimensions. Take a close-up of the signature if possible.

Folk art includes items made by untrained amateurs, done with style, vigor, form and color. Anything that is hand-crafted in decorative ways may qualify. Quality pieces bring thousands, even tens of thousands of dollars.

Art from outside the U.S. and Europe is getting increasing attention. Prices are rising fast for South Pacific masks, bowls and shields. Mexican and South American paintings and folk arts have hit record prices within the last year.

If you have a painting you think valuable, showing it to many dealers and auctioneers in hopes of getting ever higher prices is likely to have the opposite effect. Paintings often diminish in value in proportion to the number of people to whom they are offered.

The art market is volatile, risky, and rife with competition, rumor, and disagreement among experts. Top museums make million dollar mistakes. Even famous auction houses occasionally miss a "masterpiece" and sell it far below value; smaller auction houses do it frequently. Buying or selling art successfully is a matter of personal taste, luck, and market analysis.

Researching your art can be tedious work, even for those who enjoy research. So many paintings were created by unknowns, the vast majority of what you own will neither be listed nor catalogued, let alone pictured. Much research in the field of art comes to a dead end. Using experts to evaluate and sell your art is good strategy.

Good prices are being paid for good items in today's art world, even though the market is generally depressed. This is a very volatile time, and tastes are changing as a result of the movement of baby boomers into the market. Personally, I believe their impact will be felt for a long time, so I'm selling anything I consider surplus that I don't feel will have boomer-appeal.

PAINTINGS & PRINTS

★ **Paintings by listed artists of all types and periods,** including 20th century. This first rate auction house regularly handles works of art from $100 to $100,000 and may be the perfect outlet for your better quality paintings. Send a photo, give the dimensions, describe any damage and note any signature.

James D. Julia Auctions
PO Box 830
Fairfield, ME 04937
(207) 453-7904   Fax: (207) 453-2502

★ **Paintings, prints, and photographs made by artists in** *Who Was Who in American Art.* Primarily interested in American Impressionism, Peter will consider a wide range of works from 1800-1950, as long as the artist is listed. Among special interests are:

Art depicting competitive rowing ($500-$1,500);
Color woodblock prints, particularly the *White Line* prints of
  the Provincetown, MA, printmaker group ($500-$2,000);
Paintings and prints by American women artists of any
  period ($500-$10,000+);
Photos of Abraham Lincoln ($500-$10,000).
Does not want wood engravings from *Harper's, Leslie's,* and other periodicals. Send photograph and the dimensions.

Peter Falk
206 Boston Post Road
Midison, CT 06443
(203) 245-2246

★ **Old etchings and lithographs worldwide** if before 1900. American etchings and lithographs may be as late as 1950. Particularly interested in the work of **Currier & Ives,** John Sloan, Thomas Rowlandson, Thomas Hart Benson, J.S. Curry, Frank Benson, Daumier, **Audubon,** Goya, A. Horn, Millet, Piranesi, and Rembrandt. "I'll pay from $1,000 to $10,000 for large 19th century **lithographic views of Baltimore.**" He has no interest in 20th century European prints, nor is he interested in the work of Parrish, Icart, Mucha, R.A. Fox, or Wallace Nutting. You'll have to tell him the artist, title, subject, size, and condition. "While I do purchase through the mail and will make tentative offers on items before I see them, I cannot commit to purchases until I have personally examined the items. It would be unprofessional to do otherwise."

Craig Flinner
Craig Flinner Gallery
505 North Charles Street
Baltimore, MD 21201
(410) 727-1863

★ **Paintings and limited edition prints** by listed artists, particularly American and **Oriental**. Give the size and condition. Include photo.

    Ivan Gilbert
    Miran Arts & Books
    2824 Elm Ave.
    Columbus, OH 43209
        (614) 236-0002 eves

★ **Chromoliths and hand colored prints** on topics of natural history (birds, bugs, fish and animals), military, medicine, old West, Indians, costumes and fashion, Negroes, sports, and art Nouveau. Wants pre-1900 prints only, but does buy 19th and 20th century **advertising art and labels** on similar themes or with other attractive pictures. Describe fully for this major graphics dealer, known for paying high prices for quality items. Joe is author of two books on advertising labels. His *Cigar Label Art* is $40 and *Fruit Crate Art* is $20 from the author.

    Joe Davidson
    5185 Windfall Road
    Medina, OH 44256
        (216) 723-7172

★ **Prints, engravings, chromoliths, and woodcuts** before 1900 on many topics including city scenes of the U.S. and Canada, natural history (birds, bugs, fish, and animals), military uniforms, fashion, the old West, children, expositions and fairs, disasters, mining, Indians, and Oriental life in America. These are very difficult to buy by mail, and must be examined under high magnification. If your print is framed, he believes "it is wise to remove the print from the frame in order to find the publisher and date of publication." Indicate the size of the image, and the size of the overall print, including border. Include an SASE.

    John Rosenhoover
    100 Mandalay Road
    Chicopee, MA 01020
        (413) 536-5542

★ **Prints and illustrations** including **yard longs, calendars,** and prints of flowers, children and beautiful women including calendars and books before 1919. **Also illustrations by** Harrison Fisher, Francis Brundage, Newton Wells, Catherine Klein, Maud Humphrey, and others. Also wants **magazines** with fashion prints and color pictures of women and children, such as *Ladies Home Journal, Women's Home Companion, Butterick, McCall's,* etc. Buys only color prints. Prefers unframed items. Must send photocopy. Note *all* defects. Will make approximate offers, but must see to determine condition before buying.

    Linda Gibbs, Heirloom Keepsakes
    10380 Miranda
    Buena Park, CA 90620
        (714) 827-6488

★ **Prints, American and European.** Buys a wide range of prints. Generally prefers topical prints rather than scenics. Give a complete description, including size of image, size of sheet, colors, and any and all information printed or written at the bottom of the print.

Kenneth Newman
The Old Print Shop
150 Lexington Avenue at 30th Street
New York, NY 10016
(212) 683-3950

★ **Woodblock prints by European, American and Canadian artists** (1895-1950) in color or black and white. He buys only pencil signed prints created and signed by the artist whose work they are. Particular interests include:

Landscapes and marinescapes by the widely traveled artist, **Arthur Wesley Dow**, Ipswitch MA. His prints are signed but unnumbered, usually 5x7 inches or smaller, and can be worth $1,000 and more;

Prints by the Provincetown printers, especially their "white line prints" characterized by blocks of color separated by white lines. These run in size from 3x4 inches to 16x20, but are mostly from 5x7 to 8x10 inches. Values run from $1,000 to $15,000;

Prints with Oriental subjects, but only those by Western, often British, artists. People to look for include Bartlett, Hyde, Keith and Lum.

"I do not want Oriental prints from Japan and the Far East or wood engravings from *Harper's Weekly* or other magazines and newspapers. Nor do I generally buy woodblock illustrations from books." If your print is loose and unframed, a photocopy is quick and accurate. If you feel you have one of these valuable prints, the expense of a color copy may be justified. If your print is framed, try to get a good photograph by shooting outdoors in open shade. Thomas makes offers *if your item is genuinely for sale,* but is not interested in doing free appraisals. In business for

"Woodblocks are rectangular with sharply defined borders. When printed in color, a slight registration problem is often apparent. They are usually signed in pencil outside the image area."

10 years, Thomas issues annual catalogs of art for sale and will send you an illustrated wants list if you send a #10 (long) envelope.

Steven Thomas, Inc.
PO Box 41
Woodstock, VT 05091
(802) 457-1764

★ **Black and white steel engravings** of birds, animals, nature, romance, and fantasy. Will consider buying most subject matter other than city views and violence.
Gregory Mills
PO Box 2073
Hollywood, CA 90078

★ **Art Deco color prints,** posters and calendars from 1920's and 30's.
R. Bright
PO Box 449
Noel, MO 64854
(417) 475-6367

★ **Paintings depicting the industrial/machine age.** Wants paintings and signed prints depicting workers in industrial settings. He also buys **WPA paintings and prints**. Send photo.
David Zdyb
2988 William Street
Buffalo, NY 14227

★ **Damaged art of all kinds** is wanted. "If people send a good sharp photo I will make an offer on paintings, sculpture, and **Currier & Ives** prints that have been damaged but are still in restorable condition."
Alan Voorhees' Art Restoration
492 Breesport Road
Horseheads, NY 14845

★ **Paintings of the Hudson River or Catskill Mountains.** No modern works. A complete description includes the dimensions, condition, and the signature. A photo is very helpful.
Edward Sheppard
221 Water Street
Catskill, NY 12414
(518) 943-2169

> Look on the back of paintings for evidence they have been exhibited. Artist signatures and picture titles are often found on the stretcher or on the back of the canvas itself.

★ **Paintings of Indians and Eskimos.** Please send a photo for a prompt response. It's helpful if you can read the signature. Dealers price your goods; amateur sellers may request an offer.
Barry Friedman
22725 Garzota Drive
Valencia, CA 91355
(805) 296-2318

★ **Paintings and prints depicting boats** including whaling, yachting, racing, working, etc., are sought by this well known dealer in marine antiques. Give the dimensions, history, and a careful account of any damage or restoration. Photo suggested. Will give "ball park" estimates of value on ordinary items, but appraisals are for a fee. Sporadically issues a pictorial catalog for refundable $5.
Andrew Jacobson
PO Box 2155
South Hamilton, MA 01982
(508) 468-6276

★ **Engraved portraits and photographs of famous people** in all walks of life. Will consider items loose or in books. Photocopies make the best descriptions.
Kenneth Rendell
PO Box 9001
Wellesley, MA 02181
(617) 431-1776   Fax: (617) 237-1492

★ **Paintings of 18th and 19th century American political figures** or historic events. Please send a photo along with a description of the painter's signature if there is one. Only original oils or watercolors in fine condition are wanted. No paper prints, engravings or illustrations torn from books.
Rex Stark
49 Wethersfield Road
Bellingham, MA 02019
(508) 966-0994

★ **Paintings and prints depicting smoking.** Buys a wide range of prints, paintings, and other items with a tobacco theme. All sizes, all media, all nationality, all tobacco topics considered but prefers smaller paintings. Buys pre-1930 magazine illustrations, prints, advertising, signs, posters, photographs and other items. Special interest in cigars, but anything related to tobacco consumption will be considered. Buying for resale and for his personal collection.
Tony Hyman
PO Box 3028
Pismo Beach, CA 93448
(805) 773-6777   Fax: (805) 773-0117

★ **Original paintings for American magazine covers and story illustrations,** 1900 to date. "I'll buy art for magazines and stories in the following genres: aviation, western, fantasy, science fiction, adventure, erotica, detective, mystery, and movie." Also buys **art for pin-up calendars, advertising campaigns, and paperback book covers with similar themes.** These covers were generally vividly painted on 24" x 30" canvas. Rough sketches for cover or story art can also have value. Sellers should submit a photograph of the art, along with the dimensions and an accurate description of the condition of the surface (any soil, holes, dents, scratches, etc.). Note the signature, in the unlikely event there is one. Check the back of the painting because exhibit or publishing history may be recorded there. Most pulp paintings are worth $500 to $2,000, depending upon the artist, subject and condition, although some *Tarzan* and movie covers bring up to $10,000. Jim is a popular artist and comic book illustrator who writes extensively on Pop Culture and art and wrote two books on the history of comics.

"The rule of thumb is don't ever guess about what is and isn't worth something. Send us pictures and let us evaluate it for you."

> Jim Steranko, Supergraphics
> PO Box 974
> Reading, PA 19603
> (215) 374-7477

★ **Original paintings by American illustrators for magazine covers,** magazine story illustrations, or advertising, 1910-1980, including artists such as **Norman Rockwell** and all his contemporaries. Also original art for magazine or calendar pin-ups. Has special interest in sexual or sentimental themes (children, dogs, families, patriotism, etc.).

> Charles Martignette
> 455 Paradise Isle #306
> Hallandale, FL 33007
> (305) 454-3474

★ **Illustrations by well known 20th century illustrators** such as Maxfield Parrish, the Leyendeckers, Norman Rockwell, Rolf Armstrong, Vargas, Petty, Rose O'Neill, Mucha, Erte, Grace Drayton, Will Bradley, and Coles Phillips. Wants original art, prints, posters, advertising, calendars, magazines, and books, 1895-1930. Especially Maxfield Parrish calendars for *Mazda* and pin-up calendars, 1920-1960. Give dimensions and condition of your print, and tell what book, magazine, calendar, etc., it came from. Note the condition. Denis does not want "free appraisals, pen pals, or time wasters." He is the author of price guides for print artists and edits *The Illustrator Collector's News*, available for $12 a year.

> Denis Jackson
> PO Box 1958
> Sequim, WA 98382
> (206) 683-2559

★ **Paintings, drawings and original art for advertising** airlines, automobiles, gasoline, tires, soft drinks or whiskey. Especially likes paintings for ads for *Coke*, alcohol, movies, tobacco products, and other culturally significant items and events. If in doubt, call.
Charles Martignette
PO Box 293
Hallandale, FL 33009
(305) 454-3474

★ **California paintings.** Wants to purchase the work of Edgar Payne, William Wendt, Maurice Braun, Franz Bischoff, Hanson Puthuff, Elmer Wachtel, Ben C. Brown, and Clarence Hinkle.
Robert Lewis
2940 Westwood Blvd. #2
Los Angeles, CA 90064
(310) 475-8531

★ **Paintings by Cincinnati artists** and others. Buying work of Blum, Twachtman, Hurley, Sawier, Weis, Vogt, Wessel, Selden, Casinelli, Duveneck, Sharp, Farney, Nourse, Potthast, Volkert, and other American and European artists. Please send a good clear photo of items for sale. If in doubt, telephone. Have your work in hand when you do.
Cincinnati Art Galleries
635 Main Street
Cincinnati, OH 45202
(513) 381-2128

★ **Paintings by New Orleans and Gulf Coast artists.** Buys oil paintings from artists of New Orleans and the surrounding area, especially from the 1920's and 30's such as A.J. Drysdale, Clarence Millet and G.L. Viavont among others.
Sanchez Galleries
4730 Magazine Street
New Orleans, LA 70115
(504) 524-0281

★ **Sketches, drawings, and paintings by Philip Boileau and Robert Robinson,** American 20th century illustrators. Boileau is known for his 1900-1917 paintings of attractive women done for private customers, magazine covers, and other commercial purposes. Robinson worked commercially from 1907-1952 also on magazine covers and other commercial work. Please provide Bowers with a good close up color photo and as much information about the work as you can. The value of paintings varies, and Bowers will work with you to determine value.
Q. David Bowers
PO Box 1224
Wolfeboro, NH 03894
(603) 569-5095

★ **Wallace Nutting pictures, books, furniture, and other memorabilia.** Among Nutting pictures, Mike particularly wants interiors, scenes with people, animals, and houses. He does not want single pictures of common exteriors of apple blossoms, country lanes, trees, lakes, and ponds, although he will take these as part of a large collection. Collections are preferred, but single pieces will be considered. No size is too large. Mike says he'll travel anywhere to view collections of considerable size and diversity. When describing pictures, give the title, frame size, and condition. When describing books give standard bibliographic information, including title, edition, color of the cover. Mike will either buy outright or consider accepting your items on consignment for one of his Nutting auctions. The 4th edition of Mike's *Price Guide to Wallace Nutting Pictures* is available from him for $17 postpaid.

Michael Ivankovich
PO Box 2458
Doylestown, PA 18901
(215) 345-6094

★ **Wallace Nutting pictures, books and other ephemera,** including furniture, lamps, wooden dishes, postcards, calendars, and greeting cards designed, built, or used by him. "Not interested in recent items, or things that are damaged, broken, or otherwise in less than very good condition," says this 7 year veteran Nutting dealer.

James Buskirk
Eleanor's Hand Tinted Photos
312 Starling Way
Anaheim, CA 92807
(714) 998-9615

★ **Commercial printed art by J.G. Scott** who specialized in cute round faced children. Most of his work is signed JG SCOTT and can be found on the covers of women's magazines, advertising blotters and calendars from the 1920's and 30's and on children's greeting cards printed by the *Gibson Co.*

Robert Stauffer
3235 Mudlick Road SW
Roanoke, VA 24018
(703) 774-4319

★ **Maxfield Parrish printed art.** "I'll buy prints, books, calendars, cards, posters, etc., especially Edison *Mazda* calendars. If you phone, have the piece in front of you!"

Michelle Ferretta
888 Lasuen Drive
San Leandro, CA 94577
(510) 522-1823

★ **Maxfield Parrish** calendars (all years), complete books, full decks of playing cards, original prints, autographs and unusual advertising items. Not interested in book fragments or modern reproductions. Describe condition. She offers "many thousands of dollars" for an original oil painting by Parrish.
Debra Buonaguidi
540 Reeside Ave.
Monterey, CA 93940
(408) 375-7345

★ **Original art and prints by F. Earl Christy** who specialized in beautiful society women. Wants covers from movie and women's magazines, advertising, fans, blotters, calendars, postcards, and anything else illustrated by Christy.
Audrey Buffington
2 Old Farm Road
Wayland, MA 01778

★ **Paintings and prints by R. Atkinson Fox, Maxfield Parrish, and Icart.** Claims she'll pay "top cash."
Christine Daniels, La Petite
135 East Shiloh Road
Santa Rosa, CA 95403
(707) 838-6083

★ **R. Atkinson Fox prints wanted.** "I'll buy prints, calendars, postcards, or anything else with artwork by R. Atkinson Fox." Please telephone or send a photocopy.
Pat Gibson
38280 Guava Drive
Newark, CA 94560
(710) 792-0586

★ **Currier & Ives prints**, and **chromos published by Prang.** No modern reproductions are wanted.
Edward Sheppard
221 Water Street
Catskill, NY 12414
(518) 943-2169

FOLK ART

★ **American folk art** such as **carvings**, **weathervanes**, whirligigs, **duck decoys**, pre-1900 **quilts**, figural 19th century **pottery**, **fishing decoys**, windmill weights shaped like animals, figural **architectural pieces such as cherubs or gargoyles**, small hand painted boxes, **game boards**, **handmade dolls**, Indian rugs, baskets, Indian pottery, **folk paintings of children** and animals, and **hooked rugs** with pictorials rather than patterns. No damaged or repaired pieces.
    Louis Picek, Main Street Antiques
    PO Box 340
    West Branch, IA 52358
       (319) 643-2065

★ **American folk art of the 20th century.** "This is a very subjective area of collecting, and not everyone agrees on what's folk art. I like, and will buy, a variety of paintings and sculpture. They have to be well done, but naive in perspective, or quirky in subject. Narrative 'story telling' paintings are especially desirable although I don't want anything cute or fakey, and don't want 'memory' pictures done recently of some old-timely scene." If you have something you think might be good, and is for sale, send a photo along with a complete history and description. "I prefer people to state what they want for a price," says this 20 year veteran collector and expert, "as too many people have overblown expectations, and are insulted when they get fair offers."
    Linda Campbell Franklin
    2716 Northfield Road
    Charlottesville, VA 22901

★ **Ivory items of all sort,** including Eskimo and Oriental carvings, scrimshaw, ivory tusks (elephant, walrus, whale, hippo, etc.), dresser sets, poker chips, dice, and billiard balls. Dave does not want ivory jewelry, letter openers, or sewing and crochet tools, nor does he buy bone or synthetic objects. If you are selling tusks, give the length around the outside curve, and the diameter at the large end. He asks you to use a flashlight to carefully inspect for cracks in the hollow end. Follow standard description form. A sample catalog is $1. Please list your phone number and best time to call.

"Bone has fine brown specks, whereas plastic imitations will sometimes have air bubbles or pits, whereas real ivory has grain like fine wood."

    David Boone's Trading Company
    562 Coyote Road
    Brinnon, WA 98320
       (206) 796-4330   (800) 423-1945   Fax: (206) 796-4511

★ **Figures and native carvings made of ivory.** Ivory can be elephant, walrus, whale, hippo, wart hog, or narwhale, but he wants ivory art, not small useful items like pins, combs, spoons, brooches and toothpicks. Picture is a necessity, and he prefers you to set a price. Terry also buys **primitive and pre-Columbian artifacts.**
    Terry Cronin
    207 Silver Palm Ave.
    Melbourne, FL 30901

★ **Mourning pictures** in watercolor or embroidery. These are characterized by willow trees, tombstones, birth and death dates, weeping women, etc. These are often for famous people, presidents, generals, etc. Those honoring "nobodies" are more rare and desirable. Will pay at least $100 and as much as $300-$400 for better ones.
    Steve DeGenaro
    PO Box 5662
    Youngstown, OH 44504

★ **Prisoner of war straw figures** woven or plaited by French prisoners during the early 1800's. Other documented prisoner art from the 19th century, including **ivory carvings** are sought.
    Lucille Malitz, Lucid Antiques
    PO Box KH
    Scarsdale, NY 10583
    (914) 636-3367

★ **Tramp art** items made from cigar boxes or fruit crate wood which has been layered into edge-notched pyramids. Typical items include boxes, picture frames, doll furnitures, banks, wall pockets and small furniture. Especially wants large items like chests of drawers, but will buy those only if they are in fine condition with a minimum of missing pieces. He will consider painted or gilded examples (most are varnished). Original surface is important and information about its origin (such as signatures and dates) is a plus. He does not want items made from ice cream sticks, clothespins or matches, nor does he buy items recently repainted or in rough condition. "A photo is almost essential." Inspect closely for signatures and dates.
    Michael Cornish
    195 Boston Street
    Dorchester, MA 02125
    (617) 282-3853

★ **Wax carved portraits, paper cut silhouettes, and pin pricked pictures** of scenery or groups of people. Give a good description of what you have and set the price you want.
    Laurel Blair
    PO Box 4557
    Toledo, OH 43620
    (419) 243-4115

QUILTS

★ **Quilts that are graphically artistic** made before 1940 especially made before 1900. Cotton, wool, and silk quilts all have value if made well but children's size quilts are best if they do not have children's subject matter. Solid color materials and small calico patterns are most desirable. Large patterns cut into small pieces usually make the quilt of no interest. All quilts should be in mint condition, with at least six stitches per inch, preferably more. No holes, tears, stains, thin spots when held to light, fading, soft from too much washing, and no patched repairs. A photo is very desirable. Herb says he will pay $5,000 for an album quilt made between 1840 and 1860, $15,000 for an album quilt from that same period made in Baltimore, and $600 up for any navy blue and white quilts in excellent condition. Herb does not make offers.

" Most desirable colors are blue/white, red/white, red/white/blue, red/green, and pre-1900 earth tones. Yellow, orange, hot pink, and purple usually make a quilt less desirable."

> Herbert Wallerstein Jr.
> Calico Antiques
> 611 Alta Drive
> Beverly Hills, CA 90210
>   (310) 273-4194   Fax: (310) 273-1921

★ **Patchwork quilts made by African-Americans,** especially unusual or improvisational quilts. Provide a full photo of the quilt, a statement of condition, and all information you can about its history. It is probably a good idea to discuss the value of the item with Eli before setting a price. "I'll also buy **fabric sample books,** especially of printed cottons."

> Eli Leon
> 5663 Dover Street
> Oakland, CA 94609

ART OF OTHER CULTURES

★ **Folk art** including painting, sculpture, weaving, wood, etc., including **American Indian, Oriental, African, or Eskimo** art. Provide the dimensions, condition, and photos. Condition critical. Special interest in current "outsider art." Contact Ivan only if your item is for sale.

> Ivan Gilbert, Miran Arts & Books
> 2824 Elm Ave.
> Columbus, OH 43209
> (614) 236-0002

★ **Folk art weavings worldwide,** including rugs, saddle blankets, tapestries, ponchos, and other old, fine, and rare pieces. Will consider Oriental, Middle Eastern, European, Indian, and South American fine quality rugs and other weavings. Also **Eskimo and American Indian weavings.** In addition to weavings, he buys **needlepoint, paisley shawls, and hooked rugs**. Nothing after 1920 or that is machine made.

> Renate Halpern Galleries
> 325 East 79th Street
> New York, NY 10021
> (212) 988-9316

★ **Micronesian, Polynesian, and New Guinea masks, ceremonial bowls, and the like.** Some interest in scrimshaw, but none in items from New Zealand and the Maori.

> David and Cathy Lilburne
> Antipodean Books
> PO Box 189
> Cold Spring, NY 10516
> (914) 424-3867

★ **African or South Pacific tribal art** including masks, weapons, musical instruments, jewelry, household objects, bowls, furniture, feather work, textiles, and "almost anything else that was made for tribal use and not for the tourist trade." Especially old collections including artifacts with elaborate decoration and animal, human, or spirit figures. Collections of **pre-Columbian pottery from Mexico or Peru** are sought, but *only* if documented and authenticated. High quality tribal art can bring as much as $100,000 so is worth inquiry. Does not want items made after 1970, ebony carvings, tourist items, or figures of natives holding spears. A photograph is essential and Jones would like to know where the item was collected.

> Charles Jones
> African Art
> 6716 Barren Inlet Road
> Wilmington, NC 28405
> (919) 686-0717

ORIENTALIA

★ **Fine quality Oriental antiques** with special emphasis on Japanese netsuke, inro, lacquer, and fine Chinese porcelains. Marsha buys, sells, and collects all types of Oriental antiques from early ceramics to late 19th century items including furniture, Japanese swords, sword fittings, jade carvings, and jewelry. Many small ivory carvings are worth between $1,000 and $10,000. Modern or reproduction items are not wanted, nor is anything imported since 1960. Marsha is a senior member of the American Society of Appraisers, specializing in Oriental art, and will appraise for a fee. She will also help amateur sellers with fine items genuinely for sale if you make a good photo, give the measurements, and draw or photocopy all markings or signatures found on the bottom.

> Marsha Vargas
> The Oriental Corner
> 280 Main Street
> Los Altos, CA 94022
>   (415) 941-3207

★ **Antique Japanese netsuke, inro, and other art** including pouches, pipes and pipe cases, ivory and wooden statues, Japanese lacquer, metalwork, cloisonne, paintings, and ceramics. Will pay $10,000 up for ivory and wood 18th and 19th century netsuke and $500 for netsuke inlaid in various materials. No roughly carved pieces, man made materials, or factory pieces bought in hotel lobbies, airports or gift shops. If you provide clear close-up photographs of your netsuke from all angles and an exact drawing of the signature, Denis will make an offer. He is member of the Appraisers Association of America and does formal appraisals for a fee.

> Denis Szeszler
> Antique Oriental Art
> PO Box 714
> New York, NY 10028
>   (212) 427-4682

★ **Phoenix bird china** is wanted by this author of four books on the topic. She also edits an infrequent newsletter on this striking blue/white Japanese china for $12 a year.

> Joan Oates
> 685 South Washington
> Constantine, MI 49042

SCULPTURE & FIGURINES

★ **Bronzes and porcelain figures** prior to 1935. Describe all markings and give dimensions and colors. Photo is highly recommended.
> Arnold Reamer
> PO Box 26416
> Baltimore, MD 21207
>   (410) 944-6414 or (410) 486-8412

★ **Bathing beauties and "naughties" figurines.** Wants small bisque or porcelain figurines, 1900-1940, which are nude, in bathing suits, in their underwear, stockings, or dressed in lace. They are finely modeled and in coy poses. Some had actual mohair wigs. Naughties were hollow figurines, often of children or women, intended to be filled with water so they peed or squirted out of their breasts. Other naughties appeared to be innocent figurines until lifted up or turned over, displaying a risque (often explicit) side. "I am especially interested in finding Black naughties or bathers with a wig, but I am interested in *all* fine examples of bathing beauties and naughties. I am also looking for old catalogs, advertisements, and other information about them. A good wigged naughty is worth from $250-$450, depending upon the pose and execution." No Japanese figures or reproductions. Generally does not want damaged pieces, but will consider extraordinary figures with minor damage. Size and pose is important so accurate measurements and a sketch, copy, or photograph is almost essential. Include your phone number. Will buy only if you grant right of refusal after inspection. If you too collect these figures, please call. She'd love to meet you.
> Sharon Hope Weintraub
> 2924 Helena
> Houston, TX 77006
>   (713) 520-1262

★ **Female figurines, especially nudes** in bronze or porcelain in Art Deco or Art Nouveau, 1880-1930. Wants *Dresden, Meissen, Capo di Monte, Royal Dux, Amphora, Teplitz*, and other fine makers. Nothing that has been broken or repaired. No figurines of children or popular limited edition collectibles.
> Madeleine France
> Past Pleasures for 20th Century Women
> PO Box 15555
> Plantation, FL 33316
>   (305) 584-0009

★ **Nude figurines** in any material, made since 1900.
> Charles Martignette
> PO Box 293
> Hallandale, FL 33009
>   (305) 454-3474

★ *Royal Doulton* **figurines and character jugs** are purchased by this well known dealer who has been in business for 20 years. "No collection is too large or too small," he says, encouraging you to "call toll free as long as you have the name and HN number of the figurines and the name and size of the character jugs." Pascoe is especially interested in the rarest items, since they maintain a computer list of collectors worldwide who are looking for specific types of figure. Ed lectures frequently in the U.S. and England, and has edited price guides to these popular figures. He is not interested in buying dinnerware, and does not do pattern matching.

> Ed Pascoe
> Pascoe & Co.
> 545 Michigan Ave.
> Miami Beach, FL 33139
>   (800) 872-0195   Fax: (305) 532-8543

★ **John Rogers statuary.** If you have a white or putty colored plaster grouping of figures, check for the signature JOHN ROGERS, often accompanied by NEW YORK and a date and patent number. These figural groups can be from 12" to 48" high, with most just under 2' tall. Themes are Civil War, Americana, theater, etc., with a few of them comic. A few are made of material other than plaster. Perfect condition is always best, but he will consider damaged pieces, as he is a restorer of Rogers' work. He needs to know the name of the piece (which is always found on the front of the base) and the condition of the putty colored paint. When describing paint, indicate how badly it is flaking from your statue. Prefers you to telephone him with your statue in front of you.

> Bruce Bleier
> 73 Riverdale Road
> Valley Stream, NY 11581
>   (516) 791-4353

★ *Noritake* **human and animal figures** are wanted by this well known glass auctioneer and porcelain collector.

> Tom Burns
> 109 East Steuben Street
> Bath, NY 14810
>   (607) 776-7942

LIMITED EDITION COLLECTIBLES

★ *Heubach* **porcelain or bisque figurines and other items** including children's tea sets, trays, religious items, and anything else. Porcelain portraits of the Three Fates, singly or as a group, would be a treat to her and worth hundreds of dollars. Draw a picture of the mark, and give all colors. Frances is cataloging every *Heubach* product made and she'd like to hear from anyone with anything unusual by Gebruder Heubach, even if it is not for sale.

> Frances Sanda
> 5624 Plymouth Road
> Baltimore, MD 21214

★ *Hummel* **figurines** with full bee and crown markings. Please give complete information concerning condition and all markings on the bottom. He is available to restore *Hummels*.

> Donald Hardisty, Don's Collectibles
> 3020 East Majestic Ridge
> Las Cruces, NM 88001
>   (800) 827-3721

★ *Hummel* **figurines,** before 1971, especially figurines with the crown or full bee marks. Also wants *Goebel* vases, figurines, half dolls, wall plaques and especially monks in red robes. Also *Hummel* calendars from 1950 through 1975. Also *Precious Moments* **figurines** with the triangle or hourglass mark or with no mark at all. All *Hummels* must be marked. Please give all marks and numbers and note whether or not you have the original box. Please don't offer *Hummel* plates, bells, or anything that is chipped or cracked.

> Sharon Vohs-Mohammed
> PO Box 14192
> Tallahassee, FL 32317
>   (904) 385-3595

★ *Goebel* **figurines of cats.** "I don't want cats other than those made by *Goebel*. I don't want *Goebels* other than cats." Include marks and numbers on the bottom of the figurine.

> Linda Nothnagel
> Route 3
> Shelbina, MO 63468
>   (314) 588-4958

Collectors often want figurines depicting their hobbies: smoking, fishing, etc. Check the index at the back of the book and look for buyers in the appropriate category.

★ **Snow Babies.** "I'll buy any and all clean German 'Snow Babies' (little china children in pebbly snow suits), especially jointed Snow Babies and 'action' Babies with animals or engaged in some activity." Doesn't want Babies from Japan, Taiwan, or Dept 56, nor does she want damaged or faded items. Give the size and markings, if any, and note all damage, no matter how minor. "Photo would be great." Also buys **small German bisque Santas.**

Linda Vines
PO Box 721
Upper Montclair, NJ 07043
(201) 746-5206

★ *Pen Delfin* **rabbits.** This mail order dealer in modern *Pen Delfin* bunnies is always looking for retired rabbits of all types, from the middle 1950's on. Will buy all, including the larger rabbits and houses, but wants undamaged items for resale. Note the figure's name on the bottom.

George Sparacio
PO Box 791
Malaga, NJ 08328
(609) 694-4167 eves

★ **Wade figurines** including Disney characters, circus animals and performers, friars, other animals, fairy tales, whimsies, and what have you.

Ken Clee
PO Box 11412
Philadelphia, PA 19111
(215) 722-1979

★ *Osborne Ivorex* **plaques.** These are three dimensional plaster composition wall plaques that are hand painted and then waxed. They were made between 1899 and 1968. In addition to plaques, the company made statuary of people and buildings, jewelry boxes, and a few other small items. Subject matter of the plaques included individual characters to large cathedrals. Anne Hathaway's home and that of poet Robt. Burns were popular subjects, as were other buildings and monuments in the U.S., Canada and Europe. Sizes range from a few inches to over a foot, with 3"x5" and 6.5"x9" two popular sizes. Some are factory framed in wood, making them premium items. Some poor quality reproductions exist. Most, but not all, *Ivorex* plaques are marked "A/O" (Arthur Osborne) on the lower right or left corner. In the 1930's they began marking them on the back with a three line ink stamp with the company name and copyright. Small vertical oval and rectangular plaques sometimes have markings on the lower rim. Values range from $30 up, with a few reaching $200+ because there are relatively few collectors. Andy wants to hear from other collectors for purposes of starting a club.

Andy Jackson
823 Carlson Ave.
West Chester, PA 19382
(215) 692-0269   Fax: (215) 272-7040

★ *Bossons* **artware** including character heads, wall plaques and figures. These are made of plaster or *Stonite*, a vinyl/stone mixture. Figures made of the latter are marketed as *Fraser-Art*. "We buy modern figures that are still available, but are primarily interested in obtaining discontinued figures, which can be worth $85 and up, with a few rare ones valued at over $10,000." There are *Bossons* look-alikes, but only figures marked BOSSONS CONGLETON ENGLAND COPYRIGHT are wanted. Slightly damaged figures will be considered, since Dr. Hardisty is a restorer approved by *Bossons*. He is a charter life member of the International *Bossons* Collectors Society, a licensed dealer of modern *Bossons*, and author of the price guide to these popular British figures.

    Donald Hardisty, Don's Collectibles
    3020 East Majestic Ridge
    Las Cruces, NM 88001
      (800) 827-3721

COLLECTOR'S PLATES

★ **Collector's plates.** The Ernst family is one of the nation's larger dealers in collector's plates. If you have a collection of plates to sell, they will help you in one of two ways. If your plates are items they have requests for and can sell promptly, they will purchase some or all of them outright. In the more likely event that you have some plates in less demand, they will sell them for you on consignment. They will price them according to the current market, catalog them, and notify their extensive mailing list that your plates are available. The price they ask is dependent upon how quickly you wish to sell them. They charge 20% of the item's selling price for this valuable service. When you call or write, they will send you complete information plus specific instructions on how to pack and ship your plates safely. The Ernsts have been in business for 21 years and are listed in Dun & Bradstreet.

    Ross, Ruth, and Ruth Ann Ernst, Collectors Plates
    7308 Izard
    Omaha, NE 68114
      (402) 391-3469

★ **Collector's plates and limited edition figurines** such as *Hummel, Cabbage Patch, Royal Doulton, Bing & Grondahl, Anri,* and *Bumpkins.* The Selesh family deals only in limited edition items, not in antique or commemorative plates, nor in dinnerware. If offering a plate for sale, indicate if you have the original box, authenticity certificate, and other paperwork. This major dealer and appraisal service will make no free offers but may help you in other ways to dispose of what you have.

    Adam Selesh, Tiffany Steven's Collectibles
    478 Ward Street Extension
    Wallingford, CT 06492
      (203) 284-0306

Paper ephemera

If you are handling an estate, closing a business, or have piles of family papers and photos, read this section carefully to see the types of paper goods that can have value to collectors. Historical data is not always worth a lot of money, but getting it to the appropriate researchers often means your family's contribution to an industry or movement will be properly recorded. I encourage you never to throw away any paper with prices, formula, processes, or descriptions of people or travels.

Paper ephemera is bought for one of two reasons: (1) It is either pretty and collectible in its own right, or (2) it is historically interesting and provides data to the collector. Some paper is bought for both reasons.

Describing paper is usually easy. Photocopy it! If your item is too large to fit on a machine, take multiple copies and tape them together or go to a commercial copy center where larger machines are available.

Condition is critical for buyers of either kind of paper. Don't try cleaning paper yourself. It is very easy to do more harm than good. There are restorative techniques which can be used to clean foxing (little brown spots) and some stains, but the processes are always risky (some paper dissolves when you try to clean it) and seldom worth the effort for low priced items. Let the buyer do it.

Many of the items listed in this section can also be sold to more than one person, so don't give up if you don't find a buyer on your first try.

MISCELLANEOUS PAPER

★ **All paper goods in good condition** are sought by one of the West's better known ephemerists. Kenrich Company buys **postcards, posters, sports cards, scorecards, playing cards, movie lobby cards, photos, stereoviews, panoramic photos, stamps and covers, philatelic items, letters, letterheads, trade cards, signs, insurance policies, timetables, slave documents, brochures, calendars, blotters, original artwork, bumper stickers, book marks, cookbooks, menus, napkins, coasters, matchbooks, seed packets, diaries, logs, autographs, scrapbooks, games, paper dolls, souvenirs, guidebooks, almanacs, directories** and more. If it's paper, collectible, and in fine condition, Bill will probably buy it. Closed Sunday and Monday.

> Bill Colby
> Kenrich Company
> 9418-T Las Tunas Drive
> Temple City, CA 91780
> (818) 286-3888   Fax: (818) 286-6035

★ **Collections of paper** "on just about any subject." Wants any collection of the old or unusual. "Immediate answer if you include your phone number."

> George Theofiles
> Miscellaneous Man
> PO Box 1776
> New Freedom, PA 17349
> (717) 235-4766 days

★ **Accumulations of paper items** from before 1920. Especially wants stocks and bonds, but also buys bills, checks, and letters with "pretty vignettes." Buys some **Western, circus,** and **magic posters** as well. Does not buy anything made after 1940. If you have a large collection, or just **boxes of old paper**, please telephone with your items in front of you.

> David Beach
> Paper Americana
> PO Box 2026
> Goldenrod, FL 32733
> (407) 657-7403   Fax: (407) 657-6382

★ **Accumulations of paper items from before 1910.** Prefers Western items, but will consider all collections, especially related to the military, mining, railroads, energy, banking, express companies, law enforcement, and other topics generally associated with the old West.

> Warren Anderson
> PO Box 100
> Cedar City, UT 84720
> (801) 586-9497

★ **Manuscripts and printed documents with interesting content.** These need not be signed by anyone famous. "I particularly like colonial American documents from before the Revolutionary War, but will consider material from all periods. Please describe the contents and why you think the item is unusual." Photocopy advisable.

> Chris Wilson
> 2762 North Washington Blvd.
> Arlington, VA 22201
> (703) 525-5930

★ **Rare documents** from the time of papyrus to the present. Buys collections of letters, manuscript (hand written) material, land grants, photograph collections, diaries, hand colored maps, atlases, and "anything unusual in paper."

> Ivan Gilbert, Miran Arts & Books
> 2824 Elm Ave.
> Columbus, OH 43209
> (614) 236-0002

★ **Rare documents in all fields,** from autographs to stock certificates, from song sheets to pardons and passes, including handwritten documents, land grants, maps, and "most any other unusual paper items." Gordon buys lots of all sizes, from single items to entire estates.

> Gordon McHenry
> PO Box 1117
> Osprey, FL 34229
> (813) 966-5563   Fax: (813) 966-5563

★ **Paper items fringed in silk.** Buys Victorian greeting cards in any style from single sheet to little booklets, from any holiday or event, as long as they have silk fringe. Also wants sachets, menus, advertising, and similar trinkets, as long as they are silk fringed, and 1875-1925.

> Ronald Lowden, Jr.
> 314 Chestnut Ave.
> Narberth, PA 19072
> (215) 667-0257 anytime

★ **Prints, calendars, trade cards, advertising, and magazine covers** featuring the work of name artists such as Frances Brundage, Ida Waugh, Jessie Wilcox Smith, Maud Humphrey, Torres Bevins, Mabel Lucie Attwell, Henry Clive, Harrison Fisher, Coles Phillips, Rose O'Niell, Grace Drayton, Charlotte Becker, Maxfield Parrish, and others.

> Madalaine Selfridge, Forgotten Magic
> 33710 Almond Street
> Lake Elsinore, CA 92330
> (909) 674-9221

★ **Collections of labels, stickers**, and **poster stamps** pre-1960. Wants collections of colorful, smaller graphics of all types, even if many are duplicates. Immediate answer if you include your phone number.
George Theofiles, Miscellaneous Man
PO Box 1776
New Freedom, PA 17349
(717) 235-4766 days

★ **Paper puzzles in any printed format.** "I'll buy crosswords, mathematical puzzles, rebuses, tangrams, brain teasers, picture puzzles, etc. The format can be a book, magazine, pamphlet, broadside, trade card, or newspaper, but I do not want 'hidden image' puzzles or those that are too juvenile, intended for small children." In general, he is most interested in items from before 1950, the earlier the better, although value depends on the quality of the puzzle and the rarity of the material. He also wants material about the history of puzzles, directories of puzzles, and "anything with the byline 'Sam Loyd,' a famous turn of the century puzzlist." Give the date and condition, and describe the puzzle or state its objective. Not interested in jigsaw puzzles.
Will Shortz
Games Magazine
19 West 21st Street
New York, NY 10010
(212) 727-7100 days

★ **Rebus puzzles.** Rebus puzzles are combinations of pictures, syllables, and letters which create a message when decoded. Linda wants hand drawn rebus puzzles in letters or postcards. She only wants noncommercial hand drawn puzzles, not printed ones, but they can be from any period, if they're interesting. Preferably wants pencil or pen and ink rather than paintings, with less sophisticated drawings the most interesting to her. She doesn't care how difficult the puzzle is. Doesn't want trade cards, greeting cards, or puzzles printed in books.
Linda Campbell Franklin
2716 Northfield Road
Charlottesville, VA 22901

★ **Scrapbooks compiled by children or adults before 1895.** A variety of contents may be of interest, *except* if primarily newspaper clippings. Any size considered. You must write detailed descriptions of contents, noting materials that are damaged or trimmed. Your alternative is to photocopy pages from the book. He promises to return your materials promptly and unmarked if he invites you to ship it for inspection. Condition is an important factor in value for this 40 year vet.
Ronald Lowden, Jr.
314 Chestnut Ave.
Narberth, PA 19072
(215) 667-0257 anytime

★ **Scrapbooks** and collections of loose die-cut, embossed Victorian paper in suitable condition for resale.
Madalaine Selfridge
Forgotten Magic
33710 Almond Street
Lake Elsinore, CA 92330
(909) 674-9221

★ **Scrapbooks of Victorian era trade cards.**
Russell Mascieri
6 Florence Ave.
Marlton, NJ 08053
(609) 985-7711   Fax: (609) 985-8513

★ **Diplomas** and advanced degree diplomas from before 1930.
Bob Hut
PO Box 1495
New York, NY 10163

★ **Passports** and some other travel documents, pre-1940 American or foreign. Documents must be complete, nothing missing, removed or torn. Photocopy the page with the owner's description and inside pages that have been used. "No overpriced passports belonging to celebrities."
Dan Jacobson
PO Box 277101
Sacramento, CA 95827

★ **Consular and foreign service stamps on documents** of any type, 1906-1955. Send photocopy.
H. Ritter
68 Heatherwood
Norristown, PA 19403

★ **Admission tickets of all types.** "I buy sports, political, theatrical, and social tickets. Must be complete. No stubs or foreign items. No transportation tickets for trolleys, railroads, etc. Please price what you have and ship it on approval."
David Lamb
48 Woodside Drive
Rochester, NY 14624

★ **"Dirty letters."** Buyer wants hand written or typed sexy or risque letters 1800-1975, ideally with the original envelope if mailed. "Even better if any photos or other items mailed with the letters are still there."
Charles Martignette
PO Box 293
Hallandale, FL 33009
(305) 454-3474

PAPER DOLLS

★ **All types of paper dolls, cut or uncut,** one or a collection as long as they're pre-1960. Will buy commercial, magazine, or newspaper dolls. Sellers should list paper dolls by name, if possible, and indicate whether they are cut or not. Photocopies are helpful. Fran (a collector for 20 years) is available for slide shows about paper dolls.
>Fran Van Vynckt
>7412 Monroe Ave.
>Hammond, IN 46324

★ **Paper dolls of all types.** Wants to buy antique paper dolls, 1910-1960 books, greeting card dolls, magazine dolls from adult or children's publications and newspaper comic strip dolls from the 1930's and 40's such as *Flash Gordon* and *Brenda Starr*. Celebrity or not. If neatly done, will buy cut dolls. When describing your doll, give the name, if possible, and include any writing on the front or back of the doll, the box, or the book.
>Madalaine Selfridge, Forgotten Magic
>33710 Almond Street
>Lake Elsinore, CA 92330
>   (909) 674-9221

★ **Paper dolls and paper toys** of all kinds, cut or uncut, from boxed or book sets, newspapers, magazines, cereal boxes, etc. Especially wanted are paper dolls of real people. For 23 years, Loraine has published *Celebrity Doll Journal*, a quarterly, available for $6.25/year. If you really want to sell your dolls, indicate names, dates, and quantity, and whether cut or not. Also indicate condition, mentioning bends, tears, missing parts, and tape. No need to photograph or photocopy any more than the doll (not the whole set). Will buy some rare sets even when damaged, and buys some current items, but no *Betsy McCall* sheets.

"Dolls that have been cut out are desirable as long as their arms and legs aren't bent. Do not mend with tape! Numbers on boxes or dolls are useful info."

>Loraine Burdick, Quest-Eridon Books
>5 Court Place
>Puyallup, WA 98372

★ **Paper toys, figures, and buildings,** especially toys and models by *Builtrite,* but interested in any paper dolls and soldiers in good condition. In business for more than a decade, Paper Soldier publishes a large and informative catalog for $4.
>Jonathan Newman, Paper Soldier
>8 McIntosh Lane
>Clifton Park, NY 12065
>   (518) 371-5130

AUTOGRAPHS

★ **Autographed letters and documents** from ancient times to modern days in all fields. Significant medieval documents and manuscripts are always of interest. This 28 year veteran dealer does not want autographs obtained by writing celebrities, modern politicians, or movie stars. A photocopy is suggested.

> Kenneth Rendell
> PO Box 9001
> Wellesley, MA   02181
>> (617) 431-1776   Fax: (617) 237-1492

★ **Autographs in all fields** are purchased for resale by this collector and dealer. He buys old letters, envelopes, canceled checks, and various documents and photos signed by famous people.

> Bill Colby, Kenrich Company
> 9418-T Las Tunas Drive
> Temple City, CA 91780
>> (818) 286-3888   Fax: (818) 286-6035

★ **Letters, signed photos and signatures of famous people** in any category: Presidents, Hollywood, NASA, sports, Civil War, art, music, literary, scientific, historical, rock and roll, theater, aviation, old west. Also interested in old handwritten diaries, collections of letters from the not-so-famous, handwritten recipe books, and anything written while traveling across America. Wants California and New Orleans letters from 1800-1870. Offers $1,000 for signed Buddy Holly photo. Please photocopy what you have. Does not want autopen or printed signatures.

> Michael Reese II
> PO Box 5704
> South San Francisco, CA 94083
>> (415) 641-5920

★ **Autographs, signed books, and rare documents in all fields.** Particularly wants U.S. Presidents and first ladies and "investment quality items." Wants handwritten letters of Presidents while in office, particularly of William Henry Harrison and James A. Garfield, whose letters could be worth as much as $50,000! No facsimile or secretary signatures. "It is usually necessary to see the actual item, particularly in order to make a firm offer." Their monthly catalog is free.

> Michael Minor and Larry Vrzalik, Lone Star Autographs
> PO Drawer 500
> Kaufman, TX 75142
>> (214) 932-6050 from 10 to 10 Central time daily

★ **Handwritten documents and letters of famous Americans.** "We particularly want Washington, Adams, Jefferson, Franklin, Hancock, and Lincoln, and specialize in U.S. Presidents." Famous scientists, inventors, authors, and musicians are also sought. Mention all imperfections.

    Steve and Linda Alsberg
    9850 Kedvale Ave.
    Skokie, IL 60076
    (708) 676-9850

★ **Autographs in various fields** including Presidents and their wives, statesmen, scientists, inventors, entertainers, characters from the old West, and famous people in all walks of life. Especially wants handwritten letters of any President, particularly modern Presidents. Purchase offers are free. Appraisals are for a fee. His sample catalog of autographs for sale is available for a long SASE.

"Politicians' signatures are worth little except Presidents. Movie and TV stars since 1960 are also of little value, with a few exceptions such as Marilyn Monroe."

    Paul Hartunian
    127B East Bradford Ave.
    Cedar Grove, NJ 07009
    (201) 857-7275

★ **Historical documents signed by U.S. Presidents.** "I'll buy land grants, military and civil commissions, ship's papers, passports, appointments of judges, postmasters, ambassadors, etc. I search for clean documents with no holes, stains, tape or trims. I'd love a George Washington land survey (to $10,000) or a Supreme Court appointment. Every mark, every fade, every crease or wrinkle *must* be described accurately."

    Richard Lechaux
    HC-60 Box 3712
    Fort Valley, VA 22652
    (703) 933-6305

★ **Autographs in all fields** with a particular emphasis on Presidents, political, military, and historical figures. He does not want Hollywood or TV people after 1940. "The more information the better. Describe what it is written on, whether faded or bright, whether written in pen or pencil, and the wording of any inscription."

    Chris Wilson
    2762 North Washington Blvd.
    Arlington, VA 22201
    (703) 525-5930

★ **Autographed non-fiction books.** Will consider any, but is particularly interested in the Soviet Union, Eastern Europe, Asia, Communism, Socialism, and conservative authors.
> Edward Conroy , SUMAC Books
> Route 1 Box 197
> Troy, NY 12180
> > (518) 279-9638 eves

★ **American and foreign autographs in all fields throughout Western history,** including politicians, Presidents, signers of the Declaration of Independence, music and the arts, literature, the military, and scientists. Will buy one or collections. This 20+ year veteran is not interested in unsigned documents of any sort.
> Robert Batchelder
> 1 West Butler Ave.
> Ambler, PA 19002
> > (215) 643-1430   Fax: (215) 643-6613

★ **Checks autographed by any famous person** are wanted, especially bounced checks. He'll pay from $750-$3,500 for checks he especially wants from Henry Ford, Harry Houdini, Greta Garbo, Buddy Holly, President Taylor, Gerald Ford, Lyndon Johnson, Al Capone, Richard Nixon, Charles Chaplin, President Tyler, and others. "I want to know the condition, the date, whether the check is signed or endorsed, and the color of the check. If the seller has a price in mind, please quote it up front. If the seller has no idea of value, then I will make him a fair quote." He also buys pay orders, certificates of deposit, and other small size financial documents. Send a fax or photocopy.
> Olan Chiles
> 1892 Avenida Aragon
> Oceanside, CA 92056
> > (619) 724-2339   Fax: (619) 726-4964

★ **Famous people's signatures on manuscript documents, land grants, maps, photographs,** and other early paper. Has particular interest in Southern and Civil War figures and in letters signed by James McHenry, Washington's Secretary of War.
> Gordon McHenry
> PO Box 1117
> Osprey, FL 33559
> > (813) 966-5563

★ **Historic early American autographed documents,** letters, and ephemera in all fields. Also buys autographed books, maps, prints, stock certificates, and bonds.
> Earl Moore
> PO Box 243
> Wynnewood, PA 19096
> > (215) 649-1549 anytime

★ **Composers, musicians, and singers of classical music** including signed photographs, letters, musical notations, and manuscripts. Does not do free appraisals.

J.B. Muns, Books & Fine Art
1162 Shattuck Ave.
Berkeley, CA 94707
(510) 525-2420

★ **Composers, musicians, opera singers, and movie stars** from the late 1800's to the 1950's. Prefers to buy signed photos, letters with important content, or musical quotes. Among the many people they would like to find are Kathleen Ferrier, Conchita Supervia, Maria Galvany, Celestina Boninsegna, Fernando De Lucia, Guilio Grisi, and Marietti Alboni. "We are not interested in the autographs of current performers, but will pay very well for first class older items. Condition is important. We request photocopies and prefer to see the item in person, especially when large collections are involved." Will make offers for amateurs. Dealers, price your goods.

Bill Safka and Arbe Bareis
PO Box 886
Forest Hills, NY 11375
(718) 897-7275

★ **Autographs of celebrities and "newsworthy persons"** including photos, letters, checks, or other documents signed by mass murderers, assassins, spies, heads of state, Royalty, rock stars, Presidents, and other famous and infamous persons. Examples: Arafat, Jackie Kennedy, Madonna, Michael Jackson, David Berkowitz, John Hinkley, etc. Not interested in printed signatures or autopens. Photocopies are a must if you want an offer. "If I cannot tell from your copy whether the signature is authentic, it will be necessary to ship it for my inspection. Before I buy items, I expect the seller to sign a statement guaranteeing that they own the item in question and that there are no liens against it."

Sheldon Kamerman, World Wide Auctioneering Group
466 11th Street #F
Lakewood, NJ 08701
(908) 363-6161 weekends

★ **Autographs of Hollywood stars** especially young ladies. No sports personalities, although "I want *anything* signed by Walt Disney." Tom publishes address directories of famous people (mostly movie stars) and is interested in obtaining home addresses you might know. Tom prefers you to set the price wanted but will make offers. Send a photocopy. His autograph catalog costs $3.

Tom Burford, Celebrity Access
20 Sunnyside Avenue #A241
Mill Valley, CA 94941
(415) 389-8133

POSTERS

★ **Rock and roll concert posters** of all eras and all types, especially those from the 60's by San Francisco based artists. Values range from a few dollars to a few thousand, with *Family Dog's 10th Dance* one of the biggies. Also buys **handbills, postcards, and tickets** from rock and roll band concerts. "These items can be worth hundreds of dollars, so be careful how you treat them and how you dispose of them." To sell rock posters, you need to give the name of the lead band, the date, the location of the concert, and the condition. Please note all creases, tears, and soil when you describe condition, "but we'll buy the very rarest posters in almost any condition. Call anytime, leave a message about what you have, and we'll call you back."

    Bob Metzler, Flash Paradise
    PO Box 621
    Pacific Palisades, CA 90272
       (310) 472-6668 phone and fax

★ **Old posters of all types.** This 30 year veteran dealer says, "I'll pay top prices for any printed poster done before 1960, especially WWI and WWII, film, travel, theater, circus, and transportation (ocean liner, railroad, and air). Also buys poster books, periodicals, postcards, photos of posters being printed or posted. Include phone for immediate answer.

    George Theofiles, Miscellaneous Man
    PO Box 1776
    New Freedom, PA 17349
       (717) 235-4766 days

★ **Vintage posters 1880-1950, all countries and subjects,** especially U.S. posters from WWI and II and 1890-1910 American advertising. Army recruiting posters by Christy and Flagg from WWI bring $500 to $1,500. No reproduction posters are wanted. Poster Master offers an illustrated catalog for $3 which contains 800 posters for sale.

    George Dembo, The Poster Master
    9 Passaic Ave.
    Chatham, NJ 07928
       (201) 635-6505

★ **American posters of WWI.** No foreign, repros, or damaged. Give the main slogan, the size, the artist if known, and the condition.

    Ken Khuans
    155 Harbor #4812
    Chicago, IL 60601

★ **Posters which advertise magazines** pre-1940. Fine condition only.
    Leon Williams
    467 Portland Ave.
    St. Paul, MN 55102

Postcards

Postcard collecting is one of the largest hobbies, and you should be able to sell all but the most common and recent cards, as long as they are in good condition. Postcards are collected for the photograph, the greeting, the message, the artist, the stamp,and the postmark. For you the seller, that translates into a lot of possible buyers if you take the time to look.

Real photo cards (black and white real photos of people, places or events) are among the most sought as they are a valuable source of historical information. Often the only surviving photos of buildings, parade floats, and other slices of our past are found on real photo cards. If you have a card that pictures any business, occupation or vehicle, the folks interested in those topics will probably pay more for the card than will a postcard dealer or collector. Scenics picturing rivers, trees, mountains, lakes and the like, are seldom wanted, and worth only a dime or so.

Describing a postcard is easy. Make a photocopy. Describing the condition of your cards is difficult because buyers are very fussy about condition. Photocopies have the advantage of showing the condition of the corners (important to collectors) and the existence of creases and other damage. Almost all postcard buyers expect the right to return items they feel are not as described.

Because postcards are so widely available, and popular with so many of the buyers in *Where To Sell It!*, I'm including guidelines on types of cards and describing their condition.

Types of postcards

EARLY CARDS: This refers to cards from the mid 1870's to 1900. You will sometimes hear the earliest cards called Pioneer era cards. Early cards had no pictures, other than advertising, until 1893. Cards from this period are collected for their stamps and postmark as much as for the card.

POSTCARDS: In 1901, private printers were first allowed to use the word POSTCARD, and "real photo" cards were introduced. Real photo cards have a black and white or sepia photo on one side of the card and the address on the reverse. Messages were not allowed on the address side, so the picture side will often be defaced by personal messages.

DIVIDED BACK CARDS: Cards used between 1907 and 1914 are called "divided back" cards because the message was permitted to be written on the address side. The message was written on the left and address on the right. Real photo, greeting, and advertising cards can have divided backs.

WHITE BORDER CARDS: Starting just before WWI and lasting to the Depression (1915-1930), most postcards had a white border around the picture.

LINEN CARDS: During the Depression and WWII (1930-45), postcards had a textured surface, like linen. Inks from this period were usually bright. The colored printed photographs were usually of poor quality with little detail.

CHROME CARDS: Modern brightly colored, slick surface postcards start around WWII and continue today. Their colors are vivid, the details are sharp, and the cards are of little interest to collectors.

How to describe condition

MINT: A perfect card, as it comes from the press. No marks, bends or creases. No writing or postmarks. Rarely seen.

NEAR MINT: Like mint but very light aging or very slight discoloration from being in an album for many years. Not as fresh looking as mint.

EXCELLENT: Card looks like mint with sharply pointed corners (no blunt or rounded corners). It may not have any bends or creases. May be used or unused, but writing and postmark are only on address side, with clean fresh picture side.

VERY GOOD: Corners may be just a bit blunt or rounded, or it might have an almost undetectable crease or bend that does not detract from overall appearance of picture side. May have writing only on the address side.

GOOD: Corners may be noticeably blunt or rounded with noticeable but slight bends or creases. May be postally used or have writing, but only on the address side.

AVERAGE: Creases and bends more pronounced. Corners more rounded. Or it may have writing in margins on picture side, or the postmark may show through from address side but not on main portion of picture.

POOR: Card is intact, but has excess soil, stains, or heavy creases. Or it is written on the picture side, or has a cancel that affects the picture. Salable only if a very scarce card.

SPACE FILLER: Poor condition, perhaps with torn or missing corners, or breaks in the picture surface. Neither desirable nor valuable.

POSTCARDS

★ **Postcard collections, pre-1930,** especially American street views, disasters, railroad stations, fire departments, and diners. He also buys cards depicting foreign royalty, expositions, snowmen, full length Santas, and pre-jet commercial aircraft. Does not want foreign views, scenery, parks, woods, mountains, lakes, and flowers. Does not want damaged cards or those which have been pasted in albums. "If your cards are not for sale, or if my offer is not accepted, I will appraise your cards at a cost of only one postcard of my choice for each 100 cards I appraise." Cards must be shipped for inspection for purchase or appraisal. John runs auctions, postcard shows, and heads the Postcard History Society. He can supply you with many interesting free or low cost items regarding postcard collecting. For more information send a Self-Addressed Stamped Envelope for his "Postcard Opportunity" sheet.

    John McClintock
    PO Box 1765
    Manassas, VA 22110
       (703) 368-2757 eves

★ **All types of postcards,** old or modern, are purchased for resale. You may ship any quantity up to a shoe box full (about 600-700) together with your telephone number and he will make an offer. If the offer is unacceptable, postcards will be returned promptly.

    Bill Colby, Kenrich Co.
    9418-T Las Tunas Drive
    Temple City, CA 91780
       (818) 286-3888

★ **Postcards, American and foreign,** all subjects, used or unused, if before 1950. "I'll pay competitive prices for better single cards or will buy collections, box lots, accumulations, etc."

    Sheldon Dobres
    4 Calypso Court
    Baltimore, MD 21209
       (410) 486-6569

★ **Postcard albums and collections,** the older the better, in very good condition only. Interested in all topics, but does not want damaged cards. Joan conducts mail auctions and sells on approval. Wants to know the number of cards, condition, and types of subjects pictured. She's been a collector for nearly 50 years!

    Jo Ann Van Scotter
    208 East Lincoln Street
    Mt. Morris, IL 61054
       (815) 734-6971

★ **Picture postcards** before 1940 are sought by this paper dealer, who does not buy chrome cards of any type of subject matter.

    Mike Rasmussen
    PO Box 726
    Marina, CA 93933
    (408) 384-5460

★ **Postcards worldwide,** used or unused, before 1950, from any country, but especially from the U.S. and Canada. Wants street scenes, buildings, occupationals, sports, transportation, and people. Doesn't want water, forests, mountains, deserts, trees, etc. Also buys some pictorial "greetings." Pays 25¢ to $5 for most postcards, but a few European cards drawn or painted by famous illustrators can bring $100 up. No quantity too large. Prompt payment if you send approvals, and unwanted cards are returned. Neil makes all payments in the currency of the seller.

"All payments are in the currency of the seller. Just ask, if you want Canadian Postal Money Orders, good at any U.S.P.O."

    Neil Hayne
    PO Box 220
    Bath, ON K0H 1G0 CANADA
    (613) 352-7456

★ **Postcards** from the 1920's to the 1950's, both white border and linen cards which picture any of the following:

    Art Deco or Art Moderne buildings typical of those times,
        such as diners and gas stations;
    The New York World's Fair of 1939, especially buildings;
    Texas Centennial of 1936;
    City views of **Houston**, Texas;
    Products or service advertisements.

Edy has a preference for the "linen" cards with a textured surface, but will consider good white border cards. Please photocopy.

    Edy Chandler
    PO Box 20664
    Houston, TX 77225
    (713) 531-9615 eves

★ **Scenic views of Colorado, Kansas, and Missouri** before 1930. Also buys early cards of **Elks Lodges, prisons**, and **bowling alleys**. The best way to describe your cards, he says, is to photocopy them. Please note, he is not interested in chrome or linen cards.

    George VanTrump, Jr.
    PO Box 260170
    Lakewood, CO 80226

★ **Cards advertising any product or service.** "I'll buy milk, medicine, automobiles, boats, shoes, musical instruments, tourist attractions, bands and singing groups, farm products, home items, clothing, entertainment, trains, auto dealerships, restaurants, highways, sports events... the list is endless. I'll buy one or a box full." Also wants **cards showing automobiles**, especially convertibles, trucks, used car lots, dealer show rooms, and any card showing a truck or car with clearly readable advertising on the side of it, any era, from anywhere in the world. Also "better grade" **commercial airline cards** showing propellor-driven planes. Only cards issued as advertising by the airlines are wanted. Most cards are purchased for resale, although many are for Jay's private collection. Jay recently released *The American Automobile Dealership,* illustrated with 340 postcards ($25 from the author).

    Jay Ketelle
    3721 Farwell
    Amarillo, TX 79109
      (806) 355-3456

★ **Sexy real photo postcards** of women acting provocatively (such as lifting their skirts, etc.), 1880-1980. Also wants nudes, semi-nudes, and xxx-rated postcards, all periods. Photocopy what you want to sell.

    Charles Martignette
    PO Box 293
    Hallandale, FL 33009
      (305) 454-3474

★ **Views of Hong Kong and Macao before 1945.** Please photocopy and price what you have.

    Kin Leung Liu
    1517 South Angeline Street
    Seattle, WA 98108
      (206) 767-3025

★ **Postcards illustrated with original drawings by the sender.** Wants pen and ink or pencil sketches more than more fancy paintings.

    Linda Franklin
    2716 Northfield Road
    Charlottesville, VA 22901

★ **Postcards made of macerated (ground up) U.S. currency.**

    Donald Gorlick
    PO Box 24541
    Seattle, WA 98124

Photographs

Photos of "instant ancestors" (unidentified portraits of ordinary people staring stiffly into space) have little value. But those pictures will find ready markets if the sitters are in uniform or holding tools or weapons. Photos of officials, workers, events, outdoor city scenes, parades, stores, vehicles and uniforms will always find a buyer among collectors trying to learn more about an industry or era.

When reading entries in this chapter you will run across reference to various types of photographs. I've given you information on the next two pages to help you understand and describe what you have.

If you come across round photos with square mounts, you may have pictures taken by one of the first *Kodaks*. They are a curiosity as they do not exist in great numbers.

Stereoviews are popular. Of interest are earlier, larger, cards depicting famous events, disasters, important people, and industrial processes, especially related to mining, oil, or transportation. Early stereo cards (before 1890) have colored (not gray) mounts and were originally flat. After years of being stored with newer curved cards, they too become curved. Don't try to flatten them as you may crack the photographic emulsion and ruin them.

To sell a photo, make a photocopy (not a photograph) of what you have. This saves a lot of your effort. Condition of the photo and its mat are both important to a buyer. Note banged corners, stains, and the like. If the photo is faded, make certain you indicate that fact, as photocopies tend to make photos look better than they are.

Types of photographs

Daguerreotypes: Earliest photos, 1839-1854, recognizable by a silvery image on glass. The leather and early plastic cases are often worth more than the photo. Outdoor and city views are rare. Large "Dags" can be valuable. Do not clean them and do not leave them exposed to sunlight.

Ambrotypes: Photos on a glass negative backed with dark paper to make a positive image. Mid 19th century. Subject matter is the key to value. Like Dags, these often come in elaborate cases sometimes worth more than the photo.

Albumen photographs: Paper prints before 1890 usually used egg albumen in preparation of the image surface. Most folks can't tell the difference looking at the photo.

Tintypes: Cheap popular portraits, 1858-1910, printed on sheets of blackened tin. Also called ferrotypes. Subject matter is the key to value. Pictures not taken in a studio are usually more valuable.

Carte de visites (cdv): Photos on card stock measuring 2.5" x 4" popular between 1860-1890, often found in albums.

Cabinet cards: Photos on 4" x 7" cards, usually studio shots with the photographer's name at the bottom. These and cdv's were sold as souvenirs and memorials and can be found with pictures of celebrities, Presidents and Generals.

Stereoviews: Cards containing two shots of the same subject to give a 3-D effect when seen through a viewer. Older views (1860-1890) are larger, flat, have colored mounts (yellow, pink, etc.) and generally no printing on back. Later views have curved gray mounts (*Underwood* is common). Newest, and worthless, are colored printed stereoviews.

Snapshots. Printed in b/w on thin paper, popular 1920-1960, when color pictures and slides became the photo of choice.

PHOTOGRAPHS

★ **Photographs** including tintypes, Daguerreotypes, ambrotypes, cartes de visite, cabinet photos, albumen prints, stereocards, silver prints, platinum prints, cyanotypes, and photo albums. His list of "fine subjects" includes: banjo players, Russians, kids playing marbles, Brooklyn, photographers, auto racing, nudes, military, Civil War, autographed photos, funny photos, Lincoln, John Wilkes Booth, portraits taken in Philadelphia of identified people, unusual photos, Shakers, WWII, **mug shots**, writers, gunmen, artists, Philadelphia, famous people, Hawaii and Samoa in the 19th century, Puerto Rico, Indians, mining, Orientals, rockets, sports, aviation, and similar topics dating before 1915. No ordinary studio portraits, and no photo equipment is wanted. Photocopy both sides of your photo and price what you have for sale.
Richard Rosenthal
4718 Springfield Ave.
Philadelphia, PA 19143
(215) 726-5493

★ **Rare old photographs,** cased photos, stereoviews, etc., especially work by important Western photographers such as Jackson, Curtis, and others. Also buys books with actual photos tipped (pasted) in.
Ivan Gilbert
Miran Arts & Books
2824 Elm Ave.
Columbus, OH 43209
(614) 236-0002

★ **Photos and photographic literature.** Wants to buy Daguerreotypes, ambrotypes, tintypes, stereoviews, round *Kodak* snapshots, and other interesting photos from any era. No portraits. Would love to find photos of photographers at work. Buys complete unpicked photo albums, specializing in Pittsburgh and Allegheny County, Pennsylvania. Also wants early **cameras, photographic accessories and literature.**
Nicholas Graver
276 Brooklawn Drive
Rochester, NY 14618
(716) 244-4818

If you have photographs of events, businesses, industry, or sports, specialists in those subjects are often your best buyers. It could put more $$$ in your pocket to read the chapter in *Where To Sell It!* dealing with the subject matter of your photo.

★ **Original photos of Lincoln.** "I'll buy photos of Lincoln taken from life and printed before 1866. Will also purchase the Ayers photos of Lincoln printed in the 1880's and 1890's. I'll also buy photos of Lincoln look-alikes." No photos of prints, statues, or Abe's house. Send a photocopy of what you have. "Serious sellers only, please."

> Stuart Schneider
> PO Box 64
> Teaneck, NJ 07666
> (201) 261-1983

★ **Stereoview cards** "in nearly all categories" are sought. He points out that there are two types of stereo cards, printed and photographic and that he wants only photographic views of:

> Famous people;
> Ships, sailboats, riverboats, wharfs, etc.;
> Railroads, especially Western;
> Aviation, blimps, balloons, etc.;
> Automobiles, any early views;
> Fire fighting anything;
> Military, depicting equipment or arms;
> Western lore, cowboys, Indians, mining, etc.;
> Sports and games, from checkers to football;
> Music, bands, theatrical scenes, etc.;
> Street scenes from any city or town;
> Occupationals...people at work, especially photographers.

"I want any cards that capture a bygone era, people at leisure, at home, children playing, costumes, furniture, and the like. In addition to U.S. views, I will also buy fine condition photos of Canada and Europe." If your photo has a title, copyright date, or catalog number, please give them. Describe the scene or make a photocopy. Tell him the color of the card on which the photos are mounted. Describe any damage.

> Steve Jabloner
> 7380 Adrian Drive #23
> Rohnert Park, CA 94928
> (707) 795-3081

★ **Stereoview cards,** particularly older Western scenes, transportation, mining, Mt. Lowe, fires, high wheel bicycles, famous people, Civil War, and early California. "However, I buy most common stereos, too," presumably for a lot less. He particularly wants **stereos of Lincoln** published while Lincoln was alive. If you want to sell your cards, Chuck wants to know the subject of the card quite specifically, an accurate description of condition, and the publisher. If you have a price you want, say so. He does not want cards *printed* in color or in black and white.

> Chuck Reincke
> 2141 Sweet Briar Road
> Tustin, CA 92680
> (714) 832-8563 eves

★ **Photos of people and or animals with fake rural backdrops** and outdoorsy settings created with painted backgrounds and papier maché props, stumps, fences, rocks, etc. Any type photo, any period as long as it's clear and in fine condition. Also wants 1930's to 60's department store **photos of kids with Santa.** Please send a photocopy of these inexpensive items for sale, keeping your expectations reasonable.

    Linda Campbell Franklin
    2716 Northfield Road
    Charlottesville, VA 22901

★ **Bizarre photos,** such as freaks, dwarfs, lynchings, slaves, public punishment, and what have you. Especially interested in photos of **death, especially post-mortem photos, but also mourning photos, executions, lynchings, embalming and medical photos with doctors and cadavers.** Will take later photos if of someone famous. Likes to find old prints of the family gathered around the deceased. Worth from $5 to $75+ for the very early and unusual.

    Steve DeGenaro
    PO Box 5662
    Youngstown, OH 44504

★ **Stereoviews showing the development of the early West, 1860-1900:** expeditions, **railroad construction**, freighting through the Sierras, maritime scenes, **Indian portraits** and culture, **mining, logging,** and **early small town scenes** as well as cosmopolitan **San Francisco.** Particular interest in Custer, Teddy Roosevelt, Mark Twain, Bret Harte, John Sutter, artist Albert Bierstadt, and all early **photographers and their equipment.** The latter will bring "hundreds of dollars" in excellent condition. Also wants paper ephemeral advertising from early western photographers. Not interested in faded views or those with damaged mounts. No lithographed views, only real photos in excellent condition.

    Jim Crain
    131 Bennington Street
    San Francisco, CA 94110
        (415) 648-1092 eves

★ **Stereoviews.** Buys most U.S. black and white views as well as other interesting pre-1920 photos. This large paper dealer buys for resale.

    Bill Colby, Kenrich Co.
    9418-T Las Tunas Drive
    Temple City, CA 91780
        (818) 286-3888

★ **Stereoviews made on glass or tissue.**

    T.K. Treadwell
    4201 Nagle Road
    Bryan, TX 77801
        (409) 846-0209

★ **Old photos of famous people, outdoor scenes and "the odd and the unusual."** Will buy Daguerreotypes, ambrotypes, tin types and cartes de visite in fine condition. Send a photocopy.
Chris Wilson
2762 North Washington Blvd.
Arlington, VA 22201
(703) 525-5930

★ **Photographs and engravings of famous people** in all walks of life. Will consider items loose or in books. Please photocopy.
Kenneth Rendell
PO Box 9001
Wellesley, MA 02181
(617) 431-1776   Fax: (617) 237-1492

★ **Bathing beauties and nudie photos,** pre-WWI.
Steve DeGenaro
PO Box 5662
Youngstown, OH 44504

★ **Provocative or obscene photographs** including nudes, semi-nudes, candids, home made pictures, outdoor frolicking, etc, from teasing to xxx. Also pin-up photos of dancers, starlets, and sexy ladies of all ages and periods.
Charles Martignette
PO Box 293
Hallandale, FL 33009
(305) 454-3474

★ **Photos of cowboys, Indians,** and related subjects, including cattle drives, early Texas towns, outlaws, lawmen, the Geronimo expedition (especially those taken by C.S. Fly), and the Mexican War. All types wanted, including stereo. Please send photocopies.
Johnny Spellman
10806 North Lamar
Austin, TX 78753
(512) 258-6910 eves   (512) 836-2889 days

★ **Photos of Indians and Eskimos,** especially the work of Edward S. Curtis. Also buys real photo postcards on the same theme. Please send photocopies for a prompt response. Dealers price your goods, but amateur sellers may request an offer.
Barry Friedman
22725 Garzota Drive
Valencia, CA 91355
(805) 296-2318

★ **Photographs of people with guns.** Has a particular interest in Civil War and Western scenes but wants hunters, soldiers, sailors, Indians, and cowboys. All types of early images are considered, including cdv's, cabinet cards, tintypes, Daguerreotypes, etc. Send a photocopy of any image you want to sell, except those on Daguerreotypes, the cased photos with a mirror finish. SASE please.

    Charles Worman
    PO Box 33584 (AMC)
    Dayton, OH 45433
       (513) 429-1808 eves

★ **Occupational photos,** especially baseball players, firefighters, Civil War soldiers, and other occupations. "I prefer cdv and cabinet card photos, and will pay particularly well for photos of doctors, nurses and other medical topics, especially related to embalming or medical school." Only items from before 1930 are wanted. Please send photocopy.

    Steve DeGenaro
    PO Box 5662
    Youngstown, OH 44504

★ **Photos taken before 1930** of special events, parades, sports, trans-portation, people with unusual clothing, people doing "something weird," twins, children with toys and "unusual photos." Is not interested in studio photos of men and women's heads. Describe the photo's size, condition and content. Photocopy suggested, although this relatively new dealer will ask to see your photos before making final payment.

    Joe Burkart, Antique Photo Art
    143 Northwood Drive
    Hiawatha, IA 52233
       (319) 393-2206

★ **Photos in memorial matts** (ordinary portraits mounted in memorial matts after the person died). Memorial matts have printed or embossed angels, doves, Gates of Heaven, etc., and mottoes like "Free at Last."

    Steve DeGenaro
    PO Box 5662
    Youngstown, OH 44504

★ **Panoramic group photos** taken in North or South Carolina.

    Lew Powell
    700 East Park Ave.
    Charlotte, NC 28203

Watch for revenue stamps on the back of Civil War era carte de visites and other photos. Most are common, but a few are quite valuable.

Cameras

Camera buyers want the odd , old and unusual.

Amateurs find it hard to recognize the earliest Daguerreotype cameras because they often look like wooden boxes without a lens. They are quite valuable, as are hidden ("detective") cameras, popular in the late 1800's and capable of bringing premium prices today. Panorama cameras, multi lens cameras, and other early oddities will also sell readily.

If you want to sell a camera, provide the following information in your first letter:

(1) Brand name, and model name if you know it;

(2) All numbers on the body of the camera;

(3) The name of the brand of lens, and any numbers and other information printed around the front circumference of the lens. If you have more than one lens, give that same information on each lens;

(4) Whether or not the camera works;

(5) Whether or not the camera seems to be complete;

(6) Whether the case and camera is covered with wood, metal, leather or cloth, and the condition of that covering;

(7) Whether or not the camera has a folding cloth or leather bellows, and if it does, the color of the bellows;

(8) A list of accessories with the camera, such as lenses, boxes, instructions, etc.

CAMERAS

★ **Unusual and early cameras** including panorama cameras, wide angles, sub miniatures, hidden cameras, and oddly shaped or novelty cameras such as those shaped like cartoon or advertising characters. When writing, include all names and numbers found on the lens. If the camera is unusual, make certain to take a picture of it or make a good sketch. Jim is author of *Collectors Guide to Kodak Cameras* and *Price Guide to Antique and Classic Cameras*.

> Jim McKeown, Centennial Photo
> 11595 State Road 70
> Grantsburg, WI 54840
> (715) 689-2153

★ **Cameras of brass, chrome, or wood** made before 1948. Anything interesting photographic, be it camera, book, or what have you, will be considered, including pre-1930 **photo magazines**, pre-1948 catalogs, and other ephemera. *No Polaroids*. Provide any numbers or names anywhere on the object. Describe condition of wood, leather, or metal. *Must* include an SASE.

> Alan Voorhees, Cameras & Such
> 492 Breesport Road
> Horseheads, NY 14845

★ *Kodak, Polaroid,* **and other cameras.** "I buy the following *Kodak* cameras: Colored (not black) folding cameras in any size or color, box cameras other than black, *Super Six-20, Chevron, Bantam Special* with black and chrome finish, *Gift Kodak*, and other unusual or deco-looking cameras and projectors." Harry also buys quality **35mm cameras by *Legit, Nixon, Canon, Voigtlander* and *Zeiss*.**

"An early Canon *with* pop-up viewfinder is worth $3,000+ to me, even in poor condition."

He also buys **large format press and view cameras,** lenses, roll-backs, etc. He also buys **8mm and 16mm cameras** by *Angenieux, Arriflex, Beaulieu, Bolex* and *Mitchell* **only.** Harry also buys model 180, 190, and 195 *Polaroids*, and any passport *Polaroid* (with more than one lens), but only those models...no others.

> Harry Poster
> PO Box 1883
> South Hackensack, NJ 07606
> (201) 794-9606 weekdays before 7 p.m.

★ *Kodak* **cameras, advertising, and memorabilia.** "I'll buy only pre-1930 cameras in near mint condition, especially those with original cardboard or wooden cartons. I'll also buy just the empty cartons!" Frank's list of cameras he seeks is too long to print here, but if you deal in cameras or if you have an old *Kodak*, it might be worth picking up his wants list. He also wants a *Kodiopticon* **slide projector**, and cameras made by companies absorbed by *Kodak* including *Poco, Columbus, Ludigraph, Kameret* and **Rochester Optical's** *Empire State View* camera. *Kodak* newspaper and magazine advertising before 1930 may also find a buyer, as will counter top advertising, posters, signs, wooden framed pictures of people using *Kodaks*, and any of the the literally hundreds of items with the *Kodak* logo. "If it says *'Kodak'* on it, I want to know about it. That includes books which use *Kodak* as part of the title, advertising in foreign languages, instruction books, stock certificates from any camera company, *Kodak* annual reports, and anything else that is old and in fine condition related to *Kodak*."
Frank Storey
324 School Lane
Linthicum, MD 21090
(410) 850-5728 eves

★ **Cameras, accessories, and photographic literature.** Wants early or unusual cameras and photo accessories, photography books, catalogs of photo equipment, advertising for cameras and film, and miscellaneous photographic ephemera such as lapel pins, buttons, and *Kodak* items.
Nicholas Graver
276 Brooklawn Drive
Rochester, NY 14618
(716) 244-4818

Most *Kodak* and *Polaroid* still cameras have little if any value, although colored, commemorative, and very early *Kodak* cameras are worth inquiry. 16mm home movie cameras and projectors have little value.

★ *Kodak* **publications,** especially *Kodak* catalogs before 1950, advertisements in color prior to 1900, *Kodak Salesman* magazine, *Kodak* trade circulars, display counter cards, *Kodak* advertising novelties, and *Kodak* postcards. No cameras or equipment from *Kodak* or anyone else.
Wayne Ellis
754 Bob-Bea Lane
Harleysville, PA 19438
(215) 256-6888

VIEW-MASTER & 3-D EQUIPMENT

★ *View-Master* **reels and equipment** made by *Sawyers* or *GAF*, the companies that owned *View-Master* before 1980. Will buy single reels, 3-pack reels, cameras, *Stereomatic 500* projectors, and the blue Model B viewer. Also buys some *Tru-Vue* and other 3-D items. Does not want any cartoon reels or any damaged, broken, or worn items. Give numbers on the reels and state their condition.
>Walter Sigg
>PO Box 208
>Swartswood, NJ 07877
> (201) 383-2437

★ *View-Master* **cameras, reels and dealer displays** wanted. "I will pay over $100 for film punch or close-up lenses, $200 for *Stereomatic 500* 3-D projector, $5 and up for military reels in sets or for advertising reels, and over $50 each for movie preview reels and displays from the 1950's 3-D movies. I need clean single reels and 3-packs, often paying over $5 each for many newer packs. Send a list, or the items themselves, for my prompt offer."
>Harry Poster
>PO Box 1883
>South Hackensack, NJ 07606
> (201) 794-9606 weekdays until 7 p.m.

★ **3-D cameras, reels, and other** *View-Master* **equipment,** including flash, close up lenses, cases, film cutters, 3-D projectors, library boxes, adjustable viewers, and old order lists from *Sawyers* or *GAF*, the manufacturers of *View Master*. Wants early views with blue backs, view reels that look like they're hand printed, Belgian made scenic views, pre-1970 U.S., and scenics of other continents. "I don't want children's cartoon reels made after 1950 or any scratched or damaged reels." The reel number and copyright date are more important information than the title.
>Robert Gill
>PO Box 1223
>Seaford, NY 11783
> (516) 781-8741

★ **3-D stereoscopic cameras and accessories** including viewers, projectors, manuals, and books by *Airequipt, Realist, Kodak, TDC, Wollensak, Busch, Radex, Brumberger,* and other makers. Also wants books which discuss 3-D photography and dealer displays which show any 3-D image. "I will pay over $1,000 for some special 3-D items such as the *Macro Realist* outfit by David White."
>Harry Poster
>PO Box 1883
>South Hackensack, NJ 07606
> (201) 794-9606 weekdays

Souvenirs and ephemera from various places

Collectors of "places" want a wide range of items, no two exactly alike in their wants. Many "places" collectors are historians of their particular region and focus on photos and old documents, while others are just having fun collecting colorful do-dads. Collectibles of both kinds tend to be relatively inexpensive.

Content of the photos and documents, along with age, scarcity and desirability will determine value. The value of photos and documents generally ranges from $5 to $50. Particularly rare and important photos will bring more, even from historically oriented collectors.

Some collectors seek products made in their region, or traditionally associated with their area: Great Lakes shipping, Western mining, Florida citrus, and the like. A few collectors want it all, including art native to their area, guidebooks, minor paper ephemera, money and coins,

This group of buyers has been placed near the end of *Where To Sell It!*, situated after the various specialties these collectors want, and nearest to the photographs and paper items that so delight them.

I have arranged buyers into geographic regions of the country in an effort to make it easier for you to find them.

SOUVENIRS NATIONWIDE

★ **City view books.** Buys city souvenir books which show city and town scenes, 1870-1940. Make photocopies of the cover, title page, and a sample pictorial page. Describe the condition of the cover, binding, and the contents pages.
> Herbert Mitchell
> Avery Library
> Columbia University
> New York, NY 10027

★ **Roadside ephemera.** Wants ephemera from any diners, tourist courts, motels, gas stations, drive-in theaters, and other roadside businesses, with particular interest in those designed to serve the Lincoln Highway traveler between 1920 and 1970. Buys postcards, photos, guidebooks, advertising, roadside signs, and books and magazines having to do with road travel. Especially interested in Pennsylvania items and seeking all ephemera from the S.S. Grand View Ship Hotel.
> Brian Butko
> 2640 Sunset Drive
> West Mifflin, PA 15122

★ **Pennsylvania Turnpike memorabilia of all kinds.** What have you? Please photocopy or send a photo with your description.
> J.C. Keyser
> 12 Springcreek
> Westerville, OH 43081

★ **Wooden Adirondack souvenirs.** "I'll buy the weird and the wonderful! I'm seeking items made in the Adirondacks and sold all over America, usually stamped with the name of the place where they were sold." The distinguishing feature of these rustic wood souvenirs is the maker always left some bark on the piece. He wants **lamps, mugs, tankards, picture frames, smoker's stands, clocks, plaques, inkwells, towel racks, wishing wells,** and just about anything else except nut bowls

"You're not sitting on a gold mine with a handful of tourist trade souvenirs."

and salt and pepper shakers. Many of these items had decals of Indians on them and better pieces had carvings of big game animals like moose or bears. He will also buy **miniature canoes and canoe paddles** and other birch bark items of all types. All items must be completely undamaged. Price and describe fully in your first letter, realizing these are inexpensive items. He promises prompt answers to all inquiries.
> Barry Friedman
> 22725 Garzota Drive
> Valencia, CA 91355
> (805) 296-2318

NORTHEASTERN EPHEMERA

★ **New Hampshire ephemera** from before 1900. Please price and include a photocopy.
Alf Jacobson
PO Box 188
New London, NH 03257

★ **Great Barrington, Massachusetts, and Berkshire County souvenirs** including pictorial china, plates, pins, salt & pepper shakers, spoons, cups, postcards, photos and especially souvenir china from the years 1905-1916. Towns to look for are Housatonic, Van Deusenville, Risingdale, Egremont, North Egremont, Stockbridge and Sheffield.
Gary Leveille
PO Box 562
Great Barrington, MA 01230

★ **Ocean Grove, New Jersey, memorabilia** including souvenirs, maps, photos, postcards, books, glass, porcelain, and anything else from this camp meeting seaside resort located south of Asbury Park. "I want everything, including beach, hotels, auditorium, etc."
Norman Buckman
PO Box 608
Ocean Grove, NJ 07756
(800) 524-0632

★ **Hoboken, New Jersey, memorabilia** including paper ephemera, books, photographs, postcards, prints, maps, articles, letterheads, labels, and any manufactured item with the word HOBOKEN molded or printed on the item. "We buy almost everything, no matter how trivial, including **personal reminiscences of early Hoboken residents** for inclusion in various local histories we are writing." You have the Hans' permission to ship any early Hoboken item on approval. They pay postage both ways.
Jim and Beverly Hans
Hoboken Historical Museum
Box M-1220
Hoboken, NJ 07030
(201) 653-7392

★ **New Castle, Delaware** items of historic value are sought, including books, photos, postcards, etc.
Mel Rosenthal
507 South Maryland Ave.
Wilmington, DE 19804
(302) 322-8944

★ **Adirondack Mountains memorabilia** including all books, paper ephemera, photographs, stereoviews, hotel brochures and registers, transportation timetables, manuscripts, maps, guidebooks, diaries, postcards, sheet music and prints related to any mountain towns and lakes of the Adirondacks. Lake George, Lake Placid, Lake Luzerne, Old Forge, Keene Valley, Plattsburgh, and the counties of Clinton, Herkimer, Essex, Lewis, Warren, St. Lawrence, Franklin, and Saratoga are among the many places which interest him.
> Breck Turner
> With Pipe and Book
> 91 Main Street
> Lake Placid, NY 12946
> (518) 523-9096

★ **Brooklyn, New York, and Long Island ephemera.** Historically interesting paper items are sought, including county and city atlases, city directories, photos, bill and letterheads, trade and business cards and similar items.
> Brian Merlis
> 2569 West 2nd Street Suite 5B
> Brooklyn, NY 11223
> (718) 645-3743

★ **Souvenir china and glass from Western New York state,** especially Rochester, LeRoy, and Batavia, but other cities as well.
> Burton Spiller
> 49 Palmerston Road
> Rochester, NY 14618
> (716) 244-2229

★ **Coney Island souvenirs** including Dreamland, Luna Park, and Steeplechase. He particularly wants pitchers, glasses, dishes, and other cream colored diamond and peg pattern custard glass marked CONEY ISLAND. SASE appreciated.
> John Belinsky
> 84 Day Street
> Seymour, CT 06483
> (203) 888-2225

★ **Junction Canal between Elmira, NY, and Athens, PA** (1856-1872). Wants photos and all ephemera of any type about this canal. Also items depicting or related to any branch extensions of the canal, such as that along the Susquehanna River in Pennsylvania.
> F.C. Petrillo
> 95 Miner Street
> Wilkes-Barre, PA 18702

★ **West Point memorabilia.** "I'll buy almost anything made of china or metal, but also want postcards featuring West Point. Send for my list of items I'm especially seeking."
Pat Klein
5 Pasco Hill Road
Cromwell, CT 06416

SOUTHERN EPHEMERA

★ **Tennessee.** Bookstore owner Snell says, "I'll buy Tennessee history, authors, pamphlets, and ma₁s. Also books and documents **by or about Presidents Jackson, Polk, and Johnson** and books by Tennessee authors such as Alfred Crabb, H.H. Kroll, and Samuel Cole Williams." Especially wants *Charles Egbert Craddock* by Edd Parks. "I don't want books that have been discarded by libraries."
William Snell
3765 Hillsdale Drive NE
Cleveland, TN 37312
(615) 472-8408

★ **Southern souvenirs, especially Georgia, Tennessee, and Kentucky.** China, glass, postcards, sterling, pottery, and other items are among wants. Send long SASE for list of others.
Abbie Bush
PO Box 503
Elkader, IA 52043
(319) 245-2128

★ **Charleston, South Carolina, memorabilia** including letters and envelopes, maps, tokens and medals, books, pamphlets, postcards, stock certificates and other fiscal paper. Also any South Carolina item related to the Confederacy.
Bob Karrer
PO Box 6094
Alexandria, VA 22306
(703) 360-5105 eves

Do not send items without permission. Postal Regulations say if you do you are giving it away. The person to whom you mail something without permission has the right to keep it and not pay you for it! You may send to buyers in *Where To Sell It!* only when they specifically ask you to.

★ **Great Smoky Mountains National Park** in NC and TN, before 1970. "I'll buy guidebooks, maps, photos, brochures, pamphlets, and similar paper ephemera. Also souvenirs, especially plates and glassware associated with the Park. Also interested in similar items for the towns of **Gatlinburg and Townsend, TN, and the Cherokee Indian Reservation, NC.** Not interested in any color postcards, but do want real photo b/w cards of the park." Photocopies appreciated.
Doug Redding
16532 Baederwood Lane
Rockville, MD 20855

★ **Georgia, South Carolina, and Florida paper pre-1870** that is related to slavery, the Civil War, indentures, King's grants, state grants, wills, or historically interesting topics. Georgia is of particular interest and documents can bring $100-$500 depending upon contents.
John Parks
203 Tanglewood Road
Savannah, GA 31419
(912) 925-6075

★ **Eureka Springs, Arkansas, souvenirs and paper ephemera.** Wants informative or colorful paper, plates, cups, spoons, etc., from this resort capitol of the Ozarks. Wants pre-1930 items in fine condition.
Janis Watson, Bank of Eureka Springs
PO Box 309
Eureka Springs, AR 72632
(501) 253-8241

★ **Eureka Springs, Arkansas, before 1920.** "Anything wanted from souvenirs to advertising, photographs to books, but I'll especially buy any information, maps, lawsuits, newspaper reports, etc., on the early land disputes in Eureka Springs. Also the Eureka Springs railroad. Also have strong interest in **Dr. Norman Baker's Cancer Hospital** in the Springs in the 1930's and will buy all ephemera related to it."
Steve Chyrchel
Route #2 Box 362
Eureka Springs, AR 72632
(501) 253-9244

★ **New Orleans, Louisiana, and the Gulf Coast.** Wants to buy anything pre-1940 from New Orleans especially *Newcomb* **pottery,** old **oil paintings** by local artists of the 20's and 30's like A.J. Drysdale, Clarence Millet, and G.L. Viavont among others, **Mardi Gras** favors of all sorts, and **prints and photos** of the people and events of New Orleans and surrounding areas, across the Lake and along the Gulf Coast.
Sanchez Galleries
4730 Magazine Street
New Orleans, LA 70115
(504) 524-0281

★ **Florida historical paper and memorabilia,** especially items from Fort Jefferson, Florida.
>   Gordon McHenry
>   PO Box 1117
>   Osprey, FL 34229
>   (813) 966-5563   Fax: (813) 966-5563

★ **Orlando, Florida, memorabilia.**
>   Jerry Chicone
>   PO Box 547636
>   Orlando, FL 32854
>   (407) 298-5550

★ **Coral Gables, Florida, souvenirs and advertising,** especially related to land sales.
>   Sam LaRoue
>   5980 SW 35th Street
>   Miami, FL 33155
>   (305) 347-7466

COLLECTIBLES FROM THE MIDWEST

★ **Ohio memorabilia,** especially books, manuscripts, maps and photographs, from before 1900. Particularly interested in local history prior to the Civil War, especially in the Akron area.
>   Frank Klein
>   The Bookseller
>   521 West Exchange Street
>   Akron, OH 44302
>   (216) 762-3101

★ **Wisconsin china, glass, or** *Red Wing* **souvenir items,** especially from the Wisconsin towns of La Crosse, Fountain City, Waupaca, Reedsburg, and Kilbourn.
>   Dana Zimmerman
>   1411 Briarcliff Drive
>   Appleton, WI 54915

★ **Waukesha, Wisconsin, memorabilia.** Waukesha was noted for its spring waters and a number of food products, so keep your eyes open for all sorts of things marked as being from Waukesha.
>   W.E. Schwanz
>   45 W22339 Quinn Road
>   Waukesha, WI 53186

★ **Michigan and the Great Lakes** ephemera and historically interesting paper goods of all types from that region.
Jay Platt, West Side Book Shop
113 West Liberty
Ann Arbor, MI 48104
(313) 995-1891

★ **Duluth, Minnesota and the Great Lakes.** Wants books, photos, and postcards, with particular emphasis on shipping.
James Baumhofer
PO Box 65493
St. Paul, MN 55165
(612) 698-7151

★ **Midwest, especially Iowa souvenirs.** "All good items from all Iowa towns, especially Colfax, Clayton and Elkader are sought." Send long SASE for wants list.
Abbie Bush
PO Box 503
Elkader, IA 52043
(319) 245-2128

★ **Iowa souvenirs.** "Always interested in all Iowa souvenirs, especially china. Towns of Colfax, Ackley, and Sibley are particularly wanted."
Mary Yohe
6827 South Juniper
Tempe, AZ 85283
(602) 820-7442

★ **Humboldt or Rutland, Iowa,** pictorial postcards and advertising from those two towns.
Don Olson
PO Box 245
Humboldt, IA 50548

★ **Trade tokens and dog licenses from Iowa.**
Dennis Schulte
8th Avenue NW
Waukon, IA 52172
(319) 568-3628 before 10 p.m.

★ **Rockford, Freeport, and Belvidere Illinois, tokens, medals,** buttons, badges, ribbons, and other small flat collectibles. Also banks, early signs, coffee tins, bottles, etc. Loves to find larger items marked as being from Rockford. No paper or cardboard items.
Rich Hartzog
PO Box 4143 BFT
Rockford, IL 61110
(815) 226-0771

★ **Dakota Territory, South Dakota, North Dakota, Minnesota, Wyoming, and Montana photographs and small ephemera** from before 1930 in any format, including real photo postcards. Wants all historically or pictorially interesting paper ephemera, advertising, letters, books, bottles, and small objects. Especially wants items marked DT, DAKOTA TERRITORY, DAK or SOUTH DAKOTA. Buys single items or collections. Is often as interested in the photographers as the subject matter of the photo. Photocopies are recommended. If your items are in fine condition, you may ship them on approval.

> Robert Kolbe
> 1301 South Duluth
> Sioux Falls, SD 57105
> (605) 332-9662

WESTERN EPHEMERA

★ **Paper ephemera about the Western U.S.** especially related to the military, early forts, ghost towns, Mormons, railroads, mining, banking, cowboys, Indians, lawmen, cattle, courts, and financial matters. Buys letters about the West, autographs of famous Westerners, and most illustrated pre-1910 Western documents.

> Warren Anderson
> American West Archives
> PO Box 100
> Cedar City, UT 84720
> (801) 586-9497

★ **Dallas ephemera** pre-1915, including pamphlets, letters, documents, postcards, photos, and items related to **the Texas State Fair.** *The Artwork of Dallas* folio will bring $300 or more.

> Ron Pearson
> 10620 Creekmere Drive
> Dallas, TX 75218
> (214) 321-9717

★ **Texas maps and prints.** "The popular image is that people in Texas are wealthy, but they are not. Being a *thing* from Texas does not automatically make it worth a lot of money either." Mostly wants pre-1900 prints of Texas industry. San Antonio is the only Texas city she is interested in finding on general prints and maps.

> Shirley Sorenson
> 270 Sherri Drive
> Universal City, TX 78148
> (512) 658-2548

★ **Maps of Texas** from before 1900. Also trail driving maps.
Johnny Spellman
10806 North Lamar
Austin, TX 78753
   (512) 258-6910 eves   (512) 836-2889 days

★ **Nevada and Death Valley ephemera** including books, newspapers, magazines, diaries, letters, maps, promotional brochures, "and anything else printed or written on paper." Also stereoviews, merchant tokens, dog tags, hunting licenses, photos, postcards and what have you. He requests prices but will make offers.
Gil Schmidtmann
Route #1   Box 371
Mentone, CA 92359
   (909) 794-1211

★ **Colorado mining memorabilia,** 1859-1915, especially Cripple Creek and all other mining towns and camps and the railroads that served them. Wants photos, stereoviews, advertising, letterheads, billheads, brochures, pamphlets, mining papers, stock certificates, maps, badges, candlesticks, souvenirs, and other small items marked with the name of one of these towns. Photos should be of mining, railroad, or downtown activities, not people or scenery. Albums with numerous photos eagerly sought, as are Business or Mining Directories and books on Colorado mining. Does not want *anything* from the flatland Colorado towns like Denver, Pueblo or Colorado Springs, nor anything from state or national parks. Give whatever info is printed or written on the back of photos.
George Foott
6683 South Yukon Way
Littleton, CO 80123
   (303) 979-8688

★ **Colorado and Wyoming memorabilia** from 1860 to 1930. Wants real photo and advertising postcards, souvenirs, "good for" trade tokens, stereoviews, envelopes and letterheads, fancy whiskey bottles, posters, calendars, trade cards, political buttons, ephemera from the Leadville Ice Palace, *any* item from the 1908 Democratic National Convention held in Denver, items from military forts, and items from fairs, rodeos, and Cheyenne Frontier Days. All items *must* be from Wyoming or Colorado and be within the 1860-1930 time frame. "I do not want items from National Parks, items after 1930, newspapers, or magazines. Please give a complete description." He emphasizes, "Please do not send unsolicited items."
Edward Marriott
9191 East Oxford Drive
Denver, CO 80237
   (303) 779-5237

★ **Las Vegas, Nevada souvenirs and memorabilia** from before 1970. Buys gambling tokens and chips, casino playing cards, match covers, postcards, stationery, plates, business directories, showroom programs, magazines with stories about Las Vegas history, and photos of interiors of casinos, banks, hotels, motels, and restaurants. Also interested in photos of Las Vegas celebrities. Will consider other ephemera from this desert playground.
　　Marc Weiser
　　PO Box 28730
　　Las Vegas, NV　89126
　　(702) 871-8686

★ **Nevada ephemera** including mounted photos, pre-1930 postcards, law badges, bottles, railroad ephemera, fire department ephemera, cowboy relics, maps, stocks, Indian artifacts, posters, advertising, mining, military, etc. If it's early and marked NEV, Ron is interested.
　　Ron Bommarito
　　PO Box 114
　　Genoa, NV　89411
　　(702) 782-3893

★ **All Nevada memorabilia** from before 1950 is wanted, including maps, photos, postcards, stationery, tokens, and other ephemera but especially items related to banks and finance including bank bags, letterheads, documents, stocks, checks and scrip. Also interested in anything related to the history and operation of **prostitution** in Nevada.
　　Douglas McDonald
　　PO Box 20443
　　Reno, NV　89515

★ **Nevada, Utah, and Wyoming** souvenirs are wanted including china, glass, sterling silver, postcards, pottery, and other small items originating in those states. Send long SASE for wants list.
　　Abbie Bush
　　PO Box 503
　　Elkader, IA　52043
　　(319) 245-2128

★ **Idaho, Montana, and Washington items** including trade tokens, postcards, letterheads, calendars, buttons, ribbons, wooden nickels, stocks, match holders, calendar plates and other advertising china. Pays $1-$3 each for postcards with postmarks from discontinued post offices. Pays $2-$10 for cards of small towns he can use. Nothing after 1930.
　　Mike Fritz
　　1550 Stevens Street
　　Rathdrum, ID　83858
　　(208) 687-0159

★ **Yakima County, Washington, items.** "I buy pre-1950 photos, phone books, newspapers, directories, souvenirs, promotional booklets, and postcards, but no chrome faced postcards." Yakima HS yearbooks from pre-1910, 1933-34, and 1953-54 are also wanted. If in doubt, send for his wants list of 28 towns he seeks.

> Ron Ott
> 10 North 45th Ave.
> Yakima, WA 98908
> (509) 965-3385

★ **San Francisco Bay area ephemera** pre-1910, especially related to the 1906 quake. Photos, diaries, letters, family mementos, and the like are wanted with emphasis on unusual. Ron has particular interest in items associated with schools and education before 1906 and to meal tickets and other items related to life in relief camps immediately after the disaster. No newspapers or postcards. Ron heads the S.F. History Ass'n and can accept tax deductible gifts related to S.F. from any period.

> Ron Ross
> 620 Church Street
> San Francisco, CA 94114
> (415) 626-3666 eves

★ **San Bernardino, California, items** from buildings, fairs, and resorts. Wants ceramic souvenirs including cups, plates, sterling silver spoons, badges, ribbons, pins, etc. Particularly interested in items associated with the 1903 Street Fair, 1908 Festival of the Arrowhead, 1910 Centennial, and the National Orange Show, from 1911 to 1920.

> Gary Crabtree
> PO Box 3843
> San Bernardino, CA 92413
> (714) 862-8534

★ **San Gabriel Valley, CA, items.** Wants pre-1930 items from any San Gabriel Valley towns: Arcadia, Temple City, El Monte, San Gabriel, Baldwin Park, Rosemead, Pasadena, Covina, San Marino, Monrovia, Duarte and Azusa. Also wants anything related to **Emperor Norton** and **Lucky Baldwin.** He suggests you ship your items to him via UPS at 650 West Duarte, #309, to get his offer.

> SC Coin & Stamp Co.
> PO Drawer 3069
> Arcadia, CA 91006
> (800) 367-0779

★ **San Diego, California, memorabilia** including postcards, pamphlets and photographs.

> Ralph Bowman's Paper Gallery
> 5349 Wheaton Street
> La Mesa, CA 91942
> (619) 462-6268

★ **Santa Cruz, CA,** postcards, photos, souvenir plates, and other collectibles.
>Rick Righetti,
>219 Olive Street
>Santa Cruz, CA 95060
>(408) 426-3014

★ **Alaskan and Canadian memorabilia** including postcards, trade cards, advertising, labels, letterheads, and photos, especially items pre-1875. Buys for resale. Approvals welcome if nothing is damaged or dates after 1950.
>Nick Nickell
>102 People's Wharf
>Juneau, AK 99801
>(907) 586-1733

★ **Alaskan memorabilia.** "I'll buy nearly anything old about Alaska, the Yukon, or the Polar Region including books, maps, photographs, letters, souvenirs, china, spoons, and miscellaneous ephemera. One of my specialties is Alaskan postcards around 1910. I buy for resale, and seldom buy items newer than 1945."
>Richard Wood, Alaska Heritage Books
>PO Box 22165
>Juneau, AK 99802
>(907) 586-6748

★ **Alaskan memorabilia.** Wants embossed bottles with Alaskan product or business names, license plates, postcards (not scenery), Klondike novelty material, brochures from the Alaskan & Canadian Railroad & Steamship lines, and "all very early newspapers, photographs, and printed matter." Also wants *Alaska Sportsman* magazines from the 1930's and selected issues of *Alaska Journal*. Does not want Alaska-Yukon Exposition material. Give description, condition, date of origin, and indicate what cities, towns, or regions are featured. Do not send items unsolicited. Will send a wants list for SASE.
>Reed Fitzpatrick, The Paper Scout
>PO Box 369
>Vashon, WA 98070
>(206) 463-3900 days

★ **Hawaiian and South Seas ephemera.** Wants books, printed items, paintings, prints, photos, postcards, and other memorabilia from Hawaii, as long as it's pre-1920. Send insured. No Hula dolls.
>Bernie Berman
>755 Isenberg Street #305
>Honolulu, HI 96826

★ **Puerto Rico.** Wants pre-1930 books, postcards, and other memorabilia of Puerto Rico. Please price and describe in your first letter.
Frank Garcia
13701 SW 66th Street #B-301
Miami, FL 33183

FOREIGN EPHEMERA

★ **Canadian items:** calendars, stock certificates, bank notes, old letters in original envelopes, fancy letterheads, all Canadian railway, merchants' tokens from Western Canada, Canadian military or law enforcement, and postcards of BC, Yukon, NWT, AB, SK, and Newfoundland. Nothing after 1950, please. No road maps, tourist brochures, and postcards of tourist attractions or scenery. Prefers items be sent on approval or a photocopy made and included in your letter.
Michael Rice
PO Box 286
Saanichton, BC V0S 1M0 CANADA
(604) 652-9047 eves

★ **Canada, the Arctic, and the Klondike.** All information wanted including maps, paper ephemera, prints, government documents, and photographs about Canadian immigration, travel, history, fur trade, mountaineering, Indians and Eskimos. Does not make offers.
Tom Williams
PO Box 4126, Station C
Calgary, Alberta T2T 5M9 CANADA
(403) 264-0184

★ **Canadian postcards, stereoviews and other ephemera** especially from the Province of Ontario. Mainly interested in small town views, events, railroad stations, and transportation. No scenics or items after 1950. "A photocopy of the item is almost essential" to accompany your complete description. Also wants **Canadian made woodworking planes.** When offering planes, make certain to include all writing and numbers you find on the tool. Note whether it is complete or not.
Peter Cox
PO Box 1655
Espanola, Ontario P0P 1C0 CANADA
(705) 869-2441 or (705) 859-2410

★ **Panama Canal Zone and the Isthmus of Panama memorabilia** including postcards, letters, stamped envelopes, scrapbooks, tokens, medals, maps, coins, stamps, and everything else including souvenirs. Especially likes pre-1915 picture postcards with cancellations from obscure Panama post offices. "I will probably offer to buy anything Isthmus." Bob is the long time editor of the Isthmus collectors' journal.

Bob Karrer
PO Box 6094
Alexandria, VA 22306
(703) 360-5105

★ **Cuban memorabilia** before Castro including coins, stamps, money, historical documents, postcards, souvenir spoons, maps, stocks and bonds, lottery tickets, cigar bands, military decorations and insignia, "or any other collectible item including those related to the Spanish domination of the Island." He'll pay from $80-$400 for the 10, 20 and 50 peso bank notes of 1869. There is a 1916 coin and a 1944 banknote each worth more than $50,000, so it could pay you to look.

Manuel Alvarez
1735 SW 8th Street
Miami, FL 33135
(305) 649-1176

★ **Brazil.** Books, photos, and paper ephemera from the colonial period through 1945. Especially interested in travel and exploration books with early information about Rio de Janeiro and/or the Amazon. Also wants letters and diaries of military personnel who served in Brazil during WWII or in the Joint Brazil-U.S. Military Commission. Material may be in any language. Please include your phone number.

Lee Harrer
1908 Seagull Drive
Clearwater, FL 34624
(813) 536-4029 evenings

★ **Philippine Islands.** "I'll buy postcards, photos, books, magazines, maps, and other paper items, especially real photo postcards from Manila or elsewhere in the Philippines. I don't want coins, stamps, paper money, or books on the Spanish American War. It's helpful if you give me the name of the postcard publisher."

Michael Price
PO Box 7071
Ann Arbor, MI 48107

★ **Australia and Antarctica items from before 1920,** including prints, maps, photographs, ship's logs, scholarly ethnographic studies, novels, travel books, children's books, postcards and paper ephemera. No interest in items from New Zealand or the Maori.

David and Cathy Lilburne, Antipodean Books
PO Box 189
Cold Spring, NY 10516
(914) 424-3867

★ **Antarctic and Arctic ephemera** especially books but also diaries, posters, photographs, letters, pamphlets and *Aurora Austrailis*, the Antarctic newspaper 1907-09. Will buy any clean copies of the latter.

Jay Platt, West Side Book Shop
113 West Liberty
Ann Arbor, MI 48104
(313) 995-1891 days

★ **Greenland, Pitcairn Island, Hudson's Bay, Canada, Mexico, and other countries' ephemera** especially tokens and medals, but other small items, especially before 1930 are likely to be of interest. Your best bet is to photocopy what you have.

Rich Hartzog, World Exonumia
PO Box 4143 BFT
Rockford, IL 61110
(815) 226-0771

★ **Micronesia, Polynesia, and New Guinea ethnographic materials,** masks, ceremonial bowls, and the like. Also maps, mariner's charts, voyage books, and ship's logs from vessels traveling in that region, in any language. Some interest in scrimshaw if associated with the Pacific. No items from New Zealand or the Maori are wanted.

David and Cathy Lilburne, Antipodean Books
PO Box 189
Cold Spring, NY 10516
(914) 424-3867

★ **Imperial Russian antiques and memorabilia** whether religious, civil, or military. We buy Russian:
Orders, decorations, badges, buttons, medals, and other militaria;
Porcelains, bronzes, icons, prints, paintings and graphic arts;
Coronation and other commemorative memorabilia.
Items are bought for cash or brokered. "Please send a clear photo or photocopy and details, including price wanted." Mail order catalog and appraisal services available. No Soviet items.

ART Co.
PO Box 278183
Sacramento, CA 95826
(916) 366-8850

Magazines

People are attracted to magazines for many reasons. Some buy for the covers and illustrations. Others look for early articles or advertising relevant to their hobby. Some folks just collect magazines!

To describe items for sale, give the name and date of the magazines and note all tears, creases, address stickers, writing, or anything else which affects the cover or contents. If you have many issues, list them, counting only those with covers and pictures intact, no water damage, and no mildew smell. Describe the condition of a typical issue.

If you offer a magazine to someone because of an article contained in it, give the name and date of the magazine and article, the author, and the number of illustrations. It's a good idea to photocopy the cover.

DESCRIBING THE CONDITION OF MAGAZINES

VF (very fine) = fresh, bright copy without flaws except for minor aging of paper;

F (fine) = bright copy with very minor wear and only minute cover tears or creases;

VG (very good) = cover and spine wear, tiny tears and creases, minor chipping , browning of paper;

G (good) = obvious cover and spine wear, discoloration, water stains, pieces missing, tears up to 1" long;

FA (fair) = tight and complete, but longer creases, tears, rubbing, fading, and/or store stamps or dates;

P (poor) = many defects, serious damage, referred to as a "reading copy," not as a collectible.

424

MAGAZINES

★ **Volume 1, Number 1, first issue magazines,** newspapers, comic books, or miscellaneous publications including newsletters, catalogs, fan publications, etc. Also buys pre-publication issues, proofs, dummies, and premier issues. "When I don't buy, I will try to help the seller find someone else who might."
Stan Gold
7042 Dartbrook
Dallas, TX 75240
(214) 239-8621

★ **First issue and dummy issue magazines.** Seeking well known titles from before 1930. Should be in fine condition with clean covers and contents intact. Also **old magazines with beautiful covers and illustrations.** "I'm primarily interested in the period from 1910 to 1930, but will buy a few earlier or later. The quality of the artistic illustrations is the key. Mucha is a favorite, but the work of many other illustrators is sought. Titles of most interest are *Collier's* (1900-1910), *Delineator* (1910-1924), *Harper's Bazaar* (1900-1960), *Hearst's* (1912-1930), *Inland Printer* (1890-1910), *Ladies Home Journal* (1900-1930), *Ladies World* (1912-1918), *Metropolitan* (1912-1924), *Vanity Fair* (1913-1936), *Vogue* (1900-1960), *Pictorial Review* (1910-1924), and movie magazines (1900-1945). I don't buy much after 1940, and nothing less than excellent condition. I always prefer to buy whole stacks, not single issues."
Leon Williams
467 Portland Ave.
St. Paul, MN 55102

★ **Most magazines in quantity** if before 1950 and most newer fashion, movie, and quality photography magazines. Give quantity of each title and a description. Doesn't want *National Geographic* after 1910, *Reader's Digest* after 1930, *Life* after 1936, *Arizona Highways* after 1940, or *American Heritage* hardcovers. One of the largest magazine dealers, they will pick them up if you have a truckload.
The Antiquarian Bookstore
1070 Lafayette Road
Portsmouth, NH 03801
(603) 436-7250

★ **Illustrated magazines 1895 to 1930** including women's, children's, movie, pulps, theater, farm, motorcycle, and many more. Titles such as *Collier's, Esquire, Vogue, Saturday Evening Post, Vanity Fair, American* and others are wanted. Give date, condition, and price. He is not interested in giving free appraisals. "No pen pals and time wasters."
Denis Jackson
PO Box 1958
Sequim, WA 98382

★ **Bound volumes of illustrated fashion and other magazines** including *Graham's, Godey's Ladies Magazine,* and others published before 1880. Wants *Craftsman* (1900-1915), *Ladies Home Journal, Delineator, Woman's Home Companion, Vogue* and *Saturday Evening Post* from 1910-1922. Condition is important. Note cracks, tears, foxing. Include SASE for answer.

> "People overestimate the condition of magazines saying 'good for its age' when it's in fair to poor condition at best."

John Rosenhoover
100 Mandalay Road
Chicopee, MA 01020

★ **Fashion magazines** from 1890 to 1910, including *Harper's Bazaar, Delineator,* and others. Also buys pictures, postcards, and catalogs showing women's fashions of that period.
Cheryl Abel
103 Jacqueline Ave.
Delran, NJ 08075

★ **Women's magazines.** "I'll buy women's magazines such as *Better Homes & Gardens, Good Housekeeping, McCall's* and *Ladies Home Journal.* I especially want issues from the 1930's and 1940's but will consider issues from 1900-1950."
Susan Cox
800 Murray Drive
El Cajon, CA 92020

★ **Men's outdoor magazines.** "We are active and good buyers in need of magazines on hunting, fishing, archery, hunting dogs, and guns. We buy *Stoeger Shooter's Bibles* (1924-1949), *Gun Digests* (1944-1962) and gun and fishing tackle catalogs (1850-1949). We will currently purchase all fine copies, including current years, of *Guns, Man at Arms, Gun Report, Gun World, Arms and the Man, World & Recreation, Rifle, Shooting and Fishing, Shooting Times, American Angler, Handloader, Guns and Ammo* and certain issues of other similar magazines. Special wants include *Chicago Field* (1876-1880),

> "If one magazine in a group has things cut out, chances are that most of them will."

Forest & Stream before 1930, *Sports Afield* before 1932, *Field and Stream* before 1920, *Outdoor Life* before 1920 and others. "We need magazines in fine condition, both covers as originally attached, with no bad musty smell, and nothing cut out. Sometimes in the case of very old and scarce magazines we can use them in less than fine condition. Don't ship anything in advance as our wants change over time."
Lewis Razek
PO Box 1246
Traverse City, MI 49684
(616) 271-3898

★ **Men's outdoor magazines** including *Field & Stream, Outdoor Life* pre-1920, and *Sports Afield* before 1932.
> Thomas McKinnon
> PO Box 86
> Wagram, NC 28396

★ **Scandal and exploitation magazines** from 1952-1973 including but not limited to *Behind the Scenes, Bunk!, Celebrity, Exposed, Hollywood Tattler, Hush-Hush, Inside Story, The Lowdown, Naked Truth, Sensation, Top Secret, TV Scandals, Untold Secrets,* and *Whisper.* "I'll pay $35 each for complete issues of *Inside Stuff* from the 1930's." Also wants *Police Gazette* in good condition, especially bound. Nothing current, soiled, damaged or with pages clipped. Give title, date, and volume.
> Gordon Hasse
> Box 1543 Grand Central Station
> New York, NY 10163-1543

★ *Esquire* **magazine,** 1933-1959. Also buys *Playboy* (pre-1960 only), *True,* and complete years of *Cosmopolitan, McCalls, Vogue, Ladies Home Journal, Woman's Home Companion, Redbook, Saturday Evening Post, Country Gentlemen* and *Collier's.* List years and condition.
> Charles Martignette
> PO Box 293
> Hallandale, FL 33009

★ *TV Guide,* 1948-70, including early local editions. Selected issues from 1971 to 1989 also purchased. Issues of NY City's *Television Guide* from 1948 are worth $25-$50 each. Note if address label is on the cover.
> Jeffrey Kadet
> PO Box 20
> Macomb, IL 61455

★ **American humor magazines and newspapers,** 1765 to date. Wants comic material and ephemera (but *not* comic books). Humorous periodicals including satire, cartoons, or comic sketches in a variety of formats, mostly to a popular audience. No *MAD* and *National Lampoon.*
> David Sloane
> 4 Edgehill Terrace
> Hamden, CT 06517

★ *Humorama* **magazine.** Pays $1 and up. Give dates and condition.
> Jeff Patton
> 3621 Carolina Street NW
> Massillon, OH 44646

★ **College humor magazines and covers.** "Buying one and all." Send a photocopy of the cover and indicate the date if it doesn't show.
> Lisa Lisciotto
> 455 Harding Place
> Fairview, NJ 07022

★ **Magazines about diving and underwater activities.** Buys foreign and domestic magazines such as *Skin Diver, Aquarius, Diver, Scuba Times, Sport Diver, Ocean Realm,* etc. No books, hardcover or soft.

Thomas Szymanski
5 Stoneybrook Lane
Exeter, NH 03833

★ **National Geographic Society publications of all types.** Buys magazines, books, maps, article reprints, atlases, pictorials, school bulletins, advertising, invitations, slides, videos, postcards, and calendars produced by the NGS. Also buys materials published by other companies with articles about the NGS, which spoof the NGS, are funded by the NGS, or in any way refer to the NGS. He particularly wants magazines before 1913, technical books such as that on Machu Picchu (he'll pay $1,000) and the complete advertising brochure sent to prospective members in 1888. He'll pay you $5,000 for a vol. 1, No. 1 magazine. **No magazines after 1959.** Nick buys outright or accepts items on consignment. He encourages correspondence from buyers and sellers.

Nick Koopman, Collectors Exchange
10600 Lowery Drive
Raleigh, NC 27615

★ **Crossword and other puzzle magazines** before 1970. "It doesn't matter if they're filled in." Give the name, date and condition. The first 18 issues of *The Eastern Enigma* are worth $1,000.

Will Shortz, Games Magazine
19 West 21st Street
New York, NY 10010

★ **Pulp magazines.** Buys many types, especially hero, super-hero and character pulps such as *The Shadow, The Spider, Doc Savage, Captain Hazard, Captain Zero, The Wizard, Wu Fang,* etc. Also aviation pulps like *G-8, Dusty Ayres, Battle Aces* and similar titles. Other collectible pulp categories are detective, spicy, terror, and odd like *Gun Molls* and *Speakeasy Stories.* Not interested in romance or Westerns. Give the title, date, and overall condition. Include your phone number. Please don't ask about comic books or family magazines like *Post, Life* or *Readers Digest.* Also buys **pulp related items** such as pins, badges, rings, membership cards, art, displays, and autographs of writers and artists.

Jack Deveny
6805 Cheyenne Trail
Edina, MN 55435

★ **Pulp magazines.** Buys nearly 1,000 titles: adventure, aviation, crime and detective, hero, mystery and menace, **Western**, science fiction and fantasy, **romance**, spicy, sports, confession, and others. Give the title, date, and condition of each magazine, with emphasis on the cover.

Jim Steranko
PO Box 974
Reading, PA 19603

Newspapers

Newspapers seldom sell for much money, even if they're over 100 years old. A whole year of the *London Gazette* from 1800 is only worth about $300. Some 19th century publications are important, however, because they contain the first printing of stories by famous writers or artwork which has itself gone on to become collectible.

Fascinating newspapers and magazines with first hand stories of Daniel Boone and Andrew Jackson can be bought from some dealers listed in *Where to Sell It!* for less than $30. A Baltimore paper describing the burning of Washington by the British in the War of 1812 recently sold for only $15.

To describe a paper, give the name, city, date, number and size of pages, and mention any significant stories. If bound, indicate the type and condition of the binding (leather or boards, loose, split, leather crumbling, etc.). If it is a small town 18th or 19th century paper, a photocopy of the masthead is suggested.

The newspapers that are always welcome are illustrated weeklies like *Harper's* and *Leslie's* from 1855-1900. When offering 19th century illustrated papers, make certain they are complete as the value drops significantly if important pictures are missing. Tell the buyer about tears, rips, stains, cut outs, and foxing (brown spots). If the paper is dry, brown, or brittle, it is seldom of value unless it's before 1750 or the only known copy of a title.

Both newspapers and magazines can be shipped "Special Fourth Class Book Rate," which is inexpensive. Ask for the latest rates at your post office.

NEWSPAPERS

★ **Newspapers covering any important event before 1945.** Also all half year bound runs of pre-1870 papers, especially from Southern U.S., Confederate states, early West, or anywhere in the U.S. pre-1800. Wants specialty papers covering the women's movement, labor, railroads, abolitionism, temperance, or the Civil War. Also **illustrated newspapers** like *Harper's, Leslie's, Ballou's, Southern Illustrated News, London Illustrated News*, etc. Also bound volumes of British newspapers and magazines pre-1700 (although he will buy later issues if historically significant). Also issues of any American magazine before 1800. Pays $100 each for newspapers before 1730 but notes that many reprints exist so they need be authenticated. No 20th century items except mint condition reports of important events. No severely defective papers.

> Phil Barber
> PO Box 8694
> Boston, MA 02114
> (617) 492-4653 Fax: (617) 868-1534

★ **Newspapers of historical significance** especially relative to Lincoln's speeches or death, George Washington, the Revolution, the Civil War, colonial America, early Illinois and the Chicago fire. Buys individual issues of historical significance or bound volumes. Buys all *Harper's Weekly* and *Frank Leslie's Illustrated*, 1855-1916.

> Steve and Linda Alsberg
> 9850 Kedvale Ave.
> Skokie, IL 60076
> (708) 676-9850

★ **Bound volumes of American and European illustrated newspapers, 1850-1910** including *Harper's Weekly, Leslie's, Illustrated London News, Judge, Vanity Fair, Das Plachate, Jugend, Puck*, and the like.

> Joe Davidson
> 5185 Windfall Road
> Medina, OH 44256
> (216) 723-7172

★ **Bound volumes of illustrated weekly newspapers** such as *Puck, Harper's, Scientific American,* and others, but before 1890 only. Loose stacks considered, but single copies are not wanted. Fine condition only.

> John Rosenhoover
> 100 Mandalay Road
> Chicopee, MA 01020

★ **Historical newspapers** wanted in large or small quantities, bound volumes, or single issues from the 18th, 19th, or 20th centuries.

> Steve Goldman
> 11 Pheasant View Place
> Parkton, MD 21120

Books

Buyers look for books on specific topics, books by specific authors, books published by certain publishers, books illustrated in a particular manner, books from a particular period or country, and books of a specific type, such as leather bound, miniature or first editions.

When writing to potential buyers about a book, provide what we call "Standard Bibliographic Information." You can save work by photocopying both sides of the title page:

Title as found on the title page, not as on the spine;
Author, publisher, and place of publication;
All printing and copyright dates;
Number of pages;
Type and approximate number of illustrations.

Also briefly describe the condition of the (1) cover, (2) spine, (3) binding, (4) pages and (5) the dust jacket. Note bookplates, writing, and all damage. Don't offer books that are damaged, recent, or not the buyer's specialty.

A dealer's price for books depends upon his customers and present stock, the rarity of your offering, current market, and his cash flow at that moment. If you want an appraisal of your books, hire an appraiser and pay the fee. Before you hire an appraiser, understand that most family book collections are not worth the expense.

Books can be shipped Special 4th Class, or 'Book Rate, which permits three pounds for around two dollars. However, books are fragile and may be damaged in transit. It only costs $1 or so more to send a book first class. Since the buyer is paying for shipping, use the faster, safer method.

BOOKS

★ **Large collections of good books,** especially subject collections of Americana, Civil War non-fiction, Michigan history, theology, golf, chess, etc. Also wants **books with color plates, leather bound books,** and **autographed books** by famous authors. Catalogs are issued periodically. If you want to sell, give standard bibliographic information. One of the nation's largest used and rare booksellers, John does not buy *Reader's Digest* books, *National Geographic* magazines, book club editions, textbooks of any kind, encyclopedia sets, or anything in poor condition.

> John K. King Books
> 901 West Lafayette Blvd.
> Detroit, MI 48226
> (313) 961-0622

★ **Various fine and early books,** including:
> **Incunabula,** hand written books before 1501;
> **European books** before 1600;
> **English books** and manuscripts from before 1700;
> **American books before 1800;**
> **Books published in Pennsylvania** before 1810 in English or 1830 in German. Especially seek items printed by Benjamin Franklin in Philadelphia, the Brotherhood in Ephrata, or the Saurs (Sower) in Germantown;
> **Fine leather bound books** in sets;
> **Books with fore edge paintings;** "Let us hear about all fore edge paintings, no matter what era;"
> **Books illustrated in color,** especially chromoliths before 1900;
> **Books on China or Japan** if scholarly and illustrated;
> **African exploration and development** and materials devoted to problems faced by less developed countries today;
> **Arabic studies** including materials relating the spheres of Moslem influence, both ancient and modern. Buys important books in Arabic and related languages;
> **Urban studies** including all aspects about any cities everywhere and in all eras;
> **City view books** of buildings and streets of cities worldwide.

Make certain to include count of pages and photos in your description. Please make a photocopy of the title page. In business for 20 years, Ron offers a series of fine catalogs. He is a member of numerous historical and professional organizations.

> Ron Lieberman, Family Album
> Route #1 Box 42
> Glen Rock, PA 17327
> (717) 235-2134

★ **Any book, pamphlet, or tract printed in English speaking America before 1800.** "Books need not be complete nor necessarily in good condition. We will purchase damaged books or even fragments." If you own a book without a title page that you believe to be very old you may send them the book for identification. It's always best to write first, though, and if possible send them a photocopy. The Haydn Foundation for the Cultural Arts is a non profit public institution.

Michael Zinman, Haydn Foundation
495 Ashford Avenue
Ardsley, NY 10502

★ **Fine quality books from all periods** are wanted. "My book buying wants are guided by the belief that the quality of a book comes from both the printed word (the reader's access to knowledge and imagination) and from the physical object of the book itself. The books I seek are generally first or early printings or are examples of high quality hand made private press bookmaking. I am particularly interested in buying books in the fields of art, architecture, Americana and the West, science and medicine, literature and literary criticism, travel and exploration, philosophy and religion, and world history, but will consider any high quality book. I am always looking for examples of **fine binding, printing and illustration,** especially books signed by Zachnsdorf, Sangurski and Sutcliffe, Riviere, and other fine binders. Some fine private press books to look for include Kelmscott Press, Ashendone Press, Doves Press, Cranach Press, Nonesuch Press, Gregynog Press, Arion Press, and Golden Cockerel Press among others. **Books signed by the author or illustrator** are also of particular interest to me as are Chagall's *Illustrations for the Bible* and *Drawings for the Bible*, Harold Bell Wright's *To My Sons,* pre-1800 copies of *The Book of Common Prayer*, pre-1935 *Alcoholics Anonymous* books, and the Limited Editions Club books, especially *Lysistrata* and *Ulysses.* I do not want book club editions, *Reader's Digest* books, dictionaries or encyclopedia sets after 1850, Bibles after 1750, and incomplete sets of books. I generally prefer the seller to set the price, but if you want an offer, you should provide all information on the title page and copyright page. Make a photocopy of these two pages if you can do so without damaging the book. Describe the binding and format, and the condition of the cover, binding and pages." Don't forget your SASE.

Paul Melzer, Fine & Rare Books
12 East Vine Street
Redlands, CA 92373
(909) 792-7299

★ **Fine and antiquarian books,** pamphlets, and original manuscripts, especially dealing with **medicine,** travel to the old West and photography. Also **children's books** that are "old, rare and colorfully illustrated."

Ivan Gilbert, Miran Arts & Books
2824 Elm Ave.
Columbus, OH 43209

★ **Books illustrated with full page b/w illustrations,** including steel engravings, etchings, copper plates, or woodblocks. Wants views of the U.S. and Canada, North American Indians, explorations and Western America, animals, art, railway surveys, pre-1880 fairs and Centennials, architecture, Civil War, and pre-1860 Hawaii (Sandwich Islands). Indicate size along with standard bibliographic information. Note tears, foxing, etc. Count the number of illustrations.
    John Rosenhoover
    100 Mandalay Road
    Chicopee, MA 01020
    (413) 536-5542

BOOK BUYERS WANT TO KNOW

Standard bibliographic information: title, author, publisher and place of publication, all dates of printing or copyright, number of pages, who illustrated it, and the approximate number of illustrations. Describe condition of the cover, spine, binding, pages and dust jacket. Note bookplates, writing, and all other damage.

★ **Books illustrated with color pictures before 1890** depicting plants, animals, birds, fish, Indians, sports, cowboys, medicine, military, buildings, costumes, fashion, or advertising. Standard bibliographic data.
    Joe Davidson
    5185 Windfall Road
    Medina, OH 44256
    (216) 723-7172

★ **Books illustrated with color plates before 1899,** especially German before 1895, American natural history (plants and animals) before 1870, and Indians. Give standard bibliographic information, noting tears, erasures, foxing, etc. Give the number of illustrations in color and in b/w. **Books illustrated by** Kate Greenaway, Arthur Rackham, Jessie Smith, K. Nielson, Wyeth, W. Crane, Maxfield Parrish, Pogany, Dulac, Newell, Maud Humphrey, Remington, Erte, or Harrison Fisher. Books must date between 1890 and 1926. Give standard bibliographic information, noting tears, erasures, foxing, etc. Count and indicate the number of illustrations in color and in black and white.
    John Rosenhoover
    100 Mandalay Road
    Chicopee, MA 01020

★ **Books illustrated by Japanese woodblocks.**
Jerrold Stanoff, Rare Oriental Book Co.
PO Box 1599
Aptos, CA 95003
(408) 724-4911   Fax: (408) 761-1350

★ **Books illustrated with photographs tipped (glued) in,** U.S. or foreign. Also books illustrated by important photographers.
Janet Lehr
PO Box 617   Gracie Square Station
New York, NY 10028

★ **Used and rare books, manuscripts** and **maps.** "We specialize in **U.S. maps and atlases before 1870**, books on the military, aviation, lighter-than-air craft and Ohio subjects. We also have interest in obtaining old **bookbinding tools** and equipment."
Frank Klein, The Bookseller
521 West Exchange Street
Akron, OH 44302
(216) 762-3101

★ **Atlases with colored plates** before 1870 as long as they deal in whole or in part with the United States. It is important that double page plates should not have a white area separating the plate into two sections. Also interested in **commercial atlases prior to 1925** and **books of all types with foldout maps** in black and white or color, but they must be before 1870. Groups of loose color plate **maps** are also considered. Include dimensions with standard bibliographic information. Note tears, erasures, foxing, etc. Give the number of maps in color and in b/w.
John Rosenhoover
100 Mandalay Road
Chicopee, MA 01020

★ **Atlases with colored plates** published before 1870. Provide standard bibliographic data to this important dealer.
Joe Davidson
5185 Windfall Road
Medina, OH 44256
(216) 723-7172

★ **Detective and mystery 1st editions** in hardcover or paperback. Also biography, reference, and bibliography related to the detective/mystery genre. Wants Dashiell Hammett and Raymond Chandler 1st editions with dust jackets. Computerized for modem access.
Richard West's Booking Agency
PO Box 406
Elm Grove, WI 53122
(414) 786-8420

★ **Large 20th century fiction collections.** If you have many hundreds of hardback fiction books with their original dust jackets, give him a call. Has strong interest in **John Steinbeck** including signed limited editions, first editions, first printings by subsequent publishers, appearances in anthologies, spoken word records, tapes, film and theater memorabilia, and things owned by him. Does not want book club editions or items in poor condition. If a book had a dust jacket, slipcase, box, or wrap-around as originally issued, these items should still be present. Be specific about what you have for sale, giving complete bibliographic information and a full description. No interest in paperbacks or contemporary remainders.
>   James Dourgarian, Bookman
>   1595-A Third Avenue
>   Walnut Creek, CA 94596
>   (415) 935-5033

★ **Leather bound books.** "I'll buy decorator leather bound books in quantity for $3 to $5 each. Not interested in fine first editions, just old books with little other value. Must have good spines and covers, but can be in any language from any period, as I want them only for their decorator potential. Call if you've got a bunch of them."
>   Joan Brady
>   834 Central Ave.
>   Pawtucket, RI 02861
>   (401) 725-5753

★ **Books published by the Limited Editions Club.** "I'll buy all years, all titles, as long as they are in fine condition in a fine box. I'll also buy Club ephemera including monthly letters, prospectus, etc." Only *Lysistrata* and *Ulysses* are acceptable without original box. Also buys *Heritage Press* books, *Encyclopedia Britannica* published after 1980, and *Encyclopedia Judaica* (any edition). Please describe fully.
>   Lee and Mike Temares
>   50 Heights Road
>   Plandome, NY 11030
>   (516) 627-8688

★ **Any type of book from art and archery to Zen and zoology.** This important Florida dealer prefers rare books but is interested in a wide variety of topics and subject matter, especially **limited edition books by fine presses** such as Derrydale, Kelmscott Press, Black Sun Press, Grolier Club, Grabhorne Press and the like. He does not buy school books, encyclopedias, medical texts, Book of the Month Club editions, or reprints of famous novels. "Only tentative evaluations are possible without seeing your book," but give complete bibliographic information.
>   Steven Eisenstein, Book-A-Brack
>   6760 Collins Ave.
>   Miami, FL 33141
>   (305) 865-0092

★ **Sporting books.** "We are always interested in purchasing "sporting" books on hunting, fishing, bird dogs, archery, guns and gun collecting, game animals and birds, books by the Derrydale Press, and many more. We purchase for stock, so there is no delay. We do ask that if you quote a book to us, you wait until you hear from us. We answer all quotes even if we do not buy them. We are good active buyers and ask that you keep our wants in mind. Among many authors we seek are Frank Forester, Havilah Babcock, Robert Ruark, Archibald Rutledge, Robert Traver and Corey Ford." Provide standard bibliographic info.
Lewis Razek, Highwood Bookshop
PO Box 1246
Traverse City, MI 49685
(616) 271-3898

★ **Technical books and paper ephemera,** pre-1910. He wants books on trades, machines, manufacturing and technical processes.
Jim Presgraves, Bookworm & Silverfish
PO Box 639
Wytheville, VA 24382

★ *I.C.S. Reference Library* or *I.C.S. Technical Library* books on any topic are sought, as long as they are from the early 1900's and bound in brown or black leather.
Jack Zimmerly
1200 Shypoke
Fairbanks, AK 99709

★ **Encyclopedias** from any year that are in good resellable condition. She buys and sells encyclopedias of all sort and publisher, including *World Book, Britannica, Americana,* and others. She *sells* for prices varying from 10% to 60% of new cost. Your books will probably be worth from 30% to 50% of that, depending on customer demand.
Kathleen Italiane, Encyclopedias
14071 Windsor Place
Santa Ana, CA 92705
(714) 838-3643 from 10 to 10

★ **Science fiction and mystery first editions.** Fantastic adventure novels by authors such as Edgar Rice Burroughs, A.Merritt, Sax Rohmer, and Talbot Mundy with their original dust jackets. Also buys **adventure and detective pulp magazines**. Include dates in your description.
Claude Held
PO Box 515
Buffalo, NY 14225

★ **Occult and mystic science,** astrology, magic, numerology, alchemy, palmistry, spiritualism, pyramids, tarot, Yoga, Atlantis, UFO's, ESP, and anything else metaphysical. "I'll also buy art, posters, cards, games, antique crystal balls, and other mystical and occult ephemera. I'll buy one or one thousand, if in fine condition."
>Dennis Whelan
>PO Box 170
>Lakeview, AR 72642

★ **Crossword puzzle books.** It doesn't matter if the puzzles are filled in, as long as the books are hard cover and before 1955. Give standard bibliographic information.
>Will Shortz, Games Magazine
>19 West 21st Street
>New York, NY 10010
>   (212) 727-7100 days

★ **Pre-1970 crossword and other word puzzle books,** hard or soft cover, even if written in. Especially wants Simon and Schuster hardcover puzzle books 1924-60. Give the complete title, date, and series number, and how much of the book has been filled in. No crossword dictionaries, but does buy **crossword magazines**. Wants list sent for large SASE.
>Stanley Newman, American Crossword
>PO Box 69
>Massapequa Park, NY 11762

★ **Paperback books from the 1940's, 50's and early 60's.** "If it had an original cover price of 25¢ or 35¢ and it's in nice condition, we want to buy it all. We are very competitive for any books, and will travel worldwide to buy complete libraries of these books. We specialize in science fiction, mystery, Western, and 'sleaze' but will consider other fiction from this period as well. We will also consider **digest size books and pulp magazines** in these same fields. Please don't send us badly creased, soiled, water damaged, or destroyed copies, as we buy for resale. We cannot use reprints either." Give standard bibliographic information and include what the original cover price was. Describe condition of cover and binding. Gorgon books issues monthly catalogs of books for sale, sponsors the annual paperback expo, and was a founder of the paperback collector's club.
>Joe Crifo and John Gargiso, Gorgon Books
>102 JoAnne Drive
>Holbrook, NY 11741
>   (516) 472-3504

★ **Thornton W. Burgess and Harrison Cady books** and ephemera. Does not want any of their books published by Grosset & Dunlap.
>Stephen Kruskall
>PO Box 418
>Dover, MA 02030

CHILDREN'S BOOKS

★ **First editions of children's books** in very good condition. Wants books illustrated by Mabel Lucie Atwell, Jessie Wilcox Smith, Charles Robinson, Maxfield Parrish, Charles Folkard, Maurice Sendak, Edward Gorey, and Ralph Steadman, among others. Can send you a wants list.
> Joel Birenbaum
> 2486 Brunswick Circle   #A1
> Woodridge, IL 60517

★ **First editions of the *Bobbsey Twins*** series published by Mershon or Chatterton-Peck. No Grosset & Dunlap editions. Also wants **Frank Merriwell items**, especially *Frank Merriwell's Book of Athletic Development*, Merriwell postcards, and the Tip Top League badge.
> Audrey Buffington
> 2 Old Farm Road
> Wayland, MA 01778

★ **Children's series books.** Must be in dust jacket if issued that way. Seeking the last 3 or 4 titles in series. Describe condition of dust jacket.
> Lee & Mike Temares
> 50 Heights Road
> Plandome, NY 11030

★ **Children's books,** American or English, from the 1400's to 1925, including educational books such as McGuffey's readers.
> Ron Graham
> 8167 Park Ave.
> Forestville, CA 95436

★ **Children's early readers** and other colorful children's books in fine condition for resale. Wants primers and pre-primers like the Dick and Jane series: *Look and See, Come and Go, Work and Play, Good Times with our Friends, Happy Days,* and *Fun with Dick and Jane.* Also wants *Our Big Book*, a flip chart version of the readers which stood in the front of a classroom. He'll buy foreign editions, teacher's editions, and Catholic school editions (with John, Jean, and Judy). Other early readers, "dating back as far as you can go," are also wanted. "We'll buy school books other than readers, if fine condition and well illustrated." He also buys *Tom Swift* **and other children's series** books.
> Joe Perry Collectibles
> PO Box 5967
> Garden Grove, CA 92645

★ **Children's coloring books** from the 1930's and 40's if all uncolored.
> Fran Van Vynckt
> 6931 Monroe Ave.
> Hammond, IN 46324

Index of people who buy

WHERE TO SELL IT!

WHERE TO SELL IT!

Index of
things you can sell